WISDOM IN ISRAEL

WISDOM
IN ISRAEL

GERHARD VON RAD

SCM PRESS LTD
London
TRINITY PRESS INTERNATIONAL
Valley Forge, Pennsylvania

Translated by James D. Martin from the German
Weisheit in Israel
published 1970 by Neukirchener Verlag,
Neukirchen-Vluyn

Library of Congress Cataloging-in-Publication Data available

1 56338 071 4 (USA)
334 01794 7 (UK)

First published in Great Britain 1972
by SCM Press Ltd
26–30 Tottenham Road, London N1
Seventh impression 1993

Published in the United States by
Trinity Press International, P.O. Box 851,
Valley Forge, PA 19482–0851

Printed and bound in Great Britain by
Mackays of Chatham PLC, Chatham, Kent

95 96 97 98 99 00   10 9 8

*To my colleagues in the Faculty of Theology
of the University of Lund
and
my colleagues in the Faculty of Theology
of the University of Wales*

*in gratitude for receiving me into their company
by the conferring of an honorary doctorate*

CONTENTS

PART FOUR CONCLUSION

PREFACE

WHEN an author sees his book pass into the hands of a reader, he would gladly see it accompanied by a personal word from himself. He will want to say still more simply and less 'guardedly' what he believes to be really important and what – although he certainly does not consider it unimportant – he has not on this occasion placed in a prominent position. He will point to passages which he could not have written without the stimulus of others and, on the other hand, to those in which he has obviously not attained what he had in mind. But he knows that his book must appear without such a protective word.

It is often said nowadays that the study of wisdom in Israel is 'modern'. The present author is not of this opinion. Certainly there appear important monographs and many individual studies, but must one not ask whether the methods which to a large extent determine our Old Testament research are suitable for the elucidation of the didactic literature? Almost too many scholars have set themselves to master more and more comprehensive subjects, to embrace larger and larger contexts in Israel's intellectual life. Where, in all this, is there still room to consider a sentence filled to the brim with ideas? If there arises also the question which is pursued with such determination today of the prehistory of a range of ideas – and in the case of wisdom this question takes one into the broad territory of wisdom outside Israel – then the exegete's glance is diverted from the text itself to a wider context, and the text, with its claim to truth, is abandoned, for it has been made the springboard to the examination of something else, something more extensive.

In this book, not many questions will be asked about tradition-contexts, and where they are, they serve only to illuminate the claims to truth made by specific didactic statements. Even a text which is by and large satisfactorily arranged within its 'tradition' still provides us, if we set about considering it seriously, with plenty of questions.

In view of what has been achieved to date, this book does not aim at encyclopaedic completeness. (The author is fully aware that research in this field is working with fairly fine distinctions with regard

to the formal structure of the sentences.) Only certain fundamental
questions are discussed here. The understanding of Israel's didactic
literature is definitely dependent on how successful we are in making
contemporary the specific questions which it formulates and in subsequently completing its lines of thought; for Israel had to undergo the
adventure of liberating her reason in a quite unique way. It remains,
therefore, only for the author to request the reader to expose himself
to the tensions within which the teachings of the wise men operate
and to bring with him a readiness for contemplation. *Res loquuntur!*

Once again, our librarian Fräulein A. Findeiss has helped me with
great willingness, not only in procuring books but also in reading
through the manuscript before it went to press.

In certain places the ready assistance of Dr Hermann Timm of
Heidelberg has helped to clarify and improve the style.

Heidelberg, March 1970

TRANSLATOR'S NOTE

The language of this book is in some passages not as lucid as it might be and there are places where interpretation is a problem. I trust, however, that I have not seriously misrepresented the author in any respect. As far as biblical and apocryphal quotations are concerned, I have translated these direct from the German, keeping as close to the language of the RSV as Professor von Rad's renderings allowed. Where discrepancies occur between different renderings of the same passage, these are also to be found in the original German. The use of quotation marks round words which are clearly not reported speech indicate a textual problem. I am grateful to my colleague, Mr Robin Salters, for help with the reading of the proofs.

St Andrews, June 1972

ABBREVIATIONS

ANET	*Ancient Near Eastern Texts Relating to the Old Testament*, ed. J. B. Pritchard
AOT	*Altorientalische Texte zum Alten Testament*, ed. H. Gressmann
BBB	Bonner Biblische Beiträge
BK	Biblischer Kommentar
BKAT	Biblischer Kommentar, Altes Testament
ET	English translation
EvTh	*Evangelische Theologie*
JJS	*Journal of Jewish Studies*
OTS	*Oudtestamentische Studiën*
RGG	*Die Religion in Geschichte und Gegenwart*
SVT	Supplements to *Vetus Testamentum*
ThLZ	*Theologische Literaturzeitung*
ThR	*Theologische Rundschau*
ThZ	*Theologische Zeitschrift*
TWNT	*Theologisches Wörterbuch zum Neuen Testament*
VT	*Vetus Testamentum*
ZÄS	*Zeitschrift für ägyptische Studien*
ZAW	*Zeitschrift für die alttestamentliche Wissenschaft*
ZDPV	*Zeitschrift des Deutschen Palästina-Vereins*
ZKT	*Zeitschrift für katholische Theologie*
ZNW	*Zeitschrift für die neutestamentliche Wissenschaft*
ZThK	*Zeitschrift für Theologie und Kirche*

PART ONE

INTRODUCTION

I

THE PROBLEM

N O O N E would be able to live even for a single day without incurring appreciable harm if he could not be guided by wide practical experience. This experience teaches him to understand events in his surroundings, to foresee the reactions of his fellow men, to apply his own resources at the right point, to distinguish the normal from the unique and much more besides. Man is scarcely aware of this continual guidance, nor of the fact that this experience is only partly contributed by him. He grows into it, it proves true for him, the most that he does is to modify it. Least of all will he reflect that this experience, looked at more closely, is a highly complex structure. Of course, as we have said, it is constructed out of individual experiences which have been brought into play and purified over and over again. But experiences without preparation do not exist. By and large man creates the experiences which he expects and for which, on the basis of the idea which he has formed of the world around him, he is ready. Experience presupposes a prior knowledge of myself; indeed it can become experience only if I can fit it into the existing context of my understanding of myself and of the world. Thus it can even be that man misses possible experiences offered to him, that he lacks the capacity to register them, because he is incapable of fitting them into the limits of his understanding.

This experiential knowledge is, however, not only a very complex entity, but also a very vulnerable one. And this cannot be otherwise, for it renders man an invaluable service in enabling him to function in his sphere of life other than as a complete stranger and puts him in the position of understanding that sphere of life, at least to a certain extent, as an ordered system. Such knowledge does not accrue to an individual, nor even to a generation. It acquires its status and its binding claim only where it appears as the common possession of a nation or of a broad stratum within a nation. But precisely in its quality as a communal possession this knowledge finds itself on dangerous ground. Certainly, on the basis of a long period of trial, it can make for itself a claim to stability and validity. But, in so far as it becomes the possession of all, it is in danger of simplifying and generalizing truths which can be generalized only to a certain extent. Thus the sphere of order in which man is invited to take refuge is at all times under threat. It is fundamentally called in question by every contrary experience; indeed this knowledge can even become one enormous deception to the extent that it tries to shut off the experience of new reality and fights against it where possible. In this process there occur naturally, alongside periods of disclosure and of movement, periods of resistance and preservation. It cannot, however, be said that these latter are to be judged only negatively. They, too, are obedient to specific needs, those of inner development, that is, of an inward concentration. Dangers threaten everywhere, threaten not only the process of self-disclosure but also the intellectual arranging and developing of what has been experienced.

Every nation with a culture has devoted itself to the care and the literary cultivation of this experiential knowledge and has carefully gathered its statements, especially in the form of sentence-type proverbs. This, then, is one of the most elementary activities of the human mind, with the practical aim of averting harm and impairment of life from man. Not only does the outside world as an object stimulate man's desire for knowledge; its movements and reactions affect him and, at the same time, subject him to influences. In any event, man must know his way about in the world in which he finds himself in order to be able to hold his own in it.

What we have just described as one of the most elementary activities of the human mind is nevertheless a highly complex phenomenon, for the road from an experience which is considered worthy of note to the linguistic expression of it – and to this particular linguistic expression – is a long one, one which has by no means been adequately explored. Once an experience has found expression in a proverb, a sentence, a maxim or even in an aphorism, a multi-layered process has come to an end. In the interval, the validity of the experience in question must have been proved. Where does this happen? What are the given presuppositions for this type of intellectual productivity? If we disregard the proverb for a moment, then the composition of wisdom literature seems to be connected with particular periods in the intellectual life of nations. How is one to determine its relationship to other 'ideological' works of literature? Does it simply fill what has been felt to be a gap? Above all, however, by which intellectual powers is this process carried out? By the reason or perhaps, rather, by a particular type of intuition? The maxim – if we disregard, for the moment, its individual types – can function in the most varied contexts. As a trivial proverb it can belong to the world of the simple. It can, however, like a precious stone among trinkets, outshine a poem of the highest quality. The demand which it must always satisfy is that of brevity, of compactness and yet of intelligibility, with, if possible, a clear graphic quality; in short, that of being easily remembered.

Ancient Israel, too, participated in the business of cultivating her experiential knowledge. That in doing so she stumbled upon perceptions largely similar to those of other ancient peoples is no longer surprising. What is surprising, rather, is that many of the most elementary experiences appeared quite differently to her, especially because she set them in a quite specific spiritual and religious context of understanding. But was 'reality', then, not one and the same?

In this book the attempt will be made to understand somewhat more exactly what we are accustomed to include under the general term 'Wisdom in Israel'. The attempt will be made to work out some of the specific trends of thought and theological contexts in which this Israelite wisdom functioned and from the point of view of which this wisdom could be interpreted still more appropriately. The way to an understanding of this great intellectual activity on Israel's part which, as we might say, proceeds so remarkably along a razor's edge between faith and knowledge, goes beyond the examination of numerous individual texts. Many of these, by their often remarkably profound content but also by their literary form, invite the reader to pause at length over them; others appear trivial to us, and we are no longer able to see what was once important in them. This latter fact should, however, make us stop short, for in it we should be able to realize that we no longer understand correctly the decisive intellectual achievement lying behind these experiential statements. They are, in fact, concerned with the achieving of a certain distance from that which is near and everyday, from that which everyone knows and yet no one knows or understands. Indeed, it requires an art to see objectively things which have always been there and to give them expression. Is it not they which produce the greatest puzzles?

A great difficulty for the task before us is the fact that the literary material gathered in this way resists classification under overlapping headings. Basically, each sentence, each didactic poem, stands on its own and does not expect to be interpreted on the basis of similar poems. In fact, when the reader takes up these texts (and this is the way it must be with this type of literature), he must have enough time to reflect contemplatively both on the unit as a whole and on the details of it; for every sentence and every didactic poem is pregnant with meaning and is unmistakably self-contained, so that, notwith-standing the many features common to them all, they strike us as being peculiarly inflexible. Thus, these didactic poems, from the point of view of their content and the movement of their thought, are difficult to fit into a comprehensive pattern. However, one can arrange them according to certain groups of problems and treat together some of the principal teachings which clearly are of importance among these instructions. This is the way which will be taken here. It soon becomes obvious, however, that an arrangement of this kind can be carried out only to a certain extent, since no object or question can be positioned at all definitively. The next object cannot be explained on its own either; in order to be properly understood it must also be placed in the total ideological picture. For all its fluidity and variability, the ideological world to which the teachings belong is nevertheless an indivisible unity. Thus the reader must expect in this book some repetitions with respect to the basic structural ideas. A small index of key words at the end of the book will be of assistance in finding discussions which occur in different places.

This study will endeavour to grasp something of the fundamentals of the understanding of the world and of life, and not least of the under-standing of reality, in ancient Israel. What is the result if we under-stand the texts from the point of view of the specifically religious tensions which caused them to be written down in ancient Israel and on the basis of which they were understood? In trying to answer this question a difficulty dogs our steps. We lack the concepts really suited to the Hebrew world of speech and thought, concepts which would help us to expound the Israelite understanding of man and the world. We are therefore left with no alternative but to use, to begin with, the terms with which we are familiar. In what follows, therefore, frequent use will be made of 'orders', of an 'inner law' of creation, of a 'secular understanding of the world' etc. But at the same time we will be continually compelled to analyse these concepts – almost even before they are used – or at least to delimit them, whenever they are describing what Israel meant by them.[1]

The author must reach a prior understanding with the reader about yet another difficulty. If one surveys the relative review articles in our scholarly works of reference, as well as the monographs and separate studies of the last decade, then it might appear as if 'wisdom' in Israel, in Egypt or among the Mesopotamian peoples was a fairly clearly delimited subject. But this is by no means the case. On the contrary, with the increasing number of scholarly works in this field, the concept 'wisdom' has become increasingly unclear, and there are already orientalists who have completely excluded it from their sphere of investigation.[2] In the didactic books of the Old Testament, much is said about that wisdom which a man should acquire; it is recommended, differentiated from folly, etc. But – and this is something quite different – was there wisdom in Israel in the sense of an 'intellectual movement'? And if there were such a thing, would it not then be more essential to formulate the phenomena, the questions and the thought processes as clearly as possible than to apply to them the label 'wisdom' which has become so vague? If, in fact, one removes this blanket term, then one comes face to face with literary documents of the most diverse type. The designation of a text as 'wisdom', indeed this whole term 'wisdom' as a total phenomenon, is by no means directly rooted in the sources. It first emerged in the scholarly world and has since become established. It belongs, therefore, to the fairly extensive number of biblical-theological collective terms whose validity and content are not once for all established and which have to be examined from time to time from the point of view of whether they are being correctly used.[3] It could even be that scholarship has gone too far in an uncritical use of this collective term; it could even be that by the use of this blanket term it is suggesting the existence of something which never existed and that it is in this way dangerously prejudicing the interpretation of varied material.

[1] 'You are now invited to read with kindness and attentiveness . . . for things do not have the same meaning when they are read in the original Hebrew and when they are translated into another language.' Preface to Sirach (the grandson translated the grandfather's work into Greek).

[2] W. G. Lambert, *Babylonian Wisdom Literature*, 1960, p. 1; H. Brunner, 'Ägyptologie', *Handbuch der Orientalistik*, I. Abt. 1. Bd., 1970, p. 133.

[3] Misgivings about the summary use of the term 'wisdom' until now have already been voiced on several occasions, e.g. H. H. Schmid, *Wesen und Geschichte der Weisheit*, 1966, pp. 7, 185; H.-J. Hermisson, *Studien zur israelitischen Spruchweisheit*, 1968, pp. 12f.

The question is therefore justified whether the attractive code-name 'wisdom' is nowadays not more of a hindrance than a help, in so far as it disguises what stands behind it rather than depicts it properly. As matters stand today, we can only first remove the individual phenomena, as far as is possible, from under this unsatisfactory blanket term and examine them anew from what are, nowadays, rather different points of view. That wisdom has to do with human understanding, that it is a particular form of human knowledge and behaviour, is not disputed. We are thus perhaps doing a service in approaching the subject first of all in a more general way and with fewer presuppositions, in enquiring more closely after Israel's search for knowledge, that is, in what particular way and by what means Israel sought to prove herself. As far as I can see, this question has not yet been put in this way because older scholarship was not aware of the intensity and the flexibility of the Israelite search for knowledge, nor of the specific area within which this search operated.

The examination of the book of Proverbs was reached only late by the great wave of historico-critical scholarship which had washed over biblical scholarship as early as the second half of the eighteenth century. This is not surprising, for the criteria of source criticism could not be applied to these texts. Thus, in the second half of the nineteenth century, the authenticity of the Solomonic book of Proverbs could still be maintained, with at most only a few modifications. The sudden change in opinion was unquestionably produced by the historico-critical examination of the Bible, but the conviction that the book of Proverbs as a whole was to be regarded as a product of the post-exilic Jewish community could not be based on unambiguous results of textual analysis. Scholars were guided, rather, by a general picture which they had drawn of spiritual and religious movements and developments in ancient Israel.[4] It was, above all, the rigid, individual 'doctrine of retribution' that they felt obliged to regard as characteristic of a late period. It was particularly disadvantageous that at this stage in the investigation scholars were unable to free themselves from what we now see to have been a much too confused set of questions. They considered the book of Proverbs, like the psalter and the prophetical books, to be a specifically religious book which was to be appreciated primarily on the basis of its con-

---

[4] Thus, e.g., G. Hölscher still placed the older proverbial literature in the later Persian period: *Geschichte der israelitischen und jüdischen Religion*, 1922, p.148.

cept of God and of its piety. Since, however, the results of these
particular researches were not exactly satisfactory – they took exception to the rational, even opportunistic reflections, especially to the
paucity of specifically religious statements – they felt obliged to deduce
from the book of Proverbs that there had been a decided loss of
religious content in the post-exilic period.

The investigation did not emerge from the shadow of these un-
fortunate, religious judgments until scholars became aware of wisdom
texts in the great cultures which were neighbour to Israel and of the
relationship of these texts to Israelite material. Particularly in ancient
Egypt, wisdom books existed dating from the third millenium BC right
up to the late period. A somewhat revolutionary effect was produced
by the discovery that a whole passage from the wisdom book of
Amenemope had been taken over almost word for word into the
biblical book of Proverbs (Prov. 22.17–23.11). The assumption that
wisdom was a religious phenomenon of post-exilic Israel proved to
be completely wrong. Wisdom, it was now clear, was a phenomenon
common to the ancient East, a cultural commodity with respect to
which Israel was to a great extent a recipient and not a donor. At
the same time, the suspicion against its early dating in the period of
the monarchy was seen to be unjustified. It followed logically that a
great comparison of the wisdom materials should begin then and
there.[5] The result of this work, which is still not complete even today,
was the recognition of a quite unexpected range of elements in
common, of similarities, of points of dependence, which linked Israelite
wisdom to that of the ancient Near East. It was not quite so logical
that in this process of comparison the vast majority of scholars began
the hermeneutical operation from the appreciation of ancient Near
Eastern wisdom. In the course of this interpretation of Israelite wisdom, disturbing questions inevitably emerged. What was the relation-

[5] W. O. E. Oesterley, *The Wisdom of Egypt and the Old Testament*, 1927; W.
Baumgartner, *Israelitische und altorientalische Weisheit*, 1933; J. Fichtner, *Die altorient-
alische Weisheit in ihrer israelitisch-jüdischen Ausprägung*, 1933; H. Ringgren, *Word and
Wisdom*, 1947; H. Gese, *Lehre und Wirklichkeit in der alten Weisheit*, 1958; H. H. Schmid,
Wesen und Geschichte der Weisheit, 1966. W. Zimmerli set off in a new direction when
he devoted his attention to the internal problems of the book of Proverbs: 'Zur
Struktur der alttestamentlichen Weisheit', *ZAW* 51, 1933, pp. 177ff. He was followed, almost thirty years later, by U. Skladny, *Die ältesten Spruchsammlungen in
Israel*, 1962. Of particular significance were, also, individual articles by W. Zimmerli and by R. E. Murphy. The course of research in the last decade has recently
been mapped by R. B. Y. Scott, 'The Study of the Wisdom Literature', *Interpretation* 24, January 1970, pp. 20ff.

ship of this wisdom, which was partly imported into Israel, to the
Yahwistic faith, which was otherwise regarded as entirely exclusive?
Was this perhaps an intellectual activity which was more or less
neutral from a religious point of view and which could, therefore,
happily settle in the vicinity of quite different cults? Thus, for example,
the opinion is current today that Israelite Yahwism, with its strong
religious stamp, penetrated only very hesitantly the didactic wisdom
material.[6] Wisdom teaching has even been described as a foreign
element in the Old Testament world.[7] There is every appearance
that the process of comparison with the wisdom of neighbouring cultures has more or less petered out. Only when the details of Israel's
striving after knowledge have been more clearly recognized, can a
methodically exact comparison be carried out. But the foundations of
such a process of comparison must be laid considerably deeper and
more solidly.[8]

What we lack today is a work about wisdom in Israel which is
much more decisive than has hitherto been the case, which starts
with what is specific in its subject of study, which, to a greater extent
than has been the case till now, allows the themes to be announced
and the questions asked by the didactic texts themselves; in short, a
work which attempts to put itself into the specific world of thought
and values and into the tensions within which the teachings of the
wise men operated. For this, a decided effort is needed to see the
'reality' of life – how easily this word flows from the lips of exegetes –
as Israel saw it, and at the same time there is also needed a readiness
to take quite seriously the basic experiences which Israel claimed to
have had in this very 'reality' down through the centuries.

It lies in the nature of the materials that collections of sentences,
didactic poems or problem poems can be dated only approximately

[6] H. H. Schmid, op. cit., p. 148, etc.

[7] H. Gese, op. cit., p. 2.

[8] The process of comparison has been made more difficult still by the fact that
we know practically nothing of the way by which the didactic material (from
Egypt, for example) came into Israel. It may often have been fairly complicated,
for the Syrian–Palestinian literature will have to be accorded an important role as
intermediary. Recently, texts from ancient Ugarit (1500–1200 BC) have also at last
.produced the expected contribution to international (or, to be more precise,
Babylonian) wisdom. J. Nougayrol in *Ugaritica V* (*Mission de Ras Shamra*, T. XVI,
1968), pp. 273ff., 291ff. In the one case, one would have to suppose an extensive
process of infiltration; other material may have been brought directly to Israel by
travelling wisdom teachers. H. Cazelles, *Les Sagesses du Proche-Orient Ancien*, 1963,
pp. 27ff.

even in the most favourable circumstances. Nevertheless, the dating of Prov. 10–29 in the pre-exilic monarchical period is hardly ever contested now. On the other hand, linguistic evidence compels a late date for such works as the Job dialogue or even Ecclesiastes. From the outset, therefore, we shall have to reckon with profound variations in the ideas and questions contained in texts which are spread over many centuries. On the other hand, there is much that has remained the same, convictions which have continued unaltered into the latest periods. The differentiation of the old from the new, of the conventional from the emergence of new problems and, by this means, the relative dating of the formulation of a specific problem, is often difficult enough. Thus, for example, the complaint about the vanity of life and the resigned summons to the enjoyment of life are certainly not in themselves a definite indication of a late period. They are, rather, objects of reflection in the ancient Near East which are met with in the most varied periods and contexts. Nor must we be surprised to encounter, even in specifically late texts, statements which could equally well have stood in quite old texts. We shall not hesitate, therefore, whenever we feel able to justify the practice, to group together passages from books of different periods. In many cases it is quite impossible to derive individual wisdom sentences each from a different, quite specific period, since even obvious differences need not always be explained from the point of view of a chronological sequence. Scholarship was amazingly certain in supposing that Prov. 1–9 was the latest collection in the book of Proverbs, but the arguments hitherto adduced appear remarkably weak on closer examination.

The period whose literary heritage we shall examine begins with the emergence of school wisdom in the early monarchy. The existence of an older clan wisdom need not be contested in principle; its existence is, indeed, even highly probable.[9] It is, however, a phenomenon that is so difficult to define that our examination takes no notice of it as an independent factor. Besides, the acceptance of a connection between it and school wisdom has proved to be questionable. It should be stated here, as a matter of principle, that in this context we do not see it as our task to go behind the didactic poems in the book of

[9] The question of an older family and clan wisdom preceding school wisdom has recently been raised afresh by J.-P. Audet, 'Origines comparées de la double tradition de la loi et de la sagesse dans le Proche-Orient ancien', *25. Internationaler Kongress der Orientalisten, Moskau 1960,* 1962, T. 1, p.352, but especially by E. Gerstenberger, *Wesen und Herkunft des 'apodiktischen Rechts',* 1965, esp. pp. 110ff.

Proverbs to enquire whether perhaps here and there forms of a much
older wisdom may be discerned. We accept the material as it is presented by the collectors, and we are justified in understanding it, in
that form, as school wisdom. As our latest point, we take the book
of Sirach, not, of course, in the sense that it marks a conclusion – as
if there could be any such thing in this field – but as a discernible
break and as a transition to different thought-forms. There will, however, be several opportunities of indicating lines of thought which
lead considerably beyond Sirach. This will be particularly necessary
when we look at certain elements in apocalyptic literature.

One way of reaching a correct understanding of the teachings of
the wise men, which might seem promising to many, will not be
taken here, namely that of the examination of terminology. No doubt
a list of terms could be gathered, the use of which is particularly
striking in the didactic traditions; but in our opinion it would be a
hopeless undertaking to move from an analysis of the specific content
of these terms and from the way in which they are used, to any kind
of sound judgments about the nature of this instruction and of its
problems. The traditio-historical examination of Old Testament texts
has shown us how, within certain streams of tradition, of a cultic, a
forensic or a didactic nature, certain concepts will be preserved with
great consistency because they were constitutive from a terminological
point of view, but that at the same time there will be a great fluidity
in their meaning. Even if this difficulty could, at a pinch, be overcome by means of a new type of examination of terms which could
take account of this fact, another difficulty is absolutely decisive. It
is a fact that Israel, even when she is reflecting theoretically, does not
work with an array of concepts which are to any extent precise.
Israel showed remarkably little interest in working out clearly defined
terms, for she had at her disposal other methods of making a statement more precise, for example *parallelismus membrorum*, a method
which can reduce to despair any honest analyst of terms. How can
one approach, from the point of view of the history of terms, a sentence
such as this?

> I, Wisdom, am neighbour to shrewdness (*'ormā*)
>   and the knowledge of prudence (*mᵉzimmōt*) is at my disposal.
>   (Prov. 8.12)

No doubt this is a poetically exaggerated statement. It is, therefore,
difficult to transpose it into a statement which is clear to us. One has

the impression that the language of these didactic poems has a quite different relationship to these terms from the one we have. If one does not wish to write the statement off as empty bombast – and one should be warned against this – one finds oneself in considerable difficulties.

> Proverbs of Solomon, son of David, king of Israel, to learn
> wisdom and discipline (*mūsār*).
> To understand (*hābīn*) sayings of understanding (*bīnā*),
> To acquire discipline (*mūsār*) in good sense (*haśkēl*), integrity
> (*ṣedeq*), justice (*mišpāṭ*) and honesty (*mēšārīm*).
> To give shrewdness (*'ormā*) to the simple,
> knowledge (*da'at*) and prudence (*mezimmā*) to the young.
> Let the wise man hear and increase his learning (*leqaḥ*),
> and the man of understanding (*nābōn*) acquire guidance (*taḥbulōt*).
>
> (Prov. 1.1–5)

How can an exegesis which takes words seriously deal adequately with this series of statements? What do the many individual terms mean? In what sense are they associated with each other, and in what sense are they differentiated from each other? It would only be with difficulty that one would conclude that the prologue to the book of Proverbs is mere empty noise. How, then, is one to proceed? Presumably a comprehensive term, for which there is no longer any handy word, can be constructed here for the reader by the fact that, to a certain extent, into this prologue a number of known terms have been inserted so that by this cumulation the desired extension of the conceptual range is achieved.[10] Certainly the individual terms used are differentiated from each other; but perhaps not in a way which can be precisely defined, for they also obviously overlap with each other, too. By the cumulation of many terms the text seems to aim at something larger, something more comprehensive which could not be expressed satisfactorily by means of any one of the terms used. The question from the point of view of the history of stylistics, namely to which stage in the development of poetic expression in Israel such a text is to be assigned, we cannot yet answer.

In these latter considerations, there arises already a problem from which we shall not be free until the end of our search for an understanding of the didactic literature. If Israel failed, to a great extent, to arrange the multiplicity of phenomena by means of abstract terms,

---

[10] On this 'stereometric' way of thinking, see below p. 27.

then we must be all the more clear about the individuality of such an understanding of God, of the world and of man. We must not, at any rate, make uncritical use of those familiar abstract terms (nature, history, world, creation, providence, etc.); we must, rather, seek to understand how Israel confronted the world in which she found herself. For a reality which is not apprehended by means of objective, comprehensive terms, presents a different appearance; indeed, as one will already be in a position to surmise, it confronts man more rigorously.[11]

[11] Israel, too, of course, made use of abstract terms as an aid to thought (justice, fear, knowledge, discipline, etc.). The question here is simply how she proceeded with these abstract terms, how she used them and how she failed to use them. One can say, in quite general terms, that she always used certain abstract terms, but that she never reached the point of turning these into broad abstractions.

II

CENTRES AND TRANSMITTERS OF THE DIDACTIC TRADITIONS

IF ONE EXAMINES the book of Proverbs to ascertain the *Sitz im Leben* which it gives to the individual collections of proverbs, the first clues may be found in the headings which are prefixed to the different collections.[1] The one which attributes the whole book to king Solomon (Prov. 1.1) is the one which has been most determined by the general tradition. However, the separate collection which comprises Prov. 10–15 is also in Solomon's name. The proverbs in chs. 25–27, too, are designated 'proverbs of Solomon' 'which the men of Hezekiah have collected' (25.1). This note, whatever may be one's views on Solomonic authorship, is hardly ever doubted now. It records a planned editorial process carried out at the royal court and already completed during the monarchy. The 'words for Lemuel' are directed at a king (Prov. 31.1f.). If one now considers that many of the proverbs actually presuppose conditions at court, then the first result of our researches would be that the book of Proverbs itself points to the royal court as a place where wisdom was traditionally nurtured. This would correspond exactly to what we know of the courts of Egypt and Mesopotamia. There is a particularly rich representation of such didactic works from Egypt which have been attributed mainly to kings or, at best, to state officials. The situation in Mesopotamia is no different; one need think only of the wise minister Ahikar 'on whose counsel all Assyria depended' (as the narrative stresses in stereotyped fashion) and of his teachings which he directed towards his successor in office and nephew.[2] This again

---

[1] The book of Proverbs consists of nine individual collections: I Prov. 1–9; II 10–22.16; III 22.17–24.22; IV 24.23–34; V 25–29; VI 30.1–14; VII 30.15–33; VIII 31.1–9; IX 31.10–31. The various superscriptions of these collections suggest that at one stage each of the collections had its own process of tradition.

[2] The Ahikar story is translated in Gressmann, *AOT*, 1926², pp. 454ff. and in Pritchard, *ANET*, pp. 426ff. Tobit 14.10 refers to the principle figure of the narrative who was at that time universally known.

reminds us of ancient Israelite circumstances, of David's adviser Ahithophel, for example. When he gave advice, it was 'as if one consulted God himself' (II Sam. 16.23). Thus it was obviously one of the principal duties of these high officials to advise the king in political matters.[3]

> Plans are established by counsel;
> by wise guidance wage war. (Prov. 20.18)
>
> Victory comes through abundance of counsellors. (Prov. 24.6b)

To give advice in the king's presence in well-chosen words was a very responsible office which demanded precise, expert knowledge which one could acquire only after a long training. It is, therefore, no accident if, in all these didactic works, instructions about the right and wrong use of words plays such a large role. These officials also frequently went on journeys and, in political missions, had to represent with the artistry of their speech the interests of their country at foreign courts.[4] But the art of political counselling and the rules of diplomatic exchanges were certainly not the only things which were to be learned at court. On one occasion, there is a mention of the 'wise men who knew the times' (Esth. 1.13). In this case what is meant are astrologers or the science of prognostication. But that is not all. We shall have to concern ourselves further with the meaning which was given to knowledge about the right time for an undertaking. Daniel and Joseph function as interpreters of royal dreams (Gen. 41.14ff.; Dan. 1.17; 2.28). We know that the interpretation of dreams in the ancient Near East had grown into a science on its own. That such a function was practised also at the court in Jerusalem can certainly be assumed on the basis of Isa. 3.3. In the late book, Wisdom of Solomon, there are even enumerated individual branches of the natural sciences taught at that time; these are astronomy, zoology, demonology, psychology, botany and pharmacy (Wisd. 7.18ff.). One can scarcely assume that all of these areas of knowledge accrued to the teachers only in the latest period. The book of Proverbs contains only practical wisdom and is certainly only part of a search for knowledge which, in the earlier period, too, already stood on a much broader foundation.

But the matter is complicated from another aspect also. In spite

---

[3] P. A. H. de Boer, 'The Counsellor', SVT 3, 1955, pp. 42ff. There are particularly fine examples of such polished speeches in the council of war in II Sam. 17.
[4] Sir. 34.11f.; Prov. 22.21; Sir. 39.4.

of our first definition of the *Sitz im Leben*, it is simply not possible to regard the book of Proverbs merely as a product of courtly knowledge and serving for the training of high officials. The social context from which the individual sentences, and indeed whole groups of sentences emerge, but also the range of problems within which they move, the subjects with which they deal, can be more or less precisely defined, with the result that the world in which they exist is certainly not that of the court.[5] On the contrary, sentences from the fairly narrow world of court and high officials are, on the whole, only scantily represented.[6] Thus, the supposition emerges that the wise men of the court, 'the men of Hezekiah' for example, also functioned as collectors of non-courtly teaching material and that wisdom was not by any means located only at court. Obviously it must have found at an early stage centres where it was nurtured in a broader cultural level in the country and where it was concerned more with the kind of questions asked about life by the middle classes and the landowners.[7]

It would be a great help if we could deduce from the Old Testament something about education in Israel. But several careful examinations have produced rather negative results.[8] The first direct reference is to be found in the late book Sirach, where once a 'school' (*bēt hammidrāš*) is mentioned (Sir. 51.23). In spite of this, there can be no doubt that there were schools in ancient Israel, too. We can deduce this from circumstances in neighbouring cultures, even if one must be clear that these circumstances cannot simply be transferred to an Israel which, from the cultural point of view, was more modest. We can deduce it also from the high level of literary achievement already apparent in the early monarchy. This demands the assumption that a class of scribes existed. It could never have developed to such a peak without a scribal culture. In Israel, too, writing was known. But writing has to be taught. Handwriting, however, was never taught without accompanying teaching material. It follows from this that there must have been schools of different types in Israel.

[5] On this cf. especially the analyses of U. Skladny.

[6] Royal proverbs occur particularly in Prov. 16.10–15; 25.1–7.

[7] The young man whose training in music and rhetoric is so finely described in I Sam. 16.18 came from Bethlehem. From there it could be understood that Amos, too, had access to this instructional wisdom; cf. H. W. Wolff, *Amos' geistige Heimat*, 1964, and on this H.-J. Hermisson, op. cit., pp. 88ff.

[8] On the question of schools in Israel see most recently especially H.-J. Hermisson, op. cit., pp. 97ff.; W. McKane, *Prophets and Wise Men*, 1966², pp. 36ff.; L. Dürr, *Das Erziehungswesen im Alten Testament und im antiken Orient*, 1932; L. Jansen, *Die spätjüdische Psalmendichtung, ihr Entstehungskreis und ihr 'Sitz im Leben'*, 1937, pp. 57ff.

Questions of ritual and the complex distinctions between clean and unclean will have been taught in priestly schools. The temple scribes of Jer. 8.8 were certainly educated differently from the young state officials at court. The Levites must have been instructed differently again, in that they were brought up to interpret and preach on old traditions.[9] Finally, a quite different training must have been necessary for those who wished to work in Ezra's chancellery where the decrees of the great king were dealt with.

There is a specific type of interrogative sentence which, we believe, allows us, at least in an indirect way, to deduce one type of educational activity. They are scattered over almost the whole of the Old Testament, and we shall designate them here simply as school questions.

Can one carry fire in the bosom of one's clothes
    without one's clothes being burned?
Or can one walk upon coals
    without burning one's feet? (Prov. 6.27f.)

Everyone remembers the chain of questions in Amos 3.3–8 which has long been described as being of the 'wisdom' type.

Can papyrus grow where there is no marsh,
    or can reeds flourish without water? (Job 8.11)

Who has woe, who has sorrow?
    Who has strife, who has complaining?
Who has wounds without cause,
    who has dull eyes?
Those who linger over wine,
    who come to taste mixed wine. (Prov. 23.29f.)

Isa. 28.23–29 is a splendid example of the catechetical-didactic style. It deals with the complicated, yet thought-provoking activity of the countryman in seedtime and harvest.[10] In Ezek. 15.1–3 there occurs a catechism concerning the worthlessness of the wood of the vine. That we are here dealing with ambitious school lectures is clear from the so-called 'teacher's opening summons' to which attention has recently been drawn.[11] Further examples of this opening summons can be found in Deut. 32.1; Isa. 34.1; Ps. 49.2–5. It has been most extensively elaborated, comprising more than a chapter, by the author

[9] On this preaching practice cf. von Rad, *Deuteronomy*, ET 1966, pp. 18ff., etc.
[10] The text is translated on pp. 140f.
[11] On the so-called 'teacher's opening summons' see H. W. Wolff, BK XIV/1 *Hosea*, 1965, p. 122. Examples are Deut. 32.1; Isa. 28.23; 34.1; Ps. 49.2–5.

of the Elihu speech (Job 32; 33.1–3; 34.1f.). For the dating of these school lectures, it is important that the form of the teacher's opening summons is already attested in the pre-exilic period. It is possible that this instruction was terminated by a regular final examination.[12] In the later period this is mentioned once (Dan. 1.19f.). We would give a great deal to find out the range covered by that examination of the pages. In less complex examples, the answers solicited by the questions follow at once.

> What man is there who desires life
>   and would gladly enjoy good days?
> Keep your tongue from evil
>   and your lips from speaking deceit.   (Ps. 34.13f.)

It will come as no surprise to learn that the theological sphere, too, was included in this didactic instruction.

> Who ascended to heaven and came down again,
>   who gathers the wind in his fists?
> Who has wrapped up the waters in a garment?
>   Who has established all the ends of the earth?
> What is his name and his son's name
>   if you know it?   (Prov. 30.4)
>
> Who has measured the sea in the hollow of his hand
>   and marked off heaven with a span
> and enclosed the dust of the earth in a measure
>   and weighed the mountains in a balance
>   and the hills with scales?   (Isa. 40.12)

This, too, is the style of the catechetical, didactic question, a style which is obviously linked with hymnic motifs. But there we must stop.

---

[12] On the interrogation of pupils which, in Egyptian instruction, clearly culminated in an examination, see von Rad, *The Problem of the Hexateuch and Other Essays*, 1966, pp. 287ff. Cf. also Ahikar, Col. i, 10f. In Sir. 10.19 there is an example of a little catechism:
What race is worthy of honour? The human race.
What race is worthy of honour? Those who fear the Lord.
What race is not worthy of honour? The human race.
What race is not worthy of honour? Those who transgress the law.
In II(4) Esdras, there are several examples of didactic dialogue (5.43ff.; 6.55ff.; 7.1ff., 4.5ff.; 8.1ff., 35ff.). Could not also the repeated summons 'Observe . . .' in I Enoch 2–5 (each time indicating a phenomenon of natural science) originate from educational practice?
'Observe and see what all trees look like . . .'
'Observe how the trees are covered with green leaves . . .'
(I Enoch 4.1; 5.1; etc.).

Examples could be multiplied if we so desired. Here we were concerned only with the stylistic form of the school question which, as a literary, stylistic device, has also passed into quite different contexts. They are often simply what we are in the habit of calling rhetorical questions. But not always. They do, however, always deal with things which a man at all events can or should know.

Unfortunately, little that is certain can be said about the most important question which we must ask in this connection, the question concerning the transmitters of the teachings, especially those of the book of Proverbs, that is about the question concerning the role of the wise men. What are we to think of as the activity of a wisdom teacher? From what point in time can we reckon with the existence of wisdom teachers as a vocational group?

The adjective *ḥākām*, which we translate, not always correctly, as 'wise', is, as we know, not conferred only on people of a particular position. Rather, it describes men who, in some sense and in some sphere, are 'competent', 'skilled'.[13] It can be used even of manual workers or sailors. To what extent the word initially stands completely dissociated from a scale of values is clear from the reference in II Sam. 13.3 where it describes a man who is an expert in the shady tricks and dodges which at court lead one to the desired goal. It was precisely in this sphere that he was 'competent'. Even an embryo which cannot find the way out of the womb can be described as 'unwise' (Hos. 13.13).[14] The adjective used as a noun, 'the wise (man)', occurs frequently in the Solomonic book of Proverbs, but unfortunately there, too – and precisely in its pre-exilic parts – we do not find the expected clarity. In the majority of instances, the wise man is not the representative of a position, but simply the wise man who is contrasted, as a type, with the fool.[15] Such, too, is the case in the post-exilic Job dialogues where, for example, the friends are, on one occasion, addressed as wise men (Job 34.2; cf. also 17.10). However, a small group of references in Proverbs enables us to see, behind the description of the wise, men who are professionally occupied with teaching and with the collection of instructional proverbs.[16] The col-

---

[13] Ex. 36.8; 31.3, 6; 35.35; I Kings 7.14; Isa. 40.20; Jer. 9.16; 10.9; Ezek. 27.8. In addition, the situation is practically identical, from a semasiological point of view, in the case of the Greek concept *sophos*; cf. H. Fränkel, *Dichtung und Philosophie des frühen Griechentums*, 1962, p.275 and U. Wilckens, *TWNT*, VII, pp.467ff.

[14] Similarly Ex. 1.10; Jer. 4.22; Job 5.13.

[15] E.g. Prov. 14.3, 24; 15.2,7; 21.20; 29.11.

[16] Prov. 22.17; 24.23; 13.14; 15.12; see H.-J. Hermisson, op. cit., pp.133ff.

lections of proverbs which we discussed above were also used, as we
know too from ancient Egypt, in the schools for officials in Israel, as
material to be copied out or learned by the pupils. That these collections were put together specifically for the purposes of the school, that
is as school text-books, is not, however, likely.[17]

Even in post-exilic texts, the linguistic usage is still somewhat fluid.
But now the concept of the wise man as the scholarly teacher becomes
clearer and sharper and reaches its climax in Sirach. In Ecclesiastes
the effectiveness of the wise men's words is compared to that of ox-
goads (Eccles. 12.11). If one examines the great number of references
with a view to determining whether some of them are not rooted in
the institutional sphere, thereby providing us with a lead, then it is
noticeable that there were always two offices, the holders of which
are credited, in what is already almost a conventional way, with
being wise, namely that of king and that of his highest counsellors.[18]
The attribution is to be understood, therefore, less as a specific judgment of a specific person than as an old-established traditional idea:
the king is wise, as is the vizier and senior counsellor at court. Precisely this intensification to something typical makes the holders of
these two offices worthwhile objects of literary portrayal. This is clear
from that story which is widespread in the ancient Near East, the
story of Ahikar, the wise minister of Sennacherib, but also from the
tradition about Solomon's exemplary wisdom. Of greater interest for
us is the small group of passages in which the adjective 'wise' is used
as a noun to describe a vocational post. Thus, in Jer. 18.18 there is
linked with posts of priests and prophets a post of wise men, whose
function consisted in giving counsel. In the first instance here one will
have to think of the giving of political advice, and Ezek. 7.26, which
is closely related to Jer. 18.18, mentions elders as a third group alongside prophets and priests. These will scarcely have been professional
teachers. In Jer. 50.35f., the wise men of Babylon are mentioned as a
third group alongside the inhabitants and the officials (śārîm), and
this probably points to a post which had its own particular function
alongside that of the politicians.

It is only from the late period that we have texts from which details
can be deduced about what the activity of these teachers was in Israel
and about how they conceived of their office.

[17] Hermisson, op. cit., pp. 122ff.
[18] King: Isa. 19.11; 10.13; Ezek. 28.3. Officials: Gen. 41.33; Isa. 19.11; 30.4;
Jer. 50.35; 51.57.

1   On the other hand he who devotes himself
       to the study of the law of the Most High
     will seek out the wisdom of all the ancients
       and will be concerned with prophecies;
2   he will preserve the discourse of notable men
       and penetrate the subtleties of parables;
3   he will seek out the hidden meanings of proverbs
       and be at home with the obscurities of parables.
4   He will serve among great men
       and appear before rulers;
     he will travel through the lands of foreign nations
       for he tests the good and the evil among men.
5   He will set his heart to rise early to seek the Lord who made him
       and will make supplication before the Most High;
     he will open his mouth in prayer
       and make supplication for his sins.
6   If the great Lord is willing
       he will be filled with the spirit of understanding;
     he will pour forth words of wisdom
       and give thanks to the Lord in prayer.
7   He will direct his counsel and knowledge aright,
       and meditate on his secrets.
8   He will reveal instruction in his teaching,
       and will glory in the law of the Lord's covenant.
9   Many will praise his understanding,
       and it will never be blotted out;
     his memory will not disappear,
       and his name will live through all generations.
10   Nations will declare his wisdom,
       and the congregation will proclaim his praise;
11   if he lives long, he will leave a name greater than a thousand,
       and if he goes to rest, it is enough for him.   (Sir. 39.1–11)

This poem can be described precisely as an ideal portrait of a scholar
and teacher of the time of Sirach (about 200 BC). At any rate, there
are revealed here the essential characteristics of a calling whose task
it was to perceive truth. If one follows the thought-sequence of the
poem, the first object of research is the 'law of the Most High'.
Accordingly, such a teacher must have been primarily a scribe. With
certainty one can say that the old wisdom teachers were not that. If
one reflects, however, on the sequence of the individual statements of
the poem, then there definitely appear to be certain tensions inherent
in the office described, for starting from v. 1b, but with the exception

of v.8b, the sphere of the scholar's duties is described somewhat differently. At any rate, here the study of the Torah appears simply as one field of activity on a level with others. One could, therefore, almost reach the conclusion that in our text the traditional picture of a teacher has been secondarily supplemented by a new fact, namely that of competence in the law. According to this picture, the first feature was familiarity with the relevant tradition of the ancients, but also a concern with prophecy. To this office there belonged, further, the continual development in the teaching of recognized authorities, concern with the interpretation of proverbs and riddles. Occasionally such a wise man entered the service of a ruler and could then, in the course of his work for him, undertake journeys and widen his studies among other nations. All this, however, would have to be founded on a personal relationship of prayer with God, for God alone – if it was his will – could furnish him with a charisma which would enable him faithfully to fulfil his teaching office. The conclusion of the poem indicates something of his respected position in public life and of his fame, which will outlast him.

If this text, on the whole, shows us rather the outward range of the intellectual preoccupation of a wisdom teacher, Sir. 14.20–27 leads us into the heart of the matter, for this didactic poem reveals something of the internal dealings of the wise man with that truth to which he has devoted himself. This incomparable description of an academic eros is the sign of a high, intellectual culture. The description of a lover who pursues the beloved and encamps near her house begins very cautiously, for this is certainly not a developed comparison. The approach is described in a very restrained manner, as is also the fulfilment with which the search for wisdom is rewarded. A glance through her window, listening at her door, settling in the environs of her house, resting in her shade – that is all, but it is much.[19]

[19] The text is translated below pp. 168f.

III

THE FORMS IN WHICH KNOWLEDGE
IS EXPRESSED

THE HUMAN MIND has, in the course of its history, found and cultivated many different ways of assimilating and recording intellectual perceptions. When we approach the teachings of Israel's wise men, one peculiarity must strike us at once, a peculiarity which unites them above and beyond their great differences in form and content; they are all composed in a poetic form, they are poetry. And in no circumstances can that be considered to be an insignificant, external feature.[1] Indeed, this peculiarity cannot be separated from the intellectual process as if it were something added later; rather, perception takes place precisely in and with the poetic conception. One certainly cannot regard the phenomenon of the poetic expression as a transfiguration and a transformation, stemming from within a man, of experiences which, from the aesthetic point of view, are much less impressive, that is as a matter more of appearance than of reality. This radical subjectivization of the aesthetic factor which was widely current in the nineteenth century, cannot possibly do justice to poetry, certainly not that of an ancient people, for poetic expression was itself rather a specific form of the perception of truth, among ancient peoples one of the most important. It is the expression of an intensive encounter with realities or events and, in so far as it elevates the experience, expressed in words, out of the amorphous mass of experiences, is itself a part of this event. All art is, of course, imitation of reality. But in the course of this imitation there always takes place a process of transformation. Actuality is elevated to a dimension of truth, the validity of which can be recognized by all. Anyone who is of the opinion, then, that man's desire for knowledge can be validly expressed in the last resort only in the language of the so-called exact sciences, can, in view of their poetic form, rate Israel's perceptions,

[1] H.-G. Gadamer, *Wahrheit und Methode*, 1960, pp. 77ff., esp. p. 94.

with which we are here concerned, only as the outcome of a 'pre-scientific', 'pre-critical' and still very naive endeavour. There can be no question, however, that even in this poetic form a very discriminating power of intellectual distinction is at work.

Anyone who surveys the broad spectrum of wisdom forms and, in particular, closely examines their formal peculiarities, their choice of words, etc., will soon have the impression that the wise men have taken considerable care with the formal and literary presentation of their concepts, care which falls little short of that of the modern scientist. Of course, for the modern communication of knowledge in an educational context, the only possibility is to use the prosaic language of science. For it, the linguistic clothing is basically incidental. If the presentation is not in barbarous prose, then that is felt to be simply an additional attraction, for the value and importance of the concepts presented are not fundamentally affected by this. To this modern form of the communication of knowledge in an educational context, a form initiated by the Greeks, there is nothing corresponding either in the Old Testament or in the ancient Near East. The reasons for this cannot be discussed here. Let the simple, but significant assertion suffice, that Israel could not express her experience of reality in this way. The experiences of reality which confronted her could be appropriately presented only in artistic form. Thus, there was, for example, a whole group of perceptions (of natural phenomena) which could apparently be expressed only in hymnic form. We must, therefore, pay particular attention to the forms in which Israel expressed her knowledge. At the same time, we shall also take a step nearer to the material which we are trying to understand here, for one can never confine oneself to the forms alone; one always has to do with the contents at the same time. We are concerned here, therefore, with more than a simple outward recording of the specifically didactic forms. If we take seriously the idea that the forms can never be separated from the contents, then, in what follows, the reader will already be presented with something of the subject matter, even if, in the first instance, from a restricted point of view.

1. THE LITERARY PROVERB

Perhaps the almost complete disappearance of the 'maxim', of the 'adage', from the life of modern man and from recent poetry was needed to make us fully aware of the uniqueness of this strange, intellectual preoccupation which once played an outstanding role in every culture. Only rarely does one still meet men for whom a remembered stock of proverbs is more than a rhetorical flourish, whose life and thought are so rooted in such aids to living that they serve as indispensable signposts in making decisions large or small. The question is obvious enough, whether we moderns have not lost, with the disappearance of the maxim, a whole dimension of specific knowledge about the world. As far as Israel was concerned, one may ask, was such proverbial wisdom not of greater importance for the decisions of daily life and thus for orientation in the thick of everyday activity than, for example, the Ten Commandments which were pronounced over the cultic assembly only rarely on great festivals. These proverbs which Israel possessed were, of course, of very different types both as regards origin and form. Many of them may have stemmed from ancient folk-wisdom, others on the other hand came from books, even from foreign literatures, and can first have become popular only through the medium of the schools. Just as in the Middle Ages Latin authors were used for teaching purposes in monastic schools,[2] so too in schools in Israel they would work with ancient Egyptian and perhaps even Edomite proverbial material. If the popular proverb already reveals a tendency to linguistic refinement in that it happily exists in elevated language, then the literary proverb which comes from the schools differs from it by an essentially still stronger cultivation both of language and of content. It is, then, better to speak, in that case, of epigrammatic poetry. This is what we find in the Solomonic book of Proverbs, for the idea which used to be widespread, namely that its sentences are to be traced back to popular proverbs, can no longer be maintained.[3] Thus, in their present form they stem from school instruction, a fact which does not, of course, exclude the possibility that this or that popular proverb has also found its way into the collection.[4]

The most basic form of poetic expression for Israel, but also for other ancient Near Eastern peoples, was that of *parallelismus membrorum*, where the poet is forced to give expression to the subject-matter from two points of view, that is in two-verse stichoi. Enough

[2] F. Seiler, *Das deutsche Sprichwort. Grundriss der deutschen Volkskunde*, 1918, p. 16.
[3] H.-J. Hermisson, op. cit., pp. 52ff.
[4] What we designate by the term 'proverb', 'sentence' corresponds to the Hebrew *māšāl*. But the latter has a much wider range of meaning, for it can also designate a maxim, a frequently used figure of speech, even a whole didactic poem. Hermisson, op. cit., pp. 38ff.; A. R. Johnson, SVT 3, 1955, pp. 162ff.

has been said, since Herder, in praise of this 'thought rhyme', as it has been aptly described. Unquestionably, it offers the poet virtually inexhaustible possibilities of inflection of poetic thought. But is this parallelism also suitable for expressing ideas which have been assimilated? Would the constant reduplication of what is being stated not lead to a certain blurring and thus to a loss of precision? It would indeed, if the stating of these ideas were concerned with achieving as great a conceptual precision as possible. But this is certainly not the case. What is being aimed at is not precision in the concepts, but precision in the reproduction of the subject-matter, if possible over its whole range.[5] As far as that is concerned, the book of Proverbs is full of incomparably vivid and also very precise statements. Ancient Israel, too, was aware of a duty to make a given statement precise, but she demanded this precision not in the coining of terms but in the reproducing of facts.

One can designate the single line, composed of two parallel sections, as the basic form of ancient Israelite epigrammatic poetry; but one must resist the temptation to regard it as the starting point of a development to more and more extensive literary forms. The assumption that the smallest units stand at the beginning of a development and that the larger units can only have followed slowly after them has proved to be erroneous in the case of didactic poetry, too.[6] The single line often enough makes higher claims and demands a greater degree of intellectual participation than a developed didactic poem. The single line is, as a rule, much more dense and affords more room for manoeuvre from the point of view of meaning and application than the didactic poem, the content of which is much less ambiguous as to its meaning.

The balance and true scales are Yahweh's,
    all the weights in the bag are his work.   (Prov. 16.11)

It is not good to show partiality to a guilty man
    or to deprive him who is in the right of justice.   (Prov. 18.5)

A false witness will not go unpunished,
    and he who utters lies will not escape.   (Prov. 19.5)

[5] '. . . for the . . . Semites, parallelism is the equivalent of stereometry in the expression of thought, in that it is always keenly sharpened and its reflections are always highly pregnant', B. Landsberger, in: B. Landsberger and W. von Soden, *Die Eigenbegrifflichkeit der babylonischen Welt*, 1965, p. 17.

[6] Chr. Kayatz, *Studien zu Proverbien 1–9*, 1966, pp. 2ff. On this problem cf. also W. F. Albright, 'Some Canaanite-Phoenician Sources of Hebrew Wisdom', SVT 3, 1955, p. 4.

A wise man scales a city of heroes
    and throws down the bastion on which it relied.   (Prov. 21.22)

Put away from you crooked speech
    and put devious talk far from you.   (Prov. 4.24)

These proverbs are constructed in parallel form, that is, they are, precisely in their pregnant character, products of an explicit literary intention. Popular proverbs do not occur in this form. The examples cited show the simplest form of parallelism, namely synonymous parallelism, where the two parts of the sentence on either side of the caesura say approximately the same thing. The last of the examples is, in addition, constructed chiastically (verb and object are reversed); it reveals, therefore, as well, a particular stylistic refinement of which Hebrew poetry made frequent use.

He who belittles his neighbour lacks sense,
    but a man of understanding remains silent.
He who goes about as a talebearer reveals secrets,
    but he who is trustworthy in spirit keeps a thing hidden.
Without guidance a people falls,
    but there is help where there are many counsellors.
It is bad for someone to go surety for a stranger,
    but he who hates going surety is safe.
A gracious woman gets honour,
    but a woman who hates virtue is a throne of shame.
A kindly man does well for himself,
    but a cruel man harms his own flesh.   (Prov. 11.12–17)

These are examples of so-called antithetic parallelism. Something like ninety per cent of all the proverbs in the collection comprising Prov. 10–15 are antithetic in style. One can see that the contrasts are sharply opposed. But the endless possibility of variation in this literary form consists in the fact that these contrasts are not, in fact, precise opposites. What is said is not simply the opposite of what has gone before – that is, tautologically, with the elements completely reversed – that would be tedious. The antithesis has, in fact, a relative independence as a statement, while it turns the thought that has already been expressed, very freely into its opposite. In each case we have simply one possible opposite among many. In this way it stimulates thoughtful people to let its ideas play to and fro in their minds. But a particularly fine poetic form is to be found in so-called synthetic parallelism.

Grey hair is a splendid crown;
it is acquired in the way of righteousness.   (Prov. 16.31)

A judicious slave becomes master over a shameful son
and shares the inheritance with brothers.   (Prov. 17.2)

Death and life are in the power of the tongue;
and whoever loves it eats its fruit.   (Prov. 18.21)

The second part does not even say, not even in modified form, either the same as the first or the opposite of it. What is characteristic is the further development of the thought that has been expressed, mostly by way of an intensification towards a new thought. The first statement advances beyond its own limits; but the main interest is in the direction in which it is extended. Here, among the many directions in which an extension might be possible, something particularly striking must occur to the poet. Often it is an extension into the general, often a specialization, by means of which what has been said is completed.

Particular favourites, especially in the collection comprising Prov. 25–27, are those proverbs which are constructed as comparisons.[7]

A little with righteousness is better
than a large income with injustice.   (Prov. 16.8)

A dry morsel with quiet is better
than a house full of sacrifices with strife.   (Prov. 17.1)

It is better to live in the corner of the roof
than to live in a house with a nagging wife.   (Prov. 25.24)

Open reproach is better
than hidden love.   (Prov. 27.5)

Also to be taken separately are the proverbs of comparison which, however, we shall have to discuss again in another context.[8]

A breached city without a wall,
a man without self-control.   (Prov. 25.28)

Silver glaze over earthenware,
smooth lips and an evil heart.   (Prov. 26.23)

Clouds, wind, but yet no rain,
a man who boasts about a gift he does not have.   (Prov. 25.14)[9]

[7] H. H. Schmid, op. cit., p. 159, note 69, has suggested that this phraseology should be understood not in a comparative sense but in an exclusive sense: '. . . is good, not . . .'

[8] See below, pp. 119f.

[9] The verb 'to be' is lacking. To insert it in translation coarsens the statement, for in this the simplest form of juxtaposition, 'it remains quite undetermined which of the two juxtaposed phenomena is the subject of the sentence and which is the predicate' (Hermisson, op. cit., p. 145).

The phenomenon of 'gnomic apperception' (Petsch), that is, a quite particular way of acquiring knowledge and giving expression to it in a particular linguistic form, namely that of the 'maxim', exists in every culture in the world and must, therefore, be regarded as a rudimentary expression of man's search for knowledge. If one analyses it more exactly, then this form of man's intellectual preoccupation appears not uncomplicated. A decisive factor in the understanding of it is the close connection, even unity, between content and form. It is not the case that the perception lay ready somewhere and needed only its appropriate form of expression. Rather, it exists only in this form, or else it does not exist at all. The process of becoming aware of the perception and of giving linguistic expression to it in word and form are one and the same act. Thus, in this manner of formation, the main concern is not with a useful didactic means to easier retention and remembering. The constitutive meaning possessed by the word, the linguistic form, here points back to much more rudimentary noetic processes. The frequency of paronomasia in these proverbs, of assonance and alliteration, still shows us something of the magical, incantatory function possessed by the resonance of the word.[10] It cannot be denied that assonance, wordplay and the like could also become decorative, stylistic devices, especially in a period of literary refinement, which put the teacher in the position of being able to display his linguistic ability. Here, of course, it is difficult to draw the line. A similar case in point is the revelling in synonyms which we have already mentioned. One hesitates, however, to regard the piling up of synonymous expressions, such as we find in Prov. 1.1–5 and which we find strange, as a more or less empty rhetorical device. It is more reasonable to assume that the hypnotic piling up of nouns is an attempt to delimit a specific area of sense by the use of words which are full of meaning. In Job 18.7–10 there is an accumulation of technical hunting expressions, and Job 4.10f. has five words for lion (African lion, Asian lion, mother beast, cub etc.).[11] Is the wise man trying to shine in his ability with words and in his knowledge of zoology? One cannot entirely close one's mind to such an impression. But would that exclude the possibility that we are here dealing with more than mere 'empty bombast' (Duhm. *ad loc.*) and that, in fact, the multiplicity of words also has the function of widening the meaning? With only a single word for 'lion', the teacher would have been

[10] G. Boström, *Paranomasi i den äldre hebreiska maschalliteraturen*, 1928.
[11] L. Köhler, *ZDPV* 62, 1939, pp. 121ff.

unable to say what he wanted, namely that disaster assails the wicked in such and such a way.

Even if the sentences were also used in the schools, nevertheless their style is not directly didactic. Far and away the majority of them are statements which make assertions in thetical form quite neutrally, that is without any direct appeal to the listeners. They are not imperative in character but have, rather, a retrospective tendency and have, basically, only empirical value. In their own way and within their own sphere they simply wish to establish something positive, something unquestionably valid. The experiences are cited, the conclusions are drawn, and the result is produced.[12] The difference between exhortatory sentences and plain statements is unmistakable. While the exhortation suggests a quite definite mode of behaviour to the listener, statements, however forcefully presented, always have a characteristic openness, something that points beyond themselves, an element which leaves room for all kinds of associations and, indeed, in certain circumstances, even permits of a figurative interpretation.[13]

It has often been said that these observations are derived exclusively from experience. Undoubtedly it often required lengthy observation of similar processes until gradually it became possible to recognize certain natural laws, and so we only begin to understand this wisdom poetry if we see at work in it a lively intellect which asked urgent questions of the world around it and never abandoned the strenuous attempt to derive some kind of order from that world and then to give to it a fixed form. But experience alone would not be sufficient. Certainly Israel was convinced that events and happenings spoke to men, but if they already had a language, did they always speak unambiguously and in easily understandable terms? Further still, events had first to become experience, that is, they had to be comprehended. Things which were similar and homogeneous had first to be recognized as similar and homogeneous before they could be classified together. All of this then had to be expressed in words. Thus, between the events and the proverbs which deal with them there lay a wide-

[12] W. Preisendanz, *Die Spruchform in der Lyrik des alten Goethe und ihre Vorgeschichte seit Opitz* (Heidelberger Forschungen Nr. 1, 1952), pp. 13f.

[13] 'Exhortations' are considerably in a minority among the preponderance of statements in the collection comprising Prov. 10–29. They are found especially in the collection which is partly dependent on the Egyptian Amenemope, Prov. 22.17–24.22, also in 25.6–10, 16f., 21f.; 26.12; 27.1f., 10f., 13, 23. On the particular problem of 'exhortations' which are found in similar form in other parts of the Old Testament, too (e.g. Deuteronomy), see W. Richter, *Recht und Ethos* (*Versuch einer Ortung des weisheitlichen Mahnspruches*), 1966.

ranging and fairly complex intellectual activity, the operations of which are not made explicit; they can be deduced only from the end-products, that is from the thetical proverbs themselves. It involved considerably more than a mere adding together, as accurately as possible, of the available experiential material, more, that is, than simply the rather technical task of evaluating it pragmatically as well as possible. It involved also the production of a pattern of humane behaviour. In the fixing of each gnomic saying there also occurred a humanizing of man.

Thus, the interpretation of proverbial wisdom has its own problems. 'One must have understanding in order to grasp its understanding and have feelings in order to feel the beauty of its expression.'[14] It is, of course, utterly hopeless to approach the comprehension of the sentences from the side of the subjectivity of those who composed them. They contain nothing that is personally conditioned; everything has been elevated to the supra-personal level, to the level of general validity. We have to take into account the specific intellectual operations which have led to the origin of a sentence, simply because it was the product not of sudden inspiration but of intellectual effort. But this is also all that we can say in this respect. Thus the sentence has to speak for itself. Here, however, we come for the first time to the most difficult problem, namely the question of the general religious and ideological sphere, of the context from which any given sentence comes and on the basis of which it is to be understood. It is of the nature of an epigram that a truth is expressed with the greatest concentration on the subject-matter and with a disregard of any presuppositions, attendant circumstances, etc. Epigrams and sentences aim to be understood by everyone, and on this account they do not circumscribe their range of possibilities of comprehension; they offer no defence even against bold interpretations. Nevertheless, this intended general validity has its limitations. In the case of a modern sentence, we notice at once where a reliable interpretation or application stops and an unreliable one begins. How much more easily, in the case of a sentence from antiquity, can one reach the point where the meaning of a sentence is falsified for the simple reason that one has lost sight of ideological and religious factors which were constitutive for the sentence. This has happened among older exegetes who saw in these proverbs the expression of a shallow religion which had become

[14] J. G. Herder, 'Spruch und Bild insonderheit bei den Morgenländern', *Suphan*, Vol. 16, pp. 9f.

rationalistic and opportunist. But in contemporary studies, too, no satisfactory answer has been provided to the question about the specific field of understanding from which the sentences in the book of Proverbs must not be removed. A glance at Hesiod could help us to remain more flexible in this respect. The gnomic sayings in his book *Works and Days* have already invited comparison with biblical proverbial poetry.[15] Hesiod, who also wrote the *Theogony*, a work abounding in difficult, mythological references, was certainly not a man who looked at life from the point of view of trivial opportunism. Here we are in the fortunate position of finding, in one and the same author, the profound, religious and ideological context into which such proverbial poetry could obviously fit without tension or difficulty. Such a theological context must also be reckoned with in the case of the authors of Old Testament proverbial poetry. Here, of course, we neither know the 'authors' by name nor, much less, do we know anything of the theological subjects with which, in addition, they might have been concerned. Nevertheless, the attempt to reconstruct the intellectual and religious background from which the sentences arise must on no account be given up. It is, in any case, certainly not a hopeless undertaking. But this particular question can be pursued only in another context.[16]

If we have endeavoured to protect these ancient sentences from inappropriate interpretations, we must at the same time, however, remain open to the possibility that the sentences have changed in the course of their transmission in time, that their total intellectual and religious consciousness has radically altered. Basically, the sense of a sentence was never completely fixed; any attempt to understand it was always a flexible one. As an intellectual heritage from the past, the sentences were handed on. But who could prevent later generations from simply adapting a proverb to their own specific intellectual background and from bringing out that meaning which struck them particularly? Here we have to reckon with considerable flexibility and freedom in later interpretation. The wisdom sentence which states that man does not have the power to determine his way (Jer. 10.23) is taken up in the Qumran writings, that is in a vastly different religious atmosphere (1QS XI, 10; 1QH XV, 12f.). With no change in

---

[15] Most recently, O. Plöger in *Gottes Wort und Gottes Land* (Festschrift for H.-W. Hertzberg, 1965), pp. 159ff. F. Hölderlin had already dealt with this question in a master's thesis.

[16] See below 'Knowledge and the Fear of God', esp. pp. 57ff.

their wording, the sentences speak to later generations also and give them the guidance which they need.

Much rarer are the cases in which a sentence has been subjected, in the process of transmission, to a reshaping of both form and content. In the collection edited by the men of Hezekiah we read at the very beginning:

> It is the glory of God to conceal something;
> it is the glory of a king to search something out. (Prov. 25.2)

This is a fine, wide-ranging sentence which can set one's thoughts moving in many different directions. It speaks of the king's glory in investigation (at that time the king was the foremost champion and promoter of all searching after wisdom); but before this there stands the saying about God, whose glory lies in concealing, whose secrets, therefore, are to be worshipped by men. God conceals, kings discover – to both, glory is due. What a profound knowledge of God and of men is encompassed by this handful of words! In the late book of Tobit (third century BC), this proverb has become something quite different:

> It is praiseworthy to keep a king's secret hidden,
> but to reveal God's works is laudable. (Tob. 12.7)

Here, too, God and king stand opposite each other, once again characterized by secrecy and revelation. But now it is no longer a question of the right of them both, but of how man should behave towards them. Once the sentence had been modified in this direction, it was, surprisingly, the opposite sense which emerged from it, namely that one should speak of God's works but keep silent about the secrets of a king. Even the well-known sentence, that it is, in fact, a father who loves his son who disciplines him (Prov. 13.24), has acquired an entirely new content when it is applied to the relationship of God to man. One should not seek to evade being disciplined by Yahweh, 'for Yahweh disciplines him whom he loves' (Prov. 3.11f.).

2. OTHER FORMS OF DIDACTIC POETRY

It is not the intention in what follows to provide an exhaustive classification of all the literary forms in which Israel's perceptions in didactic form were put down. The possibility, indeed the necessity, of clothing one perception in one form and another in another, arose from the material itself as well as from the situation of the instructors. But one will not be able, in every case, to succeed in proving that specific perceptions could be expressed only in specific forms and not also in others. On the other hand, the chosen form was a neutral garb only in very few cases, so it is necessary to say something about particularly characteristic forms.

Numerical sayings: The counting and listing of things, of types of behaviour, of virtues, etc., is an elementary need of man in his search for order. This can be amply attested in many different forms in every culture.[17] In the case of the so-called numerical saying it is with this desire for order, planted deep within man, that we have to do, particularly in a quite specific form of proverb which was cultivated not only in Israel but also in other lands of the ancient Near East and which has increasingly attracted the interest of scholars.[18]

> These six things Yahweh hates and seven are 'an' abomination to him: proud eyes, false tongues and hands which shed innocent blood, a heart that devises wicked plans, feet which run quickly to evil, a false witness who breathes lies and a man who unleashes discord between brothers.
>
> (Prov. 6.16–19)
>
> Under three things the earth trembles and ' ' four it cannot bear:
> under a slave when he becomes king,
> and a fool when he is amply supplied with food,
> under a despised woman when she gets married
> and under a maid when she inherits her mistress's property.
>
> (Prov. 30.21–23)

The stylistic features can be easily recognized in these examples chosen at random. The characteristic feature is what is, from a thematic point of view, the very general introduction with the increasing numerical reference (from one-two up to nine-ten); characteristic, too, however, is the main body which follows and in which the empty numerical references are filled out with regard to content, always in accordance with the higher of the two numbers mentioned. The aim of this form of proverb is always the same, the collection of things which are similar where the assertion of similarity is the real surprise

---

[17] E. R. Curtius, *Europäische Literatur und lateinisches Mittelalter*, 1963[4], p. 499.
[18] On the numerical sayings, especially among Israel's neighbours, see G. Sauer, *Die Sprüche Agurs*, 1963; W. M. W. Roth, 'The numerical sequence x/x+1 in the Old Testament', *VT* 12, 1962, pp. 300ff.; ibid., *Numerical Sayings in the Old Testament*, SVT 13, 1965; H. W. Wolff, *Amos' geistige Heimat*, 1964, pp. 24ff.

element, for, regarded in isolation, the cases listed are quite dissimilar. Probably these proverbs also served in the schools for teaching and learning purposes. But in saying this we have still not answered the question concerning the stylistic peculiarity of this type of proverb. This form possesses, as one can assert with a great degree of probability, something of the nature of a riddle. The question: What is the highest? what is the worst? the quickest? etc. is found all over the world.[19] Once raised, it contains an element of stimulation, since everyone – 'I'll give you three guesses' – wants to get the answer first. Thus the introduction to numerical sayings has, for all practical purposes, the character of a challenging question, for the giving of numbers alone and the silence about what is meant stimulates the listener and keeps his curiosity in suspense.[20]

> There are three things which are stately in their tread,
> and four which are stately in their walk:
> the lion, the strong one among the beasts,
> who does not turn back for anyone,
> the cock as it struts and the he-goat
> and the king when he appears (?) among the people.   (Prov. 30.29–31)

The queen of Sheba is already supposed to have 'tested' Solomon with riddles (I Kings 10.1). A riddle has to be 'opened' (Ps. 49.5), and it is certain that riddles also formed part of the repertoire of the wisdom teachers (Prov. 1.6; Ps. 78.2; Wisd. 8.8; Sir. 39.3). From this it is only a small step to the puzzle game of which the charming story in I Esd. 3 tells. The young pages of king Darius banish the boredom of their night watch by answering the riddle, 'What is the strongest?'. Each one is to put his sealed answer under the king's pillow, and they expect a great reward for themselves as a result of his decision. The first one says, 'Wine'; the second, 'The king'; the third, 'Women'.[21]

---

[19] For the Greek cultural milieu, cf. B. Snell, *Dichtung und Gesellschaft*, 1965, p. 103.

[20] The number of objects collected together was not fixed. The one-two scheme is found (Sauer, op. cit., p.88). Contrasted with this is the nine-ten scheme in Sir. 25.7–11. The higher the number, the more colourless the proverb became. Between Prov. 30.18f. and Sir. 25.7f. there lies a sweeping, downward stylistic development. In the former there are four things which are too wonderful for the understanding but which, in one respect, can be arranged conceptually (see below pp. 122f.). In the latter there is a loose enumeration of important blessings in life (descendants, wife, friend, fear of God etc.).

[21] The answer of the third boy ('but truth is the strongest of all') has certainly been expanded secondarily along these lines. On the narrative see W. Rudolph, *ZAW* 61, 1945, pp. 176ff. The assumption that the narrative was of Greek origin does not seem to me to be necessary.

It is possible that numerical sayings belong directly to the *Gattung* of the riddle. The riddle is, after all, in the last resort, playing at discovering the truth. One person hides or disguises the truth, the other brings it out of concealment into the light,

> Who has woe, who has sorrow?
> Who has strife, who has complaining?
> Who has wounds without cause,
>   who has dull eyes?
> Those who linger over wine,
>   who come to taste mixed wine.   (Prov. 23.29f.)
> What is heavier than lead?
> And what is its name except 'Fool'?   (Sir. 22.14)

One cannot speak of a particular *Gattung* of the riddle. While we heard echoes of it above in a numerical saying, we shall also find it later, disguised as an allegory.

Autobiographical stylization: Not infrequently, perceptions are presented in such a way that they appear as an entirely personal discovery, as an entirely personal experience on the part of the teacher.

> I passed by the field of a lazy man
>   and by the vineyard of a foolish man.
> See, weeds were growing up everywhere . . .   (Prov. 24.30–34)
> I was young and have grown old,
>   but I have never seen the righteous forsaken,
>   or his children begging for bread.
> I saw an obstinate, godless man . . .
> I looked for him; he could not be found.   (Ps. 37.25, 35f.)
> When I was still young
>   and before I went on my travels,
> I took pleasure (in wisdom)
>   and sought her out.
> Before the temple I asked for her
>   and to the last I will search for her.
> She blossomed like a ripening vine
>   and my heart delighted in her.
> My foot wandered in her path,
>   from my youth I have searched for her.
> I inclined my ear to her a little and learned
>   and found much instruction for myself.   (Sir. 51.13–16)
> I, too, was the last to strive,
>   like one who gathers after the grape-gatherers have passed.

I excelled by the blessing of God,
    and like a grape-gatherer I filled the winepress.
Know that my efforts have not been for myself alone,
    but for all who seek instruction.   (Sir. 33.16–17)

Here we definitely have, rather, a traditional stylistic form in which
the teacher could, from time to time, clothe his instruction, and which
also allowed of being extended into larger units. Our modern interest
in the biographies of the biblical authors should not, therefore, be
misled, for here we are scarcely dealing with genuine experiences; at
any rate they appear in a highly conventionalized form.[22] Sirach is
the first in whom one might suppose an original, personal testimony.
But even if we were dealing with what is merely a stylistic form, it
would not be simply an unimportant, neutral element. It certainly
would enliven the teaching and awaken the listener's interest; but
probably it is more than merely a didactic device. In themselves, the
perceptions, over which these teachers took pains, possessed no personal note. We have already mentioned the endeavour to raise them
to the sphere of what is generally valid. Thus, rather, they tried to get
away from what was personally conditioned to what was supra-
personally true. To this extent, then, there almost seems to be a
contradiction between form and content. But here lies a peculiar
fascination, for the teacher shows in this particular way that such
perceptions must also be rooted in the life of the individual; in this
stylistic form the teacher makes himself personally responsible for the
perception which is being presented.

The long didactic poem: The textual material which falls under this
heading would alone provide sufficient material for a critical, stylistic
study. Till now, too much prominence has been given in research to
the various forms of the sentences. An examination of the didactic
poems which spread over a wider extent is still lacking. In the speeches
of the friends in the book of Job alone there are four didactic poems
about the end of the wicked, of the 'oppressor'; one can, therefore,
speak of a didactic prototype which enjoyed a certain degree of
popularity among the wise men. In three cases a stereotyped, didactic
allusion has been preserved ('This is the fate of the wicked man' or
the 'teacher's opening', 'I will tell you, listen to me' – Job 8.8; 15.17;
27.13). On one occasion the conclusion runs: 'That is the fate of the

---

[22] Examples: Ps. 37.25, 35f.; 73.2ff.; Job 4.8; 5.3; Prov. 7.6ff.; 24.30f.; Sir.
34.11f.

wicked man from God and the heritage of the "rebellious" man from God' (Job 20.29).[23]

> This is the fate of the wicked man (with) God,
>   and the heritage which oppressors receive from the Almighty.
> If his sons are many, it is for the sword,
>   and his offspring will never have enough food.
> Those of them who survive will be buried in death,
>   and their widows will not lament.
> Even if he heaped up silver like dust
>   and clothes like clay,
> the righteous will wear them,
>   and the innocent will divide the silver.
> He built his house like 'spiders' webs',
>   like a hut which the watchman makes.
> He lies down to sleep a rich man, but 'he will not do so again'.
> When he opens his eyes, there is nothing left.
> Terrors overtake him like floods,
>   and at night the storm carries him away.
> The east wind lifts him up, and he is gone,
>   and it whisks him away from his place.
> People throw stones at him mercilessly,
>   and he has to flee.
> They clap their hands at him
>   and hiss at him from their place.   (Job 27.13–23)

In these four didactic prototypes, with powerful, rhetorical pathos, the typical portrait of the wicked man and the typical end of his, initially perhaps, successful life are sketched. Terrors hunt him, and nemesis inevitably overtakes him at the end, so that he becomes an object of horror and loathing to those who survive him. He is under a curse, without descendants and an object of horror to a wide circle.

Each of these four didactic poems is a self-contained, artistic whole which presupposes discriminating listeners. Unfortunately, no answer can now be found to the question of who could have acted as model for these poems, to which social category this 'wicked man' (rāšāʿ), this 'oppressor' (ʿārîṣ), this 'godless man' (ḥānēp) belonged. All of the

---

[23] In relationship to Isa. 17.14, B. S. Childs has devoted an interesting study to the phrase 'this is the fate of . . .' and has seen in it an expression which stems from the wisdom school: *Isaiah and the Assyrian Crisis*, 1967, pp. 131ff. (To the examples cited there can be added Jer. 13.25 and Wisd. 2.9.) Whether it is only a concluding formula does not seem to me to be quite certain. In Job 27.13 it comes at the beginning, probably also in Jer. 13.25. In Job 8.13 and Wisd. 2.9 it comes in the middle.

elements have become too typified. In these didactic poems there is nothing specifically theological in the foreground. Their subject-matter is not so much divine punishment as the occurrence of disaster as such.

Alongside these didactic poems there are still others, which are scarcely to be compared to those we have just mentioned, such as the warning against bad company (Prov. 1.10–19), the didactic poem about the 'five-fold blessing of wisdom' (Prov. 2.1–22). Above all, however, there belong here the specifically theological problem poems (in the Egyptological field one speaks of 'contest literature'[24]), particularly certain psalms (Pss. 37; 49; 73; 139).[25]

Dialogue: By far the largest part of ancient Near Eastern contest literature consists of dialogues, for the dialogue form is the best medium for the development of a problem. Alongside the wealth of dialogue literature which we know from ancient Egypt and Meso-potamia, the didactic literature of Israel has only the dialogue of Job with his friends which, however, far surpasses its companion pieces outside Israel.[26] Whether the much simpler dialogues in the fables, for example in the Jotham fable or in the dispute between the Tamarisk and the Date Palm,[27] are literary precursors of the great dialogue poems still has to be decided. One is particularly conscious of the lack of a study of the specific nature of the thought-process which is at work in the great dialogues. Such a study would lead us out of what is, in any case, an erroneous comparison with Greek or even with modern dialogues. It is not surprising that these dialogues lack any personal, psychological delineation of the protagonists. More difficult for the modern reader is the lack of any genuine contact of the speakers with each other. In the case of Job, one often has the impression that he has not listened properly. Often, indeed, both protagonists get excited about the same thing, thus, for example, in the Job dialogue when they come to discuss the theme of divine freedom. With this lack there is connected the greatest difficulty, the lack of a clear statement of the subject of the debate and the lack of any clearly marked

---

[24] Eberhard Otto, 'Der Vorwurf an Gott (Zur Entstehung der ägypt. Ausein-andersetzungsliteratur)' in *Vortr. der Orientalist. Tagung in Marburg, Fachgruppe Ägyptologie 1950*, 1951.

[25] See further below pp. 203ff.

[26] On the 'Job theme' in Sumero-Akkadian literature see H. Gese, op. cit., pp. 51ff.

[27] Translated in H. Gressmann, *AOT*, pp. 294f.; Pritchard, *ANET*, p.410.

progress in the thought. When Job begins a lament (Job 7.14), he finds himself at once in the conventional *Gattung* of the individual lament and follows its conventional topics which often do not fit his biographical situation, so that for a while one loses sight of the problem. Now the Job dialogue certainly does not move in a circle; a progress in the thought can be discerned, but here not only one question but several are tackled and these are passed back and forth at will in the course of the speeches. However, caution is advised. Perhaps this movement of thought is strange to us rather than defective; for, after all, even we can still perceive that here questions are, rather, circled around and that precisely in this way a depth and a breadth are achieved in the discussion of the problem which could never have been intuited to this extent if the discussion had moved towards a solution by way of a linear progression. It is the intuition that is important above all. It is more important than a perception which can be formulated conceptually and then expressed in a sentence. As far as this intuition is concerned, the poet always aims at an effect of totality.

In a later period – we mention only the main points – there was composed in Israel another dialogue, one of the finest things ever written there, namely the conversation between Ezra and the interpreting angel in II(4) Esdras, which stems directly from the wisdom tradition.[28] In it, Ezra unfolds the intense despair which the catastrophe which befell Jerusalem in AD 70 had brought upon the pious Jews. The angel replies by forcing Ezra to reflect on ancient wisdom insights. We are certainly not plunged into such depths by the table-talk which was said to have been carried on in the Alexandria of the Ptolemies between learned Jews and the king Ptolemy II Philadelphus. The learned Jews are never for a moment at a loss for an answer to the questions asked by the king. From the literary point of view this is no masterpiece.[29]

Fable and allegory: With the fable, too, which was once a 'great literary force', we nowadays no longer have a direct relationship; we have to try to make it our own by the devious route of a historical understanding. But here, too, we are dealing with a primitive form of human

---

[28] G. Reese, *Die Geschichte Israels in der Auffassung des früheren Judentums* (Type-written dissertation submitted to the Theological Faculty in Heidelberg, 1967), pp. 136ff.

[29] The so-called Letter of Artisteas was written c. 100 BC. The use of older traditions is not excluded. Translated in *The Apocrypha and Pseudepigrapha of the Old Testament*, ed. R. H. Charles, Vol. II (Pseudepigrapha), pp. 83–122.

intellectual activity. It has, certainly correctly, been stressed that the fable, according to its proper character, does not pursue moral goals but tries simply to present a truth, a reality, something which is typical and which is as it is.[30] Frequently, the disclosure of the truth drives it into the realm of cruelty.[31] The poetic process is, of course, remarkable enough, for in the fable there occurs a veiling of something everyday, a kind of alienation in the direction of the unreal and the fabulous. But precisely in this strange dress the truth is more forceful than in the everyday where it is so easily overlooked. This effect is particularly marked especially where the truth presented is drawn in the direction of the comic. The yield of animal and plant fables from the literature of the ancient Near East is enormous. Of course the fable as a *Gattung* belonged originally to all and was not the prerogative of a learned class. But the schools have certainly made their contribution to its collection and further cultivation. In the Old Testament only very few fables have been preserved. This could be attributed to the religious point of view which was determinative for the collection of Israel's literature.

> The trees once went forth to anoint a king over them; and they said to the olive tree, 'Reign over us.' But the olive tree said to them, 'Shall I leave my fatness, for which gods and men honour me, and go to sway over the trees?'
> And the trees said to the fig tree, 'Come you, and reign over us.' But the fig tree said to them, 'Shall I leave my sweetness and my good fruit, and go to sway over the trees?'
> And the trees said to the vine, 'Come you, and reign over us.' But the vine said to them, 'Shall I leave my wine which cheers gods and men, and go to sway over the trees?'
> Then all the trees said to the bramble, 'Come you, and reign over us.'
> And the bramble said to the trees, 'If in good faith you are anointing me king over you, then come and take refuge in my shade; but if not, let fire come out of the bramble and devour the cedars of Lebanon.'
> (Judg. 9.8–15)

This masterpiece of the most concise reasoning and linguistic style is not popular poetry but, after its own fashion, a perfect artistic poem and is intended to be taken as such. This fable operates happily in

[30] K. Meuli, 'Herkunft und Wesen der Fabel', *Schweiz. Archiv f. Volkskunde* 50, 1954, pp.65, 68, 77. Of course, the fable, with its many different types, could fulfil very varied functions. E. Leibfried, *Fabel* (1967).
[31] One can think, for example, of the cruel fable of the hawk and the nightingale in Hesiod, *Works and Days*, ll.202ff.

the political sphere, and it is the mouthpiece of men to whom any form of kingly dominion is suspicious, if not downright intolerable. Only a scoundrel, only someone who really has nothing to contribute to the welfare of the whole will lend himself to it. But the one who has nothing to offer actually has the audacity to invite the others into the security of his protection and at the same time to utter shameless threats. The fable is extremely daring, for it exposes the monarchy – what is meant is the absolute monarchy of the Canaanite city states – to ridicule. Its great antiquity is uncontested; to determine its political setting in Israel is almost hopeless. Such a polemic must, however, have had a public which was amused by the satire.[32]

> The thistle on Lebanon sent to the cedar on Lebanon and said, 'Give your daughter in marriage to my son.' Then the wild beasts of Lebanon passed by and trampled on the thistle.   (II Kings 14.9)

This fable, too, had acquired a function in a political situation, for it appears as the answer of a king who is challenged to a war. Obviously it is incomplete; it is brief, and the action is also rather obscure. Rather, it seems to refer to a marriage proposal which is not in accord with class distinctions. One has the impression that it was reduced to those elements which alone had something to say in the political situation. What a period, when kings, in diplomatic communications, wielded the intellectual weapon of the fable!

In this context there belongs also the prophet Nathan's story of the rich man who had taken from the poor man his only lamb (II Sam. 12.1–4). Here, too, it is easy to see that the fable only very approximately fits the offence which David had committed against Uriah. The fable's dominating feature, the touchingly intimate relationship between the poor man and his lamb, has, at any rate, no obvious correspondence in the case of Uriah. In addition, David not only took Uriah's wife from him but also had him killed. There are definite signs that the fable was not an *ad hoc* creation but existed independently of the case to which Nathan applied it. Another aspect of it is, however, more important. Both here and in II Kings 14, along the

---

[32] The most recent detailed treatment of the Jotham fable is in W. Richter, *Traditionsgeschichtliche Untersuchungen zum Richterbuch*, 1963, pp. 282ff. That this fable does not fit exactly the historical situation has long been recognized. When Jotham spoke, the Shechemites already had a king and had no occasion to worry about whom to choose. But a fable was certainly not expected to correspond in all its details to reality. What was important was the main thought; the listener took care of all the rest.

lines of the Jotham fable, the speaker, by means of an added interpretation, helps the listener to the correct application of the material of the fable. In this way the fable acquires an explicitly didactic interpretation which was originally foreign to it. But such a change in meaning could, of course, happen quickly in the case of the fable. With the application of the fable to a specific biographical or political situation, a fundamental change takes place in it, for in this way it acquires allegorical features. Certainly, not every single element in the fable is equally productive when it is applied to a specific situation. But, in the case of many of them, each element challenges the listener to provide an appropriate interpretation. One skips quietly over those elements which are unproductive. A similar situation occurs in the case of the two fables in Ezekiel, the one about the great eagle who broke a twig off a cedar of Lebanon (Ezek. 17) and the one about the lioness with her whelps (Ezek. 19), for these are well on the way to becoming pure allegories. One can ask whether Ezekiel was using what was still genuine fable material. If he was, then it was in very free imitation, for here, in contrast to the fables just cited, the narrative material itself is already strongly stamped by the application. The fable *Gattung* has here been greatly disintegrated by the prophet for his own purposes.

The allegorizing of historical events, which begins in Ezekiel, was subsequently developed in apocalyptic to provide great allegorical presentations of the whole history of Israel, as for example in the vision of animals (I Enoch 85–90) where all the principal events of Israel's history are mirrored in the changing fortunes of a herd of sheep and bulls. The same is, of course, true of the vision of the cloud (Syriac Baruch 53–71). Since we are here dealing with the stylistic form of dream-visions, it may well be supposed that this form of allegorizing belongs originally to the science of dream interpretation which is very old in the East. Are, then, the dreams of Joseph about the sheaves of corn and the stars bowing down, or those of the Pharaoh about the seven cows and the seven ears of corn, which are also interpreted allegorically, so very different from these (Gen. 37.5ff.; 41.1ff.)?

But such a veiled manner of speaking, which arouses reflection precisely through its veiled character, is also encountered in quite different didactic contexts:

Drink water from your cistern
   and what flows from your well,

so that your springs are not scattered abroad,
   nor streams of water in the squares.
To you alone they should belong,
   but not to any foreigner besides yourself.
May your well be blessed
   and rejoice in the wife of your youth,
the lovely hind and graceful doe. . . .   (Prov. 5.15–23)

Here is an exhortation which, to begin with, is couched in allegorical terms. Only from the last half verse is the meaning of the image clarified. The fountain, the spring, is the man's own wife. At the same time, however, the springs and streams of water recall the power of procreation and children. Thus: keep strange women at arm's length, remain true to your wife. The allegorizing veil was a means of making the exhortation more refined from a rhetorical point of view in order to make it more emphatic.

> Remember also your Creator in the days of your youth, before the evil days come, and the years draw nigh, when you will say, 'I have no pleasure in them'; before the sun and the light, and the moon, and the stars are darkened and the clouds return after the rain; in the day when the keepers of the house tremble, and the strong men are bent, and the grinders cease because they are few, and those that look through the windows are dimmed, and the doors on the street are shut. . . . before the silver cord is snapped, or the golden bowl is broken, or the pitcher is broken at the fountain, or the wheels broken at the cistern.
> (Eccles. 12.1–6)

The famous allegory of growing old now stands under the admonition: Remember your Creator before the evil days of old age come. But here, too, we surely originally have, rather, a specific form of the riddle. What is it? The keepers of the house tremble, the strong men are bent, only a few grinders are left, etc.? Answer: It is old age. There are gathered together here separate elements, each of which requires to be interpreted on the basis of the idea of the human body as a house which is still inhabited but which has slowly crumbled. The 'keepers' are the arms, the 'strong men' the legs, the 'grinders' the teeth, then follow eyes and ears. The occasional confusion of image and object did not trouble the ancient listener. Fully worked out allegories are, of course, rare. Often an image is allegorical only in parts, only to move away from that particular style again. Above all, the transitions between what is simply metaphorical and what is allegorical are fluid. But wherever we are dealing with a number of pictorial elements, each of which requires interpretation, we are jusitfied in calling it allegorical speech.[33]

We may speak of *didactic narrative* when the presentation dispenses with puzzling literary devices and when a specific context of events is presented quite openly as far as its outward sequence is concerned. In the ways in which the didactic purpose of the narrator is expressed there are considerable differences. In this respect, the Joseph narrative shows great restraint, both at its climax and in its individual features; for example, in the description of Joseph's innocence only the person who is capable of listening sensitively really feels himself addressed. Similarly in the prose narrative in Job, it is the events, the spoken word, which instruct. Only in the summary sentences (Job 1.22; 2.10b) does the narrator address the reader from outside of the narrative. Much more powerful are the didactic emphases in a narrative which have been placed there by an event which a wise man has observed in the street (Prov. 7.6ff.). The story of Tobit also releases its teachings directly and openly, for here it is not just the events themselves which instruct; in addition, the narrator places voluminous instructions on the lips of the protagonists. Such didactic narratives have, of course, rarely been 'written' *ad hoc*; as a rule they cast old narrative material in a new form. In the case of the Tobit narrative this is generally acknowledged.[34] In the case of the Joseph narrative it cannot be proved; but it is fairly certain that the story of the vizier who climbed to power and honour must have had its earlier stages. Already, for the narrator of Genesis, it lay in the distant past.

The level of ancient Israelite narrative art can be recognized in the mastery with which narrative expositions were composed. If this is already true of literary narratives such as those in the books of Samuel, then it is certainly true also of didactic narratives. The exposition of the Joseph story sets the reader, with its very first sentences, in the centre of a scene agitated with passions, on the one hand the father's

---

[33] An interesting survey of the modern use (going back as far as Goethe and Schelling) of the term allegory has been made by A. J. Björndalen, *Tidskrift for teologi og kirke*, 1966, pp. 145ff. It would be true to say of the Old Testament that one must speak of an allegory where we have a passage containing two or more metaphors belonging to the same context of meaning and mutually interpreting one another.

[34] It is, as is well known, the story 'of the grateful corpse'. It must of course be emphasized that this old material has been so altered in the present narrative as to be unrecognizable. Thus, knowledge about the long pre-history of the material is of no help in understanding the present narrative.

love, on the other the brothers' hatred. This is followed by Joseph's two dreams, which direct one's gaze into a still veiled future. The exposition closes with the sentence, 'And his brothers were jealous of him, but his father kept the thing in mind' (Gen. 37.11). Events as such come into play only when the father sends the defenceless Joseph to the brothers who are busy far away with their herds. The most artistic of all expositions has been achieved by the narrator of the book of Tobit. It consists of two sections which run parallel to each other and which correspond from the point of view of their form. The first deals with the old man Tobit who has buried a corpse which lay near his house and who is completely impoverished by adverse circumstances which have a connection with this occurrence. The other deals with a young girl whose suitors were each strangled on their wedding night by a wicked demon. These two people, independently of each other and widely separated from each other, ask God to let them die. God, however, hears the prayers of these two, who do not know each other, and links their destinies for good (Tob. 1–3). The real action begins only in Tob. 4.

A sharp differentiation of didactic narrative from other types of narrative is naturally impossible. The points of transition are fluid. Does the militant book of Judith belong more with historical narratives? From the point of view of its material it leads the reader into the military and political sphere and, tricked out with a whole load of partly confused, historical reminiscences, tells of a woman's heroism. Nevertheless, this narrative, too, will have to be credited with a didactic purpose which goes beyond the communication of sensational events, for the theme of the book is the uniqueness of Israel's God, the questioning of it and its historical proof. Much more obviously, in this respect, are the Daniel narratives to be classified here, especially Dan. 1; 3–6. They certainly do not come from that period of terrible religious persecution by Antiochus Epiphanes (167 BC), but from a much earlier time, namely from a Diaspora situation in which the Jews were certainly not persecuted but in which, on the contrary, the way to high offices of state lay open to them. But this very loyalty to the great king concealed the possibility of quite specific religious conflicts.

Prayers: It is an established result of *Gattung*-criticism that in the Psalter, as well as in other, mostly later books, 'wisdom psalms' are to be found. Behind this assertion there remains much that is still obscure, for one cannot speak of a particular *Gattung* of didactic prayers, only of a common language and motif. We have no certain criteria for the determination of these psalms. On the contrary, these poems belong to various psalm-types which they appear to imitate. Thus it is, rather, a general impression, one of a certain erudition and didactic quality, of a preponderance of theological thoughts, etc., which entitles us to separate these psalms from the great body of predominantly cultically orientated psalms. At any rate, the *Sitz im Leben* of these poems cannot be sought in the cult. 'The problem in psalm exegesis is not the cultic psalms, but the non-cultic ones.'[35] The circle of psalms which are to be reckoned as belonging to this group sometimes becomes wider and sometimes is drawn a little tighter, a fact which is not surprising in view of the lack of definite indication as to *Gattung*. Obviously we are dealing here with a type of school poetry which, in the post-exilic period, was delivered to an audience of pupils. It is possible that the wise men wrote down such prayers also for their own edification. The impression of a certain dichotomy – prayers to God and instruction for pupils – is awakened only in the modern observer. At any rate, they are genuine prayers, and the often sublime pathos of these hymns, etc., is pure. The didactic element scarcely obtrudes.[36] Often we recognize it only in the diction and in the motifs which we encounter otherwise only in explicitly didactic texts.

Let us then be satisfied here with the fact that the teachers, in a late period, gradually dominated, from a stylistic point of view, all types of psalms, from the hymn, by way of the thanksgiving, to the individual lament, and that these forms, borrowed from the cult, became for them, in an outstanding way, vessels for the expression of their perceptions and their problems. Although the types which they adopted can be recognized with comparative ease, in actual fact something new came into being at the hands of the teachers, for here, for the first time, the prayer has been elevated to become a genuine literary form and to become, at the same time, a specific form of expression for specific perceptions. This is particularly true of the hymn. There were, for Israel, perceptions which could be expressed, strangely

[35] S. Mowinckel, 'Psalms and Wisdom', SVT 3, 1955, p.205. Characteristic indications of this *Gattung* are to be found in Gunkel-Begrich, *Einleitung in die Psalmen*, 1933, pp.389ff.; H. L. Jansen, *Die spätjüdische Psalmendichtung, ihr Entstehungskreis und ihr 'Sitz im Leben'*, 1937, esp. pp.133f.

[36] In post-canonical wisdom poetry, the didactic element comes more to the fore. Thus, e.g., in the Psalms of Solomon 15, the relationship is reversed. It is teaching rather than prayer.

enough to our ears, only in the form of the hymn. We have, therefore, every right, in the discussion that follows, to draw freely upon such hymnic texts. Typical of the way in which the prayer became a literary form, is the note that Tobit 'wrote' his song of praise (Tob. 13.1). We also know for certain that Sirach composed hymns, and he was certainly not the first to do so. A special group is formed by those poems which deal with problems or meditations, which deal with serious attacks and offer solutions for those problems which threaten faith (Pss. 49; 73; 139).[37] Another group are the Torah-psalms, especially Pss. 1 and 119, which celebrate the revelation of Yahweh's will as the source of all knowledge and as an indispensable guide in life.[38] In all these texts mentioned here, one cannot be sufficiently amazed at how easily, and almost without a break, harrowing thoughts and praise can stand side by side. Nowhere is this more impressive than in the *Gattung* of the 'judgment doxology', which was first developed into an important literary prayer-form by these teachers.[39]

Were we to continue the enumeration of the literary forms used by the teachers (and this would certainly be possible), one result would not be changed. All of these forms, together with their contents, are to be designated as poetic, as products of the poetic aspect of the human intellect. This is, of course, also true of those which are written in solemn, poetic prose. Here we must also keep in mind the fact that in the ancient world poetry was not so far removed from daily life, a fact which is still true of the East today. The step from the prose of everyday language to poetry could, at that time, be taken more easily and more naturally. Everywhere in everyday life, even in diplomatic communications between heads of state, poetry had its rightful place. This is explicable only for the reason that the phenomenon of poetry was at that time still accorded a quite different, more serious function in public life, too, in so far as one recognized that poetic expression was particularly forceful in expressing truth. Its function was not simply to transmit factual knowledge. It was capable of deriving more from the affairs and events of life. There is even an intensifying, 'compressing' element which is always characteristic of it, and therefore its fixing of perceptions in connected words can claim to possess a greater degree of truth. In that period, a wide range of basic percep-

---

[37] See below pp. 203ff.
[38] The psalms to be included in this group are Pss. 1, 34, 37, 49, 73, 111, 112, 119, 127, 128, 139.
[39] On the so-called 'judgment doxology' see below pp. 196, 211ff.

tions about life and the world could be expressed only in poetic form, and thus poetic expression was something which was necessary for life and knowledge. This poetic function of fixing perceptions was occasionally characterized by the solemnity of an oath, just as even today a poetic word can exercise a magical power.

Only the man who has allowed his senses to be dulled in his dealing with the materials or who does not know the real purpose of this poetic wisdom can be deceived as to the magnitude of the intellectual achievement of our wisdom teachers. Pindar, who also made the connection between wisdom and poetry his business, describes this way of recording knowledge as 'work', 'toil'. Here, use is made of more than simply the comprehending intellect; we are dealing here with an already acquired knowledge, a knowledge which man professes and which he lives out.[40] If, in this way, knowledge acquired such an eminently human appearance, then from this there can be explained its most remarkable feature, its character as a game.[41] In many sentences, above all in the cryptic literary forms such as the fable, the numerical saying, the allegory, in their word-plays and especially when the farcical is touched upon, this game-like character is quite evident. Even the literary forms of the wise men confirm for us the strange fact that there are perceptions which can be expressed only in the form of an intellectual game. Pindar's saying, however difficult to translate into Hebrew, was also true, as far as its meaning goes, of Israel, 'Blind is the mind of him who, without the Muses, seeks out the steep path of wisdom.'[42] Israel does not seem to have wondered at all about the phenomenon of the art of poetry as such. But in this domain she has been highly daring and also highly successful. However, we shall have to keep this aspect of the matter in mind, for it will later become clear that Israel was able to justify, in a surprising way, her right to play with the truth which was inherent in the world.

[40] 'The proverb differs from a statement which communicates only factual material in that it is able to grasp not only the factual, but a human element, an inner attitude, an intellectual relationship to the factual.' W. Preisendanz, op. cit., p. 12.

[41] H.-G. Gadamer, op. cit., pp. 97ff.

[42] The two quotations from Pindar (Paean 7b) are taken from B. Snell, *Dichtung und Gesellschaft*, 1965, p. 134.

PART TWO

THE LIBERATION OF REASON AND THE RESULTANT PROBLEMS

IV

KNOWLEDGE AND THE FEAR OF GOD

WHAT IS, in biblical scholarship, usually meant by the 'wisdom' of Israel is not designated by one single, invariable term in the didactic literature of the Old Testament. The Hebrew word for wisdom (*ḥokmā*) has no precedence among the various terms; it is only one amongst others. There are the two words from the same root, *t^ebūnā* and *bīnā*, which we translate by 'understanding'. Alongside these, the word *da'at* ('knowledge') is prominent. The word *m^ezimmā* 'plan', 'thought', 'prudence' also plays a part in instruction and has approximately the same meaning. Lastly, to mention only the most important, there is the word *mūsār* which means, initially, 'correction', but much more frequently its result, namely 'discipline', thus coming close in meaning to the Greek *paideia*.[1] How closely these and other terms are connected with each other is seen in the fact that they often appear happily alongside each other. Not infrequently, in parallelism, they become intertwined almost to the point of a synonymity which is often difficult for us to understand. Naturally these words are not, strictly speaking, synonymous, but the teachers believe that there is no better way of presenting their subject-matter in appropriate fashion, not by the use of terms which are clearly differentiated one from the other, but by the opposite means, namely by the juxtaposition of words related in meaning. Notice, in the following examples, only the almost playful coordination of the terms 'wisdom', 'understanding', 'knowledge', 'prudence' and realize what a difficult task the exegete has as a result.

> For Yahweh gives wisdom;
> from his mouth come knowledge and understanding.   (Prov. 2.6)

[1] *t^ebūnā*: Prov. 2.2, 3, 6; 3.13; 8.1; 10.23; 14.29; 15.21; 17.27; 20.5; 24.3; *bīnā*: Prov. 3.5; 9.6; *da'at*: Prov. 1.4; 9.10; 11.9; 13.16; 24.4, 5; 30.3; *m^ezimmā*: Prov. 1.4; 3.2; 5.2; 8.12; *mūsār*; Prov. 1.8; 3.11; 4.13; 10.17; 12.1; 13.18, 24; (22.15;) 15.32, 33; 23.12; 24.32.

For wisdom will enter your heart,
and knowledge will be pleasant to your soul;
prudence will watch over you,
and understanding guard you.   (Prov. 2.10f.)

He who does not waste his words is an expert in knowledge,
and a cool-headed man is a man of understanding.   (Prov. 17.27)

The beginning of wisdom is the fear of Yahweh,
and knowledge of the Holy One is understanding.   (Prov. 9.10)

An intelligent mind acquires knowledge,
and the ear of the wise seeks knowledge.   (Prov. 18.15)

A wise man is 'mightier' than a strong man,
and a man of knowledge is 'more than one full of strength'.
(Prov. 24.5)

Obviously one would not arrive at this form of speech if one insisted on taking the words, at all costs, in accordance with their various shades of meaning. A differentiation in meaning certainly comes into play, but one must also take into consideration a certain ceremonial quality in the speech, a circumstantiality in speech which has become a game. If one asks what emerges from this stylization, then it is certainly not so much nuances appropriate to the perception being expressed as a desire to convince. The use of the artistic device of repetition is obvious from the very beginning in the case of didactic speech. From the point of view of content, these sentences have, of course, much to do with the human intellect. They point to something which one can teach and which the pupil has to make his own by incorporating it into his 'understanding', his store of knowledge.

At this point many questions arise. In what way did Israel herself think about this knowledge? To what phenomena was it directed and what purpose did it serve? Was its success dependent on specific, perhaps even religious suppositions? It would be particularly important to see more precisely how the teachers accommodated this strongly committed intellectual faculty to their faith in Yahweh. Although we shall come across these questions again and again in the course of our discussion, at this stage some basic points must be made.

1. It seems a simple matter to answer the question about the unalterable presupposition and prerequisite of every possession of wisdom and understanding. Does the Old Testament not say often enough that Yahweh is the giver of wisdom? But this conviction was not universal in every period, for the passages which describe wisdom *expressis verbis* as a special gift of Yahweh obviously come from a fairly

late period.[2] From this it can be inferred that the concept that all
wisdom comes from God is to be attributed to specific, theological
considerations which came to the fore only at a fairly late stage. For
the wise men who taught in this advanced period, the endowment of
man with intelligence and with a productive ability for differentiation
was not simply on the same level as other gifts of God – honour, life,
wealth, posterity – but was recognized and thought of as a phenomenon of a particular type and, above all, of special theological significance. The statement that wisdom and understanding come from
God has the weight of a considered, theological pronouncement.
Wisdom and understanding have here ceased to be something which
is given to every man 'by nature'. Occasionally, the wise men speak
of the receiving of this gift as an inspiratory event.

> I am young in years,
>   but you are aged.
> For this reason I timidly held back
>   from telling you what I knew.
> I said to myself, 'Let age speak,
>   let many years teach wisdom.'
> But it is the spirit in man,
>   the divine breath, which makes him understand.
> It is not always the old who are wise,
>   nor the aged who understand what is right.
> So I said to myself, 'Listen to me,
>   I, too, will tell what I know.'
> Look! I waited for your words,
>   listened to your insights.
> I am full of words,
>   the spirit within me constrained me.
> My heart is like wine
>   that has no air . . .
> I must speak to give vent to my feelings,
>   must open my lips and answer. (Job 32.6–11, 18–20)

Here a young wisdom teacher presents himself in full vigour, almost,
indeed, with an apparently baroque flourish. Skilfully, he begins with
the dilemma in which he finds himself. Politeness demands that he
keep silent; truth, on the other hand, that he speak. Every listener

[2] Ex. 28.3; 31.3, 6; 35.31, 35; 36.1f.; I Kings 3.4ff, 28; 5.9ff.; Ps. 51.8; 119.98;
Job 35.11; Prov. 2.6; Eccles. 2.26; Dan. 1.17; 2.21, 23; on this see M. Noth, 'Die
Bewährung von Salomos "göttlicher Weisheit"', SVT 3, 1955, pp. 225ff.

concedes that he must decide for the latter, for – and here we come
to the relevant idea – it was God himself who entrusted him with a
perception which forced him to speak. This friend of Job's describes
the perception which he has received from God in terms which recall
a type of prophetic inspiration. The spirit within him has 'constrained'
him. The perception which had come to him is something strong
which he is unable to resist. The language selected will have to be
attributed to the cultivated erudition of the later wisdom teachers
who had at their disposal a wide range of forms and concepts which
enabled them to express their ideas artistically.

Still more strongly in the case of Eliphaz, another of Job's friends,
the act of theological perception has the character of an experience
from outside. It provides simple sentences with a theological prologue
in which are described precisely the circumstances accompanying the
reception of revelation in a way in which not even any prophet describes them, and this at a period when prophets were perhaps known
only from books. But this was what was demanded by the fastidious
literary taste of a certain cultural level in later Israel.

> A word stole into my mind,
>   and my ear received the whisper of it.
> In the broodings of night-visions,
>   when a deep sleep falls upon men,
> terror and trembling came upon me
>   and made all my bones shake,
> a breath passed over my face,
>   all the hair on my body stood on end.
> Someone stood there, but I did not recognize him;
>   there was a figure in front of my face.
> I heard a whisper,
>   'Is mortal man righteous before God?'   (Job 4.12–17)

Meanwhile we must not think that these wise men acquired cheap
renown by means of empty bombast. They were faced with difficult
problems which could be tackled only with concentrated thought,
and these men felt that they were enabled to face this exacting work
by a direct, divine impulse. It is, indeed, not difficult to see how even
the literary display keeps pace in this development with the seriousness of the questions which these teachers asked themselves. Correspondingly, the need also grew to legitimatize the perceptions gained –
they were mostly of a theological nature – as deriving from a prior act
of divine inspiration. A connection was then obvious with ideas which

were originally prophetic. Actually, in such texts is expressed a feeling for the stature peculiar to a decisive gain in knowledge. It was given a divine origin, and it was felt to be necessary to provide it with a corresponding literary form of expression. The matter did not, of course, end with the belief that God himself assisted man in his search for knowledge. Even with this divine assistance, the teachers were not relieved of the duty of being accurate in their reasoning and of explicitly refuting erroneous opinions. In addition, the teachers of the later period, such as Sirach, the author of the Wisdom of Solomon and the apocalyptists, had to appear conversant with the wisdom of foreign nations in order to remain on top of the knowledge of their time.

2. If we now turn to the older sentence wisdom as it is collected especially in Prov. 10–29, then there appears an enormous gulf between this and what we have just said, for there is absolutely no trace here of such a serious, theological motivation, in terms of specific acts of inspiration, of the knowledge acquired. In vain do we look here for specific reflections on the origin of the perceptions produced – we shall discuss shortly the important exception in Prov. 1.7; 15.33. Thus, since the objects of this search for knowledge were of a secular kind, questions about man's daily life, systematic reflection on them was held to be a secular occupation about which no more needed to be said except that it was to be pursued in an organized and careful way.

> On the lips of him who has understanding wisdom is to be found,
>> but a stick is for the back of him who lacks understanding.
>>> (Prov. 10.13)
> If the boaster seeks wisdom, it is in vain;
>> but knowledge is easy for the man of understanding.   (Prov. 14.6)
> To get knowledge is better than gold,
>> and to get wisdom better than silver.   (Prov. 16.16)
> The purpose in a man's mind is like deep water,
>> but a man of understanding draws it up.   (Prov. 20.5)
> Go about with wise men, and you will become wise.   (Prov. 13.20)

If one reads over these and other sentences, one sees at once that wisdom and the acquiring of it is here a human activity which is open to everyone. As far as these sentences are concerned, there is obviously no problem in this. The gaining of wisdom is placed entirely within the sphere of human decision. Accordingly, the pupil is addressed in the didactic sentences as one who is in the position of being able to 'get wisdom' (Prov. 15.32; 16.16). Keeping company with wise men makes one wise (Prov. 13.20); if need be, 'the stick gives wisdom' (Prov. 29.15). The question where wisdom comes from is simply not raised here. At no point do these sentences give the impression that Israel considered this intellectual faculty of hers and the refining of it to be a special privilege given her by her God. On the contrary. As opposed to the exclusiveness of her religious convictions, Israel not only was aware of the search for knowledge on the part of other nations, but also studied its products and was not above appropriating from it what seemed to be useful.

Meanwhile, precisely at the point at which the modern reader comes upon the idea of the universality of the human intellectual faculty, an idea which is familiar to him and which even seems to him to be the only possible one, there emerges a group of problems peculiar to but nevertheless completely characteristic of Israel. In order to elucidate them we must retrace our steps to some extent.

The intellectual curiosity of old wisdom, its cultural impetus and the zeal with which it studied the corresponding cultural achievements of other nations stands in considerable contrast to the spirituality of the pre-monarchical period, even of the period of Saul. Whether we speak of a process of secularization starting fairly suddenly, of the discovering of man, that is of a humanization, or of the beginning of a rational search for knowledge, at any rate this strong, intellectual movement must have been preceded by an inner decline, the disintegration of an understanding of reality which we can describe, in a felicitous expression of M. Buber's, as 'pan-sacralism'. Of course, we possess very little to enable us really to reconstruct this early spirituality in Israel, for many of the traditions from this period – one has only to think of those of the patriarchal period, of the Mosaic and wilderness periods – have already been all too strongly impregnated with the spirit of the new age. But there are also narratives which stand wholly on the earlier side of this great intellectual upheaval. We are afforded interesting insights by the comprehensive narrative which depicts one stage of Saul's military involvement with the Philistines (I Sam. 13f.). If one follows the fairly complicated course of events, it becomes immediately clear that the narrator brings every decisive event, military advantages and setbacks as well as all human conflicts, into association with the world of the sacral and the ritual: the vow of abstention which Saul imposes on the warriors, with the total cursing of any potential transgressor, the obtaining of a sign through Jonathan, the 'divine panic' which strikes the Philistine camp, the overhasty eating of ritually unclean meat on the part of the exhausted soldiers, the 'redemption' of Jonathan from the death penalty by a substitute, and much more besides. One can see that the military activity takes place in a thoroughly sacral realm of ideas. Without question, we are dealing with a very old-fashioned faith which believed that every event was encompassed by rites and sacral ordinances, and for this reason we can call it a pan-sacral faith. One can, of course, object that this is a military activity which is far removed from everyday life and that in that everyday life, even in the early period, people could use their sound, human reasoning. This can certainly not be contradicted. However, in the understanding of reality, in the whole sphere of comprehension in which men's lives operated, some decisive change must have taken place, particularly with Solomon. One has only to cast a glance at the so-called Succession Narrative (II Sam. 6–I Kings 2) which was written only two generations after the archaic military account mentioned above. What a worldly sphere it is in which men play their parts here! Disasters are no longer traced back to sacral offences. Events are determined by the political will of a great king, but equally also by his weaknesses, by ambition, political intrigues and love affairs. They seem to unfold in accordance with a closely forged chain of causality, with a law which lies within the circumstances and within men themselves. Nevertheless, the narrator points us specifically to the fact that the threads of all the events lay in Yahweh's hands.

No further arguments are necessary. As a background to this presentation of history there lies an understanding of reality, a conception of the environment, which has fundamentally altered *vis-à-vis* that of 'pan-sacralism'. It is also clear that old wisdom in Israel was influenced by that enlightened intellectuality. To the obvious question as to the way in which this new conception finds characteristically theological expression, one must unhesitatingly reply that it does so in the recognition of a relative determinism inherent in events and also in the recognition of a relative value inherent in worldly things (life, property, honour, etc.). One must again qualify this by saying that it cannot precisely have been a matter of a 'discovery' for, to be precise, a life without at least a tacit consideration of these factors would be unthinkable. And yet there is a great difference. It is seen in the ability to express clearly and objectively the factors observed;

it is seen, above all, in the much-discussed 'worldliness' of the majority of the older sentences. The reader, of course, does not expect to encounter in the phraseology of the teachers an expression corresponding, even approximately, to 'determinism'. One will not even come upon the formulation of the problem. This is due to the strictly maintained dogmatic, non-interrogative form of the teachings of the wise men. Nevertheless, the experience of inherent determinism and of intrinsic value is everywhere present in the sentences of old wisdom. Wherever it teaches the recognition of orders – and this it does in abundance – it has already objectified an inner experience of the reality of the world. The case is similar with material things which, in some cases, are regarded wholly objectively as realities which determine men's lives. (As a result of these observations one could even speak of an intrinsic harmfulness of certain things, etc.)

The decisive question for us is, of course, how faith in Yahweh's dealings with men was brought into relationship with this fundamentally altered understanding of reality. One can expect to find something about this in the teachings of the wise men. In anticipation at this point, one should note only this, that the heightened consciousness of inherent, deterministic factors at no point came into open conflict with faith in Yahweh. There is a complete lack of any indication that this awareness whittled away at faith in Yahweh's overall power, which is what one might have expected.

Here, however, we stand, for the first time, face to face with the real problem of the wisdom teachers' understanding of reality. It will be our task in what follows to enter into that understanding. The process of secularization which definitely began in the early monarchy does not, in the teachings of the wise men, go hand in hand with a disintegration of faith in Yahweh's power. That would be a simple and, to us, familiar process. Rather, we see the teachers – with what sometimes appears to us as an uncanny confidence – holding together the awareness of inherent determinism on the one hand and faith in Yahweh's power on the other, indeed even mingling the two. The idea of life completely embedded in sacral ordinances has gone. But this has by no means affected faith in Yahweh. It, rather, has become part of a completely new form of the understanding of reality.

It is already possible to see that the 'worldliness' of Israel's world, which she in fact learned to see anew, was a very specific form of her understanding of reality and that one must beware of lumping it along with popular ideas of today. Of course, the teachers' search for knowledge turned towards the vast field of daily, and sometimes for that very reason trivial, experiences, a field in which man never ceases to learn. In the community life of men, in their economic activity, but also in man's keeping company with himself, either in moderation or in excess, certain inherent determining factors can be observed which would be worth having in fixed form. But – and this is where it becomes difficult for us – the circle of these fixed perceptions was essentially wider still, for to it there belonged also experiences which man had of God, for here, too, the ancients believed they had perceived a specific order and regularity. Finally, too, God's blessing was an experience, his acceptance of but also his thwarting of human intentions. And was it not obvious that God's desire for justice could not be ignored with impunity? The fact that, in the great catalogue of perceptions, experiences of God alternate with worldly experiences, at once demands that we rethink one side of the Israelite understanding of reality, a side which is of decisive importance for the correct understanding of our texts. The modern exegete is always tempted to read into the old texts the tensions with which he is all too familiar between faith and thought, between reason and revelation. Accordingly, there has been a tendency to infer too much from the preponderance of worldly sentences over religious ones. The conclusion has, for example, been drawn that this old proverbial wisdom was still scarcely touched by Yahwism and that it was still only at the very beginning of a process of interpenetration by Yahwism. Against this, it can be categorically stated that for Israel there was only one world of experience and that this was apperceived by means of a perceptive apparatus in which rational perceptions and religious perceptions were not differentiated. Nor was this any different in the case of the prophets. The reality surrounding Israel was much more comprehensive than we would imagine, either in political or socio-ethical or any other kind of terms. The neighbouring nations, the great empires, the political and strategic events were certainly seen clearly by the prophets, even more clearly than by the majority of their contemporaries, but this was still not the full reality in which Israel found herself. Just as real for them was the burden of guilt, the involvement in evil and in disobedience and the consequences of this; and as real as anything could be was Yahweh's word which thrust deep into Israel's life as both a destructive and a constructive force. All this lay on one and the same level of man's potential experience. One can, therefore, only warn against trying to see the specific factor in wisdom simply as the manifestation of a rationality which was independent of faith. Even Amos, in his discovery of Israel's reality, brought his reason into operation in a particularly consistent way. It taught him to see in contemporary historical events a logic which was anchored in 'reality' itself. That he uncovered his logic, to which everyone else turned a blind eye, and clearly recognized in it the will of Yahweh, was his own doing. The teachers did not deal with matters of such moment, but one may ask whether their thinking and that of the prophets did not, in the last resort, start from the same presuppositions.

> When a man's ways please Yahweh,
> he makes even his enemies be at peace with him.
> Better is a little with righteousness,
> than great revenues with injustice.
> A man's mind thinks out his own way,
> but Yahweh directs his step.
> An oracle is on the king's lips,
> in judgment his mouth does not fail.
> Balances and just scales belong to Yahweh,
> all the weights in the bag are his work.
> Criminal activity is an abomination to kings,
> for the throne is founded upon righteousness.   (Prov. 16.7–12)

In this group of sayings, sentences which express an 'experience of Yaweh' alternate (certainly unintentionally) with those which express an 'experience of the world'. It would be madness to presuppose here some kind of separation, as if in one case the man of objective perception were speaking and in the other the believer in Yahweh. The discovery that, in old proverbial wisdom, sentences expressing secular experience and sentences expressing religious experience are inextricably (and in variable proportions) mixed, certainly argues against the idea of any kind of tension within the perceptive apparatus. Israel knew nothing of the aporia which we read into these proverbs. It was perhaps her greatness that she did not keep faith and knowledge apart. The experiences of the world were for her always divine experiences as well, and the experiences of God were for her experiences of the world.[3] It has been rightly said that in all knowledge faith is also at work.[4] Thus here, in proverbial wisdom, there is faith in the stability of the elementary relationships between man and man, faith in the

---

[3] One may compare with this·K. Schwarzwäller's reflections on Israel's understanding of reality, *Theologie oder Phänomenologie*, 1966, pp.139ff.

[4] E. Spranger, *Die Magie der Seele*, 1947, p.52.

similarity of men and of their reactions, faith in the reliability of the orders which support human life and thus, implicitly or explicitly, faith in God who put these orders into operation. If one understands those sentences which are expressed in wholly secular terms against their total intellectual background, then they, too, are undoubtedly dependent both on knowledge and on faith in God. Indeed, it was precisely because this knowledge of Yahweh was so strong, so unassailable, that Israel was able to speak of the orders of this world in quite secular terms. Exegetes have long set great store by the sentences which mention God or which otherwise have a religious content, because they supposed that here, above all, was Israel's own contribution over against ancient Near Eastern wisdom. For us today, the more interesting sentences are actually those in which this is not the case. Without being a-religious, but being in the last resort also, of course, linked with Yahweh, they reveal to us a freedom in their understanding of the world, a freedom to which they were entitled precisely by their faith in Yahweh.

But behind our assertion that experiences of Yahweh were, for Israel, experiences of the world, and *vice versa*, there lurks the question: Were there actually two areas of experience which Israel in the last resort did differentiate, or was there only one? That we can now no longer separate a realm of religious experience from a realm of secular experience is clear. On the other hand, Yahweh and the world were certainly not identical. Yahweh encountered man in the world. But why did there still exist parallel series of statements about 'experiences of Yahweh' and 'experiences of the world' as we saw above in Prov. 16.7–12 (an example typical of the book of Proverbs as a whole)? We can only answer as follows. Obviously Israel, in her 'enlightened' understanding of the world, has stumbled upon a dialectic of experience which could no longer be simply resolved and released. Indeed, if Yahweh and the world had been identical, then everything could have been expressed in simple terms. But Yahweh encountered man in the world always and only in the individual act of experience, and this certainly did not presuppose any identity of God and world. Again, the expressions 'experience of Yahweh' and 'experience of the world' perhaps did not entirely coincide, otherwise the statements in the sentences could simply have been interchanged. But that was certainly never attempted. Looked at in this way, that attempt to establish the 'secularity of the world' does not simply prove to be the great redeeming simplification. If one tries to see this secular understanding of the world against the background of faith in Yahweh, then it appears, for its part, to be a fairly complex phenomenon which concealed its own intellectual difficulties within it and which cannot be claimed by modern secularism.

We hold fast to the fact that in the case of the wise men's search for knowledge, even when they expressed their results in a completely secular form, there was never any question of what we would call absolute knowledge functioning independently of their faith in Yahweh. This is inconceivable for the very reason that the teachers were completely unaware of any reality not controlled by Yahweh. In fact, what the sentences teach already surpasses any objective material knowledge in so far as it is dealing with perceptions which have been acquired in connection with a truth for which one has already decided. It is, in other words, a truth to which one has already committed oneself; one could even call it a truth which has to do with character rather than with intellect. Explicitly or implicitly in the sentences, evaluations are continually being made and questions of judgment being decided; and this takes place against a background of basic knowledge which also gave one moral obligations. A man was considered to be wise only when he allowed his whole way of life to be modelled on these insights which put their emphasis on values. And here lay the task which the teachers had taken upon themselves. What was the origin of that concern of theirs, that is discernible all through the book of Proverbs, their unwearying arguing and contrasting? It lay not in the fact that they had any doubts regarding the intellectual ability of their pupil, but in the fact that they knew that he assimilated this 'training in wisdom' (Prov. 15.33) often with difficulty but were not sure whether or not he was capable of forcing himself to assimilate it. The wise man is also the 'righteous man'.[5] One has to 'walk' in wisdom (Prov. 28.26), wisdom is 'knowing the way' in which one, of course, must also walk (Prov. 14.8).

With the wise man there is contrasted the 'fool'. His behaviour, however, is determined only to a very small extent by an intellectual defect. Rather, there is, in his case, a lack of ability or readiness to accommodate himself to the orders, the knowledge of which the wise men taught. The fool is the undisciplined man, who does not control his passions (Prov. 29.11), the presumptuous man. Folly is a lack of order in a man's innermost being, a lack which defies all instruction; often, indeed, folly is regarded as something which cannot be corrected

---

[5] U. Skladny, op. cit., pp.11f.

(e.g. Prov. 27.22). 'The mind of the fool is not sound' (Prov. 15.7). This lack of 'soundness' can, of course, be observed in very different ways, in insolence, in boasting, sometimes in a false sense of security (Prov. 12.15; 14.16; 28.26; etc.). Its cause is always to be looked for in the same place, namely in a lack of knowledge; one could even speak of a lack of realism (Prov. 17.24). The fool miscalculates his potentiality; he lives in deception (Prov. 14.8). For this reason, folly is always something which endangers life (Prov. 10.21; 18.7). But this non-recognition of orders and limits which have been once for all set for man was much more than a defect for which the person concerned simply had to pay the price; it was regarded as something positively culpable. Therefore, the fool was adversely affected in his social position; he was denied respect (Prov. 26.1, 8). Where a truth is offered to man, there is no longer any free decision. Whoever refuses to accept it exposes himself to moral judgment. Lastly, this lack of realism also included a misjudging of God himself. The fool 'rages' against God (Prov. 19.3). Later, the same idea was formulated in more basic, theological terms, 'The fool says in his heart, "There is no God"' (Ps. 14.1). Folly is practical atheism. In this moral, even theological appraisal of unratified knowledge, of rejected perception, there appears in outline one of the most interesting anthropological ideas of the Old Testament.[6]

3. Our attempts to determine the specific nature of the search for knowledge, the results of which are to be found in the sentences of old, empirical wisdom, have now reached the point where one of the most characteristic didactic sentences in the whole book of Proverbs must be considered. It occurs, with minor variations, five times in the didactic literature. This is true of no other sentence, and this very fact argues for the significance which it must have had.

> The fear of Yahweh is the beginning of knowledge;
>> fools despise wisdom and discipline. (Prov. 1.7)

> The beginning of wisdom is the fear of Yahweh,
>> and the knowledge of the Holy One is understanding. (Prov. 9.10)

[6] The situation is more obscure in the case of another negative human type, the *lēṣ* (fourteen times in the book of Proverbs, several times parallel with 'fool'). In the question of how the word is to be translated the old translations unfortunately leave us in the lurch. Its basic meaning is probably 'prattler' rather than 'mocker' (so H. N. Richardson, *VT* 5, 1955, p. 166). The occurrences, as well as those of the verb *līṣ*, indicate unrestrained, boastful behaviour. 'A *lēṣ* is the wine, a brawler strong drink' (Prov. 20.1). The typical factor in this is certainly the disregard of a social order which imposes obligations. See below pp. 85ff.

The fear of Yahweh is training for wisdom,
   and before honour comes humility.   (Prov. 15.33)

The beginning of wisdom is the fear of Yahweh,
   a good understanding for all who practise it.   (Ps. 111.10)

The fear of the Lord, that is wisdom,
   and the avoidance of evil is understanding.   (Job 28.28)

The expression 'fear of Yahweh' is frequently attested in the Old Testament and has a correspondingly wide range of meaning.[7] In a few prominent passages it means simply obedience to the divine will, and it is in this sense that the teachers, too, seem to have understood the term. The modern reader must, therefore, eliminate, in the case of the word 'fear', the idea of something emotional, of a specific, psychical form of the experience of God. In this context, the term is possibly used even in a still more general, humane sense, akin to our 'commitment to', 'knowledge about Yahweh'.[8] Skladny interprets it as a positive attitude, appropriate to Yahweh; he even tends towards the concept of confidence.[9] On the basis of Prov. 9.10 ($t^e\underline{h}ill\bar{a}$), $r\bar{e}$'$\check{s}it$ is to be taken in the sense of 'beginning' and not of 'principal part', 'total', 'best part'.[10] The sentence means, therefore, that the fear of God leads to wisdom. It enables a man to acquire wisdom; it trains him for wisdom.[11]

Of the five forms, that in Job 28.28 is the simplest: the fear of God – that is wisdom. But it sounds simpler than is intended by its rhetorical heightening, for the two entities cannot simply be identified with each other. Here, too, the word wisdom has been interpreted. In contrast to this slogan-like form, the others are more subtle. If the

[7] On this, cf. the monograph by J. Becker, *Gottesfurcht im Alten Testament*, 1965. This has, in part, superseded S. Plath, *Furcht Gottes*, 1962.

[8] The expression 'fear of God' is, of course, particularly prominent in the Elohistic narratives (Gen. 20.11; 22.12; 42.51; Ex. 1.17, 21). Here, too, the attribute 'God-fearing' is to be understood in a broad, humane sense, to some extent synonymous with 'obedient to God'; cf. H. W. Wolff, *EvTh* 29, 1969, pp.62ff.

[9] U. Skladny, op. cit., pp.15f., 64. The fear of God is often mentioned in the older sentences (more often than in Prov. 1–9): Prov. 1.29; 8.13; 10.27; 14.27; 15.16, 33; 16.6; 19.23; 22.4; 23.17; Job (1.1;) 4.6.

[10] In themselves, both translations ('beginning' or 'best') are possible. Indeed, the meanings are very close. Attention has, correctly, been drawn to the fact that the idea of 'best' is included in the idea of 'beginning' ('first-fruits'). The whole discussion may be found in J. Becker, op. cit., pp.214f. It is difficult to find in $r\bar{e}$'$\check{s}it$ the meaning 'essence', 'principle'.

[11] J. Becker, op. cit., pp.216, 229. This idea is among the most characteristic of Israelite wisdom. Non-Israelite wisdom is unaware of this kind of almost programmatic rooting of wisdom in the fear of God. S. Plath, op. cit., p.70.

fear of God is the beginning of wisdom, then this says something about the starting point of wisdom. The form in Prov. 15.33 is similar: the fear of God trains a man for wisdom. In spite of – or rather because of – these variants, the basic thought is reasonably clear. It is obvious that the question about the *locus* of wisdom should be answered rather than that about the *locus* of the fear of God. It is also obvious that such a definition of *locus* can be made because of the fact that wisdom is set in close relationship to the fear of God, and finally, it is obvious that the fear of God is regarded as something which is given precedence over all wisdom. In its shadow, wisdom is assigned its place; it is, therefore, the prerequisite of wisdom and trains a man for it.

This is what happened in ancient Israel, too. There is no knowledge which does not, before long, throw the one who seeks the knowledge back upon the question of his self-knowledge and his self-understanding. Even Israel did not give herself uncritically to her drive for knowledge, but went on to ask the question about the possibility of and the authority for knowledge. She made intellect itself the object of her knowledge. The thesis that all human knowledge comes back to the question about commitment to God is a statement of penetrating perspicacity. It has, of course, been so worn by centuries of Christian teaching that it has to be seen anew in all its provocative pungency. In the most concise phraseology it encompasses a wide range of intellectual content and can itself be understood only as the result of a long process of thought. It contains in a nutshell the whole Israelite theory of knowledge. In the almost abrupt way in which it is expressed, it gives the impression that some form of polemic might be involved. Why the repetition of this firm assertion that all knowledge has its point of departure in knowledge about God, if the pupil's range of vision did not contain other possible ways of acquiring knowledge which were being firmly repulsed? But nothing specific can be said about this. At any rate, there lies behind the statement an awareness of the fact that the search for knowledge can go wrong, not as a result of individual, erroneous judgments or of mistakes creeping in at different points, but because of one single mistake at the beginning. One becomes competent and expert as far as the orders in life are concerned only if one begins from knowledge about God. To this extent, Israel attributes to the fear of God, to belief in God, a highly important function in respect of human knowledge. She was, in all seriousness, of the opinion that effective knowledge about God is the only thing that puts a man into a right relationship with the objects of his perception, that it enables him to ask questions more pertinently, to take stock of relationships more effectively and generally to have a better awareness of circumstances. Thus it could, for example, be said that evil men do not know what is right but that those who seek Yahweh understand all things (Prov. 28.5). The opinion is evidently that turning to Yahweh facilitates the difficult distinction between right and wrong. But this was surely not true only of the narrower sphere of moral behaviour. Faith does not – as is popularly believed today – hinder knowledge; on the contrary, it is what liberates knowledge, enables it really to come to the point and indicates to it its proper place in the sphere of varied, human activity. In Israel, the intellect never freed itself from or became independent of the foundation of its whole existence, that is its commitment to Yahweh. On the contrary, one can – particularly in the later didactic literature – speak of an endeavour to hold the intellect to a close dependence on the basis of Israel's life or else to lead it back to that basis and not to let it stray from it. As for the knowledge of those who despise God's word, so asks Jeremiah on one occasion, 'what kind of wisdom is that for them?' (Jer. 8.9).[12]

Only a prophet could succeed in disposing of the difficult problem of the dependence of perception on knowledge of God with a rhetorical question thrown off with such apparent ease. The statement that the fear of the Lord was the beginning of wisdom was Israel's most special possession. But this does not mean that everything is now clear. It will take the whole of this book to think through some of the consequences implied by this sentence. Starting from this basis, Israel is led into areas of knowledge of a particular type and exposed to experiences of a particular type. In a word, her thinking had to operate within spheres of tension indicated by the prior gift of the knowledge of God. All that can be said either for or against Israelite wisdom is expressed in this statement. Even Job and Ecclesiastes – each in his own way – will be influenced by the fact that Israelite wisdom began by moving along this road.

[12] I am unable to agree with McKane's interpretation (*Prophets and Wise Men*, 1965, pp. 47f.). According to him, the representatives of old wisdom, in so far as they held political office, were involved as empiricists to the extent that they could not permit themselves the luxury of religious or ethical presuppositions. The fear of God was not a constitutive factor for their wisdom. They had to take the world as they found it. But one cannot assume this opposition of real world and religiosity among ancient peoples. Did not the wise men, when they spoke of Yahweh's blessing or restriction, did not Hesiod take the world as they found it? Was this a luxury on their part, in contrast to the practitioners of *Real-politik*?

However, one must resist the temptation to attribute to the statement about the fear of God being the beginning of knowledge a paramount, programmatic significance. This is not a difficult assertion which Israel has won for herself in the teeth of experiences which spoke differently. On the contrary, it says nothing that was not already continually practised in every sentence. Fundamentally, it has added to the whole nothing new, the absence of which would have detracted from the whole. If it had not been there, the situation would have been little different, for all sentences are based on this presupposition. It was important obviously only on account of its outstanding character. At any rate, the summing up of such a comprehensive perception in a very terse statement does not have a parallel in the book of Proverbs. In the midst of teaching which is orientated towards individual, practical instructions, the statement is remarkable for its concentration on a question of principle. More strongly than many others, it gives expression to a theoretical interest. It is interesting to observe that the question of the presuppositions of genuine knowledge was asked even in old wisdom and was answered in principle. While later wisdom answered the question about the prerequisite for acquiring wisdom in theological terms (wisdom comes from God), the answer here is an anthropological one. Wisdom stands and falls according to the right attitude of man to God.

In the didactic poems which are gathered in Prov. 1–9 and which are generally thought to be fairly late, in the speeches of the friends in the book of Job and in Sirach, a certain change has taken place with respect to the object towards which the search for knowledge is directed. The varied experiences which could be gathered in the broad sphere of inter-personal community life definitely fade into the background. In this respect one could even speak about a loss of breadth. In the foreground, on the other hand, are the examination and evaluation of the experiences which could be gained from divine guidance, from divine blessing or punishment. Even in this more specific domain, experiences could be adduced and patterns could be recognized, the evidence of which could not but convince the pupil. This appeal of faith to real experiences is fully justified. If we said above that there was no understanding which did not, in practice, include faith, then it can be pointed out here that there is certainly no faith which cannot at the same time rest on insights and experiences.[13] The range of

---

[13] H. Ott, 'Glaube und Vernunft', *ThLZ* 92, 1967, cols. 401ff. (411ff.).

motifs is much narrower here, and the number of perceptions which can be justified by theological experiences is not so great. On the other hand, the insights are explained in greater detail. This was necessary because these didactic poems tend, to a much greater extent, towards theological perceptions which are of more fundamental and more general significance for men. The loss in breadth, then, is compensated by a greater intensity of theological reflection. That is the whole difference between earlier and later collections of proverbs.

The modern exegete feels, from time to time, a slight uneasiness when he sees Israel busy with the examination and rational evaluation of her religious experiences, that is with the question whether some kind of logic cannot be discerned in divine guidance. He wonders whether this is not a road which must lead to a twisting of the truth in favour of a rigid theological pattern. But we have already seen that Israel's understanding of truth was more comprehensive, that it included many more realities than that of modern man. We saw that for Israel there was only a single, unified world of experience in which the 'real' phenomena in the foreground were no more real than guilt or curse or divine blessing. Later teachers, then, are no different from the earlier ones, who already derived perceptions from experiences of Yahweh. We see them continuing along precisely the same road as the one trodden by their predecessors, except that in the examination of human reality they confine themselves to specific themes, though here intensifying their theological endeavours. The use in argument of specific, basic experiences of a religious nature must on no account impair the understanding of reality. If this argument is of the right kind, then it will start from reality (understood in its Old Testament sense) and will then actually encourage this understanding and enable men to have insights into factors and contexts which were no less real. The conflict arises only when insights which were at one stage correct become 'dogmatically' hardened; when, that is, experience no longer continues to liberate that which is known and where that which is known is not being constantly re-examined, but where knowledge itself is kept firmly under control and where a twisted, and therefore inauthentic, knowledge comes into conflict with the evidence of reality (again understood in its Old Testament sense). The question whether a rigid theological pattern is not trying to pass itself off as experience would, in principle, have to be asked with regard to every textual context and not simply about the speeches of the friends in the book of Job. There is no genuine

Yahwistic faith, the expression of which we ought to let pass uncritically simply because it seems to operate in a milieu which we accept as standard.

It will undoubtedly not be easy for us to visualize the objects of Israel's search for knowledge within the sphere of reality in which she saw them. But, as we have said, that affects not only specific concepts of the wise men but also, to the same extent, the psalms or the prophets. However we define knowledge on the basis of the objects of it, as knowledge of life, knowledge of nature or even knowledge of the world, then we are using an abstraction, an objectivization which, from the outset, presupposes the existence of an entity called 'life', 'nature' or 'the world'. Here, however, right at the very outset of our examination, we are faced with a question of principle, a question of some weight. We must not transfer uncritically our accustomed ways of thinking to Israel. We must, rather, face the exacting demand of thinking ourselves into ideas, into a 'view of life', which are unfamiliar to us. A beginning could already be made if we fully realized that Israel was not aware of this or that entity which we almost automatically take as objects of our search for knowledge, or at least always include in our thought processes as part of the given framework of that search. She did not differentiate between a 'life wisdom' that pertained to the social orders and a 'nature wisdom', because she was unable to objectify these spheres in the form of such abstractions. This can easily be shown in the case of the concept 'nature', a concept which has become so indispensable to us but of which Israel was quite definitely unaware. Indeed, if we use the term in the interpretation of Old Testament texts, then we falsify something that was quite specific to Israel's view. She never saw herself in the position of beginning by conceiving as a totality the object of her search for knowledge, a totality from the knowledge of which she could always begin when interpreting specific details.[14] If one compares with this the questions of the Ionian nature-philosophers who are known to have been concerned with the principles of the world as a totality, then it would be easy to see in Israel's intellectual ability a limitation which the Greeks surpassed at the first attempt, that is, something in the nature of philosophical infantilism. One would do well, however,

---

[14] 'For the first time (in Anaximander) we see a unified concept of the world, one which includes the whole of reality, on the basis of a natural deduction from and exploration of all phenomena' (W. Jaeger, *Die Theologie der frühen griechischen Denker*, 1964[2], p. 34).

to accept this peculiarity of Israelite perception as a unique and significant achievement.[15]

But Israel's teachings are also completely different from the ideas of ancient Egyptian wisdom. The central concept, on the basis of which the teachings of the wise men of Egypt are to be interpreted, is that of Maat, a word with a wide range of meaning. It is variously translated by 'truth', 'right', 'justice', 'basic order', 'world order'.[16] Maat guarantees the continuance of the world, of both the cosmic world and the social world of men. Gods and men live by it. Men have to accommodate themselves to it, indeed for their part they have to translate it into reality and hand it on. In our context, its status as a god is of less interest, for in actual fact its significance in the religious life of the ancient Egyptians seems to have been slight. It seems important to us that the Egyptians had conceived of the proper, creative status of the world, for at this precise point Israel possessed nothing comparable. This *differentia specifica* can scarcely be overrated. From this point of view, too, the 'teaching' about the ambivalence of phenomena, indeed a certain dialectic in the thinking of the teachers, is also to be explained, an idea to which we shall return.[17] In the domain of Israel's teachings there could be completely opposite opinions. Even the actual basis for the 'almost inconceivable strength of the feeling of security' in the thinking of the Egyptians[18] can be compared only in a limited way with what gave Israel confidence. The reason for this inability to objectivize certain entities mythically or speculatively must be sought in the special features of her faith in God. Did not Israel, in all her attempts to perceive the course of human experience, always come back to Yahweh who comprehended all things in his power? There was never a special domain in which she was alone with her understanding and the objects of her knowledge, and therefore she found herself – if one dares such a comparison at all – with her search for knowledge in an essentially difficult starting

---

[15] The 'four-part comprehensive formula', heaven, underworld, land and sea confirms this (Job 11.8f.), for it does not conceive the idea of the 'whole' but simply adds together the different areas. On this formula see F. Horst, *Hiob* (BKAT XVI/1), p.170.

[16] On the idea of Maat see H. Brunner, 'Ägyptologie II', *Handbuch der Orientalistik*, Vol. I/2, 1952, pp.93ff.; ibid., *Altägyptische Erziehung*, 1957, p.142; S. Morenz, *Gott und Mensch im alten Ägypten*, 1964, pp.66, 118f., 133, etc.; H. Gese, op. cit., pp.11ff.; H. H. Schmid, op. cit., pp.17ff.

[17] See below, pp.247ff., 311.

[18] H. Brunner, *Erziehung*, p.149. On the inadmissibility of contradictory opinions, see ibid., p.142.

position. With no possibility of anticipating what was not known or experienced, she was forced to hold fast only to what could be discerned from time to time on the basis of individual questions, at the same time always fixing the boundary which was drawn to prevent her from gaining a total picture. This means that Israel was obliged to remain open, in a much more intensive way, to the category of the mysterious. When she spoke of mystery – again the language lacks the term but not the object – she did not mean something vague and inexpressible which defied being put into words. In wisdom and didactic contexts it refers rather to something perceived by the understanding rather than by the feelings. The term is precise in so far as it refers to God's activity in the world, in which very special domain the wise men dared to look for rules. There are, as has been well said, not only depths of the abyss and of the dark; there are also depths of light: 'The mystery in what is utterly clear.'[19] We shall have more to say about this way taken by knowledge along the frontier of the mysterious.

[19] R. Guardini, *Gegenwart und Geheimnis*, 1957, p. 23.

V

THE SIGNIFICANCE OF ORDERS FOR
CORRECT SOCIAL BEHAVIOUR

THE BOOK OF PROVERBS has always been regarded as containing the concentrated deposit of ancient Israelite morality.[1] There would be no objection to this as long as one allowed the Old Testament to say what Israel understood by 'moral' and did not attempt to understand it from the point of view of the traditional conceptualism of philosophical or theological ethics (freedom, conscience, duty, etc.). If one interprets the sentences of the book of Proverbs against their own background of ideas and from the point of view of their own intention, one quickly becomes aware that they are rooted in a very specific world of values, one which is not at once familiar to us. In this respect it may be readily accepted that this instruction has little or no interest in acquiring theoretical knowledge, that it supplies, rather, pragmatic knowledge. It is, however, more difficult to answer the question whether one can approach these teachings in any really meaningful way by means of the term 'moral'. Is that term really central to them? Were they not, rather, directions for mastering life and for overcoming life's numerous difficulties? Certainly they also include many instructions which we would describe as 'moral'. But regarded in this way, the sentences contain in one respect more, in another less than instructions for the moral life. As far as the question of the moral element is concerned, one will, in any case, be able to grasp the contents of the sentences only incompletely. The form of expression which most appropriately corresponds to ethics is the admonition, the imperative. But in relation to affirmative sentences, exhortations are very much in the minority.

[1] Accordingly, in manuals of Old Testament theology, 'wisdom' is usually dealt with under the heading of 'ethics'. So, e.g., Th. C. Vriezen, *An Outline of Old Testament Theology*, ET 1958, pp. 315ff.; G. Hölscher, *Geschichte der israelitischen und jüdischen Religion*, 1922, pp. 148ff.; P. van Imschoot, *Théologie de l'Ancien Testament*, 1954: 'The wise men are Israel's moralists' (p. 100).

Since exhortations are found above all in the section which is parallel to the Egyptian *Amenemope* (Prov. 22.17–23.11), the opinion has even been expressed that exhortation was not a genuinely Israelite didactic form. Most difficult, however, – and here we anticipate – is the awareness that our term 'moral' can be laid only very unnaturally against the term 'goodness', which was very much alive, not only in ancient Israel but also in early Greece.[2]

Anyone who attempts to evaluate the rules for behaviour which were applicable to the individual in an ancient nation will invariably ask about the basic ethical norms by which that nation was guided. But although traces of such ethical norms can certainly be found in the writings of the nation in question, one must not be misled as to the actual significance such norms may have had for the life of the individual. Even in the West, the Decalogue, the Sermon on the Mount, the Categorical Imperative have not often directly determined the decisions of individuals. As a rule, the individual receives the call to ethical behaviour from a quite different direction. Every individual always possesses a family, a tribe or a town, that is, some specific form of community life. This community life has its ethical atmosphere; it compels the individual to live up to specific expectations which people have of him, it provides him with long established examples and values. As a rule, the individual conforms unthinkingly to these community-determined factors; but, *vice versa*, the rules of behaviour are also, in turn, conformed to these factors. It would, therefore, be unrealistic to try to understand the behavioural rules of a community as a more or less direct expression of specific, absolute, ethical convictions of principle. The role which a man has to play in the community into which he is born is to be great extent conditioned and determined by community considerations. But the way in which he fills this role and the way in which he is guided to fill it is the point at which we can see the decisive factor.[3] Thus, we must briefly concern ourselves with the community and historical background to the instructions in the book of Proverbs.

What can be deduced from the Solomonic book of Proverbs concerning community and economic circumstances, that is, concerning

---

[2] On the term 'goodness', see below, pp. 77f. It does not translate a specific Hebrew word, but is chosen (following H. Fränkel) in order to describe a whole range of ideas which could be expressed in Hebrew by a whole series of words, of which *ṣaddīq*, *ṣedāqā* 'correct community behaviour' is the most prominent.

[3] Th. C. Vriezen speaks correctly of a 'merging of religious and ethical elements', op. cit., p. 316.

the specific social sphere to which the sentences belong, has already been carefully compiled.[4] The life depicted is a wholly sedentary one, partly in rural situations, partly also in fortified towns. Alongside work in the fields, there are craftsmen and commercial traders. The sentences speak of the king and of how to conduct oneself in his presence, as well as of the blessing bestowed by an ordered and righteous life and of what threatens such a life. There are rich and poor, freemen and slaves. But, seen from the point of view of the freemen as opposed to that of the slaves, there is also the world of the degraded, even of the crippled or the mutilated, who were scarcely reckoned to be part of the community.[5] Everything that can be discovered about the book of Proverbs by this sociological examination corresponds, as we may confidently expect, to the circumstances of the pre-exilic monarchical period and indeed, on the whole, to those of an urban cultural milieu.

What amazes us is the fact that there is so little trace of the serious crises in the social life of this period which can be deduced from the message of the prophets, crises such as the confrontation between Canaanite economic concepts and ancient Israelite land rights, the existence of large estates and the impoverishment of hitherto free farmers. References to shifts or at least to ominous tensions in the social structure have to be looked for with a magnifying glass. The overall impression is rather one of relationships which are in all essentials stable and which, as such, can in no sense be regarded as in need of reform. It is no proof to the contrary that the poor and poverty are frequently mentioned. These exist always and everywhere; of course, where they lead to hardships in the social life, they are experienced as a sting in the conscience. On the other hand, the sentences often judge poverty very coolly and unemotionally, for often enough it is the person's own fault.[6] In a word, it is simply there (Prov. 17.5). Obviously it would be wrong to expect direct references to actual social problems in this kind of sentence literature. Its ideas are characterized by a thoroughly static quality. Its statements try to grasp life from the aspect of that which always remains the same; they are open not to daily social problems but to that which is generally valid and which survives no matter what the social circumstances. This

---

[4] Especially in the work of U. Skladny. On the exhortations, see W. Richter, *Recht und Ethos*, 1966, pp. 183ff.

[5] Deut. 23.2; (Lev. 21.16ff.;) Job 24.5–12; 30.3–8.

[6] E.g. Prov. 11.16; 12.11, 24; 13.4, 18, 25; 18.9; 19.15; 20.4, 13; 21.5, 17; 22.7; 24.34.

does not, of course, mean that what is often called the ethos of wisdom does not reveal a very characteristic shape.

But how are we to progress in our question as to what Israel, and particularly her teachers, understood by 'ethical'? A mere glance at the book of Proverbs shows us that in the world of the didactic sentence, reflections of principle as to what good action is, unfortunately cannot be expected. We do read on one occasion that the fear of Yahweh included hating evil (Prov. 8.13); but apart from the fact that the question still remains open as to what evil and good, both of which are in fact often mentioned, really are, such a statement does not require a proper definition. It is saying nothing more than that man must lead his life in the fear or in the knowledge of Yahweh and then have it as his duty to reject evil and choose the good. Any information about the ethical principles of the wisdom movement cannot be derived from such and similar statements, for the simple reason that under the teachers there could be absolutely no discussion as to what good and evil were. And this brings us back round in a circle once again.

Our question about the good as Israel understood it misses the point as long as we look for the answer in the ideological sphere and in terms of a definition. Israel encountered the good in a quite different way; the good was experienced by her quite simply as a force, as something which determined life, something experienced daily as effective, that is as something present, about which there need be as little discussion as about light and darkness. The good was therefore – and here the ancients thought much more pragmatically – in any event something which was very definitely active. 'Good' is that which does good; 'evil' is that which causes harm. Both good and evil create social conditions; in a completely 'outward' sense they can build up or destroy the community, property, happiness, reputation, welfare of children and much more besides. Here, then, it is a question not only of movements and tendencies inside a man's heart, but of life-forming forces whose power was obvious to all. It was a question of reactions which could always be identified. And once again there was no discussion among the teachers about this life-forming reality of good or of evil; knowledge of them was the prime conviction on which all individual teachings rested and from which they proceeded. It is demanded of us, however, that we abandon the rigidity of the modern, popular scientific understanding of reality and try to enter into that ancient biblical idea of reality which was aware that the world in which man lived was so much more favourably disposed towards him, towards his life and behaviour, bringing out correct behaviour, rejecting what was not useful. This is, then, a concept of reality which realized that the behaviour of an individual was connected much more intensively, much more 'organically', with the variations in his environment, of a concept of reality which was able to understand the effect of the environment on man as a challenge, but also as a response to his behaviour and which, in a word, realized that from this direction something extremely important was continually happening to man, good and evil, which addressed him and which never entirely withdrew itself from his comprehension. This enables us to answer the question about the ethos of didactic wisdom with comparative ease. The good man is the one who knows about the constructive quality of good and the destructive quality of evil and who submits to this pattern which can be discerned in the world. He is the righteous man, the diligent, the temperate, the one who is ready to help, the one for whom this goodness of his itself turns out to be good. Being 'good' and worldly 'goods' are, in this type of teaching, closely related to each other. Thus, in reality, the good is that which does good. Goodness was, therefore, always something public, never something merely internal; it was a social phenomenon. 'When it goes well with the righteous, a city rejoices.' 'By the blessing of the upright a city is exalted' (Prov. 11.10f.). The behaviour and activity of the individual are always viewed both with regard to their consequences and with regard to their effect on society.

Such a man, who behaves correctly and at the same time – we have seen that the two cannot be separated – is himself successful in life, was called by the teachers (but not only by them) a ṣaddīq. We usually translate the word by 'righteous', although we know that the Hebrew word cannot really be accommodated to our world of language and ideas. If a man was called a ṣaddīq, there were connected with that word concepts and standards of which we do not immediately think when we describe a man as 'righteous'. In Israel a man was judged by the extent to which he fulfilled the claims made upon him by a community. Here, then, lay the norm by which he was judged. The claims which are made upon a man from the direction of community life are wholly unpredictable. Often enough it may have been quite practical help which had to be offered at some personal sacrifice. If, in this way, a man lived up to what the community expected of him, then he was considered to be 'righteous' (a state which we would definitely describe by the use of different adjectives). But the Hebrew word had a wider meaning, for it did not confine itself to the 'righteousness' which the administration of justice demanded. Wherever a man recognized and fulfilled claims made upon him by the community to which he belonged, that man was 'righteous'. But the wise men (particularly in the sentences in Prov. 10–15) never tire of expressing anew the idea that everything which emanates from such a righteous man also supports him and brings him – one is tempted to say – into a sphere of blessing.[7] To speak of a 'doctrine of retribution' is, therefore, highly misleading, because this was not a question of ideological postulates but of experiences which had proved true over a long series of generations. The ṣaddīq is a man who, as we also sometimes express it, is 'in order'. We translate the word by 'righteous'. This can stand, as long as one is always aware that the 'right' with which the righteous man is content is probably also an unwritten one, since it also includes a wide range of social claims.

It is helpful to see how closely early Greek concepts come to those of Israel at this point. Aretē – which is to be translated not by 'virtue' but rather by 'goodness', perhaps also by 'merit' – always means in Hesiod and others both personal proficiency and success at the same time. It is more of a goal in life, more of a 'prize', for with the idea of goodness there belonged also the complementary idea of acquired prosperity and a position of honour.[8] Here too, then, a man's goodness is a very much more comprehensive phenomenon. Good conduct and prosperity are two sides of one and the same thing.

From the point of view of the rudiments of an ethical idealism, this circle of ideas, which was obviously common to the ancient world, is

---

[7] See further on the act-consequence relationship below pp. 128ff.

[8] E. Schwartz, *Die Ethik der Griechen*, 1951, pp. 19ff. 'The valuable man is the one who is prosperous; this is what Hesiod means by *aretē*' (op. cit., p. 23). On this, cf. also H. Fränkel, *Dichtung und Philosophie des frühen Griechentums*, 1962, pp. 475–8. 'Goodness is understood as proficiency, and the term includes also the good fortune at which it aims and the regard which the efficient man enjoys' (op. cit., p. 136). 'Good will and high endeavour are not enough to make a man "good"; there must also be achievement and visible success' (op. cit., p. 351). On the significance attributed here to what is useful, cf. also B. Snell, *Die Entdeckung des Geistes*, 1955, pp. 220ff.

The Hebrew term *tušīyā* seems to come very close to this early Greek concept of *aretē*. It is always difficult for translators because there is no real equivalent to it in English. There are contexts in which the word describes a subjective quality (Prov. 3.21;) similarly, but referring to God, Isa. 28.29; Job 11.6. But in other contexts it describes 'success', Prov. 2.7; 8.14; 18.1; et al. Cf. G. Kuhn, *Beiträge zur Erklärung des Salomonischen Spruchbuchs*, 1931, pp. 3f.

difficult to understand. If one were to suggest that its 'success think-ing' was utilitarianism or eudemonism, one could hardly misunder-stand it more.[9] Behind this concept of life there lies not the dispas-sionate utilitarian standpoint of the man who has taken his life into his own hands, but the action, which has to be constantly repeated, of pious integration into a divine order which is imposed on man and in which alone he can find blessing. One could almost say that the realization of the good inherent in men's living together in communi-ties came afresh from situation to situation, not of course, *ex nihilo* on every occasion, for there was always the contribution of earlier know-ledge and of wide-ranging experience. The teachers expend a con-siderable effort in leading young people to the right knowledge of good and evil. This does not mean that they felt the nature of the good to be a problem, but only that it required great experience to have a proper awareness of the good as such in the face of the unending variability of the situations of human life and in view of man's apti-tude for self-deception. It does not usually lie on the surface for every child to recognize. 'Many a road seems right to a man, but in the long run they were the roads to death' (Prov. 14.12). It requires, therefore, sharp eyes and an active mind in order to be able to distinguish good from evil, and often the knowledge has to be beaten into the lads (Prov. 29.15). It is always difficult, too, to live in accordance with the good that is known. In the opinion of the wise men, men can be trained to such knowledge and behaviour. In all their sentences cram-med with experience, in their exhortations and in the examples they adduce, they speak of both good and evil as of a general truth which at any rate is obvious, in the long run even directly, to the man who is willing to accept it.

This conception of the good as a force which promotes both the individual life and community life can be described as common to the whole of the ancient world. If we analyse it from the distance which separates us from it, then the whole complex of ideas appears fairly complicated. To the ancients, however, it was quite simple and self-evident. There is nothing good which does not also do good. Property does a man good, so does the blessing of children, honour, a good

[9] This has been corrected already in H. Gese, op. cit., pp. 7ff., as well as by U. Skladny, op. cit., pp. 85f. If one wishes to speak of 'success thinking', then one can, for this was also the concern in Hesiod, 'How is our environment constituted and how must we act in order to work as well as possible with the life which we have?' (H. Fränkel, op. cit., pp. 128f.).

name, a good marriage, a good friend; but the good man is the one whose behaviour brings about these results. In its 'teaching about the good things', this ethic is, in fact, astonishingly realistic. It never criticizes man's search for happiness and fulfilment, even its excesses. It simply presupposes this search as a fact. This desire for happiness – we ought, rather, to say in more restrained terms: this desire to survive without coming to grief and to know that life is secure within an order that is beneficial – is planted deep within man and is accepted without question. Indeed, the wise men themselves advocate it in that they indicate the roads which lead to it.

> Where is the man who desires life
>   and loves long life so that he can see happiness?
> Then keep your tongue from evil
>   and your lips from speaking deceit. (Ps. 34.13f.)

The teachers instruct men to gain, or to preserve or not to squander, what they call 'life', and that is simply the totality of all achievements and good things which can come to a man. Anything that is given here in the way of instruction is for all men without exception. There is here a complete lack of ethical exclusivism; there is no place for lofty ethical demands to which only a circle of like-minded men are capable of submitting; there is no place for any form of moral heroism nor for fanatics for virtue nor for ethical individualists. The thought could never arise that a man could set up his own ethos in defiance of a world that was indifferent or even hostile to him. He had, in the forces of order, a superior opponent; he found himself bound up in them and was not asked for his agreement.

Our observation that these didactic statements have a complete lack of exclusivism, that they are not orientated towards those who wish to perfect themselves over and above the crowd, that they are orientated towards all men, must not, however, be misunderstood. They are not orientated, as we so easily think, towards 'man' in the abstract. On the contrary, 'all men' are a quite specific community with historical and sociological characteristics in which quite specific examples and standards have established themselves and in which other standards, which elsewhere might stand in the foreground, are missing. In the picture of man which is expressed in these didactic statements, there is certainly also much that is of a timeless validity, applicable to all men. In making this judgment, one must, of course, consider that our Western ideas of man have, through a centuries-long course of education, become assimilated to Old Testament ones, with the result that we are more readily tempted to absolutize them. Without doubt, the picture of man presented by the sentences in the book of Proverbs has been, from the point of view of the history of culture and of society, uniquely affected, like every other one, by a whole series of factors. Another question is whether one can describe the rules for behaviour contained in the book of Proverbs as 'class ethos' or 'bureaucratic ethics', which would mean that they were, essentially, valid only for a limited upper class.[10] Seen as a whole, this question is certainly to be answered in the negative. It is impossible to establish a particular interest in the sphere of life of the upper civil servants, nor any, of course, in the sphere of life of the enslaved or even of those who were socially or cultically of the lower classes. In the foreground there appear the relationships of a relatively well-placed middle class. The decisive factor is, however, that here orders are described which not only have their validity in a specific social group but which are, in principle, valid for all men.[11] Even the male and female slaves, who are frequently mentioned, will have submitted to them without any personal reservations.

As in all nations, so too in Israel, there existed a strong feeling for honour. In Sirach, honour is actually described as the highest of all goods.

> Be concerned about your name, for it will remain with you
>   longer than a thousand costly treasures.
> The good things of life last only for a certain number of days,
>   but a good name lasts for ever.   (Sir. 41.12f.)

Certain changes in the concept of honour in Israel can be observed at once. The one which is mirrored in the didactic statements of the book of Proverbs is essentially that of a wealthy agricultural and urban community. Even the speeches of Job, from that state in which his honour has been obliterated, are thoroughly impregnated with the concept of honour that is characteristic of the urbanized landowner.

> Oh, that I were as in the months of old,
>   as in the days when God watched over me . . .!

---

[10] On the problem of a 'class ethic', see H.-J. Hermisson, op. cit., pp. 94ff. Skladny thinks that he can detect a 'mirror for princes' in Prov. 28f., op. cit., p. 66.
[11] H.-J. Hermisson, op. cit., p. 96.

> When I went out to the gate of the city
> > and took my seat in the market,
> the young men saw me and hid,
> > the aged rose and stood;
> officials refrained from talking
> > and laid their hands on their mouths;
> the voice of the nobles was hushed,
> > their tongue cleaved to the roof of their mouth . . .   (Job 29.2, 7–10)

One can see here that the honour of which Job knew himself to be worthy, was an important part of that light which God let shine over him. This honour was, however, also something which was clearly seen to exist. It was not a private privilege of Job's, but was granted incontrovertibly to the good man who was blessed with good things. It is the prize of the righteous, of the man who dispenses help on all sides (vv. 12–17). This whole concept of honour can be understood only from the point of view of a religiously based pattern of society in which 'external' worldly goods were accepted in an astonishingly realistic fashion and in which, at the same time, men had a keen eye both for the goodness of the individual and for the blessing with which God supported him. The man who is without honour is the fool (Prov. 26.1, 8), the 'disorderly' man who, possibly from some inner weakness, is unable to adapt himself to that order which is imposed on all men. But alongside this social concept of honour there is another which is essentially interiorized.

> The fear of Yahweh is training for wisdom,
> > and before honour comes humility.   (Prov. 15.33)
> Good sense makes a man patient,
> > and it is his glory to overlook mistakes.   (Prov. 19.11)
> It is an honour for a man to keep aloof from strife,
> > but every fool breaks out.   (Prov. 20.3)
> A man's pride brings him low,
> > but the humble man obtains honour.   (Prov. 29.23)

Even the poor man can have honour (Sir. 10.31). The honour of the scholar, as this is shown to Faust by 'the mob', is still unknown here. Not until Sirach can one observe the self-confidence of the scholar and his position of honour (Sir. 39.9–11). What is remarkable in this ethical instruction is the lack of education with a view to the formation of political ability.[12] One has only to compare Greek education,

[12] This is equally striking in Hesiod, who also lived in a period of social upheaval.

in which the awakening of a proper attitude to the state was of prime importance. Every individual is a member of the state and belongs, therefore, to the state. In Greece, statesmanship was considered to be the highest wisdom; not even Prometheus could bestow it upon men. It comes directly from Zeus.[13] The book of Ecclesiastes, of course, claims to be a royal testament; at the beginning, it recalls, to some extent, the duties of a king. But many possibilities which would have been of assistance in teaching the ruler remain unutilized here and are never mentioned at all in the book of Proverbs. There is also a complete lack of instruction for the young man in military and aristocratic virtues. If the didactic statements of the book of Proverbs betray nothing of education with a view to the formation of political ability, little also appears to be thought of instruction for trial in war.

> A patient man is better than a war hero,
>   and one who has self-control than someone who captures cities.
>   (Prov. 16.32)
> A wise man scales a city of war heroes
>   and overthrows the bulwark on which they relied.   (Prov. 21.22)
> A wise man is 'mightier' than a strong man,
>   and a man of knowledge is 'more than one full of strength'.
>   (Prov. 24.5)

This is not the kind of judgment that is passed in a feudal society. One could almost discern in such sentences something like resentment against the ideals of such a society. There is a king, but on the whole the attitude towards him is somewhat reserved.[14] His anger, his moods in general, are realities to which one simply has to adjust. Everything suggests that these sentences presuppose, rather, a wealthy middle class order, that is, a world in which the chief place is still occupied by the personal relations of man to man rather than by offices and institutions. The concern is with the relationship to children, women, neighbours, to clever and foolish men. It is with experiences which have been had of arrogance or of laziness, of excess, of anger and also of complaisance. There is no end to the treatment of the theme of knowing when to speak, nor to that of knowing when to keep silent; for 'death and life are in the power of the tongue' (Prov. 18.21);

---

[13] H. Fränkel, op. cit., pp. 125f., 145. W. Rüegg, *Antike Geisteswelt*, 1964, pp. 464, 531. For this reason, it was incorrect of J. Fichtner to speak, in the sub-title of his well-known book, of a 'nationalization' of wisdom in Israel. Similarly, G. Fohrer, *Introduction to the Old Testament*, ET 1970, pp. 308f.

[14] Prov. 16.14; 19.12; 20.2; 28.15.

indeed, further, 'The beginning of every activity is the word' (Sir. 37.16).[15] Of the great public institutions, only the law, that is, correct behaviour in the local legal community, above all with reference to the important office of witness, actually intrudes into the world depicted in the didactic statements and, as has been said, in a limited number of passages, the monarchy.[16]

This social order is regarded as given and is obviously stable. At any rate, it is never itself the subject of discussion. It is neither theologically justified nor subjected to radical criticism. All the more important and all the more interesting to the teachers is *what* happens in this given, social sphere and *how* it happens. Their observation of men's activities, of their behaviour in the most varied situations, of their peculiarities and of everything paradoxical, is acute, in spite of a marked tendency to didactic standardization. Their judgments are on the side of extreme sobriety, often strongly accentuated, in form often solemn. If one must mention something which appears to be characteristic of the concept of life in many didactic sentences and which is definitely also to a certain extent sociologically determined, then it is a tendency towards caution, towards wariness. Here, reticence, caution in action, is esteemed more highly than overzealous enthusiasm. Everything hasty, anything that is acquired quickly,[17] such as 'hastily won wealth', hasty speech, is suspicious from the outset. The wise men are in favour of economizing on one's forces. A useless engagement is to be avoided, unnecessary conflicts are to be sidestepped; they are without honour, and one should desire no more than what circumstances provide. Here, the wise men are aware of the dangers of every extreme, of everything radical, even of the dangers of ethical radicalism.

> When pride comes, then comes disgrace,
>   but with the thoughtful is wisdom. (Prov. 11.2)[18]

---

[15] On 'knowing how to speak': Prov. 12.14, 18f.; 13.2; 15.1f., 4; 16.24; 20.15; 24.26; 25.11, 15; 29.20; etc; on 'knowing when to keep silent': Prov. 11.12f.; 12.23; 13.3; 17.27; 20.19; 21.23; 23.9; 30.32; etc.

[16] Sentences on the office of witness: Prov. 14.5, 25; 17.23; 18.5; 19.5, 28; 21.28; 24.28; 25.18.

[17] Five sentences deal with hastily acquired property: Prov. 13.11; 19.2; 21.5; 28.20, 22.

[18] The concept of 'thoughtfulness', 'accuracy', 'moderation' is also found in Sir. 16.25; 32.3; (31.22) and, above all, in Micah 6.8; see H. J. Stoebe, '"Und demütig sein vor deinem Gott"', *Wort und Dienst, Jahrbuch der Theologischen Schule Bethel* 6, 1959, pp. 180ff.

The beginning of strife is like when one lets water loose;
so stop before the quarrel breaks out.   (Prov. 17.14)

Do not boast in the king's presence,
and do not stand in the place of the great;
it is better that you should be told, 'Move up here',
than that you should be put lower in the presence of a noblemen.
(Prov. 25.6f.)

Like someone who grabs a passing dog by the ears
is the man who meddles in a quarrel which does not concern him.
(Prov. 26.17)

The patient man will content himself till the right moment,
and then joy will burst forth for him.   (Sir. 1.23)

If you gain a friend, gain him by testing
and do not give him your trust too quickly.   (Sir. 6.7)

Warnings are often given against pride in every form.[19] Such an
attitude could be called 'unheroic' by someone brought up on different moral patterns. But it is characteristic of the whole of the
ancient world. One must remain watchful and agile in order to understand. In stubbornness and pride lie the greatest dangers which man
can make for himself.

It is no weakness for the wisest man
To learn when he is wrong, know when to yield.
So, on the margin of a flooded river
Trees bending to the torrent live unbroken,
While those that strain against it are snapped off.
(Sophocles, Antigone, ll. 710–715.
Tr. E. F. Watling, Penguin Classics, p. 145.)

A perfect example of this training of men – obviously clearly influenced by Egyptian teachings – is the 'patient' man, the one who
keeps a 'cool head', the one who is 'composed in his mind'. He is
contrasted with the deterrent example of the man who is 'short in
spirit' (we translate as 'quick-tempered'), the 'hot-tempered' man
who lets himself be driven by his emotions and passions and lets them
determine the way in which he behaves.[20]

---

[19] Prov. 11.2; 13.10; 16.5, 18; 21.24; 29.23. It is from this point of view that
we can understand the horror of the 'prattler', the 'braggart', see above p. 65. Cf.
also the monologue of the 'godless' who have reached a state of self-knowledge:
'What use has our arrogance been to us, what good have our wealth and boasting
been to us? They have all vanished like shadows . . .' (Wisd. 5.8ff.).
[20] H. Brunner, Altägyptische Erziehung, 1957, pp. 4f., 120, 122.

A quick-tempered man behaves foolishly,
  but the circumspect man is exalted.   (Prov. 14.17)

The patient man is rich in understanding,
  but the quick-tempered man gains folly.
A composed mind is life to the body,
  but jealousy devours the bones.   (Prov. 14.29f.)

A hot-tempered man stirs up strife,
  but a patient man stops quarrels.   (Prov. 15.18)

He who is sparing of words has knowledge,
  and he who has a cool head is a sensible man.   (Prov. 17.27)

Do not go about with a man who is always angry,
  and do not keep company with a hothead.   (Prov. 22.24)

An angry man stirs up strife,
  and a hot-tempered man causes much offence.   (Prov. 29.22)

This, then, is one result of our discussion up to this point. The teachers, with their perceptions and their rules, address themselves to a life which, from the point of view both of its social order and of its standards and examples, had long reposed in fixed forms and concepts. They are not concerned with modifying these given concepts or even with replacing them with better ones. Further, we have received an impression – at least as far as our terms are concerned – of a remarkable lack of principle which is a characteristic of the exhortation and of the rules for behaviour. We have found no discussion of good and evil, and similarly, the search for a common basic norm, to which the many rules for behaviour might be traced back, would remain without any satisfactory result. That this norm could not consist of a previously existing, philosophical idea is to be expected from the outset in view of the intellectual world in which Israel lived and thought. But could this norm not have been a proper Old Testament one such as the Decalogue? Did the teachers, in their rules for life, perhaps start from the statements of the Decalogue and refer what is forbidden and commanded there in general terms to the very varied individual situations of life and turn it, so to speak, into small change?[21]

[21] It was in accordance with this basic idea that H. Lamparter carried through his exposition: *Das Buch der Weisheit*, 1959, pp. 165, 201ff. The idea that in the wisdom teachings 'the application of ethical prescriptions, contained in the law as objective teaching, to the subjective life of man . . . was achieved', used to be so widely accepted that exegetes could take it as their point of departure; cf. O. Zöckler, *Die Sprüche Salomos*, 1867, p. 1(!).

In the older sentences, there are a few references to the keeping or the neglect of the *tōrā* (Prov. 28.4, 7, 9; 29.18). The word which is to be translated by 'instruc-

One can answer this question only with a blunt negative. The fact that adultery, theft or slander are, here as there, considered to be reprehensible, cannot stand as proof, for they are considered thus everywhere in the Old Testament and outside it. In addition, the actions against which the teachers warn were designated as 'sins' in God's eyes only in exceptional cases. The most prominent word for a lapse in the old book of Proverbs is *peša'*, and in no case can this be translated as 'sin', since it always describes in some form or another (even when it is a violation of property) an offence against one's fellow men.[22] It is characteristic that none of the twelve occurrences in the book of Proverbs understands this 'crime' as a sin of man against God, but as a failure of the relationship between man and man.[23] It is quite impossible to describe the Decalogue as the 'ethical norm' from which the teachers of the sentences began. But where, then, did they begin?

There is still a fairly certain way of finding out more about the norms by which, in the opinion of the teachers, men's behaviour ought to be determined. It leads by way of the motivations which are almost always attached to the exhortations in the wisdom literature. The teachers, in fact, not only urged men to be more ready to obey, but also provided their exhortations with clear motivations. These motivations, as was only to be expected, are of very different types. Since the teachers were concerned only with making the instruction clear in any given case, it is not surprising that in order to achieve this they provided arguments of different kinds.

Exhortations, which address the pupil in the imperative, are remarkably infrequent in the older collections of proverbs in comparison with affirmative proverbs. They occur with greater frequency, otherwise only sporadically, in the two collections comprising Prov. 22.17–24.34 and Prov. 25–27. The motivations with which many of these exhortations are provided deserve our particular interest.[24]

---

tion' always means, in the book of Proverbs, and thus in the later passages, too (Prov. 6.20, 23; 31.26), 'wise teaching' and not the 'law'. There is a full discussion in J. Fichtner, op. cit., pp. 82ff.

[22] H. W. Wolff, *Dodekapropheton*, BKAT XIV/2 (Amos, 1969), pp. 185f.; R. Knierim, *Die Hauptbegriffe für Sünde im Alten Testament*, 1965, pp. 177ff.

[23] Prov. 10.12, 19; 12.13; 17.9, 19; 19.11; 28.2, 13, 24; 29.6, 16, 22.

[24] Such interpretative motivations are also appended to legal statements; cf. B. Gemser, 'The Importance of the Motive Clause in Old Testament Law', SVT 1, 1953, pp. 50ff.

Do not keep company with the hot-tempered man,
  'so that you do not become accustomed to his ways
  and prepare a trap for yourself'.   (Prov. 22.25)

Do not involve yourself in financial obligations.
  'If you have nothing with which to pay,
  your bed will be taken from under you'.   (Prov. 22.27)

Do not become involved with the intemperate,
  'for the drinker and the glutton are reduced to poverty,
  and sleepiness clothes men in rags'.   (Prov. 23.21)

Do not lie in wait for the righteous man,
  'for the righteous man falls seven times and rises again,
  but the wicked come to grief in calamity'.   (Prov. 24.16)

Do not act as a witness to everything that you have seen,
  'for what will you do afterwards
  when your neighbour shames you?'   (Prov. 25.8)

Do not visit your neighbour too often,
  'in case he grows tired of you
  and then hates you'.   (Prov. 25.17)

Do not boast about the next day,
  'for you do not know what a day may produce'.   (Prov. 27.1)

Pay attention to the breeding of your small cattle,
  'for possessions do not last for ever
  nor riches from generation to generation'.   (Prov. 27.24)

If one reads through these examples, one can see at once that the attached motivations, which alone are our concern here, are not always the only possible ones which could have been given. Certainly, the exhortations could, here and there, have been differently, and probably also no less effectively motivated. That means, then, that these motivations have nothing axiomatic about them; they are attached to the exhortations for practical, pedagogical reasons. One can see this also in the fact that from time to time arguments of very different kinds are brought into play. Sometimes the uncertainty, the lack of stability in human relationships is used (Prov. 22.27; 27.1); at other times, reference is made to the undesirable consequences which might arise (Prov. 23.21; 27.24), etc. There is no need to enter into details here. The common factor in all these motivations is the fact that, without exception, they are based on experiences. Do not do yourself an ill turn through thoughtlessness or ignorance. 'The man who is kind does himself a good turn, but the cruel man does himself a hurt' (Prov. 11.17). We have to do, then, with rules for behaviour which start from a point which a man can immediately recognize. It requires no great effort on the pupil's part to see and understand these motivations. We have spoken about experiences, but here we are dealing with experiences of orders, indeed of laws, of the truth of which men have become convinced in the course of many generations. Here, then, human behaviour is determined not by general ethical norms but by the experience of inherent natural laws.

At this point, the observer will scarcely be able to suppress the question as to whether correct human behaviour can be regulated only by experience and whether, especially in the case of an ancient people, one does not have to reckon with a broad religious basis to its guiding ethical principles. And in the case of ancient Israel – one would think – were the presuppositions for this not there in plenty from the start? The question then arises: Is the ethos, as it is taught in the sentences in the book of Proverbs, not then a theonomous one and, if so, in what sense?

Now, the motivations which we gathered together above are not, in fact, the only ones. There are also those which refer to Yahweh, to his judgments and his rule.

Do not rob the poor,
  'for Yahweh will plead their case
  and deprive of life those who have deprived them'.   (Prov. 22.23)

Do not shift the widow's boundary mark,
  'for her defendant is strong
  and will bring her case against you'.   (Prov. 23.11)

Help him who has been condemned to death and make no excuses,
  'The one who examines the hearts is attentive,
  and he who preserves your life knows
  and rewards man in accordance with his action.'   (Prov. 24.12)

Show no malevolent joy when your enemy falls,
  'in case Yahweh should see it and it should displease him,
  and he should turn his anger away from him (to you)'.   (Prov. 24.18)

Fear Yahweh and the king,
  'for disaster can suddenly arise from the former,
  and calamity unexpectedly from them both'.   (Prov. 24.22)

Feed your enemy when he is hungry,
  'for you will kindle fiery coals on his head,
  and Yahweh will reward you for it'.   (Prov. 25.22)

Here at last, the modern reader believes he has found what he has been expecting for so long, for here God is mentioned, not only as the founder of law and order, but also as the one who watches over these orders and to whom man ought to know he is bound in his behaviour.

But is this handful of stray theological motivations enough to answer the question asked about the ethos of Israel (as, basically, we already knew it would be!) to the effect that the ethos of Israel was an unambiguously theonomous one? Would it not be better to admit that the available facts fall somewhat short of what we expected? It is nevertheless remarkable that Israel, who is otherwise so closely bound to Yahweh, had to allow herself to be overtaken in this respect by the Greek Hesiod, for in the form which he gave to ancient Greek folk-wisdom in *Works and Days*, the religious aspect is unquestionably clearer and less ambiguous. It is open to every pious mind to look to Zeus as the giver and guardian of the law by which all human behaviour has to be guided.[25] Let us, then, quietly admit that the ethos of the book of Proverbs simply lacks this clear-cut religious quality. An indication of this – and by no means the only one – was the fact that alongside the explicit, religious references to God and to his desire for what is right, there were also exhortations which were motivated purely and simply – one would almost say – by rules which functioned neutrally. And these latter are even in the majority. The supposition that two ethical foundations of quite diverse types are intermingled here – the one developed from the operation of inherent laws, the other directly theonomous – is quite improbable from the start. But what is the explanation of these two sides to the motivations, and to what extent is this still, in the long run, the question of a norm?

This question faces us with precisely the same dialectic as we have already encountered, namely that of Yahweh's presence on the one

[25] Plöger notes correctly that in Hesiod divine command and human instructions are much closer to each other than is the case in Old Testament wisdom exhortations (*Hertzberg Festschrift*, 1965, p. 166). Plöger, incorrectly in my view, finds the reason for this really remarkable fact in the historical development of Old Testament wisdom, namely in the lack of any deep penetration of old wisdom by Yahwism. Could the reason not be found in the precise opposite? Does it not also give rise to thought that in the translation into Greek (LXX), the accents have often shifted on to a morality and a religiosity that were foreign to Israel? The background has obviously become more religious, but, in contrast to the original text, also more rational. On the translation of Proverbs in the Septuagint, see especially G. Gerleman, 'The Septuagint Proverbs as a Hellenistic Document', *OTS* 8, 1950, pp. 15ff.; ibid., *Studies in the Septuagint: III. Proverbs*, Lunds Universitets Årsskrift, Avd. I, Bd. 52, Nr. 3, 1956, and, most recently, W. McKane, *Proverbs*, 1970, pp. 33–47.

hand and, on the other, of the laws inherent in the reality of the world.[26] Here, too, that is, in the question concerning the norm of her activity, Israel was confronted by a kind of 'in between world' whose inherent laws did not allow her simply to identify it with the utterances of Yahweh; but she did not hesitate to allow her behaviour to be regulated by the orders which could be read here. According to the convictions of the wise men, Yahweh obviously delegated to creation so much truth, indeed he was present in it in such a way that man reaches ethical *terra firma* when he learns to read these orders and adjusts his behaviour to the experiences gained. We, however, who are tracing the concepts of the ancients, must be clear that we can use the term 'experience' only in the sense which it had for Israel. If experience taught the awareness of orders, then it was teaching ultimate truths, truths about God. Correspondingly, the expression 'inherent laws', which is sometimes used, can be employed only in a restricted sense. In the long run it was always Yahweh himself with whom man saw himself confronted, and in him the indirectness of the apparently neutral event was again superseded. It is, indeed, typical that this order which controls men's actions was nowhere made the object of a theoretical definition. As a rule, the teachers only point casuistically to its functioning, that is to the place where it calls man in quite practical terms to decision. Only occasionally do the sentences rise above the level of the casuistic to what is, theologically, of general validity. We give a few examples of these for consideration by the reader, not in order to attribute, in the end, a higher place to those sentences which speak explicitly of Yahweh. (They are certainly not basically more important than those which pointed to orders which are inherently effective.) They simply raise beyond all doubt the fact that the ethos of these didactic instructions was in the last resort still a theonomous one, even if of a characteristically detached, dialectic type.

> Yahweh's eyes are in every place,
>> watching over the good and the evil. (Prov. 15.3)
>
> Sheol and underworld lie open before Yahweh;
>> how much more the hearts of men. (Prov. 15.11)
>
> All the ways of a man are pure in his own eyes,
>> but it is Yahweh who tests the spirits. (Prov. 16.2)

These are not exhortations in the formal sense of the word; but in

[26] See above pp. 59ff.

order to determine the ethos of proverbial wisdom, one must widen the circle and include also the material of the affirmative proverbs. Here it is particularly clear that, according to the sentences of the teachers, man, always and everywhere, stands in a hidden partnership with Yahweh, one which is sometimes, however, also directly and in principle explicit. What, then, is the origin of the harsh judgments on those who despise their parents?[27] It is certainly to be attributed to the experience that they are under the curse of their evil deeds, but also surely to the knowledge of Yahweh's desire for justice. The same is true of the active interest in the poor which one encounters again and again in proverbial wisdom.[28] Occasionally reference is made to the 'creator' of the poor.[29] What is the origin of the knowledge that Yahweh tests the hearts?[30] But wherever the wise men encourage men to practise good behaviour, wherever they try to prevent bad, what is characteristic is the fact that they address themselves to man's ability to think and to his better understanding, in order to reach him by the way of reflection. Here, then, we are dealing with the intelligent appropriation of what is right. Even in the domain of ethics, there is much to be learned and understood.

Whoever loves discipline, loves knowledge,
    but he who hates reproof is stupid.   (Prov. 12.1)

Wise men gather knowledge.   (Prov. 10.14)

The thoughts of the righteous
    are directed to what is right.   (Prov. 12.5)

This understanding does not always appear immediately but is perhaps the fruit of a fairly long road of realization. Men must know about the law of the act-consequence relationship. Men must sharpen their wits to be able to hear the words that can be heard spoken by misfortunes.

To our question as to what, according to the teachings of the wise men, was to determine human behaviour, there was no clear answer in the sentences. At any rate it would be impossible to name a sentence or a didactic poem or a maxim in which one could find a programmatic summary of the basis and goal of all human behaviour. This

[27] Prov. 1.8f.; 19.26; 20.20; 30.17.
[28] Prov. 14.21; 19.17; 22.9; 28.3; 28.27a; 29.7; 31.9; Job 24.4; 29.12–16; 31.16; 31.19f.; Sir. 4.1–10; 7.32; 29.9.
[29] Prov. 14.31; 17.5; 22.2.
[30] Prov. 16.2; 17.3; 21.2.

lack of guiding principles in which the quintessence of Israel's ethics might find itself succinctly formulated may surprise us. But it is in fact a characteristic of this teaching. Should one not, with respect to all this search for ethical principles, speak quite freely of a definite lack of principles, or at any rate of a highly remarkable flexibility in points of view, arguments, etc? Was the random way in which the motivations were adduced, now from the one side, now from the other, only to illuminate, to some extent, the respective exhortations, not already an indication of how little this instruction emanated from basic principles? But from what *did* it emanate? In the first instance we encounter once more the paramount significance accorded to experience. If a sentence originated from the experience of the fathers, then it could already *of* itself claim *for* itself normative significance.[31] Behind the mistrust of strong emotions and of everything overhasty which found expression in certain examples, such as that of the 'coolheaded' man, there lie, of course, experiences. But, similarly, there was a broad and deep awareness of the blessings of goodness in which, as we saw, goodness of behaviour was found alongside goodness of honour and property; and, finally, all these experiences were connected with the basic elements of a specific, highly stable, social order. Thus, these too are part of the didactic instructions. But in these instructions for correct behaviour there are included also experiences which men have had directly of Yahweh, that he proves to be the defendant of those who are without legal rights, that he quite personally 'complements' a good deed with his blessing.[32] Again, we must not forget the characteristic concept of reality as a force which continually has its effects on men. This concept would now need to be amplified only in this respect, that in these effects, orders can be discerned, from which a man can deduce norms for his behaviour. In these effects of reality Yahweh was at work, ordering and directing.[33] One could describe this reality to some extent neutrally as a definite, regulative factor which contained a challenge to men. One could, however, also speak specifically of the one who stands behind all these events and their challenge. In the realm of thought in which the rules for behaviour appear in such rational and 'secular' terms, the directness of this mention of Yahweh is rather surprising to the modern reader, especially the facility with which the Yahweh-proverbs are

[31] See below pp. 191ff.
[32] Prov. 22.23; 23.11; 25.22. On 'retribution', see below p. 133.
[33] For a further discussion of the act-consequence relationship, see below pp. 128ff.

integrated with the other sentences. Man is always wholly in the world, and he must always deal only with Yahweh. Here, of course, there is no question of an act of revelation which, with prophetic vehemence, has completely omitted to ask for man's consent. It is, rather, the reverse. The awareness of its evidence and also of its utility had become only slowly consolidated in men's minds. The ethos of proverbial wisdom originates from a knowledge which is wholly accessible to man. According to the teachings of the wise men, correct behaviour is a matter of correct understanding, but it is also a question of faith.[34] This faith – is it faith in the orders or faith in Yahweh? – is completely unshaken in the sentences. Behind the very serious exhortation not to requite evil done to one (Prov. 20.22), not to take matters into one's own hands when faced with evil men (Prov. 24.29), there does not lie – at least not in the way in which we would understand it – a lofty ethical principle, but something else, namely faith in the order controlled by Yahweh, in goodness as a life-promoting force. Men know this, and for this reason it could be said, though for us perhaps rather surprisingly, 'Understanding makes a man patient' (Prov. 19.11).[35]

By way of an appendix, a question must at least be asked, one which does not, indeed, arise directly out of the didactic literature itself, but one which is obvious enough to readers of the Bible. If the teachers believed that the good was something so obviously self-illuminating, then the narrator of the theophany at Sinai and of the proclamation of the Ten Commandments (Ex. 19f.) appears to think differently in this matter, for he depicts an event which terrified Israel. How can something self-illuminating terrify to this extent? Matters are complicated here, because it is a fairly certain result of a traditio-historical analysis of the Sinai pericope that the proclamation of the Decalogue was connected only secondarily with the Sinaitic revelation of Yahweh.[36] (Even the so-called Shechemite Dodecalogue, Deut. 27.15ff., which is possibly even older than our Decalogue, is not in the form of a divine speech.) For all that, in the present form of the narrative, the

[34] More details below pp. 191f.
[35] On the 'covering up of offences' (Prov. 10.12; 17.9; 19.11) as a specifically wisdom expression, see R. Knierim, *Die Hauptbegriffe für Sünde im Alten Testament*, 1965, pp. 119ff. To cover up an offence means to keep silent about it, to look away, perhaps also to smoothe it over. We shall return to this range of ideas under the heading of 'cause and effect'. See below p. 133.
[36] E. Gerstenberger, op. cit., p. 93, and others.

terror also extends to the communication of the commandments (Ex. 20.18–21). If, however, Yahweh himself had to come to proclaim them (in direct address) to Israel's terror, then they were thought of as something entirely new. This makes it easy to suppose that behind the insertion of the Decalogue into such a spectacular context, there is already a new, early, prophetic interpretation with a radical, theological tendency. At that period, the commandments were believed to be a direct, and therefore terrifying address by Yahweh to Israel.

VI

LIMITS OF WISDOM

OUR ATTEMPT to see at least the essentials of what was constitutive for the thinking of the wise men can be amplified still further in another direction. Already, in the course of the preceding discussion and in the texts quoted, there were numerous occasions for thinking about specific limits which were encountered by the wise men in their search for knowledge and in their instructions for mastering life and for correct behaviour. It is worthwhile pausing a little longer over this particular theme, for it appears as if the whole undertaking of this instruction can scarcely be better understood from any other standpoint than from the sentences in which the wise men speak of the limits which were encountered by their wisdom. In fact, wisdom becomes communicative, in a characteristic and interesting way, precisely at the point where such limits are experienced.

It is, of course, extremely important to see clearly from which additional intellectual point of view this discussion of limits is to be understood. One can speak in many ways of the limits which are imposed on man. Scepticism can use them as arguments and, on the other hand, an uncritical religious mind can appeal to the awareness of such limits as a means of consolation against specific attacks and intellectual difficulties. What, then, is the specific place among the early wisdom teachers for this discussion about the limits which are imposed on man?

We have already mentioned that – certainly instigated by impulses emanating from neighbouring cultures – in the early monarchy a kind of enlightenment was arrived at, a new understanding of man and the world, which manifested itself in a comprehensive literary activity which stretched far beyond the realm of the didactic.[1] At least in certain circles one can observe the emergence of a new critical sense which – even if only among an intellectual élite – led to a thorough

[1] See above pp. 58ff.

revision of accepted ideas. If we understand the word enlightenment, along the lines of a well-known definition by Kant, as the coming-of-age of man, then one would have to think of the adulthood thus achieved in Israel, too, as, in the first instance, a critical encounter with the whole world of experience and its inherent laws. Thinking entered into a new form of responsibility. It is clear that even Yahwism, which lived so intensively on experiences of a directly present God, had to express itself differently in relation to this new critical sense. Reality could no longer hide in the security of patriarchal-sacral orders. It was, instead, forced out into its own 'worldly' domain. It would appear, however, that this process of desacralization, that is, of a secularization of the world, has been greeted perhaps a little too vociferously by modern theology, because sometimes it was thought to contain a kind of biblical support for modern slogans. But what took place in Israel at that period is very little suited to the modern slogan for the reason that there was linked with what was in fact a radical secularization, an equally radical concept of God's guidance and of his presence in all parts of creation. People have not always been clear that the fascinatingly realistic presentation of history in the Succession Narrative (it is always cited in this context as the most illuminating document of this new intellectual spirit) is not to be understood quite so easily as appears to the modern reader who, in view of its rational lucidity and its consistent logical thought, would like to consider it as a forerunner of modern history. In reality, however, with its few, but carefully placed references to Yahweh's guidance of history, it is imbued with a unique and considerable theological tension. It represents a piece of genuine, secular history without in the least curtailing God's share in it. Therein lies its real theological achievement.

In this, however, we have described precisely the polarity within which also the teachings of old wisdom operate. Its proverbs are marked by the same tension between a radical secularization on the one hand and the knowledge of God's unlimited powers on the other. At one point, man's life was seen to be bound up in orders which themselves were not entirely free from a certain amount of control. Then, again, it was seen to be entirely dependent on a wholly personal attitude of benevolence on God's part. It would be easy to suppose that it must have been difficult for the wise men to maintain this tension in their teachings without loss in one direction or the other. But of this there is no trace. With effortless ease they devote themselves to the broad sweep of all that can be known. Confidently, they evaluate what has been experienced and bring every didactic aid into service in order to bring the pupil, too, to the point of trusting the evidence of the teaching in question. But this freedom in the utilization of experiences, this ability to shape life, is not their only or even their last word. Occasionally even the wise men seem to exercise a degree of self-restraint in talking, as if they were anxious to go in the opposite direction, of limits which are imposed on wisdom and on the mastery of life, even, indeed, of situations where all human ingenuity is rendered ineffective.

> All the ways of man are pure in his own eyes,
>> but it is Yahweh who tests the spirits.   (Prov. 16.2)
> A man's steps come from Yahweh,
>> how then can a man understand his way?   (Prov. 20.24)

These two sentences do not speak of something experienced or even evident, but of something unknown, that is of something which escapes human calculation. In this way the teachers take a man out of the security of his perceptions and values. What he considers to be genuine can appear quite different in God's sight, and the way which he chooses for himself is nevertheless determined by Yahweh. So do not overestimate the chances of understanding it. These are not, of course, general dogmas with which the wise men confront human stubbornness. On the contrary, behind these warnings there lie, once again, specific experiences which, although against the usual run, may not for all that be suppressed. Nor did they simply stand as exceptions on the perimeter; it was not a question of isolated cross-shots with which one had to cope as best one could. These unknown factors could be encountered at any time or in any place in life, and thus this group of sentences has its own importance within the total pattern of the instructions.

> The plans of the mind belong to man,
>> but the answer of the tongue comes from Yahweh.   (Prov. 16.1)

Here, mind and tongue are placed in a remarkable antithesis, as spheres in which the antithesis between man and God can perhaps be seen particularly clearly. To man belong – as the Hebrew text calls it – 'the arrangements of the mind', the framing of plans, the constant planning in advance. That is his field, the one in which he is master. But the projects of the mind still do not accomplish anything.

What is decisive is how man can give expression to them in words. And the meaning of the sentence is now this: the road from the constant thinking out of plans to the word, to the correct appropriate word, to the word 'at the right time', is a long one and much can happen in the meantime which is outside his control. But God is there precisely in this incalculable element, and at a single stroke which you have scarcely noticed, he has taken the whole affair out of your hands. The three following sentences can be expounded in identical fashion.

A man's mind thinks out his own way,
  but Yahweh directs his step. (Prov. 16.9)

House and property are inherited from fathers,
  but from Yahweh comes a sensible wife. (Prov. 19.14)

Many plans are in a man's mind,
  but Yahweh's decree endures. (Prov. 19.21)

Here, too, it is a question of limits of which a man must remain aware in his attempt to master life. There is no thought, however, of the well-known and much lamented limitation of man's range of vision. That would be something still comparatively harmless. It is a question not of something which a man does not know, but ought to know and perhaps even could know, but of something which he can never know.[2] Once again this simply establishes the fact as such. What it means for a man is left open. One can almost suppose that in the case of this limitation, where it becomes clear that even in every human plan God still has the last word, the wise men saw, rather, something beneficial. God could protect man even from his own plans. The ancients became aware of this limitation in that utterly incalculable and therefore mysterious factor which seemed to intrude between the preparation of a project and its realization. Here, so the teachers thought, one can experience the hand of God. Of course, such sentences do not purport to be sound doctrines about the theological distinction between human and divine activity (man in planning, God in action). They are simply examples from life by means of which one can demonstrate clearly the intervention of the divine mystery.

[2] In unmistakable dependence on such sentences, Jeremiah, too, says, 'I know, Yahweh, that a man does not have his way in his own power; no one who walks succeeds in directing his own steps' (Jer. 10.23). Similarly, the old man Tobit talks about the 'ways' of life, 'No one is capable of anything on the strength of his own will, but the Lord himself gives everything that is good' (Tob. 4.19). One has, however, the impression that what was experienced in the old sentences as antinomy has become, in Tobit, the expression of simple piety.

In no sense is there a direct, predictable road leading from a human plan to its execution. Inherited property has an element of constancy of which one can take account in one's plans. In the choice of the right wife, so much that is incalculable is at stake; one has to accept that she is a gift from Yahweh.

> There is no wisdom, no understanding,
>   no counsel against Yahweh.
> The horse is made ready for the day of battle,
>   but the victory belongs to Yahweh. (Prov. 21.30f.)

In this astonishing sentence, the awareness of the limit round which earlier sentences were already circling is expressed in extremely radical terms and is even surpassed. The astonishing element in it is clearly seen when one realizes that its aim is certainly not to warn man against acquiring and using wisdom or even to prevent him from 'making ready' the horse before the battle. If one were to remove it from its context one could even perceive in it the expression of a radical, theological agnosticism. But this would be to misunderstand it completely. Its aim is, rather, to put a stop to the erroneous concept that a guarantee of success was to be found simply in practising human wisdom and in making preparations. Man must always keep himself open to the activity of God, an activity which completely escapes all calculation, for between the putting into practice of the most reliable wisdom and that which then actually takes place, there always lies a great unknown. Is that a dangerous doctrine? Must not – we might ask – as a result of this great unknown factor, a veil of resignation lie over all human knowledge and action? This question can be answered only by the degree of trust which man is capable of placing in that divine activity which surpasses all planning. The double sentence of Prov. 21.30f. can have a comforting effect, but, with different religious presuppositions, it could have a depressing effect. Along these latter lines, Ecclesiastes will elaborate this perception in his own way.[3] In its present context, the awareness of the limitations of all human planning is certainly not depressing, but rather liberating: 'Victory comes from the Lord.' Thus, this double sentence is in no sense an isolated outpost. It must be taken together with one of the deepest insights to which those teachers penetrated. Only he is really wise who does not consider himself wise. To consider oneself wise is a sure sign of folly.

[3] See below pp. 226ff.

Do you see a man who thinks he is wise?
　　There is more hope for a fool than for him.   (Prov. 26.12)

Do not boast about the next day,
　　for you do not know what a day may produce.   (Prov. 27.1)

A rich man thinks he is wise,
　　but a poor man who has intelligence can see through him.
　　　　　　　　　　　　　　　　　　　　　　　　　(Prov. 28.11)

He who trusts in himself is a fool,
　　but he who walks in wisdom escapes.   (Prov. 28.26)

Trust in Yahweh with all your heart,
　　but do not rely on your own cleverness.   (Prov. 3.5)

Do not think you are wise;
　　fear Yahweh and avoid evil.   (Prov. 3.7)

The acquisition of wisdom and competence was stressed by none as
highly as by the teachers; but they also knew that wherever it gives
a man a sense of security or where it tempts him into boasting, wisdom
has already cancelled itself out.

No reason is given for the idea that the considering of himself as
wise betrays in a man an almost hopeless inner state. As so often, a
rule is stated without any theological reason being given for it. Is the
reason to be sought in the superior power of the unknowable, a factor
by which the wise man precisely ought to be influenced? But the
explanation is surely to be found in a different direction. Again and
again in Israel, one encounters a passionate attack on any form of
false security and on that kind of self-glorification in which a man can
badly misjudge himself. Thus, for example, before a battle, Yahweh
takes precautions that the Israelites should not 'vaunt themselves'
(Judg. 7.2). In Deut. 9.1–6, there is a whole war-sermon in which the
Israelites are warned not to attribute the guidance of Yahweh to their
own goodness and righteousness. Can, then, the axe vaunt itself over
him who wields it (Isa. 10.15)? Thus, it is not the quantitative limitation of human capabilities which forbids self-confidence and self-
glorification; it is, rather, something which can be explained only in
theological terms: self-glorification cannot be combined with trust in
Yahweh. Even the ability of wisdom to master life must inevitably
come up against this alternative. Thus, in this case too, the teaching
of the wise men is rooted in ultimate, basic convictions about faith in
Yahweh. A disparagement of wisdom would be the last thing with
which one could reproach these teachers; but the limit is drawn sur-

prisingly sharply. Wisdom itself can never become the object of trust, never become that upon which a man leans in life.

> Let not the wise man glory in his wisdom,
>> let not the mighty man glory in his might,
>> let not the rich man glory in his riches.
> But let him who glories glory in this,
>> that he has understanding and knows me,
>> that I am Yahweh who practise kindness,
>> justice and righteousness on earth;
>> for in these things do I delight. (Jer. 9.23f.)

In this presumably authentic word of Jeremiah, the prophet criticizes those things on which human self-glorification is usually based. If there is to be any boasting, then the only basis for it would lie in man's knowledge of God. One cannot say that this warning is directed against the search for knowledge on the part of the wisdom teachers whose insights are available to us in the sentences of the book of Proverbs. On the contrary, Jeremiah has correctly interpreted the deepest insights of the teachers and has given to them their keenest and finest expression.

The story of Absalom's council of war, in which Yahweh had 'broken', in dramatic fashion, the counsel of the wise man Ahithophel (II Sam. 17.14), reads almost like a paradigm of the sentence that no wisdom can prevail against Yahweh (Prov. 21.30).[4] If one consulted him, it was 'as if one consulted God himself'. Ahithophel was David's counsellor, but he had joined the rebellion against David. David knew that nothing could effect his advice. This made his position completely hopeless from the start. There was nothing moreth at men could do against this advantage, and for this reason David appealed to Yahweh to let Ahithophel's advice 'seem foolish' (II Sam. 15.31). Yahweh answered the prayer of his anointed. But on this occasion he did not allow – and events could have taken this turn – the wise man to make a mistake. As always, Ahithophel's advice was the only correct way this time, too; but, in a kind of madness, the council of war rejected it. If only we had more such narratives to clarify for us in such concrete terms the meaning of a sentence.[5] In this instance, the

[4] W. M. W. Roth, *VT* 18, 1968, pp. 70f.
[5] Ahithophel had advised the immediate pursuit of the fleeing king in order to give him no time to recover. This would prevent the need for a battle and would mean that the affair would be decided as quickly as possible. His opponent in the council, Hushai, gives completely opposite advice; the involved process of a general

frustrating of human wisdom, which is in itself superior, the making of it to appear foolish, is in a thoroughly consolatory context, for Yahweh made use of this means to rescue his anointed from the most abject humiliation. But one could unquestionably think also of contexts where the sentence could stand in a much more ominous light.

> Therefore, behold, I will again
>   do marvellous things with this people,
>   wonderful and marvellous;
> and the wisdom of their wise men shall perish,
>   and the understanding of their men of understanding shall be hidden.
>   (Isa. 29.14)

Once again we are dealing with a frustration, caused by God, of the wisdom of the wise men. Events will occur, in the face of which the insight of men of insight will be obliged to 'hide'. The context here is much darker. Isaiah sees, in conjunction with political catastrophes, a darkness falling with which human abilities at understanding will no longer be able to cope.

We have particularly emphasized the sentences which deal with Yahweh as the limit of all of man's mastery of life, because, in the context of Israel's old wisdom, they are the most impressive indications of the fact that the understanding of the world which these teachers had was not simply a predominantly religious one but that it was based quite specifically on faith in Yahweh the God of Israel. While later wisdom is differentiated from old wisdom as being 'theological', this distinction is only a relative one, for it concerns, rather, the intensity of the involvement in specific, individual, theological questions. It is not, however, a difference in principle, for even old

---

conscription is not to be omitted. Hushai was a supporter of David; he wanted to give him time to gather troops. The two speeches, especially that of Hushai, are examples of a highly cultivated rhetoric, of a precious use of language, in which the teachers trained their pupils.

Was the idea that Yahweh can make the clever man foolish also a theme of the hymn?

> . . . who frustrates the omen of prognosticators
>   and makes the soothsayers fools,
> who makes the wise men turn back
>   and makes their knowledge foolish.   (Isa. 44.25)

> He makes counsellors foolish
>   and judges he makes fools . . .
> He takes speech away from those who are trusted
>   and takes the power of discernment from the elders.   (Job 12.17, 20)

wisdom was aware that all life is determined by Yahweh and, as we have seen, reflected on his activities, activities which either challenged men or limited them.

Let us recall once again the remarkable dualism which struck us about the codification of experiences in the sentences. The teachers vacillated between two possibilities of expression: one adhered quite objectively to the causality of events, while the other was credal and spoke of Yahweh's direct dealings with men. These two types of expressions ran parallel to one another, so to speak. This appeared astonishing to us; for all that, the two types were never fused in one and the same sentence. One formulated an event in 'secular' terms; the other credally. There was never any confrontation of the two causalities in one event. But it was quite another matter in the Yahweh-proverbs which we have just discussed. Here, in one and the same sentence – a dangerous undertaking – God and man were mentioned in the same breath. Here, too, there was an awareness of God's presence, of his participation in all human events. But now it was no simple juxtaposition; now God and man – co-operating in one and the same event – suddenly parted company. This separation led the teachers didactically to the idea that they would have to break the continuity between human intentions and actual realization. The unpredictable area which lay between these two they regarded as the specific domain of Yahweh. Even this did not, of course, remove the element of doubt. A complete and, above all, unambiguous penetration of the world by God could not be demonstrated except at the price of giving up the world's secularity. Given the world in which they found themselves, the teachers considered it appropriate to speak at great length of valid rules and orders, even feeling obliged to include human activity as a factor. On the other hand, they regarded themselves equally justified in drawing attention from time to time to the hand of God intervening directly in human life. Only in this way were they able to do justice to the dialectic of all experience.

This, however, also provides an answer to our question as to the specific theological position of what was said about the limits of wisdom. The purpose of what was said in this respect was not to conceal an intellectual difficulty. Rather, it filled the gap which opened up between two types of empirical statement which were diametrically opposed to each other. Of course it approached man by way of a warning, but certainly not with the intention of making him aware of his lack of freedom. When did Israel ever complain of this mysterious presence of God in every human activity? This divine presence, on the one hand limiting human planning, on the other carrying men beyond the goal which they had envisaged – to experience human limitations in this way was, in the last resort, a comforting doctrine. By this dialectic of the two points of view, the wise men have influenced the religious thinking of the entire Western world.[6]

How could the wise men have solved this basic intellectual problem if it had not presented itself to them? It was certainly not their task to determine philosophically the relationship of a system of inherently effective laws to Yahweh's free will. Their task was a predominantly practical one; they endeavoured to place their pupils within the sphere of influence of varied and partly contradictory experiences of life. They could not give to each one of them practicable directions for the road. They were aiming at something much more important: by means of their teachings, derived from experience, they set the pupil in the midst of the constant oscillation between grasp of meaning and loss of meaning, and in this way they induced him to make his own contribution in this exciting arena of knowledge of life. In this way they probably achieved more than if they had trained their pupils to find a better solution for theological problems. Reduced to its bare essentials, these regulations of theirs for a fruitful life seem determined by a remarkable dialectic. Do not hesitate to summon up all your powers in order to familiarize yourself with all the rules which might somehow be effective in life. Ignorance in any form will be detrimental to you; only the 'fool' thinks he can shut his eyes to this. Experience, on the other hand, teaches that you can never be certain. You must always remain open for a completely new experience. You will never become really wise, for, in the last resort, this life of yours is determined not by rules but by God.

In view of all this, one must therefore be cautious in one's use of the term 'order' which we, too, have felt unable to dispense with in our

---

[6] 'Indeed, the power which is eternal moves
us imperceptibly, one way or another,
in the direction of what is beneficial to us,
of counsel, of decision, of completion,
and, as if borne along, we reach our goal.
To experience this is highest bliss.
Not to demand it is plain duty,
to expect it is comfort in suffering.'

(J. W. v. Goethe, *Die natürliche Tochter*, Act V, Scene 7)

discussion. Can one really say that the teachers were searching for a world order? Our findings, especially the discussion of the Yahweh-proverbs, suggested, rather, that one can in no sense speak of a world order as really existing between God and man.[7] What could be determined was, rather, that the statements of the teachers move in a dialectic which is fundamentally incapable of resolution, speaking on the one hand of valid rules and, on the other, of *ad hoc* divine actions.

Later wisdom, too, speaks of the limits imposed on human knowledge. Since this later wisdom scarcely ever made use of the sentence form, it did not have at its disposal the possibility of alternating between proverbs which at one point indicate the knowable and at another indicate the unknowable. The larger form of the lengthy didactic speech afforded other possibilities, namely the insertion of appropriate hymnic sections. Already in older sentence wisdom, one can describe the mystery of God's rule quite simply as a subject for study. But the later teachers became more communicative in this respect. The fascination of the phenomenon of this mystery has obviously continued to grow. The lack of transition has, of course, remained. The suddenness with which rational speeches pass into a hymn in praise of this mystery, seems rather irritating to the modern reader.

> . . . who does great things which are unsearchable,
>   wonders without number.   (Job 5.9)

> Do you think you can find out the depths of God's being,
>   or know the limits of the Almighty?
> It is 'higher than heaven',
>   what can you do?
> It is deeper than the underworld,
>   what can you know? (Job 11.7f.)

> Dominion and fear are with him
>   who creates peace in his heights.
> Can his hosts be numbered,
>   and on whom does his light not arise?   (Job 25.2–3)

> See, God is great so that we cannot grasp it;
>   the number of his years is unfathomable.   (Job 36.26)

[7] In two places in the book of Jeremiah, there have been inserted hymnic texts which are striking in so far as in them, quite unambiguously, reference is made to 'orders' in creation (Jer. 31.35f.), to orders of heaven and earth (Jer. 33.25). The dialectic which engaged our attention above is resolved here; the 'orders' (*ḥuqqōt*) actually appear as something inherent in creation.

Do you not know, have you not heard?
  Yahweh is an everlasting God,
  he who has created the ends of the earth.
He does not grow weary or faint;
  his understanding is unsearchable.   (Isa. 40.28)

If this was the same God who was at work in the laws and orders that have been perceived, then it is easy to see the tensions within which the thinking of the wise men operated. More than any other ancient people, Israel was aware that all spheres of life were encompassed in the most direct way by the power of God, by his 'zeal'. To the extent, however, to which one was aware that God was at work behind the fixed orders, the world, too, which knowledge was endeavouring to control, was drawn into the sphere of the great mystery surrounding God. Thus the teachers, especially those of the later period, were able to speak in such a lively way about the unsearchable nature of the world. So, as is well known, the divine speech in the book of Job covers every aspect of the world in order, in a didactic, interrogative style, to teach men to view the world, and whatever happens in it, in all its inexplicableness. Indeed, beginning with the intricate formation of his own body, man saw himself also as part of this mystery:

You have formed my inward parts,
  have knit me together in my mother's womb.
I praise you that I have been so wonderfully made;
  your works are wonderful . . .
My frame was not hidden from you,
  when I was being made in secret
  and wrought in the depths of the earth.
When I was still an embryo, your eyes saw me,
  every day was written in a book . . .
  when none of them as yet existed.
How precious do I find your thoughts,
  O God, how great is the sum of them.
If I tried to count them,
  they would be more than the sand.   (Ps. 139.13–18a)

This whole psalm, indeed, is a paradigm of that intermingling of faith and knowledge. The desire for knowledge is so pressing that, at the limits which are imposed upon it, it becomes itself a witness to God's inscrutability. The fear of God not only enabled a man to acquire knowledge, but also had a predominantly critical function in that it kept awake in the person acquiring the knowledge the awareness that his intellect was directed towards a world in which mystery predominated. This fear of God has trained him to openness, to readiness for an encounter even with the inscrutable and the imponderable, that is, it has taught him that the sphere in which definite, verifiable orders can be discerned is a very limited one. But one must not lose sight of the fact that the wise men never speak, in a narrower sense, of a mystery of the world. The mysteries of the world have no independent existence. In them, man directly confronts the mystery of God. Israel's intellectual powers have never escaped from the shadow of the great mystery of God. This is, indeed, the fascinating thing about this investigation of life, the fact that men dared to address themselves to a world in which they had to reckon at every step with the possibility of encountering the totally incommensurable God. Fascinating, too, is the calm, unperturbed way in which this investigation is pursued on such a terrain and faced with such a partner. Of course, hand in hand with the growing boldness in interpreting the guidance of God, there goes – remarkably enough, mostly from the same lips – solemn teaching about the mysteries of divine government. The mystery of God has now become a subject of study. Occasionally, even, the teachers could surpass themselves when they said that the mystery of God, of which they were aware, was still not the whole mystery of God, but only the outermost edge of it.

> The underworld lies naked before him,
>   the abyss is without covering.
> He stretches out the north over the void,
>   and hangs the earth upon nothing . . .
> See, these are only the outskirts of his ways,
>   what a small whisper we hear of him!
> But the thunder of his power, who can understand?   (Job 26.6f., 14)
> Who has seen him and can tell about it?
>   Who can extol him as he is?
> Much that is still hidden is greater than this,
>   for we see but little of his rule.   (Sir. 43.31f.)

If it is permissible to measure the high-water mark of a people's knowledge by what they know of the unknowable, then Israel was extremely knowledgeable. One can hardly say that ancient Near Eastern wisdom outside Israel felt itself forced into such doubt.

Whether one can describe the basic characteristic of this old instructional wisdom as optimistic in contrast to a more pessimistic, theological wisdom, is highly questionable.[8] If its optimism refers to the 'still' unquestioned connection between goodness and well-being, then one could, in all seriousness, ask whether one could not, rather, call the teaching of Job's friends, of Jesus Sirach and of the Wisdom of Solomon optimistic in contrast to old wisdom which, as we have just seen, still argues very cautiously and therefore is certainly not 'naively untamed'. Job and Ecclesiastes cannot be understood as representatives of a whole phase of wisdom, but as advocates of questions which suddenly emerge in the midst of this conceptual system. The sudden emergence of such difficult questions is not, however, something fundamentally new. One could write a whole history of such sudden appearances, of which David's question in II Sam. 24.17 would still not be the *terminus a quo*. Belief in the validity of the connection between goodness and well-being was not, in any case, a specific tenet of wisdom teaching. Not only was it spread throughout the whole world in ancient times and was, thus, not a postulate which was being propounded, but wide experience had taught men to understand this connection as a divine ordinance governing all human life. It is not possible to determine a deeper break, a fundamental revision in this concept. The difference between older instructional wisdom and later theological wisdom cannot be understood by means of an optimism-pessimism contrast. Every period has its own conflicts with reality or, better, with the concepts which it has formed of reality. But there is always something which cannot be accommodated. The search for knowledge in every age has only the confidence which it has been given and is forced to a halt at specific limits. Thus, both its optimism and its pessimism are of a specific kind. It is bad if the exegete seizes on one aspect of what is, in all periods, a very lively process of grasp of meaning and loss of meaning and makes it the criterion of two major phases in Israel's educational system.

---

[8] Amongst others, B. Gemser, *Sprüche Salomos*, 1937, pp. 55ff.; I. C. Rylaarsdam, *Revelation in Jewish Wisdom Literature*, 1963[2], p. 63; U. Skladny, op. cit., p. 82; H. Ringgren, *Sprüche*, 1962, p. 45; R. B. Y. Scott, *Proverbs, Ecclesiastes*, Anchor Bible, 1965, p. XIX; O. Plöger, *Gottes Wort und Gottes Land* (Hertzberg Festschrift, 1965), p. 172.

PART THREE

INDIVIDUAL SUBJECTS OF INSTRUCTION

VII

THE ESSENTIALS FOR COPING
WITH REALITY

AFTER THE PRECEDING DISCUSSION, primarily of principles, we are now faced with the task of considering still more closely specific individual experiences which Israel had within the wider sphere of her reality. If we use the word 'reality', we have of course, strictly speaking, already gone well beyond the range of expressions occurring in the sentences and didactic poems, for there this particular sphere is not mentioned, not, at any rate, as a homogeneous and self-contained whole, not even, as we would like to think, as 'creation'. The book of Proverbs presents us, rather, with a multiplicity of individual realities which are at first difficult to survey. The step from the many to the one, that is, to reality as a homogeneous whole, is not taken. One cannot say that this is simply due to an inability on Israel's part to think in abstract terms, for this hesitancy to classify the experience of reality in conceptual terms could be due precisely to a specific factor in her experience of the world. One could present a stronger case for the idea that the didactic form, orientated towards the practical, afforded little opportunity for indulging in broad abstractions. But we must, in every case, remain conscious of this fact, whether we judge it to be a limitation or a specific opportunity for men's experience of the world.

We find particularly aggravating the lack of any order determined by subject-matter, of any arrangements in the collection of sentences and teachings. Only rarely does the reader come upon a group of proverbs in which related material has come together. For the understanding of the sentences as a whole, these small ordered arrangements are of no significance, for they appear too sporadically. A further aggravating factor is that the didactic material which we have to discuss is, as far as we can see, the result of the intellectual activity of about eight centuries; only with difficulty, however, could it be arranged chronologically. On the one hand, we have to reckon with considerable intellectual development within this process of tradition which has spanned many centuries; on the other hand, however – and especially in the case of such specifically didactic material – also with a tenacious persistence and stability, with regard both to the way of asking questions and to the fundamental perceptions. It is fairly common, nowadays, to date the collection comprising Prov. 10–29 in the period of the monarchy. If one compares with it the didactic poems in Prov. 1–9, one might, in view of their more intensive, theological thought, consider that they were later; but this is by no means certain. The proof that only in the post-exilic period could such teaching be given has still to be produced. Perhaps, with regard to the teachings of Prov. 1–9, we must simply think of different transmitters who, at the same time, stood in different teaching traditions.

What first presented itself as an extremely important subject of research in the field of the wisdom literature was the question about the external circumstances presupposed by the didactic poems, that is, about the political, social and economic circumstances, but also, of course, at the same time, the question about the internal attitude of man to man and of man to God.[1] This, of course, raised the question about the opinions expressed in the sentences. Indubitably, by means of these questions, interesting groupings could be made among the proverbs. One can ask, however, whether there is much more to be done in this respect. It now appears more important and more interesting to examine the proverbs and teachings from the point of view of the intellectual work achieved in them. With what end in view were events examined? What was looked for in them, and what was it hoped to find? If, in fact, something of the nature of an order was recognized, how was it expressed? In this way we could succeed in understanding the sentences at a deeper level, a level at which there emerges something which they all have in common. We could, in this way, discover certain basic phenomena which were observed in more or less all spheres of life and in which the teachers were particularly interested, in that they continually come back to them. We recall that the vast majority of the sentences are in the style of simple statements, not of exhortations. They simply state what has been experienced. This is where we could begin, for it is here that the question of what the individual sentences state must be answered. Judgments? Statements of fact? Causal connections? Or how do they

---

[1] Discussed particularly in the works of J. Fichtner and U. Skladny.

regard the relationship of Yahweh or that of men to events in their environment?

I. THE EXPRESSION OF THE ACTUAL AND THE SEARCH FOR ANALOGIES

The book of Proverbs is full of sentences in which definite judgments are expressed. Beginning with the value of wisdom, the worthlessness of folly, the wise men emphasize as comprehensibly as possible what ought to be retained from one type of behaviour or another or from human characteristics. At this point, for example, there belongs the sizeable group of 'better than' proverbs ('Better a dish of vegetables with love than a fattened ox with hatred', Prov. 15.17). At this point, too, belong the tō'ēbā-proverbs ('. . . is an abomination to Yahweh') and the 'happiness'-proverbs ('happy, blessed is the man who . . .').[2] These sentences also, of course, state judgments which are self-evident within the sphere of a specific world order. There will be no further discussion of them here. With these, there are clearly contrasted other sentences in which no value judgments are passed; rather, the teacher confines himself to stating simply, as they were actually felt, specific experiences of types of behaviour. Such actualities occur so frequently that in them something of the nature of a rule may be recognized. But what is expressed is not the rule itself; rather, a typical case is presented in which the rule is immediately perceptible to those who think about it. That the rich man has many friends while the poor man is hated by his friend (singular; Prov. 14.20); that the rich man, if he needs help, always finds it, while the poor man is rejected even by his friend; that the rich man always finds listeners, while, when the poor man speaks, people say, 'Who is this?' (Sir. 13.23) – this and much more is simply so. One takes note of it, one does not alter it, one must, rather, take such facts into account and not argue about them. That the buyer first of all complains about the goods, but that, after the purchase, he boasts (Prov. 20.14), is perhaps funny, but whoever wishes to get to know men must also know about such peculiar types of behaviour; some time or another, this knowledge will be of use to him. Again and again, these sentences come back to the contradictions in social life and to the puzzles which arise within this sphere of tension.

[2] 'tō'ēbā-proverbs': Prov. 3.32; 6.16; 8.7; 11.1, 20; 15.8f., 26; 16.5; 17.15; 20.10, 23; 'beatitudes': Prov. 3.13; 8.32, 34; 14.21; 16.20; 20.7; 28.14; 29.18.

> The rich man's wealth is a strong city for him,
>   but the ruin of the poor is in their poverty.   (Prov. 10.15)

> The poor man speaks beseechingly,
>   but the rich man replies harshly.   (Prov. 18.23)

> A rich man and a poor man meet;
>   it is Yahweh who has made them all.   (Prov. 22.2)

> The rich man does wrong and boasts about it;
>   the poor man suffers wrong and must apologize.   (Sir. 13.3)

> The rich man toils to gather his fortune,
>   and when he rests he eats his fill.
> The poor man toils and exhausts himself,
>   and when he rests he finds himself in need.   (Sir. 31.3f.)

There is no appeal made here to abolish such conditions. In its place, this frequently happened in Israel, too. In these sentences, we find ourselves to some extent in a sphere where social appeals are not envisaged at all. If one were to examine these sentences with regard to the movement of thought that takes place within them, then one would encounter first of all a quite simple astonishment at actualities and at contradictions which can be observed. This does not make the poor man rich or the evil man good, but in this astonishment there is knowledge. Even if this kind of thing can still not be incorporated in a scale of values, a man does well to include such a realization in his knowledge of rules. It is understandable that it is in this type of sentence that peculiar phenomena, which are in themselves puzzling, are expressed. That it is sometimes difficult to recognize such phenomena and that they refer to difficult problems, actually lies well beyond the declaratory scope of the sentence, for with the assertion of the existence of such actualities, it has already fulfilled its self-imposed task. Its aim was neither to explain nor even to evaluate such actualities.

> Sheol and underworld are never satisfied,
>   and men's eyes are never satisfied.   (Prov. 27.20)

Here is yet another fact, though only one, which completely passes understanding. The insatiability of the eye, like that of the underworld which is always able to receive new shades, can only be stated as a highly puzzling phenomenon. This type of assertion acquires an almost uncanny quality when God is brought within its scope.

A poor man and a slave-driver meet;
  the one who gave sight to them both is Yahweh.   (Prov. 29.13)[3]

We must not omit a particular field in which the wise men have
made their observations – again only in neutral and declaratory
terms – that of man's inner life. In the psychological sphere, or faced
with the question of how a man's inner life is reflected in his outer one
and how he can, at the same time, conceal himself, how solitary he can
be both in joy and in sorrow, here the wise men have succeeded in
formulating particularly fine sentences. They have succeeded in cap-
turing just such more or less hidden truths. The author of Job dwells
forcefully on the fears and delusions which torment brutal men,[4] and
Sirach begins, on several occasions, to tackle the highly ambivalent
phenomenon of shame.[5] But similar material is already found in the
older sentence literature.

A heart knows its own bitterness,
  and no stranger shares its joy.   (Prov. 14.10)

Even in laughter the heart can suffer,
  and the end of joy is grief.   (Prov. 14.13)

A man's spirit endures his sickness,
  but a broken spirit who can bear?   (Prov. 18.14)

We can see the same process in the sphere of 'natural science'. If
we read, for example, concerning the bee, a particularly insignificant
winged creature, that we have to thank her for one of the most
wonderful things (Sir. 11.3), then this is simply the stating of an
astonishing fact and contains no moral appeal. Alongside such unpretentious sentences, one can at once place the magnificent animal
descriptions in the divine speech in the book of Job, for the difference
here is only in the more ambitious, artistic presentation.[6] We select
from the available material (ostrich, Job 39.13–18; horse, Job 39.19–
22; crocodile, Job 40.25–41.26) the description of the hippopotamus.

See the hippopotamus beside you.
  He eats grass like an ox.

[3] Cf. Prov. 29.22a. The two sentences remind us of *Amenenope*, ch. 25: '(The god)
makes 1,000 poor men at will; he also makes 1,000 men overseers.'
[4] Job 8.20ff.; 20.22ff.
[5] Sir. 4.20–26; 41.14–42.8. See below pp. 247ff.
[6] H. Richter, 'Die Naturweisheit des Alten Testaments im Buche Hiob', *ZAW*
70, 1958, pp. 1ff.

See his strength in his loins
  and his power in the muscles of his body.
He lets his tail hang down like a cedar;
  the sinews of his thighs are firmly knit together.
His bones are tubes of bronze,
  his loins are bars of iron.
He is the first of the works of God,
  'made to have dominion over his fellows'.
For the mountains provide wood for him,
  and all the wild beasts play there.
He hides under lotus bushes,
  in the covert of reed and marsh.
The lotus bushes cover him with their shade,
  and the poplars by the stream surround him.
Even when the stream rushes, he is not afraid,
  he remains calm even when Jordan flows into his mouth.
'Who' could grasp at his eyes
  or pierce his nose in the snare?   (Job 40.15-24)

As a result of its insertion into the divine speech, this passage has been placed in a definite theological light. If one removes it from this particular theological shadow, it at once becomes clear that in its original form it never gave expression to anything religious or to any moral interest. References to the animal as a model for specific human virtues – that universally acknowledged requirement of moral instruction – had a part to play in education in Israel, too, but above all in that of ancient Egypt ('Go to the ant, you sluggard . . .', Prov. 6.6ff.). In ancient Babylon, too, there were detailed descriptions of animals and their parts. There, however, they belonged to sacral literature and served the science of prognostication.[7] How different the biblical animal descriptions are! In them the concern is only with the description of the phenomenon itself and with its peculiarity. In this attitude towards a part of man's puzzling environment, in this concentration on the phenomenon itself without immediately referring it to man and his world, one can see a specific characteristic of ancient Israel's knowledge of the world, for Egyptian wisdom did not know animal descriptions of this type with no moral aim.[8] Does this particular openness to truth not also have a correspondence in the realism of so many Old Testament narratives? If one enquires about

[7] W. v. Soden in B. Landsberger–W. v. Soden, *Die Eigenbegrifflichkeit der babylonischen Welt*, 1965, pp. 70f.
[8] So E. Otto, orally.

the actual purpose of such animal descriptions, that is, about their *Sitz im Leben*, then one will need to think here too of the school.[9] Their highly-charged, poetic rhetoric does not prevent one from thinking of them as explicitly didactic poems. In this context one would need also to mention the didactic poem in Isa. 28.23ff., which deals with the various activities of the farmer.[10] If the author of the Wisdom of Solomon acknowledges that the knowledge of all earthly phenomena comes from God, the knowledge of the cycles of the year, of the stars, of the differences between plants and the virtues of roots (Wisd. 7.15ff.), he is referring to branches of knowledge which were presumably already taught in the old schools.

A further bold step towards the mastery of reality is indicated in the following sentences:

Heaven in height and the earth in depth
and the mind of kings – all are unsearchable. (Prov. 25.3)

The north wind brings rain,
and the furtive tongue glum looks. (Prov. 25.23)

Clouds and wind, but no rain;
a man who boasts of a non-existent gift. (Prov. 25.14)

Iron 'is' sharpened on iron;
one man sharpens the other. (Prov. 27.17)

Here, too, facts are stated. The structure of the sentences in Hebrew can scarcely be imitated, but in each sentence two facts are placed side by side. The facts appear to be widely separated. What has the distance between heaven and earth to do with the mind of a king? Nevertheless, something links these two widely separated statements, what we would call their unpredictability. And it is this, the making obvious of what it is that links two totally different phenomena, that is seized upon by the sentences as a gain in knowledge. To be precise, we are dealing here, then, with three affirmations, for, as the third and most important, there is the additional perception that there is something common to the two affirmations made by the sentence.

There is a similar striving after knowledge in the 'like'-proverbs, in which equations of various types are made. These sentences are to be found in great numbers both in the book of Proverbs (particularly frequently in the collection comprising chs. 25–27) and in Sirach.

[9] Is the fact that the poem places the hippopotamus in the Jordan to be explained on this basis? Many exegetes simply delete the word 'Jordan'.
[10] On Isa. 28.23ff., see below pp. 140f.

Like vinegar to the teeth and smoke to the eyes,
   so is the lazy man to those who send him.   (Prov. 10.26)

Like a dog that returns to its vomit,
   so is a fool who repeats his folly.   (Prov. 26.11)

If the wood is finished, the fire goes out;
   and if there is no slanderer, quarrelling stops.   (Prov. 26.20)

Pressing milk produces butter,
   pressing the nose produces blood,
   pressing anger produces strife.   (Prov. 30.33)

Whoever touches pitch gets dirty,
   and whoever associates with the cynic becomes like him.   (Sir. 13.1)

As smoke and reek come before the flame,
   so insults come before bloodshed.   (Sir. 22.24)

The meaning of these sentences would be grossly underrated, if one were to regard these comparisons merely as didactic and rhetorical stylistic devices used to illustrate a statement. If that were merely the case, are the comparisons then not too far-fetched? These comparisons do not have a pedagogic function, but a noetic one. They serve to bring out analogies, they are almost to be judged as discoveries of communal elements discernible even between quite different phenomena.[11] But it was precisely not a question of phenomena which could be compared quite by chance, for in that case the ranging of them together would lack the decisive factor of stringency. Here, rather, there become visible connections which point to an all-embracing order in which both phenomena are linked with each other. This, however, at once deprived them of something of the character of uncontrolled contingency. They were drawn into a sphere of order. One could almost say that the further apart the subjects being compared lay, the more interesting must the discovery of analogies have been, in so far as this revealed something of the breadth of the order that was discovered. But who can say whether our ideas of far and near correspond to those of the ancients?[12] Such

[11] This co-ordination of analogies also had a function within the realm of Greek thought. 'On the presupposition that the same logic and system operates in human life as in the world of nature, Solon argues with analogies from the connection between cause and effect in the sphere of the weather in order to determine correctly the responsibility for political events' (H. Fränkel, op. cit., p. 599). 'The power of snow and hail comes from the cloud, and the clap of thunder comes from the lightning flash. So the city is destroyed by great men' (op. cit., p. 262).

[12] There is yet another form in which concepts can be arranged together, paronomasia. Although the teachers made extensive use of it, we can no longer

references to analogous features were particularly favoured in disputes, where they had the task of safeguarding the stringency of the disputed thesis. No wild ass brays if he has fresh grass to eat; no ox lows over his fodder. From this, the friends could deduce that there was something special about Job's complaint (Job 6.5; 8.11ff.; etc.). In this respect, the most exhaustive treatment is afforded by the wonderful poem about the revolutions of the elements. Sun, wind and water are bound up in one and the same law of succession. But this is not formulated; it is illustrated.

> A generation comes and a generation goes,
>   but the earth remains for ever.
> The sun rises and the sun sets
> and hurries back to its place
>   where it rises (again).
> The wind blows to the south and veers to the north,
>   round and round goes the wind.
> All rivers run into the sea,
>   but the sea is never full.
> To the place where the rivers go,
>   there they go again and again.   (Eccles. 1.4–7)

It is not impossible that this text was originally only a poem giving instruction in natural science and had no connection with man and his questions about life.[13] In its present context, however, it is much more far-reaching. It lays open the whole area within which human life operates and, in this way, it acts as an introduction to the preacher's melancholy thoughts about human existence. Here, the analogy between events in the outer world and those in human life is not limited to one item but is all-inclusive.

Finally, in this connection, we must also mention the argument *a minore ad maius* (or *a maiore ad minus* 'if here, then how much more there'). It also links two phenomena which are unconnected with each other. Here, however, it is not a question of the establishing of

---

determine the noetic process, the gain in knowledge, which took place in the ranging together of words which sounded alike. Presumably, in this instance, the word functions both as a sound and as a bearer of meaning. We can only suppose that the similarity in sound of words grouped together was intended to have specific effects on the listener. The linguistic material can be found in G. Boström, *Paronomasi i den äldre hebreiska maschalliteraturen*, 1928.

[13] At any rate according to the attractive supposition of O. Loretz, *Qohelet und der Alte Orient*, 1964, p. 254.

analogies, but of a deduction which follows from an acknowledged order of importance. If something is already valid in an unimportant or even insignificant matter, then it is surely still more valid in a more important matter – or *vice versa*.

Sheol and underworld (lie open) before Yahweh;
how much more the hearts of men.   (Prov. 15.11)

There are poor men who are honoured for their cleverness,
and there are those who are honoured for their wealth.
Whoever is (already) honoured in poverty,
how much more in wealth.
Whoever is despised in wealth,
how much more in poverty.   (Sir. 10.30f.)

While comparison-sentences were satisfied with defining what two phenomena had in common, the so-called numerical sayings go much further. The number of phenomena classified together in some kind of analogy varies from two to ten.

There are four things on earth;
these four are the smallest on earth
and yet are exceedingly clever.
Ants are a people without power,
yet they prepare their food in summer;
badgers are a people without strength,
yet they set up their dwellings in the rock.
Locusts have no king,
yet they all march in order.
The lizard you can grasp in your hands,
and yet it is in kings' palaces.   (Prov. 30.24–28)

We have already discussed how the form of the numerical sayings is closely connected with that of the riddle. But this would make no difference to the assertion that we are here concerned with the recognition of common factors. The figurative element which characterizes every type of poetic discovery of truth comes to the fore here even more strongly than elsewhere. In the example quoted, there is no graduation in the enumeration, but the last-named phenomenon always seems to surpass the others in its oddity.

These three are never satisfied,
and four say, 'Not enough':
Sheol, a barren womb,
earth never has enough water, and fire never says, 'Enough'.
(Prov. 30.15f.)

Three things are too wonderful for me,
   and four I do not understand:
the way of the eagle in the sky,
   the way of the serpent on the rock,
the way of the ship in the middle of the sea,
   and the way of a man with a young woman.   (Prov. 30.18f.)

These two numerical sayings are remarkable in so far as the examples are not arranged with an eye to what is known. The common factor here is simply the fact that they surpass comprehension. In the first example, phenomena of insatiability are grouped together, in the second, puzzling 'ways', with regard to which (in order to understand the last examples) one must know that the Hebrew word corresponding to our word 'way' also means 'behaviour', 'conduct'. Here, too, the last example surpasses the others.

In this connection, where we have been concerned with the expressing of the actual, with the cataloguing of the real, one could also ask about Israel's share in the phenomenon of 'science by lists' which was widespread in the ancient Near East. Here, as in the Egyptian onomastica, the attempt was made, in the form of long series of substantives, to catalogue the world as completely as possible. There is no dispute that onomastica were known in Israel and were poetically constructed.[14] It is another question whether Israel continued to work independently in this domain. It is more likely that she simply made use of Egyptian models. At any rate, no onomasticon has been preserved in Israelite literature. The situation is different in the case of the so-called tables of nations which exist in a double recension in Gen. 10 and in the book of Jubilees chs. 8f.[15] One may ask whether these texts can be reckoned as still belonging to the *Gattung* of 'science by lists', since the dispersal of the nations in their territories is here presented as a historical process, in Gen. 10 as a genealogical one, in Jubilees as that of a universal allotment of land. Probably these tables of nations are dependent on actual maps. Here Israel must have

[14] G. von Rad, 'Job xxxviii and Ancient Egyptian Wisdom' in *The Problem of the Hexateuch and Other Essays*, ET 1966, pp. 281ff. More recent researches have shown how the tersely expressed description of the events of creation in Gen. 1 is based on a widely ramified knowledge of nature which was to be found expounded in texts of the 'science by lists' type: S. Herrmann, 'Die Naturlehre des Schöpfungsberichtes', *ThLZ* 86, 1961, cols. 413ff.; W. H. Schmidt, *Die Schöpfungsgeschichte der Priesterschrift*, 1967², pp. 32ff.

[15] G. Hölscher, *Drei Erdkarten. Ein Beitrag zur Erkenntnis des hebräischen Altertums* (Sitzungsber. d. Heidelberger Akad. d. Wiss., Phil.-hist. Kl. 1944/48, Abh. 3 – 1949).

followed Babylonian examples, for even the famous world map of Anaximander is dependent on Babylonian models.[16] In one way or another, the tables of nations in Gen. 10 are literary products of an interpretation, unique in the ancient world, of the broad range of historical realities with which Israel was surrounded.

2. CAUSE AND EFFECT.
THE ACT-CONSEQUENCE RELATIONSHIP

Behind the assertion of the analogous, there lay already the question of an all-embracing order. In the preceding section, we were concerned with things which were arranged side by side. In what follows, we will be concerned with the question of cause and effect, that is, the question about an order which can be discerned in the succession of phenomena.[17] In both cases we are dealing with one of the main tasks which the wise men, in their search for knowledge, took upon themselves, namely with the mastering of the 'contingent'. By the term 'contingent' we mean here simply all those events which cannot be understood by man purely on the basis of a necessity with which he is familiar. Daily, incessantly, man encounters contingent events (chance events) whose meaning and inner necessity are at first hidden from him. Only occasionally does he succeed in recognizing behind the contingent event a clear, inner necessity. Then the experience loses its contingent character, and its place is taken by the awareness of an order which is at work behind the experiences. To a greater extent than modern man, ancient man was disturbed by the awareness of the superior force of contingent events. To the extent that he regarded himself as in the power of these contingent events, so there grew the feeling of general insecurity. To him it was a threat to be ceaselessly determined and driven by events which defied all interpretation. Thus it is one of man's basic urges to limit as far as possible, with all the powers of the keenest observation, the sphere of contingency and, wherever possible, to wrest from the inscrutable, contingent event some kind of meaning, albeit a deeply hidden one.

Israel, too, took the trouble to discern in events and occurrences a recognizable set of 'inherent laws'. The next most obvious thing to do was to inquire as to what may have preceded any given event

---

[16] A. Lesky, *Geschichte der griechischen Literatur*, 1963², pp. 188f.

[17] On the distinction between a 'side by side' arrangement and an arrangement by 'succession', see H.-J. Hermisson, op. cit., p. 152.

which had to be explained. Was it perhaps possible to understand the event as something which had been caused? It is on the basis of this question that one must understand those sentences which determine what usually preceded an experience.

> Before destruction, pride;
>   and before a fall, a haughty spirit.   (Prov. 16.18)

The attempt to understand specific experiences from the point of view of what has caused them dominates the majority of all thetical sentences. Naturally, the outward life of society, with its often harsh contrasts between rich and poor, gave a particular stimulus to thought and encouraged the search for causes. The lazy man grows poor (Prov. 10.4; 24.30ff.). One must make provision in good time (Prov. 10.5). One must persevere with work in the fields and not chase after 'nothing' (Prov. 12.11). If 'hastily acquired' property does not last, then one must not be surprised (Prov. 13.11; 20.21; 21.5). Property is, therefore, not purely accidental; it is largely dependent on man's conduct. One must not regard wealth or poverty as accidental, but as something causated; one must ask about the prerequisites which men themselves have laid down. It is possible to establish rules, the ignoring of which leads to impoverishment.

Now, however, comes the surprise factor. While there was no possession in life which enjoyed such unanimous esteem in Israel as property and outward prosperity, nevertheless, experience was forced to admit, even in the case of this highly prized commodity, that it was of decidedly ambiguous value. Far from the possibility of being considered an absolute asset, it reveals itself to be conditioned.

> Wealth does not profit on the day of wrath,
>   but righteousness delivers from death.   (Prov. 11.4)
>
> Whoever trusts in his possessions will fall,
>   but the righteous will flourish like foliage.   (Prov. 11.28)
>
> Many a man is prevented from sinning by poverty,
>   and when he rests he is not tempted(?).   (Sir. 20.21)
>
> The rich man's sleeplessness wastes away his flesh,
>   and his anxiety drives away sleep.   (Sir. 31.1)

No one would suggest that wealth is here being suspected on the basis of certain principles, such as ascetic ones; the latter were completely unknown in Israel. It is not philosophical principles that find expression here but quite simple experiences of limits which have become discernible. Such assertions were of decisive significance for Israel's total knowledge of the world, in particular the awareness of the ambiguity of phenomena. Nothing, no human behaviour, no experience, no value could be recorded as being completely unambiguous.[18] Again and again it proved to be conditioned and, therefore, ambiguous. Thus, even poverty, which from earliest times had been experienced in Israel as a severe impairment of life, and with which man had never been able to come to terms, occasionally appeared in a positive light.

> Better a piece of dry bread and freedom from worry
> than a house full of sacrificial meat and quarrelling.   (Prov. 17.1)

> Better a poor man whose conduct is blameless
> than a man with twisted lips who is 'rich'.   (Prov. 19.1)

> Better a little with the fear of Yahweh
> than great treasure and unrest.   (Prov. 15.16)

In the way in which the attempt was made to cope with the phenomenon of poverty, one can see precisely a model example of wisdom thinking. In the sentences quoted earlier, it appeared as something causated and at the same time as something negative, for which man himself was responsible. But this indisputable truth had to assert itself alongside quite different truths, for, on the one hand, even wealth is not of unambiguous value, and, on the other, even poverty can, from certain points of view, appear as something of value. These 'truths', then, stand happily side by side, without affecting each other adversely, and testify to the ambivalence of the phenomena perceived.

In this discussion about effects and their causes, one could also include, from the daily intercourse between man and man, a wide range of experiences which were capable of being expressed in didactic terms. It is quite impossible, however, to enumerate all that the teachers noted in the way of reactions to or results or consequences of any given agreeable or disagreeable human behaviour. A large number of experiences are gathered there about the effects of punishment (Prov. 20.30), diligence (Prov. 13.4), association with men (Prov. 13.20), with women (Prov. 12.4; 18.22; 23.27), with unreliable men (Prov. 10.26; 12.17; 14.25; 16.27; 17.8; 24.23), with kings (Prov. 25.6) and especially about the effect of judicious and injudicious speech.

Here, too, the psychological domain occupies considerable space.

[18] See below pp. 247ff., 311.

The law of cause and effect is traced right into the hidden regions of the soul.

> Deferred hope makes the heart sick,
>   but a wish fulfilled is a tree of life.   (Prov. 13.12)

> A glad heart makes a cheerful face,
>   but with a troubled heart the spirit is broken.   (Prov. 15.13)

> A glad heart is good for the body,
>   but a broken spirit dries up the bones.   (Prov. 17.22)

> A man's heart alters his appearance
>   either for good or for evil.   (Sir. 13.25)

> Jealousy and anger shorten life,
>   and worry ages a man prematurely.   (Sir. 30.24)

> For from worry comes ruin,
>   and sadness saps one's strength.   (Sir. 38.18)

Many of these assertions of causal connections may not impress the modern reader unduly. He will, however, have to remember that his attitude to the world around him is an essentially different one. If one were to express the difference quite simply, then one could say that modern man puzzles to a greater extent over the irregularities which he is unable to fit into the general pattern. The ancients, on the other hand, were amazed if, in the confusion of daily events, inherent laws could nevertheless be discerned. It would certainly be wrong to imagine that such laws could easily be discerned everywhere in events and occurrences. There may be cases where that was actually so; in others, it required lengthier consideration, and at this very point we see the wise men's thirst for knowledge particularly at work. This can be seen particularly well in the piling up of paradoxical assertions. That someone is generous and yet acquires still more, while another is mean and yet grows poorer (Prov. 11.24), that stolen bread tastes sweet, but that later one's mouth is filled with gravel (Prov. 20.17), that a town full of warriors is scaled by a wise man (Prov. 21.22), that a gentle tongue breaks bones (Prov. 25.15), that the man who is sated despises honey, while anything bitter tastes sweet to the hungry (Prov. 27.7), that pride humiliates a man (Prov. 29.23), that blows are good for a child (Prov. 23.13f.) – these are all, at first sight, bewildering perceptions. Is good not always good, sweet not always sweet, strong not always strong? Obviously not. We are, then, dealing here once again with the awareness, mentioned above, that things can never be evaluated absolutely but are ambiguous. Even the most established experiences can be confronted at any time with something which contradicts them. But the most surprising thing is that this contradictory element still does not signify what at first sight it might appear to do, namely the irruption of chaos into knowledge. On the contrary, if one faces up to it and allows it a place in one's system of knowledge, then behind the paradox, that is, behind the apparent abnormality, a new pattern can be discerned.

In this connection, it is essential to consider once again how the wise men expressed effects of a quite specific type, namely those which, on the basis of a good or evil act, affect the author of that act himself. Only recently have we had a clearer idea of the so-called act-consequence relationship, for Israel, too, shared the widely-spread concept of an effective power inherent both in good and in evil and subject to specific laws. She was convinced that by every evil deed or every good deed a momentum was released which sooner or later also had an effect on the author of the deed.[19] To a great extent, therefore, it lay within his own power whether he exposed himself to the effects of disaster or of blessing. This idea, however, was in no way a specifically 'wisdom' one; it had, as such, long been in existence before it was formulated didactically by the wise men. It was so deeply rooted in Israelite thought that none, not even the prophets, were able to free themselves from it. On one occasion, Jeremiah describes the disaster which Yahweh will bring upon the people as 'fruit of their endeavours' (Jer. 6.19). It is her own wickedness that Yahweh pours out on Jerusalem (Jer. 14.16). It is useful to remember that this ontological definition of good and evil was widely accepted not only in the ancient Near East but also up to the beginning of the modern period.

If, in this case, as we have said, this was a perception which stood on a much broader foundation than was generally the case among the teachers in the schools, then it would be amazing if such laws, which were radically determinative for life, did not find expression again and

---

[19] Basic here is K. Koch, 'Gibt es ein Vergeltungsdogma im A.T.?', *ZThK* 52, 1955, pp. 1ff. On this, cf. the critical remarks of F. Horst, *Gottes Recht*, 1961, pp. 286ff. The question of the relationship of this 'order' to Yahweh's free will has been carefully examined by R. Knierim, *Die Hauptbegriffe für Sünde im A.T.*, 1965, pp. 85f. In its purest form – in fact as a kind of 'order' – the phenomenon of the 'sphere of activity which affects man's fate' (K. Koch) is presented by the sentences of old wisdom. In the Joseph story, on the other hand, this way of thinking is deprived of its inherent pattern and subordinated to the divine will which freely controls men (R. Knierim, op. cit., p. 85). On this contrast, see below pp. 199f.

again in the school sentences. In fact, the teachers never tire of exhorting to watchfulness in this respect and of setting before their pupils the respective consequences. This happens in a particularly decisive way in sentences such as the following:

> It is quite certain that an evil man will not remain unpunished,
>   but the descendants of a righteous man will go free.   (Prov. 11.21)
>
> Wicked men are overthrown and are no more,
>   but the house of the righteous will last.   (Prov. 12.7)
>
> Do not those who plan evil go astray?
>   but loyalty and fidelity is the lot of those who plan good.
>   (Prov. 14.22)
>
> In the house of the righteous there are provisions in abundance,
>   but the 'income' of the godless is ruined.   (Prov. 15.6)
>
> Whoever digs a pit falls into it,
>   and whoever rolls a stone, it rolls back on him.   (Prov. 26.27)

It is remarkable how objectively these assertions are made, really as if they were stating an already proved law. In fact, it would be misleading if one thought one had to understand these and other sentences theologically, as if they were stating a 'doctrine of retribution'. These sentences are not concerned with a divine, juridical act which subsequently deals out to men blessing or punishment, but with an order of life which can be experienced. If, in this context, a sentence from time to time speaks of Yahweh, of his blessing or punishment or of the fact that he rewards a merciful man for his good deed (Prov. 19.17), this does not imply a basically different conception, for of course it was Yahweh who established this order and watched over it. We shall have to discuss later those questions of a fundamental nature which have been levelled in recent times precisely at this firmly established order.

The modern observer will find it difficult to come to terms with this whole world of ideas. He is inclined to derive it from some theory that is ignorant of life, and he is astonished at its limited sense of reality. But however critically he examines it, its weaknesses are still not obvious. Certainly, many expressions of this conviction are somewhat provocative in their sharply antithetical nature; but they are supposed to be. Nor should we be allowed to take them to mean that the righteous man is, at one stroke, exempt from all hardship. Much of the apparently too naive contrast between the blessing of the righteous and the curse of the wicked is due to necessary, didactic simplification. They are not all to be understood in such a theoretical way, and there are even sentences which speak entirely of troubles which befall the righteous.

> Indeed, a righteous man falls seven times and rises again,
>   but the godless are overthrown by disaster.   (Prov. 24.16)

> Over all flesh, both man and beast
>   – but upon the godless sevenfold –
> hover plague, bloodshed, fever, sword,
>   devastation, destruction, hunger and death.   (Sir. 40.8f.)

Above all, however, these sentences were certainly not for that reason unrealistic, for they spoke on the basis of experiences which had actually been confirmed again and again in a firmly established social community. There, righteousness will always have the effect of promoting the community and will always then raise the prestige of the person concerned; similarly, all evil will very quickly be experienced by the community as detrimental, and this will have a corresponding effect upon the author of it. One must also, of course, be capable of waiting; to begin with, events are not always unambiguous.

> I have seen a fool taking root,
>   but suddenly his dwelling 'was ruined'.
> His sons remained far from good fortune,
>   they were crushed in the gate without a helper being there.
> What they reaped the hungry ate,
>   ' ' and thirsty men snatched at their wealth.
> Yes, evil does not come from the dust,
>   and disaster does not grow out of the ground,
> but a man 'generates' evil 'for himself',
>   and the sons of the flame fly upwards.   (Job 5.3–7)

> Can papyrus grow where there is no marsh?
>   Can reeds flourish without water?
> While it is still in flower, it is not cut down,
>   it withers before any other grass does.
> Such is the end of all who have forgotten God,
>   and the hope of those who are estranged from God vanishes.
>   (Job 8.11–13)

Whether good or evil, it was still a question of powers of astonishing scope, for even a man's goodness benefits not only himself but also the next generation; similarly, the children of an evil man are overtaken by destruction.[20]

We are thus faced once again with that peculiarly pragmatic concept of the essence of good and evil which we have already elucidated for ourselves in an earlier context.[21] The good, we saw, never stood alone as a moral phenomenon; being good and good things belonged together. Naturally, as part of a man's goodness, there belonged also personal excellence and righteousness, but on the other hand also success and fulfilment in life. This reality of both good and evil, which not only determined the way of life of the individual but was also of general social significance, was described by the teachers in many different ways. Specifically wisdom in origin are the arrangements of old, popular ideas in expansive, imposing didactic poems such as are to be found in the speeches of Job's friends.[22] Two things are new here, the ambitious literary form which is able to make use of strong effects, but also the extension of the old ideas to cover the whole of life. If, previously, interest was concentrated more on the consequences of a single, specific act, it is shown here what a total life looked like when it was subject to the law of disaster.

> Yes, the light of the wicked is put out,
>   and the flame of his fire does not shine.
> The light in his tent grows dark,
>   and his lamp above him goes out.
> His powerful steps are impeded
>   and his own plan 'brings him to ruin',
> for with his own feet he stumbles into the net,
>   and he strides along over a pit.
> The strap seizes him by the heels,
>   the snare lays firm hold of him.
> A rope is hidden for him in the ground,
>   and a noose for him on the path.

[20] Prov. 11.21b; 14.26; 20.7; Job 15.34; 18.16, 19; 27.14; Sir. 44.10f.

'Truly the company of the godless is unfruitful,
    and fire consumes the tents of corruption.'   (Job 15.34)

With this, cf. Hesiod, 'But whoever deliberately lies in his witness and forswears himself, and so hurts Justice and sins beyond repair, that man's generation is left obscure thereafter. But the generation of the man who swears truly is better thenceforward' (*Works and Days*, ll. 282–285. Tr. H. G. Evelyn-White in The Loeb Classical Library).

[21] See above pp. 77ff.

[22] See above pp. 38f.

Terrors frighten him on every side
and dog him at every step.
His destruction hungers for him,
and misfortune is ready for his downfall.
His skin is eaten away by disease,
and the first-born of death eats away his limbs.
He is snatched away from his tent in which he trusted,
and he is driven to the king of terrors. . . .
His memory disappears from the land,
and no fame is left to him in the street.
He is thrust from light into darkness,
he is driven forth from the face of the earth.
He has no offspring, no descendant left in his clan,
no survivor where he used to live.
Those in the west shudder at his day,
and horror seizes those in the east.
Yes, such is the fate of the wicked man's abode,
and the abode of him who paid no attention to God.   (Job 18.5–21)

The poem begins with the picture of the burnt-out hearth and the extinguished lights. The house is uninhabited. Then, unfolding destiny in reverse, it describes the snares in which such a wicked man is caught. He is at the mercy of every imaginable affliction. In a word, he has made himself the bearer of a curse. Without descendants, he becomes an object of horror for miles around. Could not all this have been spoken, in quite similar terms, by the chorus of an Attic tragedy? It is all presented as if an inherent necessity were being worked out in this complex chain of fate. There is no mention of direct divine intervention. What is also remarkable here is the interest in the psychological. The effects of disaster on a man's inner life occupied the wise men to an increasing extent. In the Wisdom of Solomon (first century BC), there is found a detailed description of all the terrors and hallucinations which assailed the enemies of the people of God 'shut up in a prison not made of iron', a prison of their own anxieties. The text is a document of uncanny psychological, even psychiatric, realism.[23] We can but let an extract from it speak for itself:

. . . for whether he was a farmer or a shepherd or a worker who toiled in a lonely spot, he was seized and forced to endure the inescapable fate; for with one chain of darkness they all were bound. Whether there came a whistling wind or a melodious sound of birds in wide-spreading

[23] H. Tellenbach, 'Sinngestalten des Leidens und des Hoffens' in *Conditio Humana* (Festschrift for E. W. Straus, 1966), p. 310.

branches, or the rhythm of violently rushing water, or the harsh crash of rocks hurled down, or the unseen running of leaping animals, or the sound of the most savage roaring beasts, or an echo thrown back from a hollow of the mountains – it paralysed them with terror. For the whole world was illumined with brilliant light and was engaged in unhindered work, while over those men alone heavy night was spread, an image of the darkness that was destined to receive them. But they were a still heavier burden to themselves than the darkness.

(Wisd. 17.17–21)

But the good was also a force, and the teachers took great pains to encourage their pupils to put their trust in this life-promoting force. There are fine and really wise teachings given here, such as that of the healing power of the good word.[24] Here, too, are linked knowledge of the healing quality of good conduct and deep insights into the human heart. One must never, however, lose sight of the fact that, in the following sentences, no lofty imperatives are promulgated, but that experiences are recorded in the indicative. The considerate turning of a blind eye preserves and promotes one's relationship with others.

By loyalty and faithfulness guilt is atoned for,
　　and by fear of Yahweh one avoids evil.   (Prov. 16.6)

Whoever covers up an offence is seeking after love,
　　but whoever stirs up a thing again alienates his friends.   (Prov. 17.9)

Good sense on the part of a man makes him patient,
　　and his glory is to overlook an offence.   (Prov. 19.11)

If your enemy is hungry, feed him with bread;
　　if he is thirsty, give him water to drink;
for you will heap fiery coals upon his head,
　　and Yahweh will complete it for you.[25]   (Prov. 25.21f.)

If the anger of the ruler rises against you,
　　do not leave your post,
for composure makes amends for great offences.   (Eccles. 10.4)

[24] Prov. 12.18 ('the tongue of the wise brings healing'); 12.20, 25; 15.1.
[25] The saying about the 'fiery coals' is to be explained on the basis of an Egyptian expiation ritual, according to which a guilty person, as a sign of his amendment of life, carried a basin of glowing coals on his head; cf. S. Morenz, *ThLZ* 78, 1953, cols. 187ff. The translation given here ('Yahweh will complete it for you') sounds unusual. But the Hebrew verb should not be translated by 'requite', as if Yahweh – from his pocket, as it were – added something to the human action. The verb *šillēm* is to be understood here on the basis of the correspondence between an act and its consequence and means 'make complete', 'finish', in the sense that it is Yahweh, in the case of a good deed, for example, who completes the act-consequence relationship. Elsewhere this is described as if it were the functioning

By way of conclusion to our discussion of the causal thinking of the wise men, mention must still be made of a remarkable hesitation, of a religious reservation with which Israel had to grapple right up to a late period; this was in the sphere of medical science. Could specific effects in this sphere not be deduced just as easily, or sometimes with just as great difficulty, from specific causes? Evidently there was a serious difficulty here. Unfortunately we have only one text which gives us informative insights into the discussions of the wise men.

> Be friendly to the physician, for one needs him,
>   and God has given to him, too, his lot.[26]
> The physician is taught by God
>   and he receives gifts from the king.
> The physicians's knowledge lifts up his head
>   and he can appear before nobles.
> God brings medicines out of the earth,
>   and a sensible man ought not to despise them.
> Was not water made sweet by a tree,
>   so that his power might be known to all men?
> Thus he gave men insight,
>   so that he might be glorified in his wonderful deeds.
> By these, the physician eases pain,
>   and with them the apothecary prepares a mixture,
> so that his work may not disappear,
>   but help might come from his soil.
> My son, do not delay in your illness;
>   pray to the Lord, for he will heal you.

---

of a neutral order. But in the case of a circle of ideas of such general distribution, we simply cannot reckon with a self-consistent range of expressions. After what we have already determined (see above pp. 62f.), there is nothing surprising in the fact that the act-consequence relationship is conceived sometimes as the operating of a rule, at other times as an occurrence directly caused by Yahweh. K. Reinhard has drawn our attention to a fine example in Herodotus of a completely unemphasized and, at the same time, very thoughtful presentation of 'retribution' overtaking the agent. The death of Cambyses corresponds exactly to the cultic outrage which he committed against the Egyptian Apis bull (Herodotus, III, 29, 64), cf. K. Reinhard, *Vermächtnis der Antike*, 1960, pp. 156f. 'According to Solon, punishment happens of itself as the outcome of an inherent mechanism' (H. Fränkel, op. cit., p. 270).

[26] Many translators prefer the Greek text here, a text which reads 'create'. But nowhere does Hebrew *ḥālaq* mean 'create'; it means 'allot' or the like. It is better to adhere to the Hebrew text, especially since the idea that man has his 'part' allotted to him by God is attested in the didactic literature (Eccles. 2.10, 21; 3.22; etc.).

Avoid evil and keep your hands clean;
    bring your offering and a memorial offering;
    make your gift as fat as you are able.
But give the physician his place;
    he should not leave you,
    for you need him too;
there are times when he is successful,
    for he, too, prays to God,
asking him to make his diagnosis successful
    and to preserve life through his healing.
Whoever sins in the eyes of his Maker,
    falls into the hands of the physician.   (Sir. 38.1–15)

What strikes the reader at once is the great variety of opinions which are presented here with little or no connection between them. In this text, then, we are dealing less with a self-contained didactic poem than with a catena of very varied, debatable opinions which could be held with regard to a specific problem. The problem here is: How should one comport oneself in an illness? What is the legitimacy of the physician? If one disregards the harsh final sentence, then the physician is accorded his rights and his indispensability. It is interesting to note, though, how hesitantly and tortuously this positive attitude is expressed. Here, obviously, the purely empirical evidence was not sufficient for a complete legitimation, evidence such as was readily available for the effect of smoke on the eyes or vinegar on the teeth (Prov. 10.26). Rather, we encounter a remarkably circumstantial array of all kinds of theological arguments: Even the physician has his sphere of life granted to him by God; he also prays to God for the success of his diagnosis, and even the medicines are made to grow by God himself. A scriptural proof for the use of medicines is even cited (the reference is to the narrative of Ex. 15.23–25).

As in the whole of the ancient Near East, medical science in Israel only succeeded very slowly in freeing itself from the strait-jacket of sacral ideas. But in Israel this process was also hampered by particular difficulties. It was expected to free itself not only from a deep-seated belief in demons or from taking renowned gods of healing into consideration (cf. II Kings 1.6), but also from what was a function and right of Yahweh's; for the idea that Yahweh alone could heal was represented in Israel in a particularly exclusive way (Ex. 15.26).[27] And was not Yahweh also the one who caused illness? Was the latter

[27] Ex. 15.26; Deut. 32.39; II Kings 5.7; Hos. 6.1; Job 5.18; etc.

perhaps a punishment? From this there arose the question whether one could prejudice Yahweh's privilege of healing. Here, in fact, the search for knowledge, otherwise active in a very impartial way, suddenly found itself confronted with a problem which touched the very roots of faith in Yahweh. Of course, even in Israel, not all healing or use of medicines was despised from the start. As elsewhere in the world, here, too, the knowledge available to the age was utilized. But healing nevertheless took place under quite specific presuppositions and was, fundamentally, not to be compared to all those techniques in which men utilized their awareness of causal connections in order to arrive at specific goals. Here, Yahweh had jurisdiction in a much more direct sense; men – priests or prophets – were entirely at his service in this matter. Thus, what was debatable was not the use of healing in itself; the question, rather, was whether the practice of the art of medicine could be accorded a secular position which dispensed with sacral authorization. Thus, one can describe the verdict of Sirach as a last, decisive step of the enlightenment. The victory, however, does not appear to have been complete, for Sirach is obliged to take great pains to show in constantly new ways that even the physician is in Yahweh's service. But the opinion which is expressed at the end threatens to nullify the carefully worked out process of legitimation.

The narrator of the book of Tobit no longer seems to be aware of this problem in this way. On the first occasion when he describes an act of healing, he shows how closely, even in such a late period, medical science was still related to magic. The liver and heart of a fish, burnt on incense, drove away the demon which threatened the bridegroom on the wedding night (Tob. 6.17; 8.2). On the other hand, the healing of the father's blindness by means of the fish gall is completely medical in character and is not described as miraculous. With great interest in the details, the healing process is described: Tobias spreads the gall on his father's eyes, 'but when they began to burn, he rubbed his eyes and the white patches scaled off from the corners of his eyes' (Tob. 11.12f.). Here we are presented with a chapter of Hebrew medicine. Besides, we know that this particular treatment was widespread in the ancient world.[28] Here it is the heavenly messenger sent from God himself who teaches it to men. Cures are then undertaken by men who have been thus instructed. It is, indeed, not impossible that the narrative has the specific intention of removing doubts and

[28] The use of fish gall to cure eye diseases is attested more than once in ancient sources. There is an Assyrian reference in F. Stummer, *Echter Bibel*, ad loc.

reservations about such treatments. The readers of the book who were trained along wisdom lines and for whom the book was written, would read the medical parts with understanding and would, at the same time, be confirmed in their conviction as to the legality of such a treatment. An angel has taught it, and men are indebted to him for this beneficial knowledge.

VIII

THE DOCTRINE OF THE PROPER TIME

For everything there is an hour,
 and a time for every purpose under heaven:
a time to be born, and a time to die;
 a time to plant, and a time to pluck up what is planted;
a time to kill, and a time to heal;
 a time to break down, and a time to build up;
a time to weep, and a time to laugh;
 a time to mourn, and a time to dance;
a time to cast away stones, and a time to gather stones together;
 a time to embrace, and a time to refrain from embracing;
a time to seek, and a time to lose;
 a time to keep, and a time to cast away;
a time to rend, and a time to sew;
 a time to keep silence, and a time to speak;
a time to love, and a time to hate;
 a time for war, and a time for peace.   (Eccles. 3.1–8)[1]

HERE IS YET ANOTHER didactic poem. At its head the thesis is formulated, the proposition itself. To the actual body of the poem there falls the task of illustrating in concrete terms, in a form not unlike that of the numerical sayings, the thesis which has been expressed in abstract and theoretical terms. This happens by means of a series of fourteen antitheses which explain clearly how the proposition, which had been stated boldly at the beginning, is to be understood. One can always do only one of two things;[2] and in order to know what is to be done in any given case, one must know that 'for everything there is a time'. This didactic poem stands within a comparatively late wisdom poem which, in an appended meditation,

---

[1] On Eccles. 3.1–11, see K. Galling, 'Das Rätsel der Zeit im Urteil Kohelets', *ZThK* 58, 1961, pp. 1ff. This also includes discussions on points of detail; on this, most recently, cf. J. R. Wilch, *Time and Event*, 1969, pp. 118ff.
[2] K. Galling, op. cit., p. 6.

draws very idiosyncratic conclusions from this very teaching. But there can be absolutely no question of this being a perception that was gained only very late. We have, rather, a statement which has stood, from the very beginning, in the centre of ancient Near Eastern wisdom.[3] Furthermore, a preoccupation with the phenomena envisaged here could, from the point of view of the history of ideas, be traced still further back. What is it about?

Once again, we are dealing with a quite elementary experience which was available to men in every period and at every cultural level, namely the experience that human activity is not equally successful and meaningful on every occasion, that its success and meaningfulness, that, in a word, all ability to act successfully, is tied to specific times. Once again it is a question, in the first instance, of the experience of a limitation which is imposed on men's energies. Man can do nothing but yield to this fact, for it is certainly not susceptible of any alteration. If he has no alternative but to recognize this limitation as a given fact, he is not, however, prevented from reflecting on it; he can go further and even attempt to derive some profit from it and to perceive in it some kind of mysterious order. In any event, this experience confirmed the awareness which has already found expression in another context, namely that in the experiences of the world in which men find themselves nothing of absolute validity can be affirmed. What is experienced on any given occasion has always shown itself to be in some way conditioned and relative.

Here, now, it is a question of the puzzling dependence of every happening on the 'appropriate time'.[4] The tree produces fruit 'in its time', the sheaves are brought in 'in their time' (Job 5.26), and migrating birds know 'their time' (Jer. 8.7; cf. Gen. 31.10). If a girl has matured, then 'her time' had come (Ezek. 16.8). Basically, it is decisive for every human undertaking that it should happen at the proper time. This is especially true of the human word which, as is

---

[3] H. H. Schmid, op. cit., pp. 33f.; 'The aim of wisdom instruction was, in large measure, the recognition of the right time, the right place and the right extent for human activity' (ibid., p. 190). On this, cf. the sentence of Pittako, 'Know the right moment'; B. Snell, *Leben und Meinungen der sieben Weisen*, 1952, p. 101.

[4] W. Zimmerli, *Das Buch des Predigers Salomo*, 1962, passim. The Hebrew word that is used, ʿēt, can be rendered only approximately by our word 'time'. On the one hand, the meaning is narrower, in that it tends towards the meaning 'set time', 'right time', 'moment of time', 'time for'. On the other, it is wider, in that the temporal aspect can recede to such an extent that it can sometimes be translated as 'opportunity for'; cf. J. R. Wilch, op. cit., p. 129 and passim.

well known, is placed by the wisdom teachers at the head of the formative factors in life.

> There is joy for a man through the answer of his mouth,
>   and a word at the right time – how good!   (Prov. 15.23)
> Golden apples in silver ornaments (?),
>   a word spoken at the right time.   (Prov. 25.11)
> Music in mourning, talking at the wrong time,
>   but punishment and discipline are wisdom at all times.   (Sir. 22.6)
> Do not withhold the word at the right time.   (Sir. 4.23)

The reverse is that if 'it is an evil time', and speech does not have a chance, then 'the prudent man keeps silent '(Amos 5.13). Even for the physician there is a time when his hand is granted success (Sir. 38.13; Jer. 8.15). The finest illustration of the statement that everything has its proper time is unfolded by the supremely artistic didactic poem about the activity of the countryman. At first glance, his activities appear remarkably obscure and lacking in cohesion. But they immediately appear meaningful when one realizes that in his operations he knows about the right time. He does not keep on ploughing; rather, he breaks off this activity in order to turn to another for which the time has meanwhile come.

> Listen, hear what I have to say,
>   pay attention and listen to my words.
> Does the ploughman plough all the time for sowing,
>   is he always opening and harrowing his ground?
> Not so. When he has levelled its surface,
>   he scatters dill and sows cummin,
> he puts in wheat and barley
>   and spelt along the edge.
> He was instructed in the right procedures
>   and taught by his God.
>
> Dill is not threshed with the sledge,
>   and one does not run a cart-wheel over cummin.
> No. Dill is beaten with a stick
>   and cummin with a rod.
> Is corn for bread threshed?
>   But one does not keep on threshing it;
> one runs a cart-wheel and one's horses over it
>   without crushing it.

> This, too, comes from Yahweh Sebaoth;
>   wonderful is his advice and great his ability.   (Isa. 28.23–29)[5]

Both strophes – the second in stronger terms – end with the remark that the farmer has received instruction in his complicated activity from God himself. Here, of course, there lies a burning question, for man can never take comfort from the affirmation of his total dependence on the appropriate time. This would throw his life back into an insecurity which would be difficult to bear, and this would happen because this particular limitation is constantly in motion and is always being experienced at different points. The information given in the didactic poem about the farmer to the effect that God transmitted to him *ad hoc* the instructions necessary for him, was true in such a pointed fashion only for this particular vocation. Unfortunately one could not apply the same *in toto* to every human occupation. Men, therefore, could do nothing but tackle for themselves, that is, with their own perceptive abilities, this element of contingency which threatened them. Do they not have before them the opportunity of ascertaining for themselves, with the help of a close examination of the circumstances, the given time for a plan and of adjusting themselves accordingly, in their actions, to the 'appropriate time'? The teachers answered this question with an unqualified affirmative. They were of the opinion that men could easily be trained to ascertain the correct time for a project, even in difficult cases, by means of a careful assessment of the circumstances and a close examination of the situation. 'My son, observe the right time' (Sir. 4.20). With this admonition, the teacher of the early period, too, certainly helped the young

---

[5] With this text one can compare Prov. 27.23–27:

Pay great attention to the state of your flock,
     be attentive to the herds,
for wealth does not last for ever,
     'and riches do not endure' from generation to generation.
When the grass has gone and the new shoots appear,
     and the mountain plants are gathered,
then there are lambs to provide clothes for you
     and goats to provide the price of a field,
and enough goats' milk for your food ' '
and provision for your maids.

This didactic poem is not nearly so artistically fashioned as that in Isa. 28.23ff. It is not so ambitious from the point of view of content either. It approximates more to a rule for honest farmers: Do not be slack in your farm work. In Isa. 28.23ff., on the other hand, it is not the farmer who is being instructed, but the pupil about the farmer's activities, so that his basic knowledge may thereby be extended.

to adapt, as far as possible, to the phenomenon of the appropriate time, to examine the opportunities which offered themselves and then to avail themselves of the rightly discerned time. If, in this sphere, one had collected experiences and had learned to allow for the risk of the time,[6] then one could also wait without anxiety for the right time.

> Until the (right) time the patient man will endure,
>> but then joy will burst forth from him.
> Until the (right) time he hides his words,
>> but the lips of many will tell of his cleverness.   (Sir. 1.23f.)

In this way what was a limitation could become an element of chance, for man acquired the opportunity of taking up what operated in his life as, in the first instance, a severe limitation and of putting it to the service of his mastery of life in order, subsequently, as far as possible, to sail a little further with the favourable wind. If the right moment is there, then one should extract from it what it offers, one should 'make the most of it' (Eph. 5.16). This, then, was to be wise, to know about the right time and then to avail oneself of it. Even of a child in its mother's womb it could be said that it is not 'clever', not 'wise', if it was unaware of the time to present itself at the mouth of the womb (Hos. 13.13).

Here, of course, Ecclesiastes intimates his disagreement. In so far as every thing and every activity has its proper time, he was still in agreement with traditional ideas. But of what use is that to the 'agent', if he 'cannot find out' for himself God's temporal order, which is undoubtedly wise and well-intentioned (Eccles. 3.11)?

In the difficult question, one must not overlook the fact that Ecclesiastes approaches the old teaching from a new and quite different direction, namely the theological. Can man become aware of the times in the way in which God allots them to him? But what the old wise men taught was not meant in this way. They understood knowledge about the time in a much more secular way, as an aspect of the art of living which endeavours to learn from experience.

In the book of Proverbs there are comparatively few references to this subject of instruction. But they can be supplemented by references from other literary contexts to such an extent that there can be no doubt as to how deeply rooted this idea was, even in the practical wisdom of Israel. If, however, one were of the opinion that the teach-

---

[6] K. Galling: 'He acquires no produce if he cannot allow for the "risk" in the time' (op. cit., p. 2).

ing about the appropriate time could have had its place only within a strict, theological determinism, then this would be difficult to reconcile with the ideas of older Yahwism. Even the Yahweh of the prophets, who, 'in a storm of activity', formed anew every historical hour and who also felt his decisions 'deeply', was not the same as the God who had prescribed in advance the right time for every event. But the knowledge that things have their proper time and that one can acquire even some knowledge of this, can be understood differently from and certainly not solely against the background and as a part of a doctrine of predestination. If there was a time when kings went out to battle (II Sam. 11.1), when the sheaves were brought in or when a good word could accomplish something, this was for a long time still not connected with the idea of a fatalistic, primeval predetermination. The knowledge about the right time rested, as indeed did all the knowledge of the old teachers, on the quite simple experience of specific orders and limits of which one could be aware. And this knowledge, like all other knowledge, was encompassed, for the old teachers, by faith in Yahweh in such a way that it limited neither the freedom of Yahweh nor that of man. In Ecclesiastes, however, the doctrine of the right time already appears to be bound up with a theological determinism; this changed it imperceptibly into a serious challenge.[7]

[7] See below pp. 264f.

IX

THE SELF-REVELATION OF CREATION

W E ARE APPROACHING now one of the most thoroughly debated problems in the whole of the wisdom literature. How are we to understand the great didactic poems in Prov. 8, Job 28, Sir. 24 and elsewhere, which speak of 'wisdom' as a personified entity immanent in creation? It is scarcely still possible to survey the scholarly literature. If one scans it, then it might appear as if the greatest puzzle lay in the question about the religio-historical origin of what is, in fact, an unusual range of ideas about a wisdom which actually calls to man. This undoubtedly important question has been answered in very different ways. It is, however, a question of secondary importance compared with the other question of what this idea, as it is now displayed in the texts, really means in the context of Yahwism. (Even if one feels obliged to speak of a hypostasis, this does not absolve one from answering the question of how Israel actually conceived of such a hypostasis.) At first sight these texts appear to be completely isolated: they seem to stand like erratic blocks on their own, unconnected with their surroundings. But one should also ask whether this range of ideas is not, nevertheless, to be understood against a wider contextual background.

No doubt the relevant texts present problems of exegesis. This is due, above all, to the fact that they do not bother to provide the reader with conceptual definitions which appear indispensable to us; but also to the intense poetic feeling which is characteristic of these particular texts. It is precisely the solemn piling up of statements which often has as a consequence the fact that the meaning of what is being said remains ill-defined and undecided. But this confusion into which we see ourselves being led in interpreting these texts could, at least partly, be attributed to the fact that the questions with which we approach these texts are not entirely pertinent. We are asking about ideas and looking for definitions of terms where Israel spoke about facts and described an occurrence. This, too, must be kept in mind.

1. WISDOM IMMANENT IN THE WORLD

1   Surely there is a place where silver is found,
      and for gold a place where they wash it.

2   Iron is taken out of the earth,
      and copper is smelted from ore.

3   Men put an end to darkness
      and search it out thoroughly . . .

4   Forgotten, without a foothold,
      they hang and swing to and fro far from men.

5   The earth, from which comes food,
      its depths are turned up 'by' fire.

6   Its stones are the place of lapis lazuli,
      and in them gold dust is found.

7   There is a path which no bird of prey knows,
      which no falcon's eye has ever seen;

8   the proud beasts have not trodden it,
      the lion has not passed over it.

9   Man puts his hand to the flinty rock,
      and overturns mountains by the roots.

10 He cuts out channels in the rocks,
      and his eye sees every precious thing.

11 He stops up the streams so that they do not trickle,
      and the thing that is hid he brings forth to light.

12 But where shall wisdom be found?
      And where is the place of understanding?

13 No man knows its value,
      and it is not found in the land of the living.

14 The deep says, 'It is not in me,'
      and the sea says, 'It is not with me.'

15 It cannot be bought for pure gold,
      nor can one pay for it with silver.

16 It cannot be paid for with gold of Ophir,
      nor with precious onyx or lapis lazuli.

17 Gold and glass cannot equal it,
      nor can it be exchanged for golden vessels.

18 No mention shall be made of coral or of crystal;
      the price of wisdom is above pearls.

19 The topaz of Ethiopia cannot compare with it,
      nor can it be valued in pure gold.

20 Whence then comes wisdom?
      And where is the place of understanding?

21   It is hid from the eyes of all living,
          and concealed from the birds of the air.
22   Abaddon and Death say,
          'We have heard a rumour of it with our ears.'
23   God understands the way to it,
          and he knows its place.
24   For he looks to the ends of the earth
          and sees everything under the heavens.
25   When he gave to the wind its weight
          and meted out the waters by measure;
26   when he made a decree for the rain
          and a way for the thunder-cloud;
27   then he saw it and measured it out (counted it)[1];
          he established it and searched it out.
28   (And he said to man,
          'See, the fear of the Lord, that is wisdom,
          and to depart from evil is understanding.')   (Job 28)

It is really a simple thought that is unfolded in this powerful expansive poem which almost luxuriates in words.[2] In contrast to the almost unlimited possibilities available to *homo faber*, he cannot determine the place where wisdom is to be found. And that would be the most valuable thing of all. Only God has seen it and brought it into action. In order to bring out this contrast as sharply as possible, the poem goes to the most extreme task ever tackled by the human mind, mining in the heart of a mountain. Man advances into unknown darkness; where even the sharp eyes of the animals give up, he still finds a way. The hardness of the stone does not frighten him, he copes with the irruption of water by hanging in shafts on ropes. Thus man is in a position to bring to light precious stones and metals. But where is wisdom to be found, where does it come from? The term 'wisdom' stands in synonymous parallelism with 'understanding' (*binā*), which again shows that there is no interest in an exact definition of terms. Obviously what is meant is already known to the reader or listener. The refrain does not sound as if it were meant to be saying anything new. The terms 'wisdom' and 'understanding' in this con-

---

[1] More precisely, 'he counted them'. Different is J. Reider, 'he tested them' (*VT* 2, 1952, p. 127).
[2] The poem has scarcely been preserved intact. Even with the help of the refrain (vv. 12, 20), it is impossible to achieve a regular division into strophes. Have refrains fallen out of the text (so G. Fohrer, ad loc.)? Do the refrains belongs at the beginning or at the end of strophes? Vv. 14–19 are missing from LXX.

text strike us as being remarkable, for here they are describing not a human virtue or something to be acquired by men, but, on the contrary, something far removed from men. One can really say nothing at all about the proper place of this idea. It is not in the deep or in the sea; no living creature has seen this wisdom. All that can be said is that God had to do with it, too, at the creation of the world. The imprecise expressions – he 'counted it out', he 'established it', he 'searched it out' – include, however, the idea that he created it. At any rate, it is contrasted with God and was subject to his ordering activity. That it assisted God at creation cannot be read out of vv. 25–26, for God's actions in relation to rain and wind on the one hand and to wisdom on the other are simultaneous; it, too, was the object of a divine action. Something must, after all, be said in solemn words about its age, about its *terminus a quo*: it goes back to the time when God gave the most mysterious works of creation their due order.

If, in the exegesis, one is not led astray in advance by the vague assumption of a relationship with apparently mythological ideas in the religions of neighbouring peoples, then there can certainly be no question in this context of considering wisdom as a hypostasis.[3] That is one of the terms, readily available from the sphere of history of religions in general, which misrepresent rather than clarify what was

---

[3] The term 'hypostasis' has become common in the study of religions to describe a phenomenon encountered in many religions. Wide recognition has been accorded to S. Mowinckel's definition, according to which 'hypostasis' is the name to be given to 'a divine being which is half independent and half regarded as a revelatory form of a higher deity, a being which represents the personification of an attribute, of an efficacy, of a part, etc. of a higher deity' (*RGG*[2] II, 1928, col. 2065). The concept has changed somewhat in recent years: 'hypostasis' can be used to describe an entity 'which participates in the being of a deity who, in turn, operates in the world through that entity, without, however, its whole nature being exhausted in the activity of this hypostasis' (G. Pfeifer, *Ursprung und Wesen der Hypostasenvorstellungen im Judentum*, 1967, p. 15).

Formulated thus, the term is of no help in the understanding of the texts with which we are concerned here, since it does not accord with the details of them, indeed it is, in fact, largely misleading. Neither in Job 28 nor in Prov. 8.22ff. nor in Sir. 24 are we dealing with the personification of a divine attribute. Is the term 'hypostasis', indeed, at all applicable to an entity which – as is the case in the texts mentioned – is the object of divine activity? But one must ask, further, whether it is sensible first of all to establish a precise definition of 'hypostasis' and then apply it to the texts. The reverse process would be a methodologically more correct one, namely to examine the texts and, if a particular discovery emerges, then to formulate a definition of it. The situation would be different if one were to decide to take the word 'hypostasis' very widely, as an objectification or personification of a concept. In that case it would be applicable to the above-mentioned texts. But since it has already become such a loaded term, we shall avoid it completely.

meant in Israel. There is nothing directly divine and nothing mythological about this wisdom. It is certainly not a divine attribute which has become independent. Nor has one any grounds for speaking of a personification. This wisdom is to be found somewhere in the world; it is there, but incapable of being grasped. If it were not inside the world, then the references to men digging through the earth would be meaningless. On the other hand – and this is admittedly remarkable – it is also again something separate from the works of creation. This 'wisdom', this 'understanding' must, therefore, signify something like the 'meaning' implanted by God in creation, the divine mystery of creation. In this connection, one must bear in mind the fact that the poem did not envisage something ideal so much as something real. God knows 'its place', he has 'measured it out', 'established it'. Something will be said below about the fact that in later Israel these ideas were scarcely formed independently of stimuli from outside Israel.

As for the teaching of this didactic poem, one must be cautious in comparing it with the other wisdom texts (Prov. 8; Sir. 24; etc.). The poem does not say everything that could have been said about this 'understanding' created in the world. It is not said that man is totally excluded from any perception of this wisdom. How, otherwise, could he speak about it? The line of thought in the poem is, rather, this. Wisdom, the order given to the world by God, is the most precious thing of all. But while man has eventually found a way to all precious things, he does not find the way to the mystery of creation. Only God knows its place, for he has already been concerned with it at creation. If man cannot determine this mystery of creation, it means, of course – this consequence is already envisaged in the poem – that it is out of his arbitrary reach. He never gets it into his power as he does the other precious things. The world never reveals the mystery of its order. One can scarcely go further than this in the interpretation.

A vast amount of experience and of solid thought must have preceded such a poem before it could have come into being at all. But nothing of that has been preserved for us.

There is unanimity about the fact that the poem has been inserted secondarily into the dialogue section of the book of Job. This makes it much more difficult to determine its point of origin; it could be late, but it could also be early. If one considers it to be a late, post-exilic text, then the question would still remain open whether such perceptions could be expressed really only in such a late period. It is highly

probable that the last line of the poem is to be regarded as an addition.
It stems from someone who did not wish to leave the reader only with
the magnificent, negative result. Its interest in wisdom remains un-
diminished. The way to wisdom is *via* the fear of Yahweh. In this way,
the person who made this addition not only departed from the theme
of the poem, but he is suddenly using the word 'wisdom' in a quite
different sense, namely the sense of human wisdom.

1 Does not wisdom call,
    does not understanding raise her voice?
2 On the heights beside the way,
    'in' the paths she takes her stand;
3 beside the gates at the entrance to the town,
    at the entrance of the portals she cries aloud;
4 'To you, O men, I call,
    and my cry is to the sons of men.
5 O simple ones, learn prudence;
    O foolish men, become sensible at heart.
6 Hear, for I will speak noble things,
    the opening of my lips is righteousness;
7 for my mouth will utter truth;
    wickedness is an abomination to my lips.
8 All the words of my mouth are righteous;
    there is nothing twisted or crooked in them.
9 They are all straight to him who understands
    and right to those who have found knowledge.
10 Take my instruction instead of silver,
    and knowledge rather than choice gold;
11 for wisdom is better than pearls,
    and no jewel can compare with her.
12 I, wisdom, am neighbour to prudence,
    and I have knowledge and discretion at my disposal.
13 The fear of Yahweh is hatred of evil.
    Pride and arrogance, the way of evil
    and perverted speech I hate.
14 I have counsel and sound wisdom;
    I am insight; strength is mine.
15 By me kings reign,
    and rulers decree what is just.
16 By me princes and nobles rule,
    and all righteous judges.
17 I love those who love me,
    and those who seek me will find me.

18   I have riches and honour,
           magnificent wealth and justice.
19   My fruit is better than gold and fine gold,
           and my yield than choice silver.
20   I walk in the way of righteousness,
           in the paths of justice,
21   endowing with wealth those who love me,
           and filling their treasuries.

22   Yahweh created me at the beginning of his work,
           the first of his acts of old.
23   Ages ago I was set up,
           at the first, before the beginning of the earth.
24   When there were no depths I was brought forth,
           when there were no springs abounding with water.
25   Before the mountains had been shaped,
           before the hills, I was brought forth;
26   before he had made land or fields,
           or all the dust of the earth.
27   When he established the heavens, I was there,
           when he stretched the vault over the deep,
28   when he fixed the clouds above,
           when he established the fountains of the deep,
29   when he assigned to the sea its limit,
           so that the waters might not flow over its edge,
       when he laid the foundations of the earth –
30   then I was beside him as his favourite,
       and I was daily his delight,
           playing in front of him all the time,
31   playing in his inhabited world
           and delighting in the sons of men.

32   And now, my sons, listen to me,
33   hear instruction and be wise,
           and do not neglect it.
34   Happy is the man who listens to me,
32b   happy are those who keep my ways,
34b   watching daily at my gates,
               guarding my doorposts.
35   For he who finds me, finds life
           and obtains favour from Yahweh.
36   But he who misses me injures himself;
           all who hate me love death.   (Prov. 8)

This great poem can clearly be divided into three parts. Part I, vv. 4–21 (vv. 4–9 are a remarkable baroque 'teacher's opening summons') contains wisdom's summons to men, in which she expounds for them her value and her indispensable nature. Part II, vv. 22–31, is comparatively self-contained: wisdom speaks of her mysterious origins which reach back to the time when the world was created, and Part III, vv. 32–36, finally returns, with the characteristic 'and now', to the paraenetic theme of Part I, to what is, in effect, a summons, in the form of an ultimatum, to listen to this wisdom, for on this depend life or death.[4] We shall deal first with the central section. Before we ask ourselves the questions raised by this part of the didactic poem, we shall notice briefly its highly artistic structure. Four subsections can be noticed. In the first and the last, wisdom speaks about herself (vv. 22f.; 30f.). In the first of the two middle strophes (vv. 24–26), the situation before creation is described ('when there were no . . .'), in the second (vv. 27–29), Yahweh's creative action ('when he . . .').

Prov. 8.22–31 has often been worked through, and both its vocabulary and the ideas to which it gives expression have been examined from all angles.[5] Seen against the background of the whole, the section comprising vv. 22–31 only serves a subsidiary function. It has independent significance only in so far as in it the voice which addresses men makes itself known. If one wishes to understand the speaker properly, then one must go right back to God's creation of the world, for here lies her origin. As 'the beginning of God's ways', that is, as the best element of creation, she was herself already a witness of creation. There is no compelling reason to depart from *nissaktī* in v. 23, 'I was set up', 'dedicated'. *ḥōlāltī*, 'I was born', is to be understood in a broader sense (as in Deut. 32.18), but even *qānānī* in v. 22 does not present any insuperable difficulty. The Septuagint translates *ektisen* (created), Aquila, Symmachus and Theodotion *ektēsato* (acquired). The Peshitta has the Syriac word corresponding to Hebrew *bārā'* (create). Behind this difference, however, there is no serious problem. One knows that *qānā* means 'acquire' (by creating), occasionally applied even to God (Ex.

---

[4] Prov. 3.13–26 is laid out in the same way as the didactic poem in Prov. 8, but in much smaller dimensions. Here, too, between the praise of wisdom (vv. 13–18) and a renewed appeal to follow her (vv. 21–26), there occurs a central section (vv. 19–20) which looks back to the function of wisdom at the beginning of time: 'By wisdom Yahweh founded the earth, and established the heavens by understanding. By his knowledge the oceans burst forth, and the clouds drip with dew.'

[5] With great care by R. Stecher, 'Die persönliche Weisheit in den Proverbien Kap. 8', *ZKTh* 75, 1953, pp. 411ff.

15.16; Ps. 74.2). A number of times it means (said of God) 'create', and here the verb seems to be a cultic-mythical relic (Gen. 14.19, 22; Ps. 139.13; etc.).[6] That the verb in v. 22b means 'create' is scarcely questioned. But what difference would it make if one abandoned this meaning? Wisdom belongs, in any case, to the sphere of that which is created. The word *'āmōn* in v. 30 has been discussed over and over again.[7] As it has been pointed by the Massoretes, it is by no means clear. The Septuagint has *harmozousa*, and from this comes the Vulgate's *componens*. This rendering supported those who thought that the Hebrew word *'ammān*= 'work-master' should be read, a word which is perhaps borrowed from Akkadian (*ummanu* = craftsman) and which is found in Jer. 52.15, an equally uncertain passage. Support for the meaning 'workman' seemed to come especially from Wisd. 7.21; 8.6 where wisdom is actually described as *technītis* = 'artist, worker'. On the other hand, one cannot maintain that this meaning fits the other statements of vv. 30f. (playing, joking). This leads to the other contending sense, namely that v. 30 is talking about a child. The disputed word must be read as *'āmūn* 'pet, darling'. This suggestion is supported by the translation in Aquila *tithēnoumenē* = 'foster-child, darling'. The differences between these readings should not be minimized. Behind them lie different theological conceptions which converge on the question: Did wisdom participate in the creation of the world as a 'demiurge' or not? This question cannot – as has long been clear from scholarly debate – be decided on text-critical principles alone. But there is another possibility by means of which the meaning of the disputed word can be determined.

The textual difficulty just mentioned is overshadowed by another, still greater one. The idea of the age-old existence of wisdom, thought of as a person and speaking self-confidently, is so strange and fits so ill with all that we otherwise seem to know of early Yahwism, that the question has long been debated whether Israel here is not being influenced by specific non-Israelite mythological ideas. One no longer hears the suggestion, which used to be confidently accepted, that an oriental 'wisdom myth' is being drawn upon here. No non-Israelite source capable of bearing such a hypothesis could be found; all that remained were extremely hypothetical, postulative reconstructions on the basis of the biblical material. One must proceed somewhat less ambitiously and enquire, in the first place, about the origin of the striking expressions in vv. 22–31. The style of a solemn address in the

---

[6] P. Humbert, *Bertholet-Festschrift*, 1950, pp. 259ff.; P. Katz, 'The Meaning of the Root *qnh*', *JJS* 6, 1955, pp. 126ff.

[7] R. B. Y. Scott, 'Wisdom in Creation: The 'AMON of Proverbs VIII 30', *VT* 10, 1960, pp. 213ff.

first person, with its characteristic repetition of 'before'-'before', is familiar to us from the way in which certain Egyptian gods present themselves. Here, then, a stylistic dependence of our text on such Egyptian texts cannot be denied. But one can go further. Recently, our attention has been drawn to Egyptian texts which speak of how a deity, as father, is embraced by a daughter, Maat, presented as a child, how he kisses her after he has 'set her at his nose'.[8] The parallel with wisdom, playing as a darling child before Yahweh and delighting him, is striking; for the divine Maat, a central concept in Egyptian wisdom teaching, embodies law, world order, justice.[9] Here, too, then, there can be no doubt that Israelite teachers have been dependent on the idea of the Egyptian goddess of order and have even borrowed characteristic, individual expressions.[10]

On the question of non-Israelite influence on our text, we can therefore say that in vv. 22–29 the style of a specific Egyptian divine proclamation has clearly been borrowed and that in vv. 30f. the Egyptian idea of a deity caressing personified truth (Maat) has somehow, though not without internal modifications, found its way into our didactic poem. It is interesting that in this text, vv. 22–31, there can be observed two different influences from two Egyptian cultic spheres which were completely independent of each other.

But what does all this prove? Only that ideas which had their roots elsewhere came to Israel's help when she needed them, in order to be able to progress in her thinking within her own domain. For in the process of this transference of foreign ideas to the Hebrew thought-world, many of them have become completely different. What is described in Prov. 8 as 'wisdom', as world order, can be compared only with difficulty with the Egyptian concept Maat. It has no divine status, nor is it a hypostasized attribute of Yahweh; it is, rather, something created by Yahweh and assigned to its proper function. Although it is clearly differentiated from the whole of creation, it is

[8] Chr. Kayatz, *Studien zu Proverbien 1–9*, 1966, pp. 76ff., 93ff. (against R. N. Whybray, 'Proverbs VIII 22–31 and its Supposed Prototypes', *VT* 15, 1965, pp. 504ff.).

[9] See above, p. 72. 'The central idea of wisdom teaching is Maat, "law", "justice", "primeval order". As a goddess, Maat belongs to the religious system of Heliopolis where she appears as the daughter of the sun-god. She came down to men at "the beginning of time" as the right order of all things'; H. Brunner, 'Ägyptologie', *Handbuch der Orientalistik*, Vol. 1/2, 1952, p. 93.

[10] This proves conclusively that the Massoretic punctuation of the word '*mn* as '*āmōn* = 'foreman' is a later theological interpretation. See below, pp. 170f. The word surely read '*āmūn* and means 'pet, darling', as has long been thought.

an entity which belongs in the world, even if it is the first of the works of creation, the creature above all creatures. This special position accorded to wisdom *vis-à-vis* all created things, a position emphasized also in Job 28, is of great significance in our didactic poem.

In this connection, exegetes almost invariably speak of 'wisdom speculation'. What they mean is that in these texts Israel's faith has reached the realm of speculation, that is, of statements which have left the sphere of religious experience and which are, rather, the products of an intellectual, creative genius which is capable of making abstract deductions. This concept, however, is in urgent need of modification. In Egypt, the idea of a primitive order, which included both nature and human life, goes back to the earliest period. Can the same not be presupposed in Israel, too? Is there really very much to be said for the suggestion that the idea of an all-embracing order could only follow, as a late speculation, the search for an awareness of individual orders? In that case, on what basis did the persistent attempts to determine individual orders operate – especially the tracing of analogies in different spheres of life – if not on the presupposition of a great all-embracing order including everything that exists, an order which can, however, never be grasped any more than only partially? Without this basic presupposition, would every endeavour towards the perception of individual orders not be illusory? Even older, practical wisdom speaks quite often of Yahweh as creator.[11] He created the poor and the human ear and eye; even the weights which are used in the market are 'his work'. Thus, there can be no doubt that even the early search for order in Israel thought on the basis of a total order and moved, in its thinking, towards a total order. This should not make us assert that the didactic poem in Prov. 8 is to be dated to an early period. There is, however, a compelling reason for asking whether the didactic poem in Prov. 8, as well as that in Job 28, really give expression to a completely new idea. Is, then, the suggestion no more than probable that within a group of early didactic texts a doctrine is suddenly represented which cannot be linked with any contemporary doctrine or with any earlier one?

There should, in any case, have been no talk of wisdom speculation, because what is being spoken of in Prov. 8 is an event, something which happens to man in the world and is actually brought upon him by the world. We have already, on several occasions, encountered the idea of the active influence of the environment on man, that is, of an

[11] Prov. 14.31; 16.4, 11; 17.5; 20.12; 22.2; 29.13.

ordering power which affects him and corrects him. Thus, these comparatively late texts are dealing with an ordering power whose existence has been felt in Israel from the earliest times. But there speaks from them a generation of teachers who obviously felt the necessity of thinking through in very basic terms and of reformulating a subject which had for long been implicitly presupposed in their teachings.[12] They speak about this order in very subtle terms, terms which already lie at the outermost edge of what it is even possible to say within the sphere of the Hebrew language. Also, Israel would never have found her way to these statements without the help of Egyptian ideas, for there were no traditional possibilities of expression available for this particular subject. Nevertheless, it would be more appropriate to consider the central portion of our didactic poem as the reinterpretation of a very old insight which had never been expressed before.

When the didactic hymn says, 'You have made all your works in wisdom' (Ps. 104.24), this gives expression to what is basically the same awareness on which Job 28 and Prov. 8.22f. simply expand in much more varied terms.

> Yahweh has founded the earth in wisdom
> and established heaven in understanding.
> By his knowledge the deeps burst forth,
> and the clouds drip with dew. (Prov. 3.19f.)

The reader will refer the expression 'in wisdom' to God's wisdom as creator; this would be to understand it as a divine attribute. But it could also be understood as an attribute of the earth, something like, 'Creation was raised by God to a state of wisdom or understanding'. Meanwhile, such a question is virtually superfluous, for it is actually impossible to separate from the former statement the idea that creation has to be credited with the attribute of wise orderliness. There is an interesting expression in Sirach to the effect that God has 'poured wisdom out upon all his works' (Sir. 1.9). The idea of 'pouring out'

---

[12] How can the application of the word ḥokmā to this object of knowledge have come about? It is difficult to imagine that we are dealing here with a word in common use. It is easier to suppose that the word ḥokmā, in this sense that is so far from normal linguistic usage, is a technical term of scholarly language. It is likely that the teachers were looking for a term corresponding to the Egyptian maat (in Job 28.12, 20 bīnā 'understanding' is also found in parallelism). Even if, on the whole, the Hebrew ṣᵉdāqā ('righteousness') was closer to Egyptian maat (H. H. Schmid, Gerechtigkeit als Weltordnung, 1968, p.61), there was, of course, no need always to translate it in this way. In addition, in this case, the word ḥokmā was nearer to what was meant.

can scarcely be understood as a free, poetic, figurative representation, but rather as the description of a real, cosmological process, namely as the bestowal of something special on creation, something which, as we learned from Job 28, now mysteriously inhabits it. Finally, one may also cite the song of the seraphim in Isa. 6.3, although this refers not to wisdom but to glory. But the statement that 'the glory of Yahweh' 'fills' the whole earth nevertheless again speaks of a quality immanent in creation, except that here, in the language of the hymn, it is described by the more strongly aesthetically accentuated expression 'the glory of God'.

In this same line of thought, there also lies the central section of the didactic poem in Prov. 8, a section which one must always consider, of course, within the context of the whole poem.[13] If we understood the teaching about 'wisdom' turning towards men from the world, as the reinterpretation of an implicitly very old idea, then we are particularly interested in what has changed in the course of this process of transmission. In the traditio-historical sense, a reinterpretation is never confined to saying the same thing, not even to saying it in 'more modern' terms. One can always discern an addition to the substance. The didactic poem in Prov. 8, in expounding the basic idea, does not simply surpass the old doctrine in that it is able to give expression to particular details about Yahweh's relationship to this world order. The most interesting feature of what is new is that this world order turns, as a person, towards men, wooing them and encouraging them in direct address. What is objectified here, then, is not an attribute of God but an attribute of the world, namely that mysterious attribute, by virtue of which she turns towards men to give order to their lives.[14] Thus, Israel was faced with the same phenomenon which more or less fascinated all ancient religions, especially, of course, the nature religions, namely that of the religious provocation of man by the world. But Israel did not agree to the mythicization and deification of the first principle of the world. Her interpretation was quite a different one, because she held fast to this phenomenon within the sphere of her faith in Yahweh as creator.

We can do no more than express in other words this thing which is

[13] The ideas of wisdom in the Wisdom of Solomon 6–9 or in Enoch 42; 91.10 are, of course, to be carefully differentiated from this. As far as these teachings are concerned, we must take into account a lively process of tradition in which new interpretations were always occurring.

[14] Against R. N. Whybray, *Wisdom in Proverbs*, 1967², p. 103; wisdom in Prov. 8 is not 'an attribute of Yahweh'.

immanent in the world and which the texts call 'wisdom'. Whether we render it as 'primeval order' or 'mysterious order' or 'world reason' or as the 'meaning' created in the world by God or as the 'glory' reflected back from the world, in every case it is spoken of in the form of a graphic personification. But this personification is anything but a freely chosen, decorative, stylistic device which the reader who is skilled in rhetoric could easily have replaced by a completely different one, with the sole aim of simplifying understanding. Rather, this form of speech was determined by the subject in question and could be fixed in words only in this way without incurring loss, for this primeval order addressed man, a factor which we shall have to discuss in a moment. There was, then, no choice, for the personal element was completely indispensable. This world reason was there before all works of creation, playing in the world like a child; like a 'favourite', she was the delight of God and, even from the very beginning, she was turned towards men in cheerful and playful disposition – a point which is particularly important for the point of the whole poem. In contrast to Job 28, this wisdom which is immanent in the world is considered less from the point of view of the economic order than from an aesthetic point of view. As 'favourite', she is God's 'delight', and she 'sports' with and 'takes delight' in men. Both texts speak of a reality which is surrounded by the most profound mystery. In the cult, it was an object of praise; in the school, an object of contemplation. What is this thing, which, on the one hand, is so deeply bound up with all created things and which seems, on the other hand, to be part of Yahweh's rule and to have a profound effect on men?

2. THE CALL

The mysterious central section of our didactic poem must be taken not only as closely as possible with the complex of statements in Parts I and III, but also with other, closely related, didactic texts. Only then does there emerge from this group of texts a comprehensive subject of instruction which is sometimes treated at great length and which, at other times, is expressed only briefly.

> Does not wisdom call,
>> does not understanding raise her voice . . .
> 'To you, O men, do I call,
>> and my voice goes out to mankind.' (Prov. 8.1, 4)

> (Wisdom) has sent out her maids,[15]
>> she invites, up on the heights of the town.   (Prov. 9.3)
>
> Wisdom calls aloud in the streets,
>> in the squares she raises her voice.
> In the noisiest places she calls,
>> at the entrance gates of the town she makes speeches.   (Prov. 1.20f.)

The facts are clear. Wisdom – we now know approximately what is meant by this – calls to men. And this brings us at last to the event which is the real subject of the didactic poem. And what an event it is! In this call we are dealing with the very opposite of something private and personal or even esoteric, which would be accessible only to initiates. She stands, not in a hidden place but 'on the heights', 'by the roadside', where 'the paths cross' (Prov. 8.2). She speaks not from the sacral sphere of the sanctuary, but in the most profane public place. And what she says is clear and precise, that men should learn from her and listen to her (Prov. 8.5f., 10, 32); she will lead men out of stupidity and idle gossip (Prov. 1.22); she teaches intelligence and truth (Prov. 8.5, 7); finally, she promises wealth and honour as well as righteousness (Prov. 8.18, 21). She even promises life, divine favour and security:

> For he who finds me has found life
>> and obtains Yahweh's favour.   (Prov. 8.35)
> He who listens to me dwells secure
>> and is safe from the terror of disaster.   (Prov. 1.33)

All this is very fine talk. One must be all the more careful, then, to ask how this was really conceived in Israel. It was obviously the opinion of the teachers that man is addressed from creation by a desire for order from which he cannot escape. This desire for order addresses, in the first instance, man's completely personal life. It is the basis and source of ethical behaviour. Listen to this voice,

> then you will understand righteousness and justice
>> and equity, every good path;
> for wisdom will come into your heart,
>> and knowledge will be pleasant to your soul;
> discretion will watch over you,
>> understanding will guard you,

---

[15] Or should this be translated 'she has dismissed them'? M. Dahood, *Proverbs and Northwest Semitic Philology*, 1963, pp. 16f.

to save you from the way of evil,
     from the man of perverted speech . . .
to save you from the strange woman,
     from the adventuress with her smooth words . . .
so that you might walk in the way of good men,
     and keep to the paths of the righteous.   (Prov. 2.9–20)

But this desire for order – it is a force (Prov. 8.14) – reaches far beyond the sphere of private life. This wisdom makes an enormous claim.

By me kings reign,
     and rulers decree what is just.
By me princes and nobles rule,
     and all righteous judges.   (Prov. 8.15–16)

This statement, since otherwise we have almost no corresponding passages, is of very great significance. One is to deduce from it that both the art of government as well as the knowledge of law – not only in Israel, but in the whole world – are to be attributed to this ordering power.[16] One may say that it is the source of all the wisdom possessed by every nation. Its sphere of influence stretches out over all peoples and nations (Sir. 24.6). But the domain over which this ordering power rules also includes the non-human sphere of nature. The dualism, familiar to us, of rules for human society on the one hand and rules for nature on the other, was unknown to the ancients. The world order rules in nature as it does through the moral law (as we would say) over men.

Even the famous self-presentation of wisdom in Sirach functions within solemn, poetic statements. It deals with our question about the relationship of wisdom to nature somewhat more clearly.

I came forth from the mouth of the Most High
     and covered the earth like a mist.
I pitched my tent on the heights,
     and my throne was on a pillar of cloud.
Alone, I wandered round the circle of heaven
     and entered into the depths of the abyss.

---

[16] In this context one can think of Cicero's 'prayer hymn', in which he celebrates philosophy as *inventrix legum* and as *magistra morum et disciplinae* (*Tusculans*, V, 5). A connection with oriental ideas (Posidonius) cannot be excluded; on this cf. H. Hommel, *Ciceros Gebetshymnus an die Philosophie* (Sitzungsberichte d. Heidelberger Akademie d. Wiss., Phil.-hist. Kl., 1968, Abh. 3), esp. p. 13.

In the waves of the sea, in the whole earth,
among every people and nation I have acquired a possession.

(Sir. 24.3–6)[17]

From the point of view of the basic idea of the existence and function of wisdom at the beginning of time, these sentences scarcely add anything to the ideas of Prov. 8.22f. (the difference comes only when Sirach identifies this wisdom with Torah).[18] Here, too, she is, as the poem clearly explains, created (v. 8 'who created me', v. 9 'he created me', cf. Sir. 1.4, 9). So, too, the statement that she has come out from the mouth of the Most High (v. 3a) is along the same lines as the first account of creation, where creation by the word is so strongly emphasized. That she covered the earth like a mist must be understood as a bold exegesis of Gen. 2.6.[19] At any rate, it says something about how closely wisdom belongs to earth. If she speaks of a throne, then this cannot refer to anything outside of what has been created. All that can be deduced from such a statement is that she is represented here not as a child, but as a ruler. In this connection, the statement that she walked round creation, from heaven down to the primeval deeps, is important. The expression 'to walk round a place' formerly belonged to legal symbolism. It signified the completion – either real or only spoken – of a legal action.[20] In this way, then, wisdom formally

[17] H. Conzelmann has suggested the possibility that in Sir. 24.1–6 an Egyptian hymn to Isis has been used; cf. *The Future of Our Religious Past. Essays in Honour of Rudolf Bultmann*, 1971, pp. 234ff. This assertion fits in well with what has been said above (pp. 152f.) about the traditio-historical backgrounds of Prov. 8.22ff. From a hermeneutical point of view this is highly interesting, in so far as a text, probably taken over *verbatim*, could in Israel be inserted into a quite different context of meaning, so that now every detail of the text gives voice to greatly altered senses. Whether there ever was a myth of a searching and disappointed Wisdom, the existence of which has been taken as certain since Bultmann's famous essay in *Eucharisterion für Gunkel*, T. 2, 1923, pp. 1ff. (see U. Wilckens, *Weisheit und Torheit*, 1959, pp. 160ff.), has become highly questionable. It leads to disastrous distortions if one interprets texts such as Prov. 1.20ff.; Job 28; Sir. 24 on the basis of and with an eye to this 'wisdom myth'. Job 28 must be left completely out of account for it talks of a wisdom hidden in creation (and not in heaven). Prov. 1.20ff. yields nothing in this respect either (Chr. Kayatz, op. cit., p. 128). The idea is clear only in I Enoch 42.1–3. Hesiod, however, also speaks of the return to heaven of two disappointed goddesses, *Works and Days*, ll. 197–201.

[18] Cf. P. van Imschoot, 'La sagesse dans l'Ancien Testament – est-elle une hypostase?', *Collationes Gandavenses* 21, 1934, p. 10.

[19] Gen. 2.6: 'An 'ēd went up from the earth to water the whole surface of the ground'. The LXX translates the difficult word 'ēd by 'spring', in Job 36.27, on the other hand, by 'cloud'. The Targum translates 'ēd in Gen. 2.6 by 'cloud'.

[20] Gen. 13.17: 'Rise, go through the length and breadth of the land, for to you shall I give it'; on this cf. D. Daube, *Studies in Biblical Law*, 1947, pp. 37f.

assumed her proprietary rights, which cover the whole world. But she does not only rule, she also speaks.

Yet another aspect of this puzzling subject is opened up by means of another important text. The voice of primeval order does not address man in such a way that he has at his disposal, whenever he might require it, an ever-flowing well of truth. She can also withdraw herself from a man who does not heed her.

> Because I have called and you refused to listen,
>   have stretched out my hand and no one has heeded,
> but have thrown all my counsel to the winds
>   and despised my reproof,
> then I will laugh at your destruction,
>   mock when terror comes upon you.
> Then men will call upon me, but I will not answer,
>   they will seek me but will not find me.
> Because they hated knowledge
>   and did not choose the fear of Yahweh,
> would have none of my counsel,
>   and despised all my reproof,
> then they shall eat the fruit of their way
>   and be sated with their own devices.   (Prov. 1.24–31)[21]

The loss of this organizing voice will have catastrophic consequences. Horror, terror, distress will come upon men. They will be thrown back upon themselves and will have to live by their own initiative, that is, they will destroy themselves. Even if they then come to realize that they need to be thus addressed to be able to live at all, then this voice will remain silent for them. Here, too, we have the presentation of something that actually takes place.

We shall pause here for a moment before drawing out of the texts the final component of the relationship between wisdom and man. This wisdom, which we have understood as the primeval world order, as the mystery behind the creation of the world, rules in a similar fashion in the non-human creation as well as in the sphere of human society. If one wishes to understand it as the Logos of the world, an idea which indeed suggests itself to the modern reader, then one must simply remember that the texts do not exactly speak of an ideal, such as a principle or a rationality in the world, but of something created

---

[21] The didactic poem in Prov. 1.20–33 is, as far as its form is concerned, a remarkable hybrid, for in parts it strongly resembles the prophetic invective and threat. As far as its subject matter is concerned, on the other hand, it is clearly 'wisdom'. Details in Chr. Kayatz, op. cit., pp. 119ff.

which is as real as other works of creation. But this primeval order does not exist only in creation; it is orientated towards man, offering him help; it is concerned about him, indeed addresses him directly. This address is not a mystery which can be deciphered only by man; it is uttered with full publicity 'in the noisiest places' (Prov. 1.20f.). All these statements leave us in no doubt that this address can be understood by man without the slightest difficulty.

All this raises the question which a biblical theology must first ask. We encounter the idea that the world is not dumb, that it has a message, in the hymn. The world proclaims itself before God as a created thing; the heavens 'tell', the firmament 'proclaims' (Ps. 19.2). 'All his works praise God' (Ps. 145.10). Within the context of the description of a theophany, it could be said, 'The heavens proclaim his (God's) righteousness' (Ps. 97.6). This speaking by part of creation appears here as an accompaniment to the divine self-revelation. But it is improbable that the heavens were empowered as witnesses only in the context of this occurrence and that they were previously dumb.

In Ps. 148, Israel, as leader of the choir, summons all creation, right to its furthest limits, to join in the hymn of praise. What finds expression here is not simply poetic exuberance, but the idea of a real witness emanating from the world. This brings us for the first time to a very close connection between hymns and wisdom. The sole difference is that this witness on the part of creation, according to the teaching of the wise men, is directed not at God, but at men, though this element is also included in the idea in the hymn context.[22]

> But ask the wild beast, and he will teach you,
>   and the birds of the air, and they will show you.
> Or the plants of the earth will teach you,
>   the fish of the sea will tell you.
> Who among all these does not know
>   that Yahweh's hand has done this?   (Job 12.7–9).

How many verbs there are, meaning 'speak'! With this idea of something being said to men by creation, we find ourselves very close to the doctrine of the call of the world order to men. Of course, in the one case it was a witness which was to lead men to acknowledge and worship the Creator; in the other, however, it was the invitation to let oneself be guided in all the decisions of life by the instructions of the primeval order. But perhaps these two are not so very far apart. If,

[22] The relationship of wisdom to the hymn and its subject matter has long been noted. Sirach was not the first wise man to compose hymns.

according to Job 12.7ff., the world presents itself to man as creation, then, at the same time, it must also speak of its wonderful order. But even what we understand by 'moral order' was, in the opinion of the didactic poem, rooted in the basic order from the beginning of the world. This call from the mysterious order to men is, as we have seen, perfectly clear; although it is actually a voice speaking out of what has been created (and speaking of Yahweh in the third person, Prov. 8.13), it nevertheless bears all the marks of a divine address. It resounds everywhere; it is impossible to escape it; and the way in which it presents man with the decision between life and death is something like an outright ultimatum. Even the gifts which it promises can only be described as gifts of salvation, and here lies the problem: an 'I', who is certainly not Yahweh, but who nevertheless summons men to itself. What prophet would have taken it upon himself to call men to himself? And who, apart from Yahweh, can say to man, 'Whoever finds me, finds life' (Prov. 3.18; 8.35; 9.6; Sir. 4.12)? Whoever is not open to this call is lost. And finally, this saving voice is not at man's disposal whenever he wishes; he can forfeit it through disobedience, and then it will deny itself to him (Prov. 1.24–27).

In the text with which we have been dealing here, however – and to begin with this can only be asserted categorically – it is not Yahweh who is speaking. This is puzzling, for in these texts we find the form of divine self-revelation. Obviously the situation here is considerably different from what it is in the prophets, who never addressed their readers in the first person. Only occasionally does the prophetic 'I' appear, more or less on the fringe of those messages which have the style of a divine address. A new phenomenon in our texts is that a bearer of revelation intervenes in the dialogue between Yahweh and Israel, someone who has not hitherto been heard in this role. His speech proceeds in a highly elevated first-person style; but he is much more than the greatest of the prophets, he is, indeed, the mystery inherent in the creation of the world. In the opinion of the teachers, Yahweh had at his service a quite different means, besides priests and prophets, whereby he could reach men, namely the voice of primeval order, a voice which came from creation, and this means of revelation was of particular interest to the wise men. In addition, the whole of God's speech in the book of Job proceeds from the same presupposition, for here, too, God allows his creation to speak and gives to it the task of opening Job's eyes.

We are at once faced with the question of the relationship between this self-revelation of creation and the voice of other bearers of revelation which spoke through the medium of cult or history (narrators) or the voice of those who spoke out of free charisma. We can only state that this question, for whatever reason, was never asked by the wise men. They were completely engrossed by the call of this voice and by the task of letting it be heard. There is no basis for the suggestion that, polemically and exclusively, they set this bearer of revelation up against all others that were thus far known in Israel. One may, rather, suppose that the voice of this revelation filled a gap and satisfied a theological need which had begun to be felt.

If one considers the ultimatum-like nature of this claim and the importance of the benefits promised, then it is difficult to imagine that this teaching about the self-revelation of creation could have accommodated itself, entirely free of tensions, to the old traditions about Yahweh. Nor can one accept, on the other hand, that it had a completely antagonistic relationship with them, for in other contexts the teachers speak quite freely of Yahweh, and that was a name which was always heavy with tradition. It would be difficult to imagine that this name, in the mouths of the teachers, would have shed all of the content with which, as far as we can see, it was indissolubly associated. On the other hand, the outlines of these didactic texts must not be blurred, for they speak not of Yahweh, but of a voice which has all the characteristics of a revelation. There must have been circles in Israel, and especially in the schools, which must have regarded it as their main task to refer the individual to that voice which sounded through the medium of creation and to bring him to the point of entrusting to this form of revelation his life with all its possibilities of conflict. The teachers do not entertain the slightest doubt that this self-revelation of creation can be heard. It can, in Paul's words, be 'clearly perceived' (Rom. 1.20).

The monarchy ushered in a period of specific individualization in which the individual's interest in Yahweh was questioned much more urgently than in the era of older Yahwism. Older Yahwism was, on the whole, scarcely prepared for this question raised by the individual, for even the Decalogue and related codes of law were of no help in the thick of individual life, nor were they ever intended to be. This movement towards independence on the part of the individual, with all the questions that arose as a consequence, can be followed to a certain extent in many Old Testament texts.[23] As the individual

[23] G. v. Rad, *Old Testament Theology*, Vol. II, ET 1965, pp. 263ff.

gradually became aware of his isolation, his release from old ties took place in quite different ways. The process placed men in the range both of new religious possibilities and of unforeseen problems. Accordingly, the spokesmen of Yahwism faced the changing situation in very different ways. The wise men made a contribution, certainly not the least important, to coping with the questions which were to be expected, namely the teaching about the self-revelation of creation. In their attempt to illuminate the reality which surrounded men, they had, in the depths of creation, stumbled upon a phenomenon which was possessed of a highly developed declaratory power. Creation not only exists, it also discharges truth.

But this truth is turned, if we once again visualize its offer according to the great revelation-discourse in Prov. 8, primarily to individuals, to 'men', specifically the men of the upper classes. It promises cleverness, understanding, righteousness, reliability, wisdom, counsel, success, strength, wealth, honour. It was for this voice that the wise men sought to provide a place in their didactic poems. In this way they have unquestionably exposed an aspect of creative reality with which Yahwism had not yet concerned itself in this particular way. Its task was so great and so new that the other task, the establishment of a compromise with the Yahwistic traditions about salvation history, faded, for the time being, completely into the background. This task was tackled only in what one might call a second operation.

Only much later, as far as we can see, first by Sirach, was this harmonization brought to completion. He has expressed the union of the two in a well thought-out way. The great discourse in which wisdom presents herself, the beginning of which we have already considered above, continues as follows:

> Amongst all these (people) I looked for repose,
>   in the possession of which I could tarry.
> Then the creator of all things commanded me,
>   and he who had created me
>   made my tent come to rest.
> He said, 'Pitch your tent in Jacob
>   and find a possession in Israel.'
> From of old, from the beginning he had created me,
>   and to all eternity I shall not cease.
> In the holy tent I served in his presence,
>   and thus I gained a firm abode on Zion.

In the city which he loves as he loves me
    I was brought to rest,
    and in Jerusalem is now my dominion.   (Sir. 24.7–11)

One can see how here the line is drawn from the primeval order right through to the revelation of Yahweh in the tabernacle and in the Jerusalem temple, a great, ambitious sketch of salvation history. The primeval order (wisdom) sought a dwelling among men and was directed by God to the people of Israel. Only here could she develop, for only here were men open to her, only here did they serve her aright, for in Israel the primeval order had revealed herself in the form of Torah. But is it correct, when it is said over and over again that in this way Torah-theology invaded the domain of wisdom and assimilated it? The opposite has occurred. Wisdom has attempted to explain, on her own terms, the phenomenon of Torah and has done so in very untraditional terms.[24]

3. INTELLECTUAL LOVE

After these considerations we return once again to the question of the relationship between man and wisdom immanent in the world. A whole range of statements has still to be heard, in which Israel has expressed what is surely the final and most astonishing word about this relationship. This mysterious order in the world not only addresses man; it also loves him. The motif of love-language spreads out so widely in the texts from Prov. 1–9 *via* Sirach and on to the late Wisdom of Solomon that we are obviously here dealing with a range of ideas which the teachers have developed along a broad front.[25] One must first of all consider the texts in which wisdom is presented as a woman who calls to men quite openly in the streets and squares and invites them to come to her in her house.

[24] See below pp. 245ff. One cannot therefore say that wisdom is here being controlled by covenant ideas; cf. N. Lohfink, *Das Siegeslied am Schilfmeer*, 1965, pp. 205ff.
    Sir. 24 is not a unit. The section which begins in v. 23 ('All this is the book of the covenant, the law which Moses gave us . . .') has obviously been added to the self-presentation of wisdom. The first-person style of the speech breaks off, and now it is the teacher who speaks, interpreting wisdom's speech. Clearly Sirach is here addressing an already existing tradition. V. 23 reads as if a figurative speech were about to be interpreted.
[25] On this range of ideas cf. G. Boström, *Proverbiastudien*, 1935, pp. 156ff.: 'Wisdom as the Bride'; U. Wilckens, *Weisheit und Torheit*, 1959, pp. 174ff.

Wisdom has built her house,
    has 'set up' her seven pillars. [26]
She has slaughtered her beasts,
    mixed her wine and set her table.
She has sent out her maids, she invites,
    up on the heights of the town.
Whoever is inexperienced, let him turn in here;
    whoever has little understanding, to him she says,
'Come, eat my food
    and drink the wine which I have mixed.'

                         (Prov. 9.1–5; cf. 1.20ff.; 8.1ff.)

It is surely correct to say that this remarkable allegorization was developed by the teachers as a contrast to and a defence against customs which had appeared in Israel, too, from the cult of the goddess of love, the goddess Astarte. The didactic narrative in Prov. 7.1ff. shows clearly enough how women enticed men to themselves in fulfilment of a fertility vow. [27] But – such is the instruction of the teachers – those who accept this invitation walk a road which leads to death (Prov. 9.13–18). The true partner who calls men to herself is wisdom. One cannot, of course, say that everything which was said in Israel about the love relationship of wisdom to men was derived from this polemic against a foreign cultic practice. We know from Egyptian texts so much about the love of Maat, the goddess of order, for men, [28] that it is impossible to deny the influence of Egyptian ideas, not to mention, in addition, the influence of the subject matter of secular love poetry. But without denying these interconnections from the direction of the history of religions, we are interested here in Israel's ideas, which have their own character *vis-à-vis* those of Egypt. If one tries to understand the idea of a wisdom who invites against a purely Israelite background, the result is something like this. Something remarkable happens to reason as it starts out in search of knowledge of the world. It encounters an opposite, indeed it is at once overtaken by the voice of the divine, primeval order, for this voice is already directed towards men; it is already on the way to them and addresses them from the place for which reason is, in fact, searching, but which it can never reach by its own efforts (Job 28). And because the mystery of the world moves towards man and seeks his ear, for this reason

[26] What the significance of the 'seven pillars' is has yet to be satisfactorily explained.
[27] G. Boström, op. cit., pp. 108ff.
[28] Chr. Kayatz, op. cit., pp. 98ff.

wisdom must, indeed, may now be loved by man. For this reason
the teachers urge, 'Love her, and she will guard you' (Prov. 4.6), 'Say
to wisdom, "You are my sister", and call insight your confidant'
(Prov. 7.4).[29] 'Approach her with your whole heart' (Sir. 6.26). 'She
will honour you if you embrace her' (Prov. 4.8). Whoever turns to
her she welcomes 'like the wife of his youth' (Sir. 15.2). And wisdom
will answer, 'I love those who love me, and those who seek me will
find me' (Prov. 8.17). 'Whoever pays heed to me will lie down in
my innermost rooms' (Sir. 4.15). She congratulates him who, like a
lover, watches day after day at her doors (Prov. 8.34). The teachers
even speak, in the style of biographical confessions, of her wooing
and of the wonderful success of her efforts.

> When I was young, I delighted in her
>   and sought her . . .
> My soul clung to her,
>   and I did not turn my face away from her.
> My hand opened her doors
>   and went into her presence and gazed upon her . . .
> Put your neck under her yoke,
>   let your soul bear her weight.
> See how little I have toiled,
>   and how I have found much rest.   (Sir. 51.13, 19, 26f.)

> I fell in love with her and sought her from my youth
>   and sought to take her as my bride
>   and became a lover of her beauty.
> When I enter my house, I shall rest beside her,
>   for there is no bitterness in keeping company with her,
> nothing sad about companionship with her,
>   only gladness and joy.   (Wisd. 8.2, 16)

In Israel, too, then, there was formed a highly remarkable, ideal
picture of man in his search for knowledge. Almost voluptuously there
is depicted what awaits the man who associates with the world, if he
offers her the trust which she solicits and pays heed to the words with
which she turns towards him. Nowhere has this picture of a man
motivated by a love of knowledge been drawn more beautifully and
more modestly than by Sirach.

> Blessed is the man who meditates on wisdom
>   and cares about understanding . . .

---

[29] The loved one is also called 'sister', S. of S. 4.9f., 12; 5.1; etc.

enough to penetrate all her secrets;
    who observes all her entrances,
who peers in at her windows
    and listens at her doors,
who encamps near her house
    and knocks his tent-pegs into her wall,
who pitches his tent by her side
    and lives well-protected,
who builds his nest in her foliage
    and spends the night in her branches,
who seeks refuge from the heat in her shade
    and lives in her abode.   (Sir. 14.20–27)

If there was, somewhere in Israel, a surrender, verging on the mystical, of man to the glory of existence, then it is to be found in these texts which can speak of such a sublime bond of love between man and the divine mystery of creation. Here man throws himself with delight on a meaning which rushes towards him; he uncovers a mystery which was already on its way to him in order to give itself to him.

She comes towards him like a mother
    and receives him like a young wife.   (Sir. 15.2)

Radiant and unfading is wisdom,
    she is easily noticed by those who love her,
    and found by those who seek her.
She presents herself to those who desire her
    and makes herself known.
He who rises early to meet her will have no trouble;
    he will find her sitting at his door.
To think about her is perfect cleverness,
    and whoever lies awake on her account
    will soon be carefree,
for she goes about, herself seeking those
    who are worthy of her.
She appears as a friend to them on their paths
    and comes towards them in every thought.   (Wisd. 6.12–16)

The 'Doctrine of the Self-Revelation of Creation' is, as we have seen, developed in many, very different texts. It is no wonder that we are struck by the many theological refinements which give to almost every text its own character. This impression of the independence of the individual texts would have been strengthened if we had not confined ourselves to all too brief paraphrases, but had really been able to reproduce the sayings in all their ramifications, so that we could have marvelled at the fine gradations of ideas from one sentence to the next. There can be no doubt that this subject of instruction was constantly in a state of fluidity and was presented from time to time in different forms. And yet one must not overlook the stable element alongside the variable. There were, indeed, far fewer new ideas presented from text to text. It was, rather, an extension of what had already been presented in embryo but which had not yet been expressed in that particular way in ancient Israel; it was more a drawing out of lines, occasionally even a combination of separate ideas, but not a breakthrough to a completely new perception.[30] In this respect, the doctrine of the self-manifesting primeval order could be regarded as a model case of the way in which wisdom material was handed on. One certainly cannot imagine that this doctrine was uttered one day for the first time by an original mind, or even that it was taken over from Egypt. Its roots are old, even within Israel. They lie, as we have seen, in the basic conviction from which even the oldest practical wisdom began, namely that there is an order in things and in events and that this order is not a mystery, but makes itself known. In this, the doctrine is close to the ideas of the hymn, according to which the majesty of creation makes itself known. What is new here is that this order, which, in the older practical wisdom, by and large, was still uncritically presupposed, has now itself become the object of a thorough, theological development.

In what it says about the original state of wisdom at the beginning of time, even Sir. 24, however, apart from a few learned extensions, scarcely adds anything decisive in theological terms to Prov. 8.22ff. Here, too, wisdom is a creature of God. The author of the Wisdom of Solomon – otherwise, in many respects, a reliable custodian of Palestinian tradition – was the first to abandon, in this regard, the line which had been adhered to hitherto and take a decisive step along the road to a mythical, speculative deification of wisdom. She is 'creator' (Wisd. 7.12) and God's 'consort' (9.4). This is a definitive abandonment of the tradition, and in contrast to it a new element has made its appearance.[31]

---

[30] This is also true of the 'playing' of wisdom in Prov. 8.31. Already in old wisdom one could constantly discern a desire for fun in the vicinity of truth, a delight, a fascination for a truth that entices men. See above p. 50; cf. H.-J. Hermisson, op. cit., p. 136.

[31] 'Sapientia leaves wisdom, which is regarded as the constant expression of the nature of God and as a principle of the world, completely in God's presence and in a world wholly divorced from the world of appearances. This duality meets us

With a series of interesting Greek terms, the author tries to describe more accurately this 'cosmic' wisdom: she is 'spirit' (1.6), she is a 'breath' of the power of God, an 'emanation' of the power of the Almighty, *atmis aporrhoia* (7.25), a 'reflection', *apaugasma*, of the invisible light, a 'spotless mirror' of the divine mystery (7.26). But a conceptually clear definition did not just happen. The transformations in the ideas about this wisdom after the time of Sirach can be shown to have been a very lively process, one which will not, however, be pursued further here. The fine didactic poem in Bar. 3.9–4.4 is, from a literary point of view, heavily dependent on Job 28 and Sir. 24. In Enoch 42.1–3; 91.10 the tradition question seems more complex.

Let us endeavour, nevertheless, to reconstruct something of the process of tradition from old practical wisdom to the doctrine of the self-revelation of creation which eventually took shape in Job 28; Prov. 8 and Sir. 24. The sentences of practical wisdom were able to mention all kinds of benefits which could entice the pupil to obedience: wisdom protects against all kinds of harm, bestows honour, safeguards the future, etc. In whatever situation one follows her, she promises improvement of life and fulfilment of life. In this respect, the great theological poems in the collection comprising Prov. 1–9 are, in the first instance, in the tradition of the old teachers. But one immediately notices interesting changes. It strikes one at once that 'wisdom' is talked of here in a predominantly different sense than was the case in the older collections. Obviously didactic thought has been hard at work here, and decisive steps have indeed been taken in three directions.

1. The order which was formerly perceived in a vague and unthinking way and as existing in many different forms must itself have more and more become the object of thought. It was objectified as something which was uniform and which could be perceived in every separate experience, and it was conceptually determined (as 'wisdom').

2. This wisdom, immanent in creation, was differentiated in the three great didactic poems (Job 28; Prov. 8; Sir. 24) from the 'real' work of creation (wind, springs, sea, mountains, etc.). This ontological separation of the phenomena within creation is the most interesting element. Obviously what the teachers perceived as a 'summons from

already in the first chapter, and it soon becomes clear that what is meant is a dualism of God's world as the real, everlasting creation, and the world of the devil as an unreal, perishable world' (D. Georgi, in *Zeit und Geschichte, Festschrift f. R. Bultmann*, 1964, p.270). On this, see also below pp. 305f.

creation', as the 'self-evident nature of its order', was not simply identical with the 'real' works of creation.

3. Even the relationship of man to this phenomenon had shifted. What we have occasionally called the provocation of man by the world was, of course, experienced at all times. But while this phenomenon was approached, in a predominantly active manner, by the old teachers in their search for knowledge (for the purpose of 'discovering order'), the later teachers regarded themselves much more as the object of its assault. She, this wisdom, was the one who dealt with men in her address to them, in her offer of the good things of life, in her invitation to lodge with her.

> Whoever finds me, has found life
>   and has obtained favour from Yahweh;
> but whoever misses me, injures himself;
>   all who hate me love death. (Prov. 8.35f.)

Certainly, even in the practical sentences, much is said about the preservation or winning of life, life often in a general and absolute sense. Righteousness leads to life (Prov. 11.19), life and death are in the power of the tongue (Prov. 18.21), he who hates bribes will live (Prov. 15.27), etc. To speak of the gain or loss of life in this way corresponds to the teachers' habit of thinking in impressive and typifying antitheses. But in Prov. 8.35f., things are different, to the extent that here what ensures life is not an activity on man's part appropriate to the situation, but the primeval order itself, on whose offer the gaining of life depends, who in fact turns to the individual with this offer in a direct appeal of the most personal kind. Life, then, does not depend simply on wise behaviour, but on man's 'finding' of 'wisdom'.[32] It is also by means of wisdom that man wins 'favour from Yahweh' (Prov. 8.35); it is she, therefore, who brings order to the whole of life in God's eyes. This sentence expresses the result of far-reaching, theological thinking and is far removed, both in form and in content, from the didactic sentences in Prov. 10ff. That wisdom is the highest good, that the acquisition of her is more valuable than gold and silver could also be said there (Prov. 16.16) and can be easily understood against the background of these didactic sayings. Almost word for word, the passage 'more precious than gold', than 'choice silver', returns in Prov. 8.19, but in a vastly different context. Now it is the primeval order itself which commends itself to man in highly personal

---

[32] Prov. 1.28; 2.5; 3.13; 4.22; 8.12; 8.17.

terms as the donor. It is the mysterious 'I' who had earlier said, 'I love those who love me' (Prov. 8.17).

With this last sentence we are back again at the range of ideas where there are to be found the strongest and, at the same time, the gentlest statements about all that man has to face in the created world around him. The existence in the world of the man who seeks knowledge is in a relationship of love to the mysterious order. It is in a state of tension through being wooed, through seeking and being sought, through having to wait for and, at the same time, anticipating precious intellectual fulfilment. The offer made by wisdom as she woos men includes everything that a man, in his isolation, might need: wealth and honour (Prov. 8.18, 21), guidance and security in life (Prov. 1.33ff.; 2.9ff.; 4.6; 6.22; 7.4f.), knowledge of God and rest for the soul (Prov. 2.5; Sir. 6.28; 51.27).

> Come to her with all your soul,
>   and with all your might keep to her ways.
> Ask, enquire, seek and find,
>   seize her and do not let her go.
> For in the end you will find she is rest,
>   and she will become bliss for you.   (Sir. 6.26–28)

And, in this sublime, unending dialogue of love, she replies:

> Whoever pays heed to me
>   will lie down in my innermost rooms.   (Sir. 4.15)

In order to assist men in every possible way, this wisdom has to set out to meet him like a lover (Sir. 15.2; Wisd. 6.13–16), she even waits at his door. What she has to offer to man, indeed what she brings to man, can only be described, with the full theological weight of the word, as 'salvation benefits'. Here, all striving for success, for mastery of life, fades into silence. This invitation on wisdom's part to give oneself intellectually to her and this gift of hers to men are no longer means towards a purpose for life, they have become ends in themselves.

In order to be able to express all this, the teachers allowed themselves to be stimulated by all kinds of ideas which had their home in the intellectual life of neighbouring peoples; they could even at times take over whole passages. And yet all this was radically alienated from its original conceptual context. The fact that not only individual Egyptian concepts, but occasionally also a whole series of sentences was taken over and could be preserved in their original, unaltered wording and that these same words and sentences could be completely emptied in Israel and then filled with an essentially different content, is a hermeneutical phenomenon which has certainly not yet been studied in sufficient detail.[33] Who – apart from modern biblical scholars – in the course of meditating on Prov. 8.22ff. or Sir. 24.2ff. would ever reach the stage of thinking of the self-presentation of an Egyptian deity? Nor was the Egyptian Maat doctrine simply being complemented in Israelite terms. Here, especially, new formulations had to be found on the basis of Yahwism. One has only to remember that the idea of Maat addressing men was totally foreign to the Egyptians.[34] But this was what was the main constitutive element of the doctrine of primeval order. Without the address to men, the whole Israelite range of ideas would collapse. One can see here how deep a gulf existed between the Egyptian Maat and the range of ideas which developed in Israel (though probably not without some stimulus from Egypt). Also, the relationship between the primeval order and Yahweh had to be determined quite differently from that between Maat and the god Amun, for the primeval order belongs to the realm of creation. And finally, the personification of the primeval order on Israel's lips was neither a mythological residue which unconsciously accompanied the idea, nor, as we have already said, was it a free, poetic and didactic use of imagery. The personified image was the most precise expression available for the subject matter to be explained. Only in this form could the teachers give adequate expression to this highly remarkable thing that happened to man in his encounter with the primeval order. It was much more than simply the objective realization of such a primeval order; it was, rather, a question of crystallizing specific experiences which man had had in his encounter with it. He had experienced it not only as a static organism of order, he felt himself assailed by it, he saw it concerned about man, he experienced it as a bestower of gifts. He saw himself led by her into a confessional state in which he, within the context of his whole existence, had to come to a decision.

If we are on the right track with what we suggest, namely that the idea of the primeval order testifying to itself is connected with, perhaps even has its origin in, the old hymn-motif of creation bearing witness to itself, then this would also shed light on the independence of this subject of wisdom instruction in Israel. However many con-

---

[33] See above pp. 152f., 160.   [34] E. Otto orally.

tacts can be established between hymns in Israel and hymns in neighbouring religions, the idea of a testimony emanating from creation is attested only in Israel. The doctrine of the primeval revelation with its distinctive element – namely the address to men – stands, therefore, on a genuinely Israelite basis. It is precisely at this most significant point that the analogy with the Egyptian Maat breaks down.

On the other hand, the idea, in the form in which it was developed in the teaching of the wise men, was again fundamentally different from what was elsewhere understood by 'revelation' in Israel. The main difference consists in the fact that there is developed the doctrine of a revelatory experience which happens to men not through a specific, irreversible sign of salvation in history, but which, rather, emanates from the power of order which is held to be self-sufficient. It is this power and not, therefore, priests, prophets or actualized traditions of the saving history, that is the great mediator. Through her address, which is delivered with great topicality, and her gifts, man has an interest in Yahweh. The addressee of this revelation is not therefore an Israel summoned to Yahweh by means of a covenant relationship – Israel is never discernible here as a theological entity – but man himself (cf. Prov. 8.15f.). The transmitters of these theological concepts must surely have been men who were heavily committed as far as knowledge was concerned, cosmopolitan wisdom teachers who had been greatly stimulated by their contact with the wisdom of foreign nations. But more interesting than their dependence on this stimulus is surely their independent theological achievement.

Thus, a great arc is clearly stretched from the sentences of old practical wisdom to the doctrine of the primeval order. The reality to which every individual life is inescapably bound has in all periods stimulated men. Israel, too, experienced this stimulus and certainly not only first in the late period. Israel, too, accepted it; she did not surrender in the face of the often apparently impenetrable outward appearance of the world; rather, she did not neglect the quest for meaning, for an order effective in the world. And what did she find? The final answer which Israel was able to give was the doctrine of the primeval order. She found a mystery in the world which was turned helpfully towards her, which was to be found already on the way to her, which was already seated waiting for her at her door.

How much man feels at home in the world! Whatever happens to him from that direction simply awakens trust, bestows order and

healing. Of course, the teachers can also, in these contexts, speak of
getting lost and of death. But this does not approach man from outside;
it is the quite particular potentiality of his own inner nature. What
kind of world is this, we ask, from which nothing evil happens to
man? We shall take up this question again later (see below pp. 304ff.).

X

THE POLEMIC AGAINST IDOLS

OUR CONSIDERATIONS have now reached a point at which a discussion of the polemic against idols may fairly appropriately be inserted. This topic was unknown to the cultures neighbouring on Israel's teachers, but it nevertheless occupies considerable space in didactic texts, at least those of the later period. It is of interest for the reason that it belongs explicitly to the specifically Israelite wisdom material. On the basis of what internal and external presuppositions is this polemic to be explained, and how was it conducted? We are conscious of the fact that, with our didactic texts, we touch only a part of that debate, which flared up again and again in many places and over a wide period. Furthermore, the idol was not undisputed in the Graeco-Roman ancient world either, and, especially in the eastern church, the dispute over the use of images in the cult was waged, sometimes with subtle, theological arguments and sometimes with brutal force. We find ourselves, then, in the midst of an intellectual debate which was carried on over many centuries.[1]

> Cursed be the man who makes a graven or molten image – an abomination to Yahweh – a thing made by craftsmen's hands – and sets it up in secret. (Deut. 27.15)

This is the first prohibition of what is surely the oldest series of prohibitions in Israel, the Shechemite Dodecalogue. But this prohibition, as one can at once see, has been expanded by means of additional, interpretative elements. On the basis of the much shorter form of some of the following prohibitions, one can conclude that in its original form it probably read, 'Cursed be the man who sets up an idol in secret.' These interpretative elements are a sure sign of how inten-

---

[1] J. Geffcken, 'Der Bilderstreit des heidnischen Altertums', *Archiv f. Religionswissenschaft*, 1916–19, pp. 286ff.; H. Freiherr von Campenhausen, 'Die Bilderfrage als theologisches Problem der alten Kirche' in *Tradition und Leben*, 1960, pp. 216ff.

sively later ages, too, were concerned with this prohibition of images. The first of the two parentheses is still within the realm of sacral concepts. The formula 'an abomination to Yahweh' originally indicates the violation of a statute of the sacral law. The situation is different in the case of the second parenthesis. In so far as the idol is described as a work of human hands, this naturally also implies a negative judgment, but this judgment is from a quite different point of view. The fact that idols were manufactured by men was not, for ancient Israel, the really important thing (who else could have manufactured them?), but that behind this, there lay a specific declaration of will on the part of Yahweh. If one rejected the cultic image as absurd because a man cannot make a god, then a decisive change in the argument had already taken place, for now it was no longer the direct will of God but the logic of a secularized understanding of the world which prohibited such an activity. But it is this very argument that we shall encounter again and again from now on. When Hosea says, 'They make for themselves a molten image from their silver . . . all of it the work of craftsmen' (Hos. 13.2), and when Isaiah says, 'They worship the work of their hands' (Isa. 2.8), it is clear that already the eighth-century prophets were wholly of this way of thinking.

> The idols of the heathen are silver and gold,
>   the work of human hands.
> They have mouths but cannot speak,
>   eyes but cannot see.
> They have ears but cannot hear,
>   nor is there any breath in their mouths.
> Let those who have made them be like them,
>   everyone who puts his trust in them.   (Ps. 135.15–18)

This text is undoubtedly much later. We quote it here because, in form, it is a curse (v.18), because it has preserved still a small fraction of the old sacral idea and of its curse ceremony. Of course, the treatment of the subject matter itself is rational, to the point of tedium. But we should hold on to the fact that the idol is regarded as the object of human trust. This theme, too, that of disappointed trust, we shall encounter again.

We encounter additional references to a polemic against the manufacture and worship of idols in certain prophetic books. On one occasion in the book of Habakkuk, the use of a graven image is questioned, one that has indeed been made with precious materials but which is dumb and has no 'spirit' (Hab. 2.18f.). Similarly, Jer. 10.1–9: one need not be afraid of a piece of wood, cut in the forest and artistically worked by men. These images even have to be fastened with nails so that they do not wobble; they have to be carried because they cannot walk. How, then, could they bring about disaster and therefore have to be feared? This polemic occupies considerably more space in Deutero-Isaiah. Once again we encounter the remark that the idol is manufactured by men and has to be secured (Isa. 40.19f; 41.7). Not without grandeur is the flash which the prophet conjures up of the coming capture of Babylon; the idols will be loaded by the victors on to the beasts of burden which almost collapse under them. The gods abandon dishonourably the city which was made sacred by their presence, but which they are unable to protect, and go off into captivity (Isa. 46.1f.). The most important text is, of course, Isa. 44.9–20. Even if the arguments used here are not essentially different from those used in the passages mentioned so far, nevertheless, in this case, the literary form of the text invites attention. One could call it a satirical tract on the folly of manufacturing and worshipping idols. The theme is treated in great detail, an indication of the author's intention to present the effects in a skilful manner. The comic side of the situation is worked out here more strongly than in the other texts. We are not intended to be indignant, but to laugh at the way in which the artist is so engrossed in his work that he forgets to eat and drink and so becomes exhausted, and at how he uses half of the wood for baking and roasting, but makes the rest into a god.[2]

In spite of appearances, this theme is scarcely specifically a prophetic one. There are good reasons for regarding the texts in Habakkuk and Jeremiah as 'wisdom' interpolations. The case of Deutero-Isaiah is different, for here the polemic can be regarded to some extent as part of the total message of that prophet. But even if we attribute Isa. 44 to the prophet, though that is by no means un-contested, he is obviously following here a pattern of instruction which emanated from teachers and not originally from prophets.[3] It can be

[2] In this connection, the commentaries are fond of citing the parallel in Horace (*Satires* I, 8.1ff.) '*Truncus eram . . .*' The craftsman, uncertain whether to make it into a bench or a god, decides for the latter. More severe is the story of Amasis' basin. Used first as a spittoon and a chamber pot, it was then melted down and made into an image (Herodotus II, 172).

[3] Deut. 4.28 is to be located in roughly this same period and it, in its turn, is again related to Ps. 135.15–18. Here, too, the arguments are on exactly the same lines as in the passages so far discussed.

assumed that this polemic became current in the schools only from the period of the exile, for it was only then that Israel found herself in the midst of a religion where idols were worshipped. One should not be misled by the preponderance of mockery; those to whom these instructions were addressed were not the worshippers of the images, but Israel herself who in no circumstances was to allow herself to be influenced by the aura surrounding these great cult images.

Perhaps, however, the modern reader of this polemic should not concur in it too readily, as if the question of the rightness or wrongness of idols could be decided at that time quite as simply as might appear today. That something of the divine is revealed in the image is a point of view that has been represented with great seriousness both before and after Israel. In the religions of Israel's wider environment, images were considered to be possessed of a soul and filled with a divine aura. Men were convinced that the image was fully capable of punishing the sacrilege of those who despised and offended it.[4] Israel's voice, as that of a whole religious community, was a lone one in the ancient world. Thus, the polemic against idols was completely topical for an Israel which lived in ever closer contact with the international world. This must be kept in mind with regard to all of these texts.

It can be accepted as a matter of course that the late didactic texts, with one exception, scarcely add anything to what has already been said against the worship of cult images, namely that idols are dead and are made by men. As an example, one might cite the apocryphal story of Bel.[5] In conversation with the king of the Babylonians, Daniel denies that the god Bel actually consumes all the food which is deposited every day at the foot of his image, since he is made only of brass and clay. A wager is agreed upon. The next day both of them go to the temple which, meanwhile, has been sealed. The king believes that he has won his wager, for the food has disappeared. Daniel bursts out laughing; he had earlier had ashes scattered on the ground and is able to show to the king the footprints of the priests and their wives and children who removed the food during the night through a secret door. What is new in this almost burlesque narrative is only the fact that in this image-worship, not only is ignorance operative, but also obvious deception on the part of the priests. The so-called Letter of Jeremiah,

---

[4] K.-H. Bernhardt, *Gott und Bild*, 1956, pp. 46ff.; on the divine aura, see pp. 24ff.
[5] The narrative is one of the additions to the book of Daniel found in the LXX.

which comes, at the earliest, from the third century BC, but perhaps only from the second, also deals with the folly of image-worship.[6]

The images are dressed 'in clothes, like men; but they cannot even protect themselves from verdigris or from being eaten by worms; they are wrapped in purple garments, but they have to have wiped from their faces the dust which (is raised) in the temple and which settles particularly thickly on them.' They have to be protected against theft by means of bolts and locks; lights are lit in front of them, but they cannot see them. 'Their faces are blackened by the smoke in the temple; bats, swallows and other birds light on their bodies and even on their faces; so do cats.' 'Since they have no feet, they are carried on men's shoulders . . . and in this way they reveal to men their own ignominy. Even those who serve them must be ashamed; for if one (of the idols) falls to the ground, he has to be lifted up by them.'

(Letter of Jer. vv. 11ff.)

All this is witty enough and affords us, at the same time, a view of such cult places, for the description of images blackened by the smoke of the sacrifices and being sat upon by cats is certainly not invented. However, one cannot shut one's eyes to the fact that the intellectual foundation of this whole mode of argumentation is slight. It stands or falls on the assumption of the complete identity of deity and image. Since, however, the images are made from earthly material, the teachers found no difficulty at all in building their mockery around this fact. That this mockery avoids the serious nature of the worship of idols is obvious. What participant in a solemn procession would have taken offence at the fact that the image was carried? The obvious question as to what in fact impelled men to worship images is practically never asked. The reason is their clouded, benighted intelligence; they are led astray by evil spirits, says the Book of Jubilees.[7] The polemic is directed in remarkably schematic and unrefined fashion against the individual image. The exegete will never succeed in discovering, behind otherwise communicative texts, specific cults which

---

[6] The 'Letter of Jeremiah' appears in the Vulgate and in the Authorized (King James) Version as ch. 6 of the book of Baruch.

[7] Jubilees 11.4; 22.18. The book of Jubilees (second century BC) backdates the criticism of the idols to Israel's earliest beginnings. Already Abraham saw through the madness of idol worship in the family in which he grew up (Jubilees 11.16). Even his departure from Haran and from his family is psychologically prepared by Abraham's aversion to the idol worship in his family (Jubilees 12). Similarly, in the still later Apocalypse of Abraham: Abraham sees his father Terah planing an image; the food is cooked with the shavings. Abraham makes fun of it all (Apoc. Abr. 1–6).

might have served as models for such a polemic.[8] These texts are important to us, of course, because they make clear in negative terms, by describing what the idols cannot do, the advantage which these teachers believed Israel to have in Yahweh. He delivers (Isa. 44.17), he sets up kings and deposes them, he bestows wealth, he fulfils vows, he saves from death, rescues the weak from the strong, makes blind men see, takes pity on widows and does good to orphans (Letter of Jer. vv. 34–38).

There is a remarkable difference between all these polemics, with their fairly modest battery of arguments, and the thoughts of the Wisdom of Solomon which emerges from the Hellenistic Jewish diaspora of Alexandria (chs. 13–15).[9] Certainly here, too, the folly of worshipping images is the main theme. How foolish is the action of the sailor who worships a piece of wood which is more fragile than his ship (14.1). Similarly, the traditional theme of the manufacture of images is again taken up in considerable detail (13.10–19; 15.7–10) and yet how much more thoughtfully, in how much more refined a manner the theme is treated here. There are, first of all, those who consider the elements, that is, fire, wind, water or the stars, to be gods, whether they are influenced by their beauty or by their terror of them. Even if they cannot be excused, for they ought to have recognized the Creator in what he created, yet it can be said in their favour that they are searching for God and wish to find him (13.1–9). This mild reproach could even be levelled at the Old Testament itself, namely at Deuteronomy (4.19), where it is said, with a tolerance that is never attested anywhere else, that God himself gave the stars to the nations as objects of cultic worship. Of course, the influence of popular Stoic philosophy might have been stronger here.[10] Quite

[8] O. Eissfeldt is of the opinion that the description in the Letter of Jeremiah refers to Babylonian cults; cf. *The Old Testament. An Introduction*, ET 1965, p. 595.

[9] H. Eising, 'Der Weisheitslehrer und die Götterbilder', *Biblica* 40, 1959, pp. 393ff.

[10] F. Ricken, 'Gab es eine hellenistische Vorlage für Weisheit 13 bis 15?', *Biblica* 49, 1968, pp. 6of.

The share of Hellenistic thought in this can never be precisely defined. The use of totally un-Hebraic terms from Hellenistic popular philosophy leads first to the assumption of a whole-scale Hellenization of Hebrew concepts. Recent scholarship has abandoned this idea. Explicitly Greek terms must have been used by the author in the presentation of his Jewish heritage. O. Eissfeldt speaks of the 'thoroughly Jewish core' of the book (op. cit., p. 601). Similar opinions are expressed by Fichtner, 'Die Stellung der Sapientia Salomonis in der Literatur-und Geistesgeschichte ihrer Zeit', *ZNW* 36, 1937, pp. 113ff. and J. Geyer, *The Wisdom of Solomon*, Torch Commentary, 1963, pp. 18f. In the passage which we have cited, the stimuli of

beyond comprehension, on the other hand, is the behaviour of those who worship images made by men, that is, something lifeless (13.10–19). In this context there are also inserted thoughts about the motives which caused the artists to construct such works at all. There is, on the one hand, the striving after gain (14.2; 15.12); on the other hand, ambition may have had an effect (14.18). What is fascinating is that the writer even attempts an aetiology of the worship of images. Could such worship not have arisen when a father had a statue erected to his recently deceased child and ended by honouring it as a god? From this there developed a mystery cult, and the whole eventually became a fixed rite. Or else, perhaps the image of a ruler was set up and was then worshipped as a god by those who had never seen the ruler in the flesh (14.15–17)? But with all the flexibility of his line of thought – the satirical element is thrust almost entirely into the background by the serious way of thinking – the author judges the worship of idols basically almost as severely as the Palestinian teachers. Indeed, in one respect he even surpasses it, in that he also regards the worship of idols as the root of all moral degeneracy. But this judgment, too, is premeditated. Since the images do not have the status of gods, they are, of course, also incapable of keeping men in the true fear of God (14.12, 23–31).

Although all these texts which we have briefly discussed show, on the whole, a very unified line of thought, they do present us with one question. It is well-known that the characteristic of the Yahweh cult from the earliest period was its lack of images. According to the prohibition of images in the Decalogue and the Dodecalogue, the worship of Yahweh in the form of an image was on a par with murder, adultery or theft (Ex. 20.4f.; Deut. 27.15). Thus, it might appear as if the polemic of the wisdom teachers against any worship of images were simply a continuation of this old tradition. But things are not quite so simple. Is it not remarkable that not a single one of these polemics refers, in its argument, to this old prohibition of images? But, further, could a reference to that prohibition ever really be

---

Greek thought on the author are unmistakable. Fichtner's assertion (op. cit., p. 129) 'that the philosophical elements are only rhetorical figures' goes too far and does not do justice to the real problems in this work. A much higher evaluation is given to the Hellenistic components by C. Larcher, OP, *Etudes sur le livre de la Sagesse* (Etudes bibliques, 1969). It is difficult to define more precisely the general background of understanding against which the philosophical terms used here are to be interpreted.

connected with this type of argument? Did one need such a strong, divine prohibition to keep one from something which appeared simply laughable or at least incomprehensible? The principal argument of these polemics certainly did not lie in saying that a divine command should not be violated, a divine command which is directed sharply against a temptation which is inherent in human worship, but, as we have seen, in an appeal to sound, human intelligence. Basically, it requires no great effort in order to make clear the folly and ridiculousness of the worship of images as this appeared to the teachers; it was, after all, a truth which each one would have to see for himself. But this was certainly not how the ancient prohibition of images understood itself. What deadly earnestness hangs over the narrative of the so-called golden calf (Ex. 32)! Here, as the narrator sees it, there is still a real threat. Israel – left alone by Moses only a short while before – immediately asked for a cultic image. She has yielded to a temptation and has thereby seriously disturbed her relationship with her God. An appeal to sound, human intelligence would have been out of place here, for the narrative still presupposes a concept of cult and sacral reality which was determinative for the religiosity of the whole of the ancient Near East and which could certainly not be tackled by means of a simple appeal to reason. In the whole atmosphere of the narrative of the golden calf, Israel was still far removed from Daniel's superior laughter (Bel v. 5).

How is this transition from a cultic prohibition to a completely rational method of argument to be explained? There is no doubt that the ancient Israelite prohibition of images proclaims, even if still within a completely sacral sphere, a specific, exclusive idea of the relationship of Yahweh to the conditions in Israel's environment. Indeed, it can be assumed that the prohibition of images was not the first expression of this idea; the prohibition itself is already a concentrated expression of a sacral understanding of the world whose specific quality lies in the fact that there must not be linked with it any pictorial representation of the deity, anything of the nature of a self-manifestation of god-like powers.[11] The knowledge that Yahweh transcends the world theologically must surely have been substantiated by the very first experiences of Yahweh which Israel ever had. This, as we have said, completely sacral and cultic range of ideas about a world which was incapable of offering any figure as a representation

[11] G. von Rad, 'Some Aspects of the Old Testament World-View', in *The Problem of the Hexateuch and Other Essays*, ET 1966, pp. 144ff.

of God also became of immense importance for the understanding of the world in later Israel too, for the simple reason that not only did it persevere, through all the attacks of enlightenment, and arrive at a rational understanding of the world, but also it changed at the same time. We have, then, the interesting case of an originally religio-sacral concept of the relationship of God to the world being accepted by reason and finally helping to construct a rational picture of the world, a picture of impressive clarity. At that point it was also possible to bring into service the arguments of a purely rational way of thought. The mode of argument used by the teachers, and of which we have spoken, is therefore neither free-thinking in the sense of an enlightenment which is basically unfavourable to religion; nor, much less, is it philosophical in the sense of a separation of the material from the spirituality of the deity. It is, in the last resort, still a theological one in that it denies to the creature the possibility of providing a representation of the Creator. The argument that the worship of images is foolish because the true Creator can be recognized in what he has created, is expressed nowhere so explicitly as in the Wisdom of Solomon (13.1-9); it is, however, no real novelty, if we recall the doctrine of the self-revelation of creation, which was discussed in the preceding section, especially its wooing voice directed at men. Whoever understood the world in this way – so full of testimony, full of evidence for the Creator – for him the erection of an image of God made out of the elements of creation was real folly. With this conception of the relationship of God to the world, Israel definitively separated herself from the cults of the surrounding nations and showed herself more and more incapable of doing justice to these cults. But is this total inability on Israel's part to understand any form of image worship not also a phenomenon?

XI

WISDOM AND CULT (EXCURSUS)

WHILE THE TEACHERS inveighed against worshipping God in images, a practice which, in their opinion, was basically wrong, it must actually have been, in these contexts, but a short step to saying something, as opposed to these offences, about what was considered in Israel to be worship fitting for God. Is it not amazing that these polemics continue so entirely in negative terms, as if there were nothing more to be said on the positive side? This is surely a sign that the existence of idols was, for the teachers, basically not a cultic problem, but – expressed perhaps not inappropriately in our language – a question of a philosophy of life. If this polemic were to be understood as cultic in the narrower sense, then at some point the idols would have to emerge as rivals of Yahweh, rivals who threaten Yahweh's exclusive claim to cultic worship. But cultic matters, with all their complex questions, have never been among the subjects of the wise men's teaching, and we have therefore no real reason, at this point where we are dealing with individual 'subjects of instruction', to append a section on wisdom and cult.

However, there are a handful of sentences in which, for example, the prayer of the righteous is preferred to the sacrifice of the ungodly (Prov. 15.8; 21.27), just as a piece of dry bread is preferred to a house full of sacrificial meat and strife (Prov. 17.1); men are warned against being too hasty in making vows (Prov. 20.25), and it is affirmed that even a man's prayer is of no avail if he is incapable of listening in life (Prov. 28.9). Along the same lines, there is also Sir. 34.19f., where the sacrifice of the ungodly is subjected to criticism especially when it includes some of the property of the poor. If someone purifies himself and then makes himself ritually unclean again, what was the point of the purification (Sir. 34.25)? But in all this, the concern is not with the cultic, but with human presuppositions which are indispensable for cultic participation. Do not construct the approach to cultic acts out of actions which are devoid of order. The way in which cultic matters can be discerned here on the fringe of the instructions is, of course, interesting, for here cultic activity appears purely as a completely personal concern of the individual. It depends upon the individual's resolve and is threatened by all the dangers which could rise up against it from the individual sphere (undue haste, lack of moral preparation, etc.). The patriarchal world of the cult is shattered by the category of the personal. Nevertheless, these sentences show that the teachers addressed men who had cultic obligations. In the Letter of Aristeas (142–171; *c.* 130 BC), the boldest attempt is made to disintegrate the old ritual ordinances by humanizing, moralizing and symbolizing means. The rules for purification and for sacrifice which were made binding in the Mosaic law symbolize human attributes or types of behaviour. But the ordinances are recognized as such and admired. Certainly these Diaspora Jews, if they ever came to Jerusalem, took part in the great cultic celebrations in the temple. If the spiritual conceptions of the cult in the Letter of Aristeas mark an extreme point of view, they nevertheless show us how difficult it is to draw a line between an 'unbroken' and a 'broken' relationship to the cult. In any case, what do we really know about the thoughts, in so far as they thought at all, of those who participated in the Jerusalem cult in, say, the year 600 or the year 400?

A further conclusion can be drawn directly from the teachings of the wise men. We occasionally hear terms which originally had their roots in the cult but which are now all used in a very generalized, moralized or intellectualized sense.[1] The question is simply what conclusions can be drawn from such an altered use of language. Two possibilities, which are to some extent mutually exclusive, offer themselves. The wise men had, intellectually, outgrown the world of cultic action. Expressions which were essentially part of the cultic world could then be used by the wise men, if at all, only in a new sense, one which had been 'spiritualized' and transferred to other spheres of life. One would then have to speak of a broken relationship of the wise men to the cult.[2] It is more reasonable to find the cause of the gulf between the wise men and things cultic quite simply in the sphere of

---

[1] Thus it is said, e.g., that pleasant words are 'pure' in Yahweh's eyes (*ṭāhōr*, Prov. 15.26), that guilt is atoned for by means of love (*kippēr*, Prov. 16.6), that a wise man 'atones for', 'covers' the king's anger (Prov. 16.14). The verb *'ākar* – attested otherwise only in the sense of 'to make taboo' – means 'destroy' in the sentences (Prov. 11.17, 29; 15.6, 27).

[2] H. H. Schmid, op. cit., p. 53.

duty to which the teachers felt themselves committed. They were not priests and one cannot, therefore, expect anything else than that cultic expressions were at their disposal only in that humanized, generalized sense in which they stood transformed in everyday language. The cultic sphere always leaves a linguistic deposit in everyday speech, and the use of such a linguistic deposit certainly indicates no acknowledgement of the cult and no programmatic position with regard to it. In the interest which the wise men had in relations between men, there was no opportunity at all for using the expressions in their original cultic meaning. Thus it is by no means a foregone conclusion either that the teachers intended these expressions to be understood only in this new sense. The question about their relationship to the cult cannot, therefore, be answered on the basis of this material. There remains, therefore, only the sentence, 'To do righteousness and justice is more pleasing to Yahweh than sacrifice' (Prov. 21.3). But a rejection of the cult cannot be deduced from this either.[3] The fact that it separates ethical and cultic actions, that it is capable of weighing the one against the other in such a way that one can actually put a higher value on ethical actions, all this is an expression of a decidedly enlightened intellectualism. This brings us once again face to face with the question of the intellectual and religious background to which the teachings of the wise men belonged and apart from which they cannot be correctly understood.[4] Unquestionably we are in danger of understanding this background in terms which are too modern and too 'intellectual' and of failing to recognize the possibilities of an ancient world of ideas.

Since, in this book, we are basically concerned only with questions which arise directly from the didactic materials themselves and from the tensions in which these operated, there is no 'wisdom and cult' problem discernible at all within this framework. This is not, of course, to deny that, in a broader sense, there is a 'wisdom and cult' problem, which is, indeed, still unresolved. What was the relationship between the wise men's desire for knowledge, which began from the fear of Yahweh, and the traditions of the cultic officials? Both, each in their own way, were aware of order and worked to achieve an awareness of that order.[5] This question could only gradually be brought nearer to solution by means of a careful and thorough examination of all

---

[3] H.-J. Hermisson, *Sprache und Ritus im altisraelitischen Kult*, 1965, pp. 123f.
[4] See above pp. 32f.
[5] See above pp. 164f., 173f.; see below, pp. 289, 295, 314.

possible source material, and this would go well beyond the limits of our discussion. It may, however, be mentioned that the connections between wisdom and the hymn are numerous. Here, it was the wise men who did the borrowing.[6] But the connection with the individual psalm of thanksgiving is also striking. Here, with an inclination to sentence-like phraseology, the situation is reversed. The cultic psalm utilizes wisdom forms of expression, a fact which is not, of course, very surprising, for whenever the individual wished to deliver himself of a solemn speech, this pregnant type of expression was available to him.[7]

[6] The question of the connections between wisdom and the hymn will need to be re-examined in the light of F. Crüsemann's convincing distinction between 'imperative' and 'participial' hymns; cf. F. Crüsemann, *Studien zur Formgeschichte von Hymnus und Danklied in Israel*, 1969. The participial hymn can be found partly in the prophetic books (sometimes as a style adopted by the prophet, sometimes in the form of interpolations). Otherwise we encounter it in the book of Job. From the point of view of content it is determined by a persistent theme: God's wonders in creation, his rule in the events of nature and his sovereign shaping of human destinies. Both in style and motif, this type of hymn is found throughout the ancient Near East. A setting in the cult of pre-exilic Israel can only be deduced as probable. The great mass of material is rather to be thought of as a specific type of literary poetry, cultivated in specific circles. From there, the step to the use of this hymnic style in long didactic poems is but a short one. A direct relationship with the world of the cult would no longer exist.

[7] E.g., Ps. 32.1f., 10; 40.5f.; 41.2; 118.8; etc.

XII

TRUST AND ATTACK

I. THE BASIS OF TRUST

IN THE PRECEDING discussions, much has been said about experiences gained and perceptions achieved. This has made it increasingly clear what a great difference there is between this search for knowledge and the search for knowledge which determines our present-day relationship to the world. Israel's search for knowledge did not approach objects in an objective and cautious way simply in order to range itself with them in one way or another. The objects to which her knowledge addressed itself did not allow a man to adopt an objective spectator's role. They compelled commitment, they demanded, astonishing as this may seem to us moderns, man's complete trust. Only with the presupposition of the giving of complete trust could life, as it faced men, be hazarded. This question was a real, live issue wherever the wise men spoke. And the teachers left their pupils in no doubt as to what was at stake in this undertaking; it was nothing less than the gaining or losing of 'life'.[1] Their didactic sentences demanded commitment and, accordingly, they had, implicitly or explicitly, the character of acknowledgments of orders which were experienced as beneficent because they bestowed life. The basic attitude towards a reality experienced in this way was thus, in the last resort, one of complete trust. In this trust the teachers knew that they were absolutely secure. It is quite impossible to discern in their teachings any feeling of insecurity such as might be experienced in the face of a great risk, or even an uneasiness such as might be experienced when abandoned to some dark unknown. On what, however, did the teachers base themselves when they sought to convince a pupil beyond all doubt that he would be successful in tackling life?

For the answer to this question, one will, of course, in the first

[1] E. Schmitt, *Leben in den Weisheitsbüchern Job, Sprüche und Jesus Sirach*, 1954.

place, turn to those sentences which speak quite explicitly of trust in God and of the advantage of such an attitude.

Whoever pays heed to the word finds prosperity,
and happy is he who trusts in Yahweh.   (Prov. 16.20)

The greedy man stirs up quarrels;
but he who trusts in Yahweh will be satisfied.   (Prov. 28.25)

Fear of men brings ensnarement;
but he who trusts in Yahweh is protected.   (Prov. 29.25)

Trust in Yahweh with all your heart,
and do not rely on your own insight.   (Prov. 3.5)

To these may be added similar sentences:

In the fear of Yahweh lies the trust of the strong man,
and to his children it is a refuge.   (Prov. 14.26)

Commit what you do to Yahweh,
then your plans will succeed.   (Prov. 16.3)

The name of Yahweh is a strong tower,
to which the righteous run for protection.   (Prov. 18.10)

These are fine, important sentences, but one cannot maintain that they provide an immediate answer to our basic question for, even if one were to enlarge their circle, which would be possible, they are, nevertheless, fairly isolated and certainly have no programmatic significance for the teachings as a whole, to the extent that one could see in them any hint of more to come. To express it more pointedly, if this handful of sentences about trust in God were missing, it would make no decisive difference to the material with which we have to deal. It would scarcely shatter the optimism which lies behind all the teachings of the wise men. In any case, what the teachers have to say about trust in God must be interpreted still more precisely on the basis of their own specific ideas. This must be our next task.

In answer to our question about the optimism, the trust on which their teachings are based, the wise men, if we have understood them more or less correctly, would probably have pointed, not in general terms to the advantages of trusting in God, but to something apparently quite different, namely the reality and the evidence of the order which controls the whole of life, much as this appeared in the act-consequence relationship. This order was, indeed, simply there and could, in the last resort, speak for itself. The fact that it quietly but reliably worked towards a balance in the ceaselessly changing state of human relationships ensured that it was experienced over and over again as a beneficent force. In it, however, Yahweh himself was at work in so far as he defended goodness and resisted evil. It was he who was present as an ordering and upholding will in so far as he gave a beneficent stability to life and kept it open to receive his blessings.[2] Thus, for example, Eliphaz concludes his first great reply to Job with the summary statement, 'Look, we have examined this, and that is how it is' (Job 5.27). This evidence was all the more forceful because these sentences were not dealing with an individual's subjective concept of what was true. If they had been, they would have lacked any ultimate binding force; for in order to contribute a valid knowledge of experience, the span of an individual life is much too short; it requires the reflection and the sifting of generations. The legitimacy and worth of these teachings really resides primarily in the fact that they are validated by a long teaching tradition.

> Do you not know this from of old,
>   since he set men upon the earth,
> that the rejoicing of the godless is of short duration,
>   the joy of those who forget God lasts but a moment?   (Job 20.4f.)

> But inquire of past generations,
>   'pay attention' to what the fathers found out,
> for we are of yesterday and know nothing;
>   our days on earth are but a shadow.
> Will they instruct you and tell you
>   and declare words from their heart?   (Job 8.8–10)

> Do not despise what the aged hand on to you,
>   for they too learned from their fathers.   (Sir. 8.9)

> I will declare it to you; listen to me.
>   I will tell you what I saw,
> what the wise men proclaim
>   and what 'their fathers' taught 'them',
> who alone occupied the land,
>   to whom still no stranger came.   (Job 15.17–19)

The last of these four texts is interesting in so far as it shows that the wise men did not simply accept the traditions uncritically, but made

---

[2] In the didactic model, Job 8.11–21, the 'godless' man is reproached with living in false security. His trust is 'a spider's web'; 'he leans against his house, but it does not stand; he holds fast to it, but it does not stay standing' (Job 8.14f.). It is unlikely that what is being referred to here is a lack of trust in God as we would understand it.

distinctions. The completely pure traditions are the old ones which are still uncontaminated by foreign influences. If we knew what was meant by these foreign influences from which Eliphaz dissociates himself, then we would be able to make a substantial contribution towards the highly problematic reconstruction of the development of doctrines within Israelite wisdom.

The following is now clear. The credibility of the wise men's teachings consisted in the fact that they dealt with perceptions and experiences which had achieved definitive expression in the course of a long, careful development. Trust in life and, in the last resort, in Yahweh could, therefore, so the teachers were convinced, be supported by specific perceptions and experiences. This perhaps somewhat surprising theory is amply confirmed by the little prologue which prefaces the collection of sentences in Prov. 22.17–24.22.

> Incline your ear and hear 'my' words,
>   and apply your mind to 'knowledge',
> for it is pleasant if you keep them within you,
>   like a 'tent peg' they will stick on your lips.
> So that you may place your trust in Yahweh,
>   I proclaim to you today 'his ways'. (Prov. 22.17–19)

We know that in this collection, and also in the preface to it, an Israelite teacher has copied fairly exactly an Egyptian model.[3] It is all the more remarkable that the passage about 'trust' has nothing corresponding to it in the Egyptian text. It is obviously a form of words which the Israelite teacher has put in the place of a very general, pedagogical remark. But precisely this correction contributed by Israel is of interest to us. Set in programmatic fashion at the head of a whole collection of proverbs, it states that the aim of the teachings that now follow is to establish trust in Yahweh. If one gives oneself to the proffered perceptions and experiences; then trust in Yahweh can only grow; a man can hear them say to him that he lives in a world in which he does not need to be afraid. In order correctly to grasp the extent of this trust, we must once again recall how Israel understood this experiential reality to which she was incessantly exposed. She knew, as we have seen, only a homogeneous environment which was determined by divine ordinances and decrees. Events in this environment did not follow a rigid system of laws; they were, rather, turned towards man, encouraging and suppressing in a highly

[3] See above p. 9.

active manner; they were, that is, always a part of direct, divine activity towards man. If this experiential reality could only be approached, from the point of view of acquiring knowledge of it, from the direction of knowledge of God, then knowledge of the world could, in turn, also consolidate knowledge of God. The statement that the fear of God is the beginning of wisdom could even be turned round, to the effect that knowledge and experience lead to the fear of God.

> My son, if you accept my words
>   and keep by you what I command you. . . .
> then you will understand the fear of Yahweh
>   and will find knowledge of God.   (Prov. 2.1, 5)

For Israel, there was no insight which did not imply trust, faith, but there was also no faith which did not rest on insights.[4] It is interesting that even this 'theological' wisdom which we allow to speak here, held fast to this constitutive role of reason.

> Look on previous generations and see:
>   Who trusted in the Lord and was ruined?
> Or who persevered in the fear of him and was abandoned?
>   Or who called to him, and he overlooked him?   (Sir. 2.10)

What is being discussed here is the question of God's faithfulness. Does he not, nevertheless, leave in the lurch those who cling to him? This difficult question is answered, not, as would have been possible and as we would, at any rate, rather expect, by a reference to the self-revelation of God, but by a reference to the experience of many generations, that is, by means of a rational insight. This is how God is shown to be worthy of trust. The statement quoted, which is, after all, concerned with the central question of faith, is a paradigm of the role which Israel accorded to experience even in matters of knowledge of God and trust in God. It would be a good thing in the first place simply to take from the teachers this concept of theirs; it would at any rate be better than to attribute to them at the outset a basic error on the basis of a definition, familiar to us, of the relationship of reason to faith. We shall have to accept that a comprehensive and critically examined knowledge was accumulated by the wise men, knowledge which set up many warning signs in the direction of the limits imposed upon it, but which, in accordance with its ultimate intention, nevertheless suggested complete trust in the reliability of

---

4 See above p. 69.

the order and, at the same time, trust in God who put that order into operation and who was operative in it. It is in this way that the question, which we asked above, about the meaning of 'trust in God' is to be answered.

2. ANSWERS TO EXPERIENCES OF SUFFERING

While we may hope that in all this we have correctly grasped an important aspect of the ancient Israelite understanding of reality, no one, on the other hand, will think that this understanding of reality is a completely closed circle of ideas into which every possible occurrence imaginable can be effortlessly slotted. At this point, exegetes have taken the easy road and have attributed to the teachers the crudest rationalism, whose short-circuited arguments could not be concealed from even the most unpretentious mind. The situation was precisely the same in Israel, too. Wherever man sets out to know his world, he remains in the last resort in conflict with the objects of his knowledge. His calculations are never ended; he must always express what is known in new terms. Indeed, that which evades calculation, the absolute puzzle, is never one and the same thing; every time, rather, it appears differently. The search for knowledge, which manifests itself in every age, has its specific area of confidence and sees itself forced to capitulate before specific limits.

Our concept of Israel's wisdom is still encumbered by a remarkably constructive theory. Old Israel, it is said, happily resolved the anguish of her existence by means of her faith in her God. Then, however, came the wise men who, with theories alien to life – especially with their 'doctrine of retribution' – constructed a doctrinaire system which could only end in theological catastrophe. One should not, of course, think that in the early period Israel was immune to attacks and could rest secure in her faith and not feel the need of such explanatory theories. The puzzle, the threat to life was experienced in every age. In this respect, the situation of the theological teachers was not new. The reaction to the many threats could appear in very varied ways in the early periods, too. It could be satisfied with the almost fatalistic commonplace that, after all, all men must die and that they are like 'spilt water' which cannot be gathered up again (II Sam. 14.14). It could also lead to the tremendous statement of resignation, 'It is Yahweh; let him do what seems good to him' (I Sam. 3.18). But beyond this, the question 'Why?' had also long since led to insights into specific contexts, especially those of sin and suffering, of guilt and punishment, insights with which we see Israel occupied in the very earliest period. The awareness of the act-consequences relationship was one of the most basic perceptions. Particularly in the case of monstrous human crimes, it was known that, sooner or later, disaster would return to the person who had committed it. One should realize that the whole prophetic proclamation of disaster rests upon this awareness. The prophets applied it to the lives of individuals; a man is punished in the measure in which he sins. But, above all, they extend this perception to the lives of the nations which, in their opinion, would have to perish because of their own guilt and pride.

Of course, the insight into the act-consequence relationship was certainly not a general conclusion, at any rate not for the smaller adversities of life. But it was rooted so deeply in the consciousness that great disorders such as national disasters immediately raise the retrospective question of a corresponding guilt, and this led, in the great cultic fasts, to a revision of the relationship of the cultic community to God and to solemn confessions of sin. Similarly, in the life of an individual, sometimes a severe illness could give rise to such a confession of sin, e.g. a so-called judgment doxology. The situation would be as follows. Behind such cultic performances there lay a calamity which inspired men with terror. As such, it was not unambiguous; all that was known was that it came from God and was intended for those who were afflicted by it. It was only the way of thinking occasioned by the disaster, perhaps a specific cultic inquiry, that connected it with a guilty deed and, very soon, with a quite specific guilty deed. This retrospective question from a severe disturbance in life back to a guilty action behind it, of which the friends of Job have always been harshly accused, did not, therefore, arise from the doctrinaire reflections of committed theologians, but had its roots in ancient and universally valid concepts. The defeat which Israel suffered at the city of Ai forced Joshua to turn to Yahweh. As a consequence of this, he first discovered the terrible sin committed by Achan (Josh. 7.6ff.). Yahweh's silence in response to an oracle sought from him could only have its reason in an as yet unknown sin (I Sam. 14.38ff.). Particularly clear is the sequence of events in the narrative in II Sam. 21. The events are begun by a three-year famine. David enquired of Yahweh and found out that blood guilt still lay on the house of Saul. He immediately made arrangements to expiate the country's guilt. The seamen in the Jonah story, too, connect – correctly, in the narrator's opinion – the great storm with a grave sin which must be discovered (Jonah 1.4ff.). Indeed, man is always guilty with respect to the deity, and for this reason a meeting with a man of God, for example, also has its dangers because he could 'bring to God's remembrance' hidden sin, the existence of which was never doubted (I Kings 17.18). We are already led into very close proximity to the Job problem by sentences from certain laments of the individual.

> There is no soundness in my body because of your wrath,
>   no soundness in my bones because of my sin,
> for my offences have grown over my head,
>   like a heavy burden they are too heavy for me.   (Ps. 38.4f.)
>
> I said, 'Yahweh, be gracious to me;
>   heal me, for I have sinned against you.'   (Ps. 41.5)

Here, suppliants are speaking out of a situation of severe illness, and here, too, from all that we know of these texts, it was a great disturbance at the root of life which forced those who were afflicted by it to a confession of their sins. According to Elihu, illness is one of the means used by God to turn towards a man and warn him (Job 33.14, 19ff.).

If one tries to determine the specific place of the theological efforts of the wisdom teachers, then one must not imagine that they had built up their world of ideas entirely on their own. They, too, lived within the Yahwistic tradition and shared fully, in their own way, in the freedom and the burdens which Yahwism gave to man. Their situation was a peculiar one only in so far as they held a teaching office. They stood in relationship to the sufferings of men and to all the adversities of men more as observers, and considered that they were called to mobilize every possible means of reaching understanding. In order to be able to reach perceptions of a more general nature here, they had to achieve a certain distance from individual adversities. To this end, the counting up of many experiences with individual sufferers and a careful sifting of what had been perceived were necessary until, with reference to the varied nature of the sufferings which afflicted men, specific rules, specific truths of universal validity could be determined. It was their duty to draw up, on the basis of the great number of experiences, definite theories about suffering, its origin and its function with regard to men, and to form them into easily-remembered rules. It is superfluous to add that this activity was an exacting one, threatened by the danger of shielding oneself from life with theories that had been deduced from life. Nor, as we shall see, did this activity reach an end or come to any unambiguous result. One had better, therefore, not speak of optimism or pessimism, for, precisely in the older sentence-wisdom, one can determine, in the attempt to control the contingent factor, a sometimes almost uncannily clear knowledge of the limits of human understanding and a knowledge of the ambiguity of phenomena.

If we intend, in what follows, to examine the explanations which the teachers were able to give for the problem of human suffering, then it is useful to think about the sphere within which these various interpretations were able to operate. It was, in fact, comparatively limited. Israel did not, even in its later wisdom, attempt to achieve anything like a total understanding of the world and of life. We see her still only occupied in confirming partial perceptions and in developing further on such a basis. But, one might ask, was Israel, as a result of her belief in a creator God (freed from the fear of demons), and of her awareness of the oneness of creation, not provided with a marvellous principle of order for which the presuppositions did not exist in the other religions of the ancient Near East? There is nothing in the ancient Near East comparable to the doctrine of the unity of all creation or to the doctrine of the unity of all mankind in Gen. 10. The reason why the teachers in Israel did not go on from there and try to achieve, on that basis and from the partial perceptions, at least the outlines of a total knowledge of the world, why assessments which might have been useful to her lay unused, can, of course, only be answered hypothetically. One can scarcely look for the reason simply in a lack of logical deduction. We shall have to assume that it was possible for Israel to take this step to practicable conclusions because of all the decidedly non-speculative presuppositions on which her understanding of the world was built. We have already mentioned how deeply her world was also involved in the mystery of God, a mystery by which even the most firmly-based knowledge was threatened. And was the position of man in the world as a creature among creatures not established in such a way that he could never take up either an entirely objective position in relation to the world or the position of a mere observer? It was the way in which he was tied to the experiential basis of his knowledge which prevented him from moving towards any type of gnosis. Thus, here too, we see Israel, in spite of a faith which encompassed the world, at the mercy of the adversities of life as if she were engaged in defensive warfare rather than provided with the weapon of a comprehensive idea of the world. The unity of the world was experienced by Israel not in the realm of pure speculation, but somewhere completely different, namely in the hymn, in which all creatures join with each other. All this should be kept in mind if one wishes to pass a fair judgment on the position of the wisdom teachers, on their perception and, at the same time, on their awareness of the limits imposed on their knowledge. They were neither superficially rationalistic nor doctrinaire, alienated from life and ready with an answer for every question. They stood, as we have said, in that forward line of human experiential knowledge, where it was a question of finding a meaning for life, but where one also risked the loss of meaning. As long as it was merely a question here of discovering laws which existed, so to speak, within society and which were discernible within the context of community life, this struggle was indeed exciting; but even setbacks, even the discovery of contradictions, did not seriously affect faith in God. It was different when it was a question of the evaluation of experiences which a man, under God's control, had had on his own. Here the discovery of contradictory experiences must have had a more disturbing effect. If, in this sphere, experiences were ambiguous or even contradicted each other, then, in view of the important and basic role which experience had in Israel, even in religious matters, faith in God and in his rule could be seriously threatened.

Of course, faith is not shaken or even broken by every attack. It knows that much that is incalculable has to be attributed to the freedom of God. 'Who can say to him, "What are you doing?"' [5] And, in addition, many occurrences, in the opinion of the wise men, could in no sense escape explanation. We shall say no more here about the act-consequence relationship. Even for the later theological teachers this insight was unassailable. But already the didactic Joseph story is concerned to let its readers see in what a strange way a crime which has been committed can follow men down through the years and can eventually catch up with them. Because the brothers terrified Joseph so much, they in turn must now be terrified of him. [6] They did, of course, realize this without, however, really getting to the bottom of the connection. But the point of the story is not exhausted once it has shown the correspondence between sin and suffering. It is unique, in that in it several possibilities of explanation sound contrapuntally. For there is also the thought of purification. The brothers' sufferings

[5] II Sam. 16.10; Job 9.12; Dan. 4.32; Wisd. 12.12.   [6] Gen. 42.21.

are caused by Joseph. Twice Joseph manoeuvres them with uncanny skill into a situation where he gives them the opportunity of betraying yet another brother. But the brothers stand the test. Furthermore, however, the most important factor in the whole event was that in all the calamity and confusion, miraculously, a beneficent divine plan was at work. What was planned as evil, he turned to good (Gen. 50.20). Not only did God have an overall hand in the situation, but in the evil, a divine guiding force succeeded in bringing about deliverance (Gen. 45.5). Such a bold mixture of divine activity and guilty human deeds was never attempted again by the teachers.

But also in the case of sufferings which are not caused by any recognizable sin, that is, which affected men for apparently no comprehensible reason, a very solemn explanation presented itself to man's search for knowledge. In such sufferings, God is secretly, but in the end clearly, pursuing the task of training men. The idea that God organizes, in the life of the individual, a beneficent training – the idea of its being a testing is closely related to this – occupies in the Old Testament only a limited space. It is, for example, almost wholly foreign to the struggles of the suppliants with their sufferings in the psalms of lament.[7] On the other hand, the wisdom teachers take up the theme gladly. Since they themselves were concerned with the training of men and thought so highly of its usefulness, it is understandable that the idea of divine training or correction through suffering was particularly cultivated by them.[8]

> Happy is the man whom God rebukes.
>   Do not despise the discipline of the Almighty,
> for it is he who wounds and who binds up,
>   who smites, but his hands heal.
> In six troubles he will deliver you,
>   and in seven no harm will touch you.   (Job 5.17–19)
>
> Yahweh's discipline, my son, do not refuse it . . .
> For whom Yahweh loves, he rebukes,
>   and he allows the son whom he loves to suffer.   (Prov. 3.11f.)
>
> The crucible is for silver and the furnace for gold;
>   but the one who tests hearts is Yahweh.   (Prov. 17.3)
>
> My son, if you come forward to serve the Lord,
>   be prepared for temptations . . .

---

[7] Ps. 118.18.
[8] Prov. 4.13; 13.1; 13.24; 19.18; 23.13; 29.15, 17; Sir. 2; 4.17; 18.13; 23.2; 31.10; 36.

Gold is tested in fire,
    but the man who pleases God in the furnace of suffering.   (Sir. 2.1, 5)

Here the disturbing element, that which threatens life, is wholly incorporated in a great trust in the rule of God who, even in sufferings, pursues beneficent intentions. In this business, God has numerous means at his disposal. Sometimes he warns a man in terrifying nocturnal visions, at other times 'he rebukes him' by means of pains, loss of appetite, loss of strength (Job 33.15f., 19ff.). If one speaks of training through suffering, one must also ask what the aim of such training is. It is certainly not some form of 'sanctification' or the renunciation of the good things of life. In the text just mentioned, Job's friend is thinking of a return to God, to prayer and to cultic confession. 'Return', however, means restoration of the original status, return to the community which God has provided for men.[9] Training, then, presupposes that the life of the man in question was not in order. It was offered in order to 'turn man aside from his deed and wipe out his pride' (Job 33.17). More simply and more impressively, Eliphaz shows how the life of the man who accepts correction returns once more to God's blessing; for if he is in a right relationship with God, then every single adversity turns to good.

You are hidden 'from' the scourge of the tongue,
    and do not need to fear devastation when it comes.
Even with the stones of the field you are in league,
    and with the wild beasts you have an agreement.
You will find that your tent is secure;
    if you inspect your pasture ground, you will miss nothing.
In ripe old age you will come to your grave,
    as one brings in sheaves at the right time.   (Job. 5.21, 23f., 26)

In a notably different way, Jesus Sirach has divided up this occurrence into separate actions. First of all, the divine wisdom is hidden from men. She inflicts harsh discipline on them; in the end, there is enrichment in the revelation of hidden knowledge.

. . . for she walks in disguise with him,
    she brings fear and despair upon him
and she tests him by means of her discipline
        until she can trust him,
    and she tempts him with her statutes (?).

[9] H. W. Wolff, 'Das Thema "Umkehr" in der alttestamentlichen Prophetie', *Gesammelte Studien*, 1964, p. 153.

> But then she comes to him by a straight path again
> and gladdens him
> and reveals to him her secrets.   (Sir. 4.17–18)

Thus, trust in God and in the efficacy of his orders had a wide range of activity and could provide strength to enable men to bear life and to persevere.[10] But even when a man could not explicitly regard adversity as a disciplinary activity on God's part, there was always yet another possibility whereby one could hold fast to faith, that of waiting, of 'hoping in Yahweh'.

> Do not say, 'I will repay evil.'
> Hope in Yahweh, and he will help you.   (Prov. 20.22)

> Be still before Yahweh and hope in him.
> . . . those who wait for Yahweh shall possess the land.
> Wait for Yahweh and keep to his way.   (Ps. 37.7, 9, 34)

> Trust in the Lord and he will care for you;
> hope in him, and he will make your way smooth.   (Sir. 2.6)

Hope is simply man's lot; all men hope, good and evil alike (Prov. 10.28; 11.23). One can never judge life in accordance with the appearance of the moment, but one must keep 'the end' in view. This important term, which is so characteristic of thinking which is open to the future, cannot always have referred to death.[11] One can also translate the word by 'future'. What is meant, therefore, is the outcome of a thing, the end of an event for which one hopes.[12] If, of course, Job's

---

[10] Historical reminiscences, too (though in simplified form), are illuminated by this type of interpretation. Past periods of distress were tests made by God; he has acted in this way from the very beginning. 'On account of all these things, let us give thanks to the Lord our God who has tested us as he did our fathers. Remember what he did with Abraham and how he tempted Isaac and all that happened to Jacob in Syrian Mesopotamia when he was keeping the sheep of his mother's brother Laban. For he has not punished us as he tested them to search their hearts, but the Lord disciplines those who are near him in order to teach them' (Jud. 8.25–27). The idea of Jacob, when with Laban, being 'tested' by God is an aspect of which the Genesis tradition was unaware. But already in Ex. 20.20 the Sinai event is interpreted as a 'temptation', a 'trial'. Ecclesiastes has provided a hideous caricature of this idea, which was becoming more and more central, of a divine testing, for he regards the serious ravages wrought in judicial life as a 'test' (really a 'sifting') imposed by God on men 'to show them that they are like cattle' (Eccles. 3.18). God's testing, then, serves to show man his futility.

[11] Not, at any rate, in the sentence, which is certainly borrowed from wisdom circles, Jer. 17.11: 'In the middle of his days he must leave it (his wealth) and at his end he appears as a fool'.

[12] Prov. 23.18; 24.14, 20.

complaint were true, that God destroys even man's hope, then this
would be a really terrifying perception (Job 14.19; 19.10)

Again, the attack assumed a different form when the disturbing
experience was discernible less in one's own life than in the lives of
others; when men whose ties with Yahweh were, to say the least,
decidedly questionable, were obviously blessed by God, and when
even those who placed their whole trust in him, lacked this blessing.
In such cases it was more difficult simply to surrender oneself to the
divine will, and even the idea of discipline was no longer sufficient.
The problem was pushed more and more on to the level of theoretical
reflection. It is clear that a faith which attempted, in such an intensive fashion, to examine experience and tried to see its validity confirmed by that experience, would have to face this problem. Then,
of course, this faith often resulted in a 'bigotry' about which the teachers warned. The most obvious answer to such questions was: Wait; you
cannot see the 'end' yet (*'aḥᵃrît* = that which comes after, the future).

> Do not grow heated at the wicked,
>   do not fly into a rage at the ungodly,
> for the wicked man has no future (*'aḥᵃrît*),
>   the light of the ungodly goes out. (Prov. 24.19f.)

> Do not grow heated at him for whom everything prospers,
>   at the man who carries out evil plans. (Ps. 37.7)

There are three great poems in the Psalter which are wholly
determined by these questions and which, for this very reason, must
be understood as didactic wisdom poems.[13] They deal with the problem of the good fortune of the wicked. It is interesting that all three
expound – notwithstanding great differences in detail – the teaching
of the sentence just quoted: Only the end brings the answer to the
question. The psalms in question are 37, 49 and 73.

Psalm 37 is an acrostic psalm and is, therefore, almost more of a
collection of sentences. But, even if the construction is not strict, it
sticks to its theme. Do not grow heated at the prosperity of the wicked
(vv. 1, 7b), trust and hope in Yahweh; the righteous will not be
ruined, but will possess the land (vv. 3, 7, 19, 22, 34).[14] The wicked,

---

[13] On these didactic prayers see above pp. 39f.
[14] What is meant by this idea of possessing the land, the inheritance, to which
the psalm returns again and again (vv. 3, 9, 11, 18, 22, 27, 29, 34), is not clear. Are
we dealing with small farmers who (cf. Micah 2.2) are afraid of losing their inheritance to landed proprietors? Cf. P. A. Munch, *ZAW* 55, 1937, pp. 37ff.;
G. Boström, *Proverbiastudien*, 1935, pp. 53ff.

however, come to a bad end; in a short time the wicked man is no longer there (vv. 2, 10, 20). The thoughts in the psalm are simple and are not developed in any complex way. Its conclusion is that it is the end that is important. The end ('*aḥªrît*) of the wicked is destruction, the end of those who trust in Yahweh is salvation (vv. 37ff.). By 'end' the psalm obviously means the conclusion of a way of life in which God's salvation and judgment are then finally visible to men.[15]

Psalm 49 begins with an imposing 'teacher's opening summons', and this clearly shows that this is a didactic poem. Again, it deals with rich and wicked people who are obviously a direct threat to the author (vv. 6f.). Here, too, the problem is tackled by means of an intellectual elucidation. The faith that has been disturbed should strengthen itself once more in the knowledge of an order which is fundamental in life and which governs all men.[16] Here, too, attention is directed towards the end, this time towards death which men forget (vv. 13, 21) and from which they cannot escape (vv. 8–10). That is one side.[17] The other is expressed in the confession:

> But God delivers me from the power of Sheol,
>   for he will snatch me away.   (v. 16)

The meaning of this sentence is debated. There can, of course, be no thought of deleting it entirely. Neither, however, can the confession be taken to mean that the poet hopes, in an acute situation of need, that is temporarily, to be saved from death, for it would be impossible to understand the resultant antithesis to the idea that the thoughtless rich must die. The verb in question means (with reference to death) 'snatch away'.[18] The most likely solution, then, is to understand the sentence as the expression of a hope for a life of communion with God which will outlast death. In any case, we have no sufficient knowledge of the ideas of post-exilic Israel about what happens after death to say that this interpretation of the confession in Ps. 49 is *a priori* impossible.

Psalm 73, too, is a didactic poem. At its head there stands a sentence

---

[15] So, too, Sir. 9.11: 'Do not envy a godless man, for you do not know what his day will be.' 'His day', that is the day which will reveal the whole situation.

[16] The psalm contains enormous textual difficulties. No one has provided a satisfactory solution for v. 11 ('the wise men must die; fools and those who lack understanding perish together'). On Ps. 49, cf. most recently G. Fohrer, *Kerygma und Dogma* 14, 1968, pp. 256ff.

[17] Similarly, Prov. 11.7; 'On the death of the godless, hope vanishes.'

[18] 'Take away', 'snatch away', Gen. 5.24; II Kings 2.3ff.

about Yahweh's unadulterated goodness towards Israel. On the one hand this stimulates the reader, while on the other it anticipates the goal towards which the reflections and experiences of the author will lead. Then follows, in vv. 2–17, a report in the first person which passes, without any clear break, into a prayer. This account of experiences which have made the author reflect, an account which then leads to a result, to a 'solution', is a particular literary form of wisdom literature.[19] Similarly, the teachers also composed prayers. Here, too, it is the 'prosperity of the wicked' (the expression occurs in v. 3b) which gives rise to the threat. Unfortunately, the detailed description of the wicked – it is the most detailed that we have – does not allow us to see any more clearly what type of men it really envisages. Here, too, the problem is approached from the direction of the search for knowledge.

> I reflected in order to understand this;
>> but it was too difficult for me.   (v. 16)

This failure of the author's intellectual efforts obviously reveals a low-water mark. He has obviously had a different experience from that of the authors of Pss. 37 and 49. He was at his wits' end, and it needed more than simply a backward thought to a point where his faith had been valid. This paralysis of his continued until an external event brought about a turning point; it continued 'until I entered the sanctuary of God and became aware of their end (*'aḥªrīt*)' (v. 17). What it was he became aware of there we do not know; obviously it was an external experience which came to the help of his faith, perhaps a divine judgment in a sacral process of law. Freed from this severe attack, the suppliant can return to a relationship with God which surrounds him more wonderfully than ever: I am with you; you hold me, you lead me and then you take me away. Body or soul may vanish but God remains his portion and his refuge.[20]

Even the great number of textual difficulties and the fact that much remains obscure cannot seriously detract from the great arch which spans the whole poem from the attack through to a quite new confidence. The poet of this psalm also clings to experience, with regard both to divine judgment and to salvation, and he too looks to the *'aḥªrīt*, to what comes after, to the end. But in the description of the

---

[19] See above pp. 37f.
[20] On this cf. H.-J. Hermisson, *Sprache und Ritus im altisraelitischen Kult*, 1965, pp. 110ff.

gravity of the attack and above all in the expression of absolute security in God, this poem far surpasses the point of view of Pss. 37 and 49.

These three psalms have to be understood against the background of a broad intellectual sphere in which faith and long experience led to the knowledge of specific orders. They do not break away from this sphere, but they are sufficiently flexible to see and to give expression to questions and discrepancies which require particular elucidation and particular answers. There was the old question of the correlation between a man's act and its consequence which demanded, if not exactly a new response, then at least a modified one. The psalms gave such a response in that, in the face of confusing experiences, they taught men, in a more decisive fashion than had hitherto been the case, to look to the end of God's ways with a man. To this extent, then, by means of the modification of a no longer entirely sufficient perception, they strengthened anew faith in the divine order, while they succeeded in propping up the sphere of order in the face of attack. Man always stands, as we have already said, in a situation of conflict with his environment. The events which he has to record are never entirely unambiguous, and the way in which he copes with the incalculable depends on his inner powers of resistance. This sphere of order which has been constructed by his search for knowledge is always in danger. It is never absolutely secure, it is always in motion, since the questions which it must satisfy also change in the course of time. Such changes in the awareness of problems at different periods often take root, for reasons which are difficult to define, in the depths of a nation's intellectual life and can also, in fact, lead to considerable inner tensions.

3. THE BOOK OF JOB

There are signs that, from the end of the monarchy onwards, the unfathomableness of the conduct of individual lives was presenting more and more difficult problems for faith in Yahweh. This uneasiness reaches far beyond the circles of the wisdom teachers. It is well known that the prophets also had to grapple with it, as we know from Jer. 12, Ezek. 18 or Mal. 3. It would, indeed, rather appear that the teachers were by no means the most prominent victims of it, and that the questions were perhaps rather forced upon them from the outside. Although we have at our disposal a considerable number of texts, all of which are concerned with such ominous points of incursion, we still do not see sufficiently clearly to be able to tackle the phenomenon as a unit and to make it intelligible against a wider context. We are certainly correct in speaking of a certain gaining of independence on the part of the individual within the cultic community and also of a transition on man's part to the offensive against God. The question of the relationship of the individual to God was posed more sharply and more critically. One may speak here of a crisis, but there was clearly never any general awareness of such a crisis, for every one of these numerous texts mentioned above stands on a completely individual basis. While otherwise the teachers stand on a broad, traditional basis of understanding, this is by no means the case in this question. In each of these texts an individual, standing outside any teaching tradition and very much on his own, wins through to a specific solution or seeks to help others where they are attacked. This is, of course, very characteristic of the nature of Yahwism, a religion which, precisely in the later period, revealed itself less and less as a firm complex of connected ideas. Yahweh's will, his purposes for men, were not sufficiently self-evident that a correct understanding of them could easily be differentiated from a false one. In the book of Job – in the prose narrative as well as in the dialogues – we are completely incapable of naming any teaching traditions with which these tremendous thoughts could be connected.

The prose narrative deals with a very pious, but also richly blessed man. Completely unexpectedly there occur disasters which rob him of his possessions, his children and finally also of his health. But he cannot see, either in the total loss of every blessing or in his severe bodily suffering, any reason for wavering in the slightest from his trust in God. If God gave, then he can also take away (Job 1.21). It is, after all, impossible to accept the good from him and refuse the evil (Job 2.10). With these two confessions of faith Job is not uttering reflective, possibly mysterious truths. The narrator, rather, puts into his mouth the quite simple, self-illuminating logic of a faith in which he was unassailably secure. Job could not know that there was a special reason for the disasters which had overwhelmed him. On one of the audience days in heaven, Yahweh had spoken to the accuser, whom we have to imagine as a kind of heavenly public prosecutor, about Job and his blameless piety. The latter had not denied the fact of that piety, but had raised all the more insistently the question of its motive. Job was not devoted to God 'for nothing'. The situation would look completely different if God once withdrew his blessing from him.

Although the first test ordered by God did not produce the result expected by the accuser, the latter did not admit defeat. Job himself had not yet been affected; he, too, was an egoist, and 'all that a man has he will give for his life' (Job 2.4). But even the much harder test which was at once set in motion reveals nothing new: Job clings firmly to his 'wholeness', i.e. piety. Now the case has been sufficiently clarified. Job's earlier state of blessedness can be restored. He saw children and grandchildren and died at a ripe old age.[21]

This prose narrative, from the point of view of its type, is certainly to be understood as a didactic narrative. It is not a simply-formed 'folk narrative' but highly cultivated literary prose. Is there such a thing as selfless piety ('without reward, even in the greatest need'[22])? The question is answered in the affirmative. It is, of course, very important that Job has no inkling of the whole heavenly prologue to his suffering and also that he never found out about it. He did not know that God had already answered for him and that all the heavenly beings who had listened to the conversation were waiting anxiously for Job's reaction. Without knowing it, Job, with his two confessions of faith, justified the 'word of honour' with which God had answered for him in advance. This man on the ash-heap, disfigured by illness, 'suffers as the glory and pride of God'.[23] Thus the narrative portrays Job as a fitting witness to God. In a moment of the greatest importance, he has clearly taken up a position with regard to something that was of concern to God. To utter anything 'unseemly' about God would be something to be detested. It was a duty, in a critical situation, to say the 'right' thing about God.[24] Thus, behind this narrative there doubtless stand subtle thoughts about suffering; but one does not have the impression that it already stands within the sphere of that specific attack from which the teachers, as we have seen, had to fight through to a state of faith in Yahweh. There is no trace here of an inner struggle or of theological tension. How ingenuously it expects its readers to accept that a notoriously innocent man – God himself testifies to this innocence – has had to suffer so severely.

[21] The narrative has gone through a fairly complex literary process before reaching the form in which we now have it. The approximate literary development of the material from older, simpler stages can be reconstructed with the help of a few, small inconsistencies; see G. Fohrer, *Studien zum Buch Hiob*, 1963, pp. 26ff., 44ff.

[22] A quotation from the final verse of the hymn by Johann Scheffer (1624–1677), 'Ich will dich lieben, meine Stärke'. Tr.

[23] J. G. Herder, *Vom Geist der ebräischen Poesie* (Bibliothek theologischer Klassiker, Vol. 30), p. 137.

[24] Job 1.5, 22; 2.10; 42.7ff.; cf. G. Fohrer, op. cit., pp. 35f.

Into this Job-narrative the huge literary block of the dialogues and the great divine speech has been inserted (probably centuries later).[25] One must first learn how to read these dialogues. First of all one must answer for oneself the question how they are to be understood from the beginning. Certainly not as 'contentious debates'. The basic situation is clear enough: they are conversations between a sufferer and his friends. What we have to expect, therefore, are complaints from the one side and pastoral words of comfort from the other.[26] What Job himself so often used to do is now the duty of the friends towards him, namely to exhort and raise up with words him who stumbles (Job 4.3f.). This expectation is confirmed by the speeches and replies. It is true that both the complaint and the consolation take on a very passionate form and, again and again, degenerate into open quarrelling. But one must not see in this the main characteristic of these dialogues. In the laments in the Psalms, too, there are complaints that erstwhile friends have become enemies.[27] It is particularly surprising to note how Job, too, even with regard to details, adopts the style and the subject-matter of the psalms of lament. There is very little in the speeches of Job which, from the point of view of form-history, is really new poetry without analogy, and yet from the whole something completely new and unique has emerged by means of a certain shift of emphasis or of a radicalization of traditional forms of speech, especially, however, by means of the skilful manner of composition. Every speech of Job's and also of the friends' consists of a whole series of formal units which even the unpractised eye can usually easily separate. Here, however, lies a difficulty for the modern reader. Since these various formal units, although by no means unreflective, are ranged one after the other without transition, there occur within these speeches sudden changes of thought, many of them very abrupt. But the poet is not, in Job's speeches, sketching a 'spiritual biography' which could satisfy modern claims from the point of view of psychology, but lets Job and the friends voice their concerns entirely in the forms of expression of their time. Even in the case of such a peculiar

---

[25] It will never be possible to provide an entirely satisfactory link, from the literary point of view, between the Job narrative and the poetic dialogue. That in attempting this, the narrative suffered minor textual losses and corrections is not to be wondered at; cf. G. Fohrer, op. cit., pp. 7ff.

[26] C. Westermann, *Der Aufbau des Buches Hiob*, 1956, pp. 4ff.

[27] E.g., Ps. 31.12; 88.9, 19. The literary forms which can be determined in the dialogues have been compared by Westermann with the corresponding forms in the psalms of lament; cf. op. cit., pp. 25ff.

concern as that of Job, the ancient poet could not but make use of the conventional forms of speech. In no sense do the friends emerge as clearly delineated personages. Alongside the protesting individual their task is simply to represent traditional concepts. As they listen to each other, both partners in the dialogue scarcely have more than very loose connections with individual, characteristic hypotheses. In their own train of thought they do not adhere closely to that of the other. This means that, on the one hand, the argument often fails to advance and that, on the other, the intellectual ground covered becomes more and more extensive. The speeches are repetitive and, to a certain extent, move forward only in a circular fashion.

All of these observations which, in the first instance, emerge rather in the sphere of form, indicate that the debate moves in an intellectual sphere which was most strongly determined by conventional concepts, values and meanings, that is in a sphere in which there were far fewer wholly personal opinions, represented by only one individual, than the modern reader imagines. Even Job is deeply rooted in the thought-forms of his day, and he has, as we shall see, a good deal in common with his friends. It is all the more amazing that he was able to achieve a much more grandiose outburst. One may ask whether Job's arguments would from the outset have received as much agreement and understanding in the ancient world as they do from the modern reader. Many examples may be adduced to show that the ancient world was much more conscious of the danger of such individuality (Antigone). There was always considerable reserve towards criticism of traditional values and, in addition, the opinion was widespread that such a hardening of an individual in radical positions was a destructive factor. The teachers in Israel also had their worries in this respect. They called the taking of intellectual offence at the unexplained, from which starting point the road to revolt against God was not far, 'being resentful'. They saw in this, no doubt with regard to the good fortune enjoyed by the godless, something false and blameworthy. Even Job had to have said to him, 'Vexation kills the fool and resentment slays the simple' (Job 5.2). In fact, how can one call what Job did anything else but resentment?[28]

The dialogue consists of three long cycles of speeches in which Job replies to the speeches of each of the three friends (chs. 5–14; 15–21; 22–27). Thus Job speaks much more often and, for the most part, at comparatively greater length. The second half of the third cycle, from

---

[28] On 'envy', see Prov. 3.31; 23.17; 24.19; Ps. 37.1; 73.3.

ch. 24 onwards, is only a torso. The expansive speeches of a fourth friend, Elihu, in chs. 32–37, are a secondary poetic addition which separate somewhat harshly Job's challenge to God (31.35–40) and God's reply (chs. 38ff.). God is, therefore, beside Job and the friends, the third participant in the debate.[29] Only at the end does he have recourse to speech. It is, however, correct to realize that this mysterious third party is already present and addressed from the beginning. His speech is therefore prepared well in advance.

Job and his friends are equally convinced that the suffering which has overwhelmed Job comes from Yahweh and that it is saying something. On the basis of this statement, which is not subjected to discussion, the whole dialogue starts. From then on, however, opinions differ sharply. The three friends are as one. Even if they expound their opinions separately, it was hardly the author's intention to differentiate dogmatically between these opinions of theirs. All that they have to say to Job moves along a comparatively uniform theological line. Their consolation divides, however, on the one hand into theoretical instructions and, on the other, into practical suggestions as to what Job's next task should be. The theoretical considerations reach far into what is generally valid and what has been tested of old. Precisely in this lies their strength. The friends hope that Job will be unable to escape the evidence which they have produced and will have to draw the right conclusions from it. Their arguments and their consolation may be summarized in the following way.

No one is sinless and pure before God. Not even the angels are, with the result that God does not trust even them; how, then, can man 'who drinks evil like water' be just before God (Job 15.16)? The situation of this man, who is in addition deeply rooted in transitoriness, is therefore unfavourable before God, for he cannot approach him with questions or demands. His perishableness and his sin prevent this. God, however, punishes the sinner. In the correspondence of act and consequence the friends saw a central, God-given rule of life. They never weary of presenting it to Job, especially in those typifying, didactic poems about the end of those who commit outrages, poems which have already been discussed. They do not maintain that Job is such; but Job is addressed as one in so far as they demand that he examine his life, too, with the help of such models. They are firmly convinced that in Job's severe suffering God has passed judgment and the thought that God could have done something unjust is com-

[29] C. Westermann, op. cit., pp. 6, 15.

pletely inconceivable to them.[30] From this there follow quite logically the practical suggestions with which they are trying to help Job. This judgment of God was directed only towards Job; thus only he can understand it and apply it to himself. The important thing is that it leads him to repentance. Hence the exhortation reaches its climax in the demand, 'Submit to this divine correction and admit that God is just.'[31]

In order to understand better the thoughts of the friends, one must be aware that the form of a sacral confession, the making of which they so pressingly urge upon Job, became, especially in the later period, more and more common as a basic form of prayer. The process was as follows. The individual (or the community), afflicted by a severe misfortune, acknowledges that his suffering is a beneficial, judicious action on the part of God. In this way he brings to a halt, to a certain extent, the proceedings which have been set in motion against him and may hope to be able to return once more to God's blessing.[32] Whether one understood such an action on the individual's life more in the sense of a punitive or of an educative, that is corrective, act on God's part was an unimportant distinction. This, then, was the consolation offered by the friends. Submit to God's correction, and it will be a blessing to you. If you resist it, then you will be broken by God.[33]

At this point it is worth taking a look at that part of the Deuteronomistic prayer offered by Solomon at the dedication of the Temple (I Kings 8) in which are enumerated the various cases in which repentance is to be made. The section is built up on a fixed pattern:

> When your people Israel are defeated before the enemy because they have sinned against you . . . (v. 33)
>
> When heaven is shut up and there is no rain because they have sinned against you . . . (v. 35)
>
> If they sin against you – for there is no man who does not sin – and you are angry with them and give them to an enemy . . . (v. 46)

The second element in the pattern deals with the repentance induced by the punitive event:

> . . . if they turn again to you and praise your name . . . (v. 33)

---

[30] Job 8.3; 34.10, 12, 31ff.; 36.23.
[31] Job 5.8f.; 8.20f.; 11.13–15; 22.21–30; 36.8–11.
[32] On the so-called judgment doxology see above p. 196.
[33] Thus, e.g., Job 5.17ff.; 33.13–20; 36.10, 22.

. . . if they pray towards this place and praise your name . . . (v. 35)
. . . if they lay it to heart and repent of their sin . . . (v. 47)

The third element speaks of the forgiveness which has been prayed for:

then hear in heaven and forgive their sin . . . (v. 34)
then hear in heaven their prayer and their supplication . . . (v. 45)

Apart from the fact that this is dealing not with an individual but with Israel as a whole, it does map out step by step the way in which Job, according to the friends' advice, should go. At the beginning there is the shattering disaster. This is followed by a reaction on the part of the conscience which interprets the event (cf. the interesting passage 'each knowing the affliction of his own heart', v. 38) and by repentance. This return to the divine mercy, which is available at all times, brings to a close the movement which was begun by the sin. Even the reference to the fact that all men sin is not absent (v. 46).[34]

Job, too, is convinced that his suffering is a direct attack by God, indeed a judgment passed by God. But the situation appears differently to him than it does to his friends. If one seeks to distinguish the main thoughts from the stream of laments, reproaches, protestations and abuse which he hurls at his friends in turn or directly at God, one will need to mention the three following groups of thoughts. Job feels that he is in the right with regard to God and continues to protest his innocence. By this he means that he feels himself unable to admit in his own case the correspondence which is asserted by the friends between guilt and punishment. He cannot admit that the breach in his relationship with God has emanated from him, that is from some heinous sin on his part. 'I was at ease when he shattered me' (Job 16.12). With great passion and quite without regard for any possible consequences, Job protests his 'righteousness' (*tummā*) before God.

I am in the right and have no regard for my life,
I despise my being. (Job 9.21)

As God lives, who has taken away my right,
and the Almighty who has made me bitter,

[34] As argument of the friends, e.g., Job 4.17–21; 25.4–6. The 'liturgy' of the great drought in Jer. 14 also reveals the same sequence in the outer and inner event. At the beginning, the disaster is described (vv. 2–6), then follows the supplication which begins almost as if it were asking the reason for the disaster: 'if (in case) our iniquities testify against us, Yahweh, act for your name's sake' (v. 7).

> my lips will not speak falsehood,
> > my tongue will not utter deceit.
> Far be it from me to say that you are right;
> > till I die I will not surrender my integrity;
> I hold fast to my righteousness and will not relinquish it,
> > my conscience disparages none of my days.   (Job 27.2, 4–6)

> Indeed he knows the way on which 'I stand'.
> > If he were to try me, I would come forth as gold.
> My foot has held fast to his steps;
> > I have kept his way and have not turned aside.
> I have not departed from the commandment of his lips;
> > I have treasured in my bosom the words of his mouth.
> > > (Job 23.10–12)

This completely unshaken conviction leads Job to the next consideration. He must achieve a discussion between himself and God. If God
has 'taken his right away' from him, then things cannot possibly
continue in that state:

> But I wish to speak with the Almighty,
> > and I desire to argue my case with God.   (Job 13.3)

> I take my flesh in my teeth,
> > and put my life in my hand.
> If he wishes to slay me than I have no hope,
> > but I should like to defend my ways to his face.   (Job 13.14f.)

> Oh that I knew how I could find him,
> > how I could reach where he is.
> I would lay my case before him
> > and fill my mouth with arguments.
> I would learn what he would answer me,
> > and hear what he would say to me.   (Job 23.3–5)

If God would only let him speak, then he would speak and not be
afraid (9.34f.); he would ask him, 'Let me know why you contend
against me?' (10.2), 'Why do you hide your face and count me as
your enemy?' (13.24). If he could present his case in this way (13.18),
then he would force God to speak. Was God not his creator, and could
he not 'long for the work of his hands' (14.15)?[35] Further, is God not
the legal helper of all sufferers? This question can be answered only
in the affirmative. The reader is almost taken aback by the violence
with which the same Job suddenly announces the certainty that in

---

[35] Elsewhere, too, Job appeals to God as his creator, cf. Job 10.3, 8–11, 18.

every circumstance he is secure in the legal protection of God, even if this means that God has to appear against himself and on Job's behalf as counsel for the defence.

> Even now, behold, my witness is in heaven,
> and he that vouches for me is on high. (Job 16.19)

But Job is still not able to find peace in this conviction. On a much broader basis there appears in his laments the argument that it is hopeless and impossible to expect justice from this God (and this is the third of these groups of thoughts). He will not even listen to his arguments, far less answer them (9.16, 3). God is so free that he establishes his own justice and does not bother about what men think justice is.

> It is all one; therefore I say,
> he destroys both the blameless and the wicked.
> When the whip brings sudden death,
> he mocks at the calamity of the innocent . . .
> If I wash myself with snow,
> and cleanse my hands with lye,
> then you would plunge me into the 'mire'
> so that my own clothes would abhor me. (Job 9.22f., 30f.)

In this dispute there is no arbitrator to put both parties on oath (Job 9.33). This God is so free and arbitrary that he can never be pinned down by men.

> If he passes by me, I do not see him;
> if he moves on, I do not perceive him.
> If he snatches away, who can stop him;
> who can say to him, 'What are you doing?'. (Job 9.11f.)

The conclusion is: If this God is unwilling, then man can do nothing to enter into a peaceful relationship with him. And it is clear in the case of Job that God is unwilling.

We can now no longer avoid the difficult task of answering, at least in broad outline, the question about justice and injustice which this dialogue poses to every reader. It is superfluous to issue a warning about the necessity for extreme caution in setting out one's thoughts, for the poet does not raise a finger to guide the reader through this confusion of theological opinions. He lets the men unfold their positions and lets the dialogue end without a conclusion. Indeed, at the end the disagreement is greater than it was at the beginning. Only in the fact that the poet allows Job to reply to each speech of the friends and therefore lets him speak more frequently, lies an indication where the centre of gravity of the dialogue lies.

Where do the differences between Job and his friends lie? That Job laments while the friends advise, lies in the nature of things. The one who comforts will always, in his words of comfort, refer to what has been generally experienced. The circumstances of Job's lament are, of course, quite special. First of all Job joins in the ancient, universal lament about the brevity and anxiety of life (14.1). Hard service is man's lot upon earth. Like a slave he longs for the shade. When he lies down, he thinks, 'When will it be morning?'. When he gets up, he asks, 'When will it be evening?' (7.1–4). Job joins in this universal lament because to a great extent it expresses his sufferings, too. In this he proves himself to be completely human in that he refuses to allow himself to be deprived of the right to give expression to his grief and does not shrink from a truth, however desperate that truth may be. But there are particular circumstances connected with this truth with which Job found himself face to face. Indeed, a spectacular display of rhetoric was necessary even to give expression to it. The realization that in his suffering he was dealing with God was, as we have seen, not new. It was, however, both incomprehensible and unbearable that God should attack him, who was just, and seek to kill him with the blind rage of an enemy.

> His anger tore me and persecuted me,
>> he gnashes his teeth at me;
>> my adversary sharpens his eyes against me.
> I was at ease, but he shattered me.
>> He set me up as his target.
> His arrows whistle round me.
>> mercilessly he splits open my kidneys
>> and pours out my gall on the ground.
> He breaks me with breach upon breach;
>> he runs upon me like a warrior.
> I have sewed sackcloth upon my skin
>> and have laid my horn in the dust.
> My face is red with weeping,
>> and on my eyelids is deep darkness,
> although there is no violence in my hands,
>> and my prayer is pure.   (Job 16.9–17)

No one in Israel had ever depicted the action of God towards men in this way before. Those who prayed the prayers of lamentation were not exactly prudish when they reproached God with his severity. But here is a new tone which has never been sounded before: God as the direct enemy of men, delighting in torturing them, hovering over them like what we might call the caricature of a devil, gnashing his teeth, 'sharpening' his eyes (the Greek translation mentions 'daggers of the eyes') and splitting open Job's intestines. One cannot but affirm that Job stands face to face with a completely new experience of the reality of God, an experience of something incalculable and fearful, of which ancient Israel and some of the prophets were aware, but faced with which Job's friends were utterly helpless, because such experiences were no longer familiar, not just to wisdom but to this whole age. It was not that more was being demanded of Job than had ever been experienced in Israel before. But the question of the intellectual sphere out of which this kind of conflict arose and in which it was to be overcome is decisive. In the case of Job, this sphere was narrowly confined. It was the realm of experience of an individual thrown entirely back upon himself, who was no longer reached by the voice of his neighbour. And what was really new was that Job involved God, in a quite different way, much more deeply and more terribly, in the suffering. This was no longer the sovereign, punitive God, the God who fulfils human destinies; Job, rather, envisages a God who quite personally and with all his powers enters into the suffering and becomes involved in it. That is the only thing that he really knows and, indeed, it nearly drives him out of his mind.

The hermeneutical question as to how the poet himself wished the dialogues to be read and understood has never been clearly answered. In the first place, one would have to take up a more critical position with regard to the reactions aroused by the debate in the modern reader. Is it so certain that only Job's protest should be held up as an example, while the friends appear as the joyless representatives of the conventional? Can we presuppose in an ancient reader such unmitigated pleasure in a religious rebel? What was the purpose of the author of the dialogues and of the divine speech, where and how does one manage to grasp his meaning? He would no doubt lay considerable emphasis on the declaration of repentance which Job uttered after he had heard God speaking (Job 40.3–5; 42.2–6). But where and how did the author (not we) see the right and the wrong? The way in which he uniformly expounds the most contradictory ideas is no argument for the point of view that he intends to lead the reader to differentiate between a clear white and a clear black.[36] The situation is certainly not as simple as that. But even the contrary supposition is unsatisfactory, namely that he intended the reader to select, item by item, from speech to speech, what is true and correctly stated. The right and the wrong certainly cannot be counted out piece by piece in this way. Rather, he wished to point out the limits and doubts of a basic position (indeed, the dominant one) by setting up in diametric opposition to it a revolutionary position, but also to point out the doubts inherent in Job's position. Both positions conceal truths. What was topical and pressing for the poet, as we have already said, was the revolutionary position. But, from the point of view of its substance, was it so completely revolutionary?

The whole quarrel between Job and his friends is due to different conceptions of the righteousness of men before God. The point of departure of the friends' argument was: No man is righteous before God, therefore all must suffer.[37] This point of view of the friends was, as we have seen, in no way specifically characteristic of 'wisdom'; it was common in Israel, even common in the whole of the ancient world. By suffering, men are forced to turn to God and confess their sins. Then God will receive them, and their relationship to God will be in order. One cannot, therefore say, that the friends are completely unaware of any righteousness of men before God. It consisted in their turning to God and in their being accepted by him. Job, on the other hand, says: I am righteous before God. God, and not I, has broken the relationship. The answer to the question how this 'holding fast' of Job to his 'integrity' (Job 27.5) is more precisely to be understood, needs a more thorough examination. In these declarations, Job asserts in the first place that he is unaware of having committed such a grievous sin as could explain the severity of his suffering. It is also clear that with this assertion he is not intending to declare that he is absolutely sinless. 'Righteousness' before God was certainly not a title which would be conferred on the basis of a counting up of moral achievements. In the last resort, it was God who granted that title to

[36] It is alarming to see to what extent we lack definite criteria for evaluating the speeches of the friends. Has the author of the Elihu speeches included specific caricaturing traits (Job 32.18ff.)? Is he, as many commentators have thought, to be understood as an arrogant boaster? Others have praised him for his modesty and for his deep understanding of suffering; cf. C. Kuhl, *ThR* 21, 1953, p.258.

[37] The passage, Job 32.1f., is of particular hermeneutical significance because in this the friends are agreed.

a man either on the basis of his faith or on the basis of his confession of him. If Job asserted that he stood in a right relationship to God, then this was not the product of a moral balance sheet drawn up *ad hoc*, but he was seeking, by means of a confession, to find security in a relationship with God which had been available to him long since and of which he at least knew enough to be able to claim it for himself. Even Job knows that this is not achieved with all his declarations of innocence. Everything depends on the justificatory verdict of God. Therefore Job has to force him to speak, no matter what it cost him. It is interesting to see to what extent Job here is still living among specifically cultic ideas, perhaps to an even greater extent than his friends.[38]

Thus Job, too, is a righteous sufferer who sees his whole case dependent on God, and we have seen how, in spite of his horror, he is again and again pushed towards God. Here alone can he receive the sentence which can free him of all blame and which can restore order both to his relationship to God and, at the same time, to his whole existence on earth. His conviction that he is free of all blame is almost disconcerting in the way in which it remains unshakeable. 'Who is there that will contend with me?' (13.19). With a very similar call, the Servant of Yahweh in Deutero-Isaiah also challenged any potential opponents:

> He who vindicates me is near.
> Who will contend with me?
> Let us stand up together.
> Who is my adversary?
> Let him come near to me.
> My right is with Yahweh.   (Isa. 50.8; 49.4b)

One presumes that Job could not have spoken in this way, for he is not aware that the God who vindicates him stands thus close, for this God with whom Job has to do must first of all have become completely different, he must have undergone a radical transformation. From this God Job expects nothing at all for himself, at the most only death as a release (Job 6.8–10). He disputes his right to treat a man in this way and despises him because he lowers himself to become a caricature of himself. The expression 'God must' recurs again and again in his speeches. Again and again he starts to force God to reveal himself to him in such a way that he, Job, can actually recognize him

---

[38] Precisely in his professions of innocence, is Job not very close to the professions in the psalms of innocence? Cf. Gunkel-Begrich, *Einleitung in die Psalmen*, 1933, pp. 215f., 238; C. Westermann, op. cit., pp. 78ff.

as his God. We said a moment ago that Job drew God down into suffering in an incomparably more radical and more complete way and sees him involve himself directly in it, and that he in this way revealed an aspect of God's reality which was hidden from his friends and probably from all his contemporaries. That was his new realization. On the other hand, he disputes God's right to approach him in this form; he accuses him of being cruel and positively malicious and refuses to see in this God his own God. He is, therefore, incapable of following God down into such hidden depths.

How do the friends react to this eruption of a new awareness of God and also to the continual frustration at this awareness? They are easily incensed at Job's lack of restraint, for they see neither the one thing nor the other, neither Job's right nor his wrong. In order to understand the great distance between the courses of the speeches of the participants in this debate, one must have clarified the utter disparity between the starting positions. The friends start from the very old, and yet ever new, question about orders, that is from the question whether certain rules cannot be recognized in the life which man lives in relationship to God. The fact that they answer this question in the affirmative with reference to the relationship between an act and its consequence is not an error peculiar to them. One would also need to be prepared to pronounce the same verdict on large tracts of the prophetic proclamation of judgment. And they are scarcely to be blamed for propagating the old perceptions in an ambitious rhetorical art-form. It is quite different in the case of Job. He starts from a quite personal relationship with God in which he once stood and which he now sees shattered. He longs for an act of judgment on the part of God which would personally vindicate him, and he regards it as unworthy of God to deny him this word and to allow his creature to perish in incomprehensible grief. For this reason he goes to the limits of piety and blasphemy in order to force this God, whom he nevertheless continues to regard as his God, out of this ambiguity. In order to give suitable expression to this need of his, he makes extensive use of the language of the psalms of lamentation which he often sharpens far beyond the conventional meaning under the weight of his own much more radical experience.

While Job's involvement in 'wisdom' questions is unmistakable, it nevertheless recedes in view of the fact that Job introduces into the debate theological points of view of a quite different type. The picture of God which destroys that involvement does not arise from the experience of orders, nor does the image of God for which he struggles with himself. It does in fact arise in the last resort from the dialogue which Israel has had with her God for centuries in the cult; it has taken shape in the hearing of the continuous exhortation from generation to generation that Yahweh is Israel's God, her defending counsel and saviour. Job thus reaches far beyond the questions of the friends to the fundamental question whether that force which had affected him was still Israel's Yahweh. As long as he finds no answer to that question, the experiential truths of the friends are of no help to him, since they always presuppose a Yahweh who is beyond dispute. He thrusts them aside because they obstruct his view of his main problem. What he demands to know he cannot be certain of by a mere adding together of everyday experiences. In a much more elementary form the question poses itself in the depths of his suffering; Yahweh *pro me*? How much easier (and how much more untrue) everything would be if he could somehow have expressed this experience of God in religious terms. But for Job this encounter with God in the depths of his suffering was fundamentally the greatest certainty of which he could speak, and from it he will not be moved right to the end of the book.[39]

One could also say that Job experienced 'God's anger' in a new way. 'Anger' was indeed for Israel more than a meted-out punishment, it was above all a reality which could no longer be accommodated to human ideas of order. What was new in this experience, over against those experiences which ancient Israel had already had of God's anger, was the fact that now this anger affected a completely isolated individual.[40]

What concerned Job above all else was the credibility of God. For this reason he was passionately concerned with the question, 'Yahweh *pro me*?' It is not suffering, as has so often been said, which has become so utterly problematical, but God.[41] That Job's faith could

---

[39] '. . . the amazing thing about this book is precisely the fact that Job makes no move to flee to some better kind of God but sticks it out in the direct line of fire from the divine anger. Without moving, Job, whom God treats as an enemy, in the midst of his darkness, in the midst of the abyss, appeals, not to some higher authority, not even to the God of his friends, but to the very God who is crushing him.' (R. de Pury, *Hiob – der Mensch im Aufruhr*, Bibl. St. 15, 1957, p. 23.)

[40] In fact, the term 'anger' (*'ap, ḥēmā, ka'as*) plays a much greater role in Job's speeches than in those of the friends. Cf. Job 9.5, 13; 10.17; 14.13; 16.9; 19.11; 21.17, 20 with 4.9; 20.23, 28; 35.15 (uncertain passages have not been cited).

[41] It is certainly not wrong to maintain, as it is over and over again, that the book is dealing with 'the problem of suffering'. But this is true only in a very limited sense, namely as the question about the imposition of this suffering on this man.

become involved in such a catastrophic test can be explained only from the fact that Job, too, lives and thinks and struggles against a broad background of old Yahwistic traditions. One can even ask whether his link with the old Yahwistic traditions was not stronger than was the case with the friends. He appeals against the terrible God of his experience to the God who, from of old, had offered himself as saviour of the poor and the sick and as the defending counsel of those who had been deprived of justice. He can live and breathe only if it is this Yahweh who reveals himself to him.

We have already discussed how great a role the question of faith played in the doctrines of the teachers. Job had to pose the question of faith afresh once again, since he saw himself thrust into the sphere of a completely new experience of God. In the sphere of a spirituality which inclined so strongly towards intellectualism and empiricism and in which knowledge of Yahweh (as opposed to the earlier periods) had transferred to the doctrine of creation, the experience of the hiddenness of God would of necessity produce a completely new feeling of terror. If Job's dialogue with the friends broke off without having reached a solution, then this was equally true of Job's dialogue with God, which he had continued far beyond his friends' comprehension. But right to the very last he refused to withdraw from the assertion of his innocence.

Let us return once again to the friends. With what are they to be reproached? That their teachings were 'rigid'[42] cannot be proved on an exegetical basis. Indeed, did the course of the argument in Job 4f., with its constantly changing points of view, not prove to be extremely flexible? There remains, then, the indisputable fact that Job's experience of the freedom and terror of God was not only strange to them in this most extreme form, but that they were completely incapable of understanding it. More precisely, their error lay, therefore, not in the experiences which they had propagated; these were legitimate enough in their own place. Their error began only in their confrontation with Job's experiences, that is, in their inability to listen and respond. To be quite fair, however, one must at this point remember the limitations imposed by the form at the poet's disposal, that of a dialogue. This form certainly afforded the opportunity of a broad development of the opposing positions. It did not, however, offer much more than that. Even if the Israelite dialogue rises considerably above the comparable Mesopotamian form in flexibility and

[42] So H. H. Schmid, op. cit., p. 178 and many others.

dramatic quality, it would nevertheless be asking for something which simply lay outside the capabilities of this art-form, if one were to expect a real, mutual involvement, a response to the arguments of the other, a working out of their deficiencies, etc. The poet confined himself to a confrontation of the positions, giving precedence to those of Job. Obviously the experience with which Job confronted those of the friends, that is the experience of a God hidden *sub specie contraria*, was not being adequately treated at the time when the poem was composed.

Yahweh accepted Job's challenge and deemed the rebel worthy of a long address.[43] What an act of condescension on the part of him who is thus called in question! This response consists, however, apart from several descriptive passages which have perhaps been interpolated, of a stream of counter-questions all concerning the wonderful power of God in his creation, the structure of the world, the stars, meteorological phenomena, animals, etc. Do you know, are you aware, are you able, do you decide? The tone of these questions is one of the most supreme irony: Teach me; you are so clever; the number of your days is great. Job's particular concern, that of receiving a justificatory verdict from God, is nowhere taken up, and indeed no reference is made to the wider circle of themes broached in the dialogues. The result of this is that there is a fairly large number of possible ways in which this divine speech can be interpreted. It is, of course, clear that the speech contains a rejection of Job. Job himself understood it in this way. But even the question as to where the divine blame attaches cannot be answered clearly. Above all, however, one has to ask whether the aim of the speech is only to pass judgment on Job's presumption or whether it is not, perhaps, to be interpreted in a more positive sense.[44]

The divine speech, which otherwise presents its challenge in such a remarkably indirect way, expresses direct blame in only two pas-

[43] It is certain that the divine speech has often been subject to secondary expansion. The fact that the text consists of two speeches, each with a solemn opening (Job 38.1–39.30 and 40.6–41.26), would lead us to suppose that the speech existed in two recensions which, in the course of the editorial process, were then placed side by side. This is all the more likely since Job's submission also exists in two forms, 40.3–5 and 42.1–6.

[44] According to H. Richter (*EvTh* 18, 1958, p. 321), the divine speech states that the judgment pronounced against Job and the punishment inflicted on him were justified. For this reason, it compels Job to withdraw his demand to be pronounced innocent.

sages. The first time is right at the beginning of the first divine speech:

> Who is this that darkens counsel
> by words without knowledge?   (38.2)

The word which is translated here by 'counsel' was an important word for the wise men. Referring here quite absolutely to God, it means the planning of God in relation to his creation and also includes what we understand by providence.[45] The question is asked ironically, for one cannot 'darken' a plan if it deserves this name at all, certainly not a divine one. Above all, however, this term, which is important for all that follows, contains a sharp challenge to Job, for the latter had expressed himself extensively to the effect that God treated men with sheer caprice and had exceeded every limit. The other reproach introduces the second divine speech:

> Will you really destroy my right,
> put me in the wrong that you may be right?   (40.8)

Job, in his speeches, has challenged God's right, one might even say his freedom. Here, in the first instance, one thinks of the complaints of Job that God was depriving him of his right (19.6 etc.). It is not that he demands after all to hear a justificatory verdict, but that he considers God as his enemy and contests his right to treat him as he does. Basically, both accusations come to the same thing: Job has improperly and 'without understanding' interfered in God's affairs.

At this point it could appear as though the divine speech were simply relegating all divine activity on behalf of men to the realm of the incomprehensible. The consequence of this would simply be a resigned submission, a total theological agnosticism and the end of any positive relationship between man and God. It is, however, remarkable that in the divine speech thoughts characteristic of the friends reappear, and no one ever reproached them with being theologically agnostic. They even remonstrated with Job that God could not be put in the wrong by man, nor could he be summoned before any court.[46] Similarly, it was they who used as an argument against

---

[45] M. Pope (The Anchor Bible, 1965), ad loc., translates the word by 'providence'. Yahweh's 'plan' is already mentioned in Isaiah, although there it refers to Yahweh's purposes in history: Isa. 5.19; 30.1; cf. Isa. 46.10. On the guidance of the individual: Prov. 19.21.

[46] Job 34.10, 12, 17b ('will you condemn the righteous and mighty?'); 34.29, 31–33; 36.23; 37.23b.

Job the incomprehensibility of the divine activity in creation.[47] Thus the divine speech cannot be understood in such a radically dismissive way, that is, as excluding man from any understanding of God.

All commentators find the divine speech highly scandalous, in so far as it bypasses completely Job's particular concerns, and because in it Yahweh in no way condescends to any kind of self-interpretation. Whether ancient man reacted in this way is not so certain. It could be that he marvelled less at this sign of divine freedom. Even Job himself understood the great speech more quickly and more directly than the modern reader will be able to do. In order to remove misunderstandings, God refrains from saying anything in explanation of his 'decrees'. Rather, he poses counter-questions concerning creation, its order and its preservation. He is not, therefore, speaking of anything theoretical, of particular principles of divine action or the like, but of something factual which happens every day. Thus God makes creation bear witness to himself.[48] Once again we encounter the idea that creation itself has something to say which man can hear. It is to this that Job is referred. In a somewhat different way from Ps. 19 or from the doctrine of the primeval order and its testimony, this self-witnessing of creation is understood as a flood of urgent questions which refer man back to the mystery of creation and of divine guidance. Here, what creation says is understood not as praise ascending to God (although this is also mentioned, Job 38.7), but as a word which turns towards the human mind. While Job is unable to answer any of these questions, the rebel thus, to a certain extent, puts the whole world back into the hands of God, for whom it exists and who alone supports it and sustains it. He has thus ceremoniously withdrawn his complaint, obviously because he now knows that his destiny, too, is well protected by this mysterious God. He could feel himself secure with this God all the more so because the speech which was addressed to him was by no means intended simply to accuse him. It is at the same time an overwhelming testimony to a serene turning of God to

[47] Job 11.7–9; 36.22–30; 37.2–16.
[48] God allows creation, that is, someone other than himself, to speak for him. 'He lets these other things speak and causes them to speak . . . eloquently of themselves. He obviously counts upon it that they belong so totally to Him, that they are so subject to Him and at His disposal, that in speaking of themselves they will necessarily speak of Him . . . He is so sure of them as His creatures . . . to be sure at once of the service which the creatures will quite simply render Him in His self-manifestation' (Karl Barth, *Church Dogmatics*, IV 3, 1st half, ET 1961, p. 430).

a world which despises all standards of human rationality and economy, to a serenity which also includes the unpleasant ostrich 'to whom God gave no share in understanding' (Job 39.17). Is there not also there a divine striving for a share in this joy?[49] In this way, then God has turned to Job, and Job has immediately understood him. Here, too, then – as has been so finely said – God has bet on Job and, in doing so, this time too he has not been wrong and has not lost his bet. It could have turned out that Job would have closed his mind to this speech, and then God would have been the loser.[50]

The insertion of the long poetic dialogue into the much older Job-narrative produces for the commentator questions which are difficult to answer. Should one take the dialogues on their own? Must one not, in expounding them, always take account of the light shed upon them by the narrative? A. Jepsen, in his careful study *Das Buch Hiob und seine Deutung*, 1963, has taken this hermeneutical principle seriously. Behind the interpretation which we have presented here, there lies the conviction that the poetic dialogue is completely independent of the narrative. The differences in various places are too great for us to be able really to look at both together. In the one place Job is quite submissive; in the other he is rebellious. And can one really refer God's praise of Job's words (42.7), praise which refers to the confession in 1.21 and 2.10, also to Job's complaints and attacks, especially after God has already rejected these outbursts in his great speech? Would it not also lead to forced interpretations if one attempted to understand the suffering, about which Job debates so passionately with his friends, primarily (as does the narrative) from the idea of it as a divine test? The concept of the suffering as a test imposed by God is expressed in the dialogues by the friends only occasionally (5.17ff.; 33.13ff.). Job has completely rejected such a positive interpretation of his sufferings.

4. ECCLESIASTES

The book which designates its author by that expression which has still not been satisfactorily explained, namely Koheleth (translated by Luther as 'the preacher'), is, according to its outward form, an offshoot of a literary type which was cultivated particularly in ancient Egypt, namely the Royal Testament. It contains a number of fairly

[49] In Ps. 104.31, what is found here between the lines is made explicit, namely that 'God rejoices in his creation'. On this passage, Calvin says, '*Status mundi in Dei laetitia fundatus est*'.
[50] K. Barth, op. cit., p. 496.

long didactic poems or short sentences which, expressed predominantly in the first person, purport to be a wise man's personal experience of life. After the commentaries appear finally to have freed themselves from the assumption of a self-contained intellectual context and of a progressive inner structure and to have arrived at the conviction that the literary units were to be explained from within themselves, yet another change appears to be on the way here.[51] There is, to be precise, an inner unity which can find expression otherwise than through a linear development of thought or through a logical progression in the thought process, namely through the unity of style and topic and theme, a unity which can make a work of literature into a whole and which can in fact give it the rank of a self-contained work of art. This is all the more so in the domain of ancient Near Eastern literature which, in any case, must be measured by different standards. A specific, unifying function is fulfilled by a small number of leading concepts to which Koheleth returns again and again, concepts such as 'vanity', 'striving after wind', 'toil', 'lot' etc. Nor can the modern reader escape the quite dispassionate – in contrast to Job – restrained solemnity and weight of his diction. Thus the book is more than a secondarily edited collection. No other collection of proverbs, not even that of Sirach, presents such clearly defined intellectual characteristics. In the questions that he asks, Koheleth stands firmly in the wisdom tradition. He is concerned to 'investigate' events and happenings, and he asks himself what then is 'good' for man.[52] One difference from the old wisdom is interesting: he is less concerned with determining and discussing individual experiences than with life as a whole and with passing a definitive judgment on it. In this respect, then, Koheleth has become, from a theological point of view, much more ambitious. Koheleth, for his part, understands his admittedly very negative judgment of the whole as the end-result of many individual experiences. But it is, meanwhile, clear that such an unequivocal judgment of the life and destiny of man cannot be based exclusively on experiences. Here, quite different factors come into play. Of this more will be said shortly. If we first let him speak for himself, there emerge three basic insights round which his thoughts continually circle. 1. A thorough, rational examination of life is unable to find any satisfactory meaning; everything is 'vanity'. 2. God determines every event. 3. Man is unable to discern these decrees, the 'works of God'

[51] O. Loretz, *Qohelet und der Alte Orient*, 1964, pp. 212ff.
[52] He uses the verb *tūr* 'spy out', 1.13; 2.3; 7.25.

in the world. It is clear that these insights are all interconnected, that even if the emphasis of a statement lies only on one of them, they nevertheless belong indissolubly together.

1. Life is vanity. The toil which is endured bears no relationship to what is gained from it (1.3; 2.22f.). A glance at the social structure of humanity affords a cheerless outlook. Injustice rules in the place of justice (3.16). It is of no advantage that the high official is supervised by a higher and that the latter is supervised by a still higher one (5.7), that a man has power over another (8.9); there is no one to dry the tears of the downtrodden; there is no comforter (4.1). Good order and honesty are of no avail. The wicked man often comes off much better, and in the end death makes everyone the same (7.15; 8.10, 14; 9.2). The worst of all is that man is incapable of controlling the future and that he stands unprotected at its mercy. He does not know what will happen, for who will tell him what is going to happen (8.7; 9.1; 10.14)? Behind the problem of the future, there lies for Koheleth the still more difficult question of death which casts its shadow over every meaningful interpretation of life. Whenever Koheleth speaks of fate (*miqreh*), death is always envisaged at the same time.[53] Such is the case, for example, in the famous passage where he asks whether the fate of men is really any different from that of the beasts (3.19). In the great allegory of 12.2–6, he mercilessly reveals how the manifestations of human life diminish with age, how it grows darker and darker around a man until 'the silver cord snaps and the golden bowl breaks'.[54] In view of such ideas, it is not surprising that what was the securest possession of the aged, namely the value of wisdom in the face of all kinds of folly, also became questionable. Certainly, even under very favourable conditions, wisdom is occasionally to be accorded a position of pre-eminence. But of what use is it if it lies unrecognized and therefore unused (9.13–16)? And is not thinking about wisdom and folly basically also a striving after wind? For, 'in much wisdom is much vexation', and 'he who increases knowledge increases sorrow' (1.16–18).

2. In spite of all these depressing observations, Koheleth is far from holding that events in the world are simply a haphazard jumble. He is aware of something which mysteriously rules and orders every event; he usually refers to this phenomenon by the neutral word 'time' and thereby touches on the fact that every activity and every

[53] The word for 'fate', 'occurrence', otherwise in 2.14f.; 9.2f.
[54] The text above p. 145.

event is subject to a certain determinism. We recall the great text which we have already discussed in another context and which states that a time and an hour have been set for everything, for every intention under heaven (3.1–8, 17). Koheleth returns to this idea again and again. For everything there is a time and a way (8.6). There is, however, no comfort in this determination of every phenomenon, for often enough, as a result of it, what man has learned by hard toil is rendered useless.

> Again I saw that under the sun the race is not to the swift, nor the battle to the strong, nor bread to the wise, nor riches to the intelligent, nor favour to the men of skill; but time and chance happen to them all. For man does not know his time . . . (Eccles. 9.11f.)

There is no way of combating this mysterious decree. Man is totally subjected to it. 'Whatever happens – it has long since been named' (i.e. it has been summoned into existence). Man 'is unable to argue with one who is stronger than he' (6.10). Here it becomes clear what lies behind the irrevocable decree; it is God himself who determines the 'appropriate times'. God has 'made' not only the days of prosperity but also the days of adversity, and thus they have to be endured (7.14).

> I know that whatever God does endures for ever; nothing can be added to it, nor anything taken from it; God has made it so, in order that men should fear before him. (Eccles. 3.14)

Here, too, the emphasis is on that which is completely unalterable, on that to which man has to submit. Thus we find ourselves face to face with the strangely paradoxical fact that to Koheleth the world and events appear to be completely opaque and that, on the other hand, he is aware that they are completely within the scope of God's activity. The point at which this divine activity becomes obvious to him as an actual power and reality is precisely the realization that there is a time set for every occurrence. To what extent Koheleth is aware that the world is controlled and encompassed by the free activity of God is made completely clear by the sentences which we can only now adduce in what follows.

3. For Koheleth, this knowledge about God and his control over the world does not, at any rate, conceal, as one might suppose, anything in the nature of a point of repose for his thoughts which, in their search, range from one phenomenon to another. The opposite is the case. With this knowledge about God there is linked his deepest

intellectual need. Here lies the real cause of all his toil. In order to gain a proper view of this problem, let us begin once again with that great text which deals with the time that is set for every activity. It has, indeed, a very characteristic continuation in which Koheleth draws his own conclusions from this truth. What follows from all this, especially for the man who sets out to master life, that is, for the 'worker'? This is Koheleth's answer:

> What gain has the worker from his toil? I have seen the business that God has given to the sons of men to be busy with. He has made everything beautiful in its time; also he has put the distant future (?)[55] into man's mind, yet so that he cannot find out what God has done from the beginning to the end. (Eccles. 3.9–11)

To the question of what man derives from all this (*yitrōn*), Koheleth replies, 'Toil'. This is not the fault of the objectives God has in view; they are 'beautiful', as Koheleth says. The trouble is that man cannot 'find out what God has done'. By this, Koheleth means that man is unable to adjust to this, that he is unable to take into account what has been decreed in any given situation by God. This is exactly what he means when he says later that 'man does not know his time'. Blind and unsuspecting, like animals blundering into a net, he is suddenly overtaken by an 'evil time' (9.12). It is, of course, God who has also 'made the evil day', but that is no consolation, for man is unable to discover what comes after him (7.14).

> There is something vain which happens on earth, namely that there are righteous men to whom it happens as if they had acted like godless men, and that there are godless men to whom it happens as if they had acted like righteous men. I said that this too is vain. Then I recommended enjoyment, for there is nothing better for man under the sun than that he should eat and drink and enjoy himself. (8.14f.)

Here Koheleth has certainly spoken the last word on where he sees the real burden, the toil of human life. It is not the adversities in themselves; it is, rather, an insurmountable barrier which is set against man's search for knowledge. Every reader asks uneasily what is left for Koheleth with such a view of things, against the background of such depressing insights. Is there any value left in life at all? One

---

[55] How the word *'ōlām*, which we usually render with 'eternity', although it means, rather, the 'distant future', is to be understood in v. 11, still could not be satisfactorily explained. Cf. the list of the different ways of taking it in O. Loretz, op. cit., p. 281, note 277. Is what is meant the trouble to ask in advance about when one has to take the future into consideration (so Zimmerli, op. cit., ad loc.)?

can almost work it out for oneself. Since God has 'made' both the good day and the evil day (7.14), man can still hold himself ready, with a completely open mind, for whatever good thing God is ready to grant to him. 'In the day of prosperity be joyful' (7.14). This is yet another theme to which Koheleth returns again and again with remarkable insistence. And no wonder, for here at last is a point at which the way in which God deals with man becomes reasonably clear. The question of man's 'lot', i.e. of the place in life assigned to him, one would say today the question of meaning – at this one point Koheleth has a positive answer, for here man can recognize a divine intention directed towards him for good. This is the only thing that man can call 'good', 'that a man should enjoy his work, for that is his lot' (3.22; 5.17).[56] It has rightly been stressed that this exhortation to be aware of happiness and of anything that enhances life is not to be confused with that zest for life which so often settles in the shadow of despair. The situation is, rather, the reverse. Here for the first time, Koheleth is aware that he is in accord with a divine purpose; here he sees himself face to face with a beneficent God, 'for there is nothing better for a man than that he should eat and drink and enjoy himself. I saw that that, too, comes from God's hand' (2.24). How excitedly this unyielding theologian speaks about God when he comes to speak on this subject.

> Go, eat your bread with enjoyment, and drink your wine with a merry heart; for God has already approved what you do. Let your garments be always white; let not oil be lacking on your head. Enjoy life with the wife whom you love, all the days of your fleeting life which he has given you under the sun, because that is your portion in life and in your toil at which you toil under the sun. (Eccles. 9.7–9)

It is certainly difficult for us, who in Western literature have scarcely anything to compare it with, to interpret such a work satisfactorily. All that is certain is that Koheleth is not presenting any self-contained compendium of instruction, but that he is carrying further the old didactic tradition, even if his questions and theses are peculiarly his own. He himself does not envisage a clear distinction between what is intellectually his own and what he has inherited from the past. However, his own revolutionary position can be delimited fairly clearly. One should also be clear about yet another difficulty which hinders a satisfactory interpretation of the book. This is not to be

---

[56] On the question about man's 'lot' in life, Eccles. 2.10, 21; 5.18; 9.6, 9; 11.2.

found in the text, but the commentator himself brings it into play. In his own feeling about life, he finds himself so directly addressed and justified by Koheleth's melancholy that he is almost won over to it in advance. Koheleth's sentences make such good sense to him that he is inclined to see in them something like a breakthrough from a forced, 'dogmatized' wisdom to a more realistic and truer view of the world. It is clear, however, that in an approach which is burdened with such an obvious bias, inappropriate, ideological presuppositions can become entangled in the exposition and can lead to problematical assessments. To counteract this, one must always again and again attempt to ask about the specific value of Koheleth's teaching against the background of the teachings of his time.

How directly Koheleth stands in the didactic tradition is clear from the way in which he speaks of God. Were one to understand his teaching as a self-contained 'philosophical system', then one would have to reproach him with being inconsistent in view of such weak theological premisses. But in this matter – that God exists and rules in the world – he shares completely the point of view of the older teachers. What is new and also alarming is his opinion of the relationship of man to what we have called the continuing divine 'activity', namely that to his way of thinking it is completely beyond man's perception and comprehension and that man, therefore, is also incapable of adapting himself to it.[57] The consequences of this conviction – measured against the confidence of old wisdom – are catastrophic. The strong urge to master life – a main characteristic of old wisdom – has been broken. Man has lost contact with events in the outside world. Although continually permeated by God, the world has become silent for him. What happens in the world is always in motion, sometimes turned favourably towards man, at others rejecting him, and is now sealed up deep in his inner thoughts. 'That which happens is far off, deep, very deep; who can find it out?' (7.24).[58]

[57] On the wide-ranging term 'the work of God' see G. von Rad, *Studia Biblica et Semitica, Festschrift für Th. Chr. Vriezen*, 1966, pp. 290ff., esp. pp. 296f.

[58] 'Thus the essential element in the chance character of the temporal realization of destiny for men is the inscrutability of the future. As an agent, man is anxious to be able to plan and organize the future. In so far as the future withdraws itself from this attempt on man's part to impose a fixed plan on the shape of the world and on life, and changes from being a medium of human realization to an occurrence which itself makes demands, which is predetermined in advance by a strange determinant and which simply happens to man, all human action comes to grief on it' (E. Wölfel, *Luther und die Skepsis. Eine Studie zur Kohelet-Exegese Luthers*, 1958, pp. 49f.).

Even in his own loving and hating, man is unable to understand himself (9.1). Man never achieves dialogue with his surroundings, still less with God. Is he even still a 'Thou'? Even if he grants fulfilment in life, it is no more than a silent acceptance of a gift silently handed over. Koheleth has come to terms with this situation, even if it is with a resignation that can leave no reader unmoved. In sharp contrast to Job, there is no sign of any attack on God, of any rebellion against a relationship of God to man which bears no resemblance at all to that known in old Israel.[59] Koheleth no longer poses Job's question as to whether this God is still his God.

What has happened here? The difference from the teachings characteristic of the book of Proverbs is so great that at least an attempt at an explanation must be made. As has already been indicated, the most common view of the radical theses of Koheleth has been to see in them a counter-blow to older teachings which believed, too 'optimistically', or better, too realistically, that they could see God at work in experience. That Koheleth turns against the prevailing teachings is beyond doubt, but the reason for his opposition must be made still clearer. According to the prevailing point of view, it would appear as if he were turning only against untenable statements, as if he were challenging a few, no longer justifiable sentences which presented the divine activity as too rational and too obvious a phenomenon. Such sentences may in fact have existed. Every understanding of the world that is formulated in comprehensive terms always carries within it the tendency to a certain stiffening, and, in zeal for the didactic emphasis, certain theses are often completely transformed into something one-sided. But the same is equally true of Koheleth. This explanation breaks down, however, for the reason that Koheleth is turning against not only outgrowths of traditional teaching but the whole undertaking. If that undertaking attributed to experience a certain ability to see the hand of God in events – a certain ability! No wise man asserted that he could understand 'the whole work of God' as Koheleth appears to do (8.17) – then he would contest this ability with regard to human experience all along the line. Anyone who agrees with him in this can scarcely avoid the conclusion that the whole of old wisdom had become increasingly entangled in a single false doctrine.

In order to cope with this difficult question, let us, lastly, take up once again that doctrine which was so important for Koheleth, the

---

[59] Zimmerli sees the beginnings of a rebellion against God in 1.13; 3.10; 6.10.

doctrine of the times which God has decreed, especially the statement that they are completely unrecognizable to man and that he can derive no profit from them for his life. These decrees, which are hidden from man, signify only toil for him. The older teachers, on the other hand, were of the opinion that man certainly needed great vigilance in order to recognize the right time for his activity but that this was certainly not a hopeless effort and that from time to time he had the opportunity, by seizing the right time, of advancing himself a little or of letting himself be carried forward in his undertakings.[60] Who is right? Can one really say that Koheleth's observation has been keener and more sober? Is the reason really only that he has been the first to succeed in freeing himself from 'dogmatic' prejudices? The reason for this alarming contradiction lies much deeper. It lies in the different presuppositions of faith in the two cases. To be more precise, the experience in which the older teachers put their trust was of a different kind from that which finds expression in Koheleth. The former was an experience which was in constant dialogue with faith; reason was at work, reason which never set itself up as an absolute but which knew that it was based on knowledge about Yahweh and that it was secure in Yahweh's power. There is, however, absolutely no way of telling to what extent such reason, surrounded by faith, can be corroborated by experience. In the case of Koheleth, the situation is completely different. If he felt himself unprotected from events and 'vulnerable on every side' (Zimmerli), then this was not due to the greater sharpness of his gifts of observation but to a loss of trust. We have already seen how earnestly the old representatives spoke to God about their confidence and how closely their intellectual efforts connected with faith. Since they taught experiences which were included in faith, they saw the aim of their teaching as being to strengthen faith in Yahweh (Prov. 22.19). They also knew that the world is encompassed within the incalculable mystery of God. But that did not disturb their faith.[61] Koheleth, however, is deeply troubled by this. Was not the future, in the whole of Israel and therefore also in the eyes of the teachers, the domain of Yahweh alone, a domain which man must confidently yield to him? Koheleth, on the other hand, experiences the hiddenness of the future as one of the heaviest burdens of life.[62] Thus he arrives at what is, as far as Yahwism is concerned, the scandalous sentence, 'All that comes is vanity'

---

[60] See above p. 139.   [61] Cf. Prov. 21.30f. (text above p. 101).
[62] Eccles. 3.11; 6.12; 7.14; 10.14.

(11.8). From this standpoint he could even agree with the age-old complaint about the vanity of life. Those who are to be praised are the dead, and it is even better not to have been born at all (4.2). Koheleth's greatest predicament lies in the fact that he has to set out to answer the question of the meaning of life, the question about man's 'lot', with a reason which is almost completely unsupported by any confidence in life. He confronts that question with the totality of life and simply makes it responsible for answering the question about salvation. The old teachers, in their search for understanding, were more modest and certainly also cleverer. They did not see it as their task to answer, by means of their still only partially valid understanding and experiences, the ultimate question, the question of salvation.

Unfortunately, we are unable to define from a traditio-historical point of view to what specific extent the teachers participated in Yahwism. The reason for this lies in the didactic material, which did not demand of them that they should provide anything even approaching a self-contained body of instruction. It is not, however, open to doubt that they stood in a broad stream of Yahwistic traditions and that they drew on their knowledge and their experiences of these. But in the case of Koheleth this is obviously quite different. His work is not the expression of any school; we are, rather, justified in considering him as an outsider completely free of tradition, and this is, indeed, what he claims to be. Not often in ancient Israel has the question of salvation been posed so inescapably to a single individual as was the case with Koheleth. He has answered it (in the way of which we know) mainly on the basis of the experiences which the world around him afforded. Anyone who has listened carefully to Koheleth's dialogue with the traditional doctrines should not find it quite so easy to give one-sided approval to the lonely rebel. He will, rather, be deeply preoccupied with the problem of experience to which both partners in the dialogue urgently referred and yet arrived at such different observations. He will realize how narrowly tied man is as he moves within the circle of experience which is offered from time to time by his understanding of the world. In view of this fact, one will, in the first instance, more readily believe that an outsider who swims against the stream is more likely to advance in realms of experience which remain unexpressed in or are even suppressed by conventional teaching.

On the other hand, limitations are once again placed on Koheleth's attempt to think in such a determined fashion against the background

of his isolated situation. In the radicalism of his questioning he has
become completely the spectator, only observing, registering and submitting. In contrast to the older wise men, he has overstepped a limit
which was drawn – for whatever reason – for them. While they, in
order to interpret the realities of their life, did not make use of any
all-embracing, abstract terms, Koheleth immediately goes the whole
way. In order to find the definitive formula, he lumps the whole of
life's experience together, and the result is 'vanity' (*hebel*). This word
runs like a pedal-point through the whole book (about thirty times).
His reason is on the look-out for a final abstraction; but that same
reason exposes itself to the counter-question as to whether it is still a
medium suitable for the answering of man's question about salvation.
The question is all the more justified because Koheleth has withdrawn
from every active development in life and has thereby excluded himself, from the outset, from a wide range of conclusive experiences.
The questions posed by Koheleth cannot, however, be answered on
the basis of pure theory, for the issues on which man's contemplative
eye fixes are not objective destiny, and, above all, they evade and
exclude themselves from any overall reckoning on the part of a distant
observer. On the contrary, they are orientated, ceaselessly and in
their great variety, towards man. The world, like a monster, presses
in on him and challenges him. To one who is secure in a fundamental
position of faith, events can appear differently from what they do to
one who is assailed by doubt. One must indeed go further and say
that they not only 'appear' different, they are and even become
different. The one who has faith encounters only that which is worthy
of his trust. Well and good! What someone considers to be paradig-
matic among the complex number of happenings and what he accordingly sets up to serve a didactic purpose, is dependent on a basic
position which the observer has previously taken up. But in no circumstances can this statement be understood in such a way that a
man is thought to be basically dependent on the ideas of the outside
world which he has made for himself. In this respect there is nothing
that is either purely subjective or purely objective. Whether one event
shuts itself off from one person, while another – apparently as similar
to the first as it possibly could be – opens itself out to someone else,
addresses him – in short, whether it sets up with him living relations
which appear meaningful to him – this is surely to be explained
not solely on the basis of the temperament and range of ideas
of the person concerned. It is to be traced back to the mysterious

realm of that dialogue between an individual and the world in which he lives, a dialogue which stands in sharp contrast to the monologue of the man who is thrown back upon his own resources. In this dialogue, that world in which he lives is a forceful partner. Koheleth, however, was incapable of entering into a dialogue with the world which surrounded him and pressed in on him. It had become for him a silent, unfriendly, outside force which he was able to trust only where it offered him fulfilment of life.[63] The wise men, however, were of the opinion that, through the medium of the world as it addressed man, God himself spoke to man, and that only in this dialogue was man shown his place in life.

5. EPILOGUE TO JOB AND ECCLESIASTES

We have analysed two works which are not only to be regarded as isolated peaks in the literary production of ancient Israel, but about whose worth even in the literature of the world as a whole there can be no dispute. Each of them goes its own way. They are comparable not even in their negations, only in their opposition to the didactic tradition. How obvious it seems to enquire about their direct effect on the thinking and teachings of their time. Must they not – one thinks involuntarily – have caused a powerful sensation and have terrified all thinking men? But we know very little about the opportunities for effect open to such works in the ancient Near East. How many copies of Job would have been in circulation? The book can surely not have been accepted among the literature used in the schools. From the outset, therefore, one would have to reckon its diffused effect as very slight. And is it at all feasible that two individual works will have brought about a rethinking of later Israel's understanding of the world? Could an understanding of the world which was not simply the elaboration of a few thinkers be changed in such a way? There is also the fact that these two works did not even represent what was obviously true as opposed to what was obviously false. Works of such a kind indicate difficult problems and theological doubts; but there is, in peoples' thought-processes, no compulsion to think things out logically until more satisfactory solutions are achieved.

---

[63] This lack of connection between Koheleth and the events of his environment with all their consequences has been impressively presented by H. Gese, 'Die Krisis der Weisheit bei Kohelet', *Les Sagesses du Proche-Orient Ancien*, 1963, pp. 139ff. On this see also below p. 303.

Out of any individual understanding of the world – constructed over centuries – there can break out unexpectedly, from unfathomable depths, eruptions whose lack of moderation prevents, from the outset, any compromise and whose sole function seems to be to point to the fragile nature of any understanding of the world, no matter how carefully it may have been thought out.

Sirach is supposed to have known Job, but every educated man at that time would have known that Job had 'kept to all the ways of righteousness' (Sir. 49.9). If, of the great number of passages in Sirach which scholars believe they have found, one or another should really prove that Sirach has read Job, then the whole affair is all the more disappointing, for then he has kept such a reserved distance that it would be difficult to understand him even simply as an interlocutor of Job.[64] Nothing has made sufficient impression on him to force him to rethink traditional teaching in the light of Job. In the case of Koheleth matters are scarcely any different. An attempt has, indeed, been made to see in a section of the Wisdom of Solomon a more or less direct polemic against one of his arguments.[65] But that is also uncertain. Can the statements quoted, about the transitoriness and vanity of life, and the summons to enjoy what is possible, come only from Koheleth? If they do, they have been distorted. But the subject of these statements is a long-standing one in the ancient Near East, and as such it is not Koheleth's private literary property. The observer who looks back, with only a handful of literary works surviving from long periods, yields all too easily to the temptation of assuming too close relationships or cross-connections which, in view of the polemical character of these works, are not really to be expected. It even seems, therefore, doubtful whether Job and Koheleth give us the right to speak of a crisis in wisdom in Israel.

Finally, a word about Job in Christian theology, not the Job of the framework narrative, for the 'story of Job's patience' (James 5.11) has, of course, always had its place in Christian preaching. But what of the poetic dialogue? Impressions are conflicting. Undoubtedly, in the course of the centuries, an immense amount of interpretative work has been accomplished, work whose scope and erudition – begun with questions about the correct form of the text – can only put modern interpreters to shame. On the other hand, however, the theological impact of the book on the teaching of the church has obviously always

[64] References in C. Kuhl, *ThR* 22, 1954, p. 266, note 5.   [65] Wisd. 2.1–20.

been slight. Apart from a few isolated voices which, however, had no lasting effect – Luther's 1524 Preface must certainly be included amongst these – one is faced with the fact that neither Job's questions nor his theology were really taken up and used by the church. One may even ask whether the church, if it had also remained open over the centuries to the theological perspectives of the book of Job, might not have been able to confront the fierce attacks of modern man more effectively and more calmly.[66] The situation is different in the case of Koheleth. In fact, in recent years it has begun to gather round itself a company of literary and philosophical connoisseurs.

[66] 'Surely all ancient and modern sceptics, pessimists, scoffers and atheists are innocuous and well-meaning folk compared with this man Job. They do not know against whom they direct their disdain and doubt and scorn and rejection. Job does. As distinct from them, he speaks *en connaissance de cause* . . . How strange it is that none of them has ever tried to learn from Job! If they had, they might have begun to realize at least what it is that they are attempting, and thus been able to give more forceful expression to their cause' (K. Barth, op. cit., pp. 404f.).

XIII

THE WISDOM OF JESUS SIRACH[1]

CONSIDERABLE LIMITATIONS have been placed on the study of the didactic books simply by the anonymity of the teachings and the difficulty or impossibility of dating them. This is not the case with Jesus, son of Eleazar, son of Sirach (usually called Jesus Sirach). Here we have an author, we know his period (180 BC), his home (Jerusalem, Sir. 50.27), and we know from his book, and from his grandson's preface, about his occupation and about his studies, as well as about his scholarly and poetic activity. One cannot, of course, expect an individual author who is original in the modern sense. Sirach, too, is determined by 'the discourse of the elders, who (in their turn) have learned from their fathers' (Sir. 8.9). He regards himself as their custodian; one may even ask whether he was at all aware of either the fact that, or at what points, he himself had developed, not inconsiderably, the tradition which he had received. The most important question which we must, therefore, ask of his book, because it leads directly to the specific elements in Sirach's teachings, is precisely the question about its relationship to the received tradition, that is, the question about the nature of its reproduction. Is it possible to recognize new tensions within which the thinking of these teachers found itself placed, and in which direction did productive developments take place? In fact we can see that the teachings in Sirach are still highly mobile. At every turn he was forced – obviously in the face of a changing intellectual situation – to expand along topical lines.[2]

[1] This section originally appeared as an article in *EvTh* 29, 1969, pp. 113–33.

[2] His book, too, defies all attempts to impose a scheme on it. But it is a characteristic of Sirach that he deals with specific 'themes' in fairly comprehensive units (respect for one's father: 3.1–16; relations with the poor: 4.1–10; with friends: 6.6–17; with women: 9.1–9; on rulers: 9.17–10.18; on physicians: 38.1–15; etc.). But even these units reveal no inner structure; they are to be thought of, rather, as bodies of traditions in which all kinds of material – relevant, old and well known, but also new and surprising – have come together.

A good point of access to the thought-world of the book – at this stage it can involve only the indication of certain characteristics – is provided by the prologue.

1 All wisdom comes from the Lord
   and is with him for ever.

2 The sand of the sea and the drops of rain
   and the days of old – who can count them?

3 The height of heaven and the breadth of the earth,
   the underworld and wisdom – who can penetrate them?

4 Wisdom was created before all things,
   and clever insight is from the beginning of time.

5 The root of wisdom – to whom has it been revealed?
   Her cleverness – who knows it?

7 There is one who is wise, greatly to be feared,
   sitting upon his throne, the Lord.

9 He created her, saw her and numbered her,
   and poured her out upon all his works.

10 She dwells with all flesh according to his gift,
   and he gives her to those who 'fear'[3] him. (Sir. 1.1.10)

This small section has a highly complicated traditio-historical pre-history. First of all there is the statement that wisdom is with God, and that is referring to God's own wisdom. She is completely inscrutable (vv. 1–3). From v. 4 onwards, the concept has altered, and statements are made about the wisdom that is created as part of the world, that is, of the primeval order, of the first of creatures which God has shared out, in exact proportions, to all his created works (vv. 4–9). Only in v. 10 is reference made to wisdom's appearing in the form of a specific human aptitude. She is of a different type from that of the primeval order bestowed upon the created world, for she corresponds to a type of human behaviour towards God. In fact, Sirach seems occasionally to think of her as a charisma bestowed by God.[4]

These brief statements recall, after the manner of propositions, practically everything of importance that had been achieved in the didactic tradition. Sirach extends the concept 'wisdom' in broad, programmatic terms. This is possible for him because he has a rich inheritance into which he can dip. 'The men of Hezekiah' (Prov. 25.1) could not, in their period, have developed the term 'wisdom'

[3] On this translation, see J. Haspecker, *Gottesfurcht bei Jesus Sirach*, Analecta Biblica 30, 1967, pp. 51ff.
[4] Sir. 16.25; 18.29; 24.33; 39.6; 50.27.

as broadly as this. Sirach himself was aware that he was a 'late-comer' in the long didactic tradition (33.16). Modestly he considers himself to be only someone who gathers the last of the grapes after the vintagers (33.16a). Furthermore, the section is also an instructive example of a way of teaching and thinking which is so foreign to us in that it is so remarkably uninterested in a clear-cut definition. On the contrary, the relevant statement is not limited (de-fined), but remains open and in the balance and is simply joined to the one next following. The statements which we would like to differentiate sharply almost merge with each other. In this way, however, the author can achieve what he wishes; he circles round the phenomenon in the totality in which it can be experienced by man and which removes it still further from a precise, conceptual definition because, no matter how much one tries to define it, it becomes lost again in mystery.

In this way Sirach has presented the subject with which his teaching will be concerned, namely wisdom. That it is wisdom, and not, for example, the fear of God, that is the fundamental theme of his book is stated by Sirach once again in the epilogue (50.27-29).[5] In what sense Sirach uses the term 'wisdom' at any given moment, whether in the sense of a primeval order which confronts man objectively, or in the sense of a wisdom which has to be practised by man, the reader himself must observe. There is no doubt that the understanding of wisdom as a human characteristic which one should be anxious to acquire is in the foreground. With a great array of exhortations, Sirach urges his pupil never to lose sight of this highest good.[6] Alongside these, however, there are statements which do not understand wisdom as the object of human endeavour. On the contrary, the decisive activity is on the side of wisdom, and man is her objective. She comes towards him, welcomes him, feeds him, exalts him (15.2-7). Sometimes she disguises herself before him, tests and terrifies him until she is able to trust him and reveal her secrets to him (4.11-18). How can one give an ontological definition of wisdom in this guise? Only as a beneficent, ordering power within creation to which man, in his world, is exposed, which woos him and leads him to knowledge. The book, then, deals with this strangely ambivalent phenomenon which is called wisdom.

But it also deals with something else, something which almost has the status of an independent theme in the book, namely with the way which leads to this great goal, the fear of God. The idea that true

[5] Against J. Haspecker, op. cit., pp. 87ff., 93, etc.   [6] Cf., e.g., Sir. 6.18-33.

wisdom was linked with the prerequisite of the fear of God was firmly asserted in the tradition. The maxim that the fear of God was the beginning of all wisdom was already for the old teachers the basis of all search for knowledge. Sirach even repeats the statement verbatim on one occasion (1.14). And yet, what a difference there is between the prologue of the book of Proverbs (Prov. 1.1–7) and that of Sirach (Sir. 1.1–30)![7] What a profusion Sirach needs in order to develop what he understands by the fear of God! For the old teachers, all that was necessary was adequately expressed by the statement that the fear of God was the beginning of wisdom. Men knew what was meant by the fear of God. For Sirach, things were no longer quite so simple; he had to say what the fear of God was and what it meant for men, and, above all, he had strongly to recommend it. It is honour and fame, gladness and a crown of joy (1.11f.), it is the root and crown of wisdom (1.18, 20). In the excitement of exhortation, the fear of God is occasionally even simply identified with wisdom and learning (1.16, 27). In this rhetorical profusion we recognize, in the first instance, a piece of linguistic history. Sirach no longer has at his disposal the basic compactness and clarity of language which was the prerogative of earlier periods. Words are more hackneyed and must, therefore, be multiplied. But there is more to it than that. The old ideas need to be interpreted afresh, they must be adapted to the ideas and to the taste of a different age, and this at once raises the question whether, then, Sirach means the same by the fear of God as did the old teachers.

In actual fact, a marked change in the ideas meets the eye. In old wisdom, the fear of God was taken to mean man's knowledge about his dependence on God, especially his obligation to obedience in respect of the divine will. At that period, this expression described an existential attitude, but in Sirach it is interpreted and described very much in accordance with experience, that is, in the direction of the content of his consciousness, of his feelings and inclinations. The fear of God is joy (1.11), the fear of God is humility (1.27), the fear of God is love for God (2.15f.). One can see that the term can be defined along various lines, and behind each of these definitions there lies a long tradition of experience which we could reconstruct at least in its main aspects.

---

[7] The two prologues are obviously constructed according to the same scheme: they outline the subject of instruction and point to the presupposition to which the gaining of the highest good is connected. Similarly also Haspecker, op. cit., p. 103.

The fear of God seeks God, is orientated towards God (32.14f.), and it trusts him and hopes in him (2.6). Unquestionably the term appears in Sirach in a much broader and more general sense. Above all, however, the fear of God complies with the Torah. This brings us to the point where the specific difference between Sirach and old wisdom has generally been thought to lie. In Sirach, the Torah – and obviously in the form of law established in writing – plays an important role.[8] In the older didactic collections any hint of this is totally lacking. Has not a highly significant change taken place here? The norms of behaviour are now no longer inferred from the advice of the teachers or from the store of experience of the olders, but from the Torah. The alliance between nomism and wisdom seems firmly established.[9] But this interpretation is incorrect. It is remarkable how tenaciously it has held its ground, for a glance at the book could invalidate it. Where, then, among the vast number of exhortations and counsels has the legal material penetrated wisdom, at what point is the Torah to be discerned as a new norm which has penetrated wisdom?[10] And would not a fairly fundamental conflict of norms have immediately arisen between the absolute, divine Torah and that process of appraisal and evaluation in which wisdom takes all the pros and cons into consideration? But such questions are superfluous. The didactic material presented by Sirach arises solely, as is abundantly clear, from didactic wisdom tradition and not from the Torah. Specific developments of this tradition still have to be discussed, but no changes are made in the conventional, carefully weighed assessment of phenomena.

All this should not, of course, be taken to mean that the Torah plays only a negligible part in Sirach's thought. It is simply a question of determining the theological point at which it exercises its specific function. One is immediately struck by the way in which it always appears in remarkably formal terms, as an entity *sui generis*, as 'the Torah', 'the commandments'. Nowhere does Sirach deal with it in any greater detail, but he does consider it necessary to refer to it. He needs it, in fact, in order to give a more precise definition of and to clarify the idea of the fear of God. By fear of God, as we have seen,

---

[8] References: 1.26; 6.37; 10.19; 15.1, 15; 19.17, 20, 24; 21.11; 23.27; 24.23; 26.23; 28.7; 29.1, 11; 32.15, 17, 23f.; 34.8; 35.1, 5; 37.12; 39.8; 41.8; 42.2.

[9] J. Fichtner, *Die altorientalische Weisheit in ihrer israelitisch-jüdischen Ausprägung,* 1933, and many others. On p. 97, Fichtner speaks of 'nomistic wisdom'.

[10] O. Kaiser, 'Die Begründung der Sittlichkeit im Buche Jesus Sirach', *ZThK* 55, 1958, p. 58.

the old teachers understood primarily obedience to the divine will. This divine will, however, existed for the later period in the form of God's Torah. All that differentiates Sirach from the older teachers is that he reinterpreted the expression 'fear of God' for an age to which the will of God spoke from the written Torah. Basically, however, his thoughts about the correlation between fear of God and wisdom are no different from those of teachers in earlier centuries.

> If you delight in wisdom, then keep the commandments,
>   and the Lord will give you it.   (1.26)
>
> Reflect on the fear of the Most High,
>   and consider at all times his commandments,
> and he will give understanding to your heart
>   and will make you wise, as you desire.   (6.37)

This, then, is the relationship between wisdom and fear of God envisaged by Sirach. Certainly, in his didactic zeal, Sirach allows himself to be carried away to total identifications: Torah is fear of God, and wisdom is Torah.[11] This does not, however, absolve us from keeping in mind the precise value of the theological position which Torah has in his book; it defines and interprets the term 'fear of God'. By including the Torah, therefore, Sirach has not taken a new and momentous step; in the language of his time, he preserves a concern which was from the outset of great importance in the teachings.[12]

It is certainly not, therefore, the case that the specific functions of wisdom have been replaced among the teachers by Torah. These functions are regarded by Sirach, as will be made clear shortly, somewhat differently than by the old teachers. This is not, however, the fault of the Torah. It can, fairly simply, be expressed thus. It is not that wisdom is overshadowed by the superior power of the Torah, but, *vice versa*, that we see Sirach endeavouring to legitimatize and to interpret Torah from the realm of understanding characteristic of wisdom.[13] At this point, the magnificent didactic poem of Sir. 24 would have a contribution to make. In it there is described how primeval order, created before all the other works of creation and filling the whole world, searched for a resting place among men in

---

[11] Sir. 1.16; 19.20; 21.11; 23.27.

[12] In any case, the fear of God was not awakened only by Torah. The observation of the great works of creation also leads men to the fear of God; cf. Sir. 43; J. Haspecker, op. cit., p. 153.

[13] In the light of this, the arguments of E. G. Bauckmann, ZAW 72, 1960, pp. 33ff. are greatly in need of revision.

order to be able to reveal itself, and that God allotted to it the people of Israel: 'Pitch your tent in Jacob and acquire property for yourself in Israel.' This is not simply a legitimatization of Torah. The question is not, 'Where does Torah come from?', but 'To what extent is Torah a source of wisdom?' The answer is, 'Because Torah is a self-presentation of primeval order, it is able to help men towards wisdom.' In the final section (vv. 25–34), the poem returns once again to the praise of wisdom and of its fullness.[14] If one approaches this from the direction of the traditional presentation in the saving history, from the exodus of Israel from Egypt into the desert, from the divine revelation at Sinai, one cannot marvel enough at how differently Sirach regards the prehistory of the Mosaic Torah. It is the primeval order inherent in the whole world appearing in a new guise. In this provenance lies its worth. How his tongue is loosened when he allows this primeval wisdom, transplanted to Israel, to speak!

> And I took root among an honoured people,
>   in the portion of the Lord, in his inheritance.
> Like a cedar on Lebanon I grew tall,
>   like a cypress on Mount Hermon.
> Like a terebinth I spread out my branches,
>   and my branches are full of glory and grace.
> Like a vine I caused loveliness to bud,
>   and my blossoms became glorious and abundant fruit.
> Come to me, you who desire me,
>   and you will eat your fill of my produce,
> for to think of me is sweeter than honey,
>   and to possess me is better than honey in the comb.
>   (Sir. 24.12–13, 16–20)

Notice that it is wisdom who speaks here, not Torah, and this is where Sirach's heart beats. Primeval wisdom is here regarded as a fascinating, aesthetic phenomenon. Where Torah is concerned, Sirach does not rise to such enthusiastic statements. In another passage he speaks in somewhat greater detail about the Sinai theophany and the revelation of the Torah. But that very passage (as well as the corresponding one in the 'Hymn of the Fathers', 45.5) shows, or so it

---

[14] The material of the poem betrays an unevenness which may possibly indicate a complicated process of tradition leading to its formation. In v. 22 wisdom's first-person address ends, and the transition in v. 23, 'all that is (true of) the law which Moses gave', is very abrupt. The sentence sounds like the interpretation of a figurative speech. But would vv. 1–22 then have to be understood as an allegory and not as the description of very real processes?

appears to us, how little Sirach is capable of developing the idea of Torah. If one compares the rhetorical vitality which grips him whenever he can praise wisdom, the effect when he describes the content of the Torah is poor.

> And he said to them, 'Beware of all unrighteousness,'
> and he gave to each of them commandments concerning his
> neighbour. (Sir. 17.14)

No, the Torah is not a subject of particular interest to Sirach. He knows about it, it has a part to play, but basically for Sirach it is of relevance only in so far as it is to be understood on the basis of, or as it is otherwise connected with, the great complex of wisdom teachings.

If we ask about the range of duties is which Sirach is engrossed, we encounter first of all the problem with which the teachers have been concerned from the very beginning, namely the control of the element of contingency, that is, the question of how one is to act in the face of events which cannot be understood on the basis of any clearly discernible set of laws, and the still more difficult question of whether behind these events there is not, nevertheless, at work a hidden order. Sirach does not allow himself to be outshone by the old teachers in the sobriety with which he observes realities and occurrences, even although he is fully aware of their ambiguity, a factor which militates against every human endeavour to establish a pattern. On the contrary, one has the impression that in Sirach's case the critical sense has become intensified. Certainly the old sentences, too, had much to say about, for example, how difficult it often is to judge things and that outward appearances are deceptive: someone in distress can laugh (Prov. 14.13) and someone who appears to be rich can be poor (Prov. 13.7); that silence in itself cannot be clearly evaluated, for even a fool who keeps silent one might think to be wise; or else about how silence towards a fool can be right but how it can also be wrong.[15] This is the kind of thing that Sirach, too, brings to mind. But it is precisely here that we come upon something new, for the way in which Sirach often sharply confronts things in all their ambivalence reveals something of a consciously applied, didactic method.

Sir. 29.1–13 deals with borrowing and going surety. The passage begins with a clear warning not to shirk the duty of helping, but then goes on to say a great deal about the trouble one has with the debtor.

[15] Prov. 17.27f.; 26.4f.

The case of going surety is clearer still. A kind man will go surety for his neighbour; but shortly after that, we read that going surety has ruined many. It is said, further, that the sinner comes to grief when he goes surety (in so far as he is simply out for gain). All this the pupil should keep in mind, so that later he will be able to do the right thing. The situation is exactly the same in the case of people who give advice (Sir. 37.7–15). In life, one is constantly dealing with such people. On the one hand, it would be foolish to pay attention to them; on the other, it would be foolish to ignore them. And then there is also 'the advice of the heart' (vv. 13f.). One must pay particular attention to one's conscience, to the heart enlightened by God. Silence can be very ambiguous. One man is silent because he has nothing to say, and in this way he can even be thought to be wise, while another is silent because he is waiting for the right moment to speak (20.5–7). Completely ambiguous is the vocation of the physician. The passage begins with the exhortation to remain in touch with the physician for he, too, has been created by God. And it closes with the statement, 'Whoever sins before his creator will fall into the hands of the physician' (38.1–15). In two passages, Sirach expatiates on the phenomenon of shame, which is capable of completely contrary interpretations. If one lives righteously, then one should not be ashamed, one should not even be ashamed to confess one's sins; one should, however, be ashamed of one's folly (4.20–26). Not every kind of shame, then, is 'seemly' (41.16). One should be ashamed of every kind of evil, but not of one's faith, nor of one's correctness in housekeeping and domestic affairs (41.14–42.8). 'Death is bitter to the man who lives at peace on his property, but is a blessing for the old and those who suffer pain' (41.1–2). In other cases, where the judgment of a thing is unequivocal, such as the case of children or friends, Sirach can actually even confine himself to dwelling more on those aspects which are often thought about less. Many a friend turns into an enemy (6.9). 'It is better to die childless than to have ungodly children' (16.3b).[16]

Behind this didactic technique, of which many more examples could be cited, there lie perceptions of which the older teachers were not conscious in these terms. Things and events in man's environ-

---

[16] This contrast of completely opposite evaluations of one and the same thing reminds us very much of the Old Babylonian dialogue between a master and his servant (*ANET*, pp. 437–8), in which the question about what is the right thing to do is lost in playful scepticism.

ment are by no means neutral in value or meaning. But they do not make their meaning and value directly discernible to man. On the contrary, they confuse him, for they glide, so to speak, constantly to and fro between good and evil, between useful and harmful, between meaningful and meaningless. This, however, is the task which the wisdom teacher takes upon himself, namely to realize the specific value of each of them from case to case, from situation to situation. In this ambivalence of appearances Sirach sees the greatest problem, for in any given situation there is always only one that is right. Koheleth would say that to determine the situation correctly in different cases is toil. In actual fact, in the development of the negative aspects, Sirach gives expression to perceptions which Koheleth could have expressed in identical terms. One can think, for example, of his scepticism about the desire for descendants (16.1–3). He, too, can give expression to the idea that one man toils without success and achieves nothing, while another, who has no means and lacks the proper ability, prospers, simply because the eyes of God have been upon him for good (11.11–12). Here Sirach even speaks about God in connection with an experience which is very difficult to understand. In another passage he warns men not to judge by mere outward appearances.

> Do not praise any man for his beauty,
>   and do not loathe anyone for his appearance.
> The bee is small among winged creatures,
>   but she produces the greatest sweetness.
> Do not make fun of what an unfortunate man wears,
>   and do not despise him who is in mourning,
> for the power of the Lord is wonderful,
>   and his power is hidden from men.   (Sir. 11.2–4)

Here, too, Sirach extends the thought impressively into the realm of the theological. Precisely because things are other than they seem – even unpleasant men, grief-stricken men and those who are pursued by misfortune are honoured – this very fact corresponds to the order which God has given to his works. 'His power is hidden from men.' Here it becomes particularly clear how much Sirach, too, knows about what weighed so heavily on Koheleth. God's power is 'hidden' in so far as its logic is not evident in events and occurrences. Should one not think – we shall have to return again later to this important text – that in the things of everyday life, that is, in water, fire, salt, oil, etc., we are dealing with neutral objects? No, says Sirach; even they are not neutral. For some they turn out to be good, but for others they become evil (39.26f.). And this, of course, on the basis of an enigmatical decree of God. Sirach has no doubt as to its wisdom and goodness.

> As clay in the hand of the potter . . .
> so men are in the hand of their creator,
> to give to them as he desires.
> Opposite evil there is the good
> and opposite death there is life,
> so opposite the good man there is the sinner.
> Look on all the works of the Most High;
> they are always in pairs, one the opposite of the other.
>
> (Sir. 33.13–15)

That is surely one of the most illuminating texts. Like Koheleth, Sirach too sees man in the grip of God with no way out, and in Sirach the idea of predestination also comes into play. There can be no doubt that in these statements the emphasis lies on the freedom and validity of the divine decrees. But this does not simplify things in the sense that, for example, those destined for good by God do good. If this were the case, Sirach would have no need at all to write his book. Rather, one could say that it is here that the problem of life first begins. For the divine decrees, as is expressed here in astonishingly clear terms, are completely opposed to each other. Man, however, has been set right in the middle of this enormous tension, between the good and the evil, between that which preserves life and that which destroys it. 'Fire and water have been placed before you' (15.16). In this hard-pressed position, Sirach offers man no moral platitudes (and he has often been accused of doing just that). He teaches the difficult art of finding the right way of looking at things in the midst of ambiguous phenomena and occurrences, and of doing what is right in the sight of God. In order to train his pupils in this, Sirach makes use of what is so characteristic of him, namely that ambivalent, didactic method, that remarkable 'both-and'. In actual practice, only one of them can ever be right.

It will be readily admitted that Sirach does not take life easily, that is, the task of hitting the right mark among events in a world in which God's power is hidden. But Sirach's teaching is neither gloomy nor tormented; it is, rather, underpinned by a great confidence. The mystery, too, about which he knows much, disposes him to adoration.

He does not renounce what is for him the urgent task of mastering life. Sirach's confidence in wisdom, that is, in the help which a properly based and a properly operated intellect offers to man, is almost unlimited.

How could man ever find his way in an environment in which, as we have just seen, all the phenomena are constantly changing with regard to their value and meaning, if he did not know something about the 'time' to which all this change is subject? Again and again Sirach speaks of the *kairos* which man must discover both in the minor tasks of daily life and in the ultimate questions of the divine decrees and which – here he differs sharply from Koheleth – he *can* discover.[17] It is not surprising that in this context much is said about knowing when to speak and when to keep silent. Many keep silent because they know that there is a proper time to speak. The fool does not do that (20.6, 19f.). One can see that wisdom and folly here are not measured by the content of what is said, but only by whether a man speaks at the wrong time (22.6) or at the proper time (4.23). Similarly, one must remember, in the case of both friends and enemies, that time has a part to play (6.8; 12.16; 19.9). Everywhere it plays its part, a part of which one should never lose sight; in borrowing and repaying (29.2–5), in drinking wine (31.28), in medicinal therapy (38.13). But, above all, there are times of need which a man should never face unprepared.[18] Thus Sirach can exhort in a very comprehensive way, 'My son, observe the right time' (4.20), for 'from morning to evening times change' (18.26).[19] Once again we see that knowledge as such is very old and is still the concern of the late periods. But the sphere of understanding in which the old knowledge is placed has changed drastically. Thus, Sirach is not content with the simple experience of the change in times and in the tasks which grow out of these times, but he places the knowledge, at the same time, in important theological contexts. It is God who allocates to man 'his time'. In the political sphere, too, he appoints rulers 'for the time' (10.4). Sirach expands on this in the greatest detail in an impressive didactic poem.

16   The deeds of the Lord are all good,
          and they suffice in their time for all that is necessary.

[17] About sixty times according to the Greek text.
[18] 2.2, 11; 3.31; 5.7; 10.26; 18.24f.; 22.23; 37.4; 40.24; 51.10, 12.
[19] 51.30 is difficult to interpret. According to the Hebrew text it should be translated: 'Do your works before the time (*beלֹō* *ʿēt*), and then he will give you his reward in his time.'

17 At his word the water stood up like a wall
   and his storerooms at the utterance of his mouth.
18 At once whatever pleases him is accomplished,
   and nothing can stop his help.
19 The action of all flesh is before him,
   and nothing is hidden from his eyes.
20 He sees from the distant past to the distant future,
   and nothing is too wonderful in his eyes.
21 One cannot say, 'What is this?', 'Why is that?',
   for everything has been chosen for its use.
21b One cannot say, 'This is worse than that',
   for everything is marvellous in its time.
22 His blessing overflows like the Nile,
   and like the Euphrates, it waters the earth.
23 In this way his wrath drove away the nations,
   and he made the irrigation water salty.
24 For the righteous his ways are straight,
   just as they are stumbling blocks to the lawless.
25 For the good, he decreed good from the beginning,
   just as he decreed good and evil for the wicked.
26 The first essentials for man's needs in life are
      water, fire, iron, salt,
   wheat flour, milk and honey,
      the blood of the grape, oil and clothes.
27 All this is good to the good,
   but to the evil it turns to evil.
28 There are winds which are intended to punish,
   and in their wrath they overturn mountains.
   At the time of destruction they pour out their power
   and placate the anger of their creator.
29 Fire, hail, hunger, and plague
   they too are made for punishment.
30 Devouring beasts, scorpions and vipers
   and the sword of vengeance to root out the ungodly.
   All these are created for their use,
      they are stored up and are summoned forth at the proper time.
31 When he commands them they rejoice,
   and when he orders they do not resist this word.
32 For this reason I have been convinced from the beginning,
   I reflected on it and set it down in writing.
33 The deeds of God are all good,
   they suffice in their time for all that is necessary.
34 One cannot say, 'This is worse than that,'
   for everything is marvellous in its time.

35   Rejoice, then, with all your heart
         and praise the name of the Holy One.   (Sir. 39. 16–35)

In provocative fashion, the poem opens with the main thesis, and
at the end – apart from a brief doxology – this is solemnly repeated
as if it were a *quod erat demonstrandum* (v. 33). The theme that is dealt
with is the power of God, and the thesis presented is that this power
is beneficent in every circumstance.[20] The actual instruction is rather
polemical. The repeated 'one cannot say' (vv. 21, 34) shows that
Sirach takes, as his starting point, opinions which are different from
his own. In doing so, he attacks the claim of certain who believe they
can judge the divine power differently in different cases, sometimes
as good and sometimes as less good, who believe, therefore, that they
can ask the critical question as to why this or that has happened. One
will not go far wrong if one thinks here of men whose faith has been
shattered and who cast doubt on the goodness and the meaning of
many divine actions. Thus Sirach, too, had to face up to the problem
of theodicy. His attack on such doubt is, however, and this is nothing
new to us, not very solid, in so far as several arguments are merged
with each other. There is, first of all, the well-known reference to the
power and blessing of the divine rule in creation and history (vv. 17b–
23). Somewhat abruptly, this is followed by the argument that
Yahweh's ways are right for those who belong to him, that is, that
faith and obedience are the presuppositions for understanding them;
and then there is a reference to a primeval, divine determination for
good and for evil, or at least to a prescience, an idea which appears
occasionally in Sirach.[21]

But the real argument of this didactic poem has not yet been stated,
and it is by far the most interesting. 'All divine rule is good, and it
suffices for every need in its time.' The decisive statement lies, of
course, in the final word: 'in its time'. Sirach has made the old idea
of the 'proper' time theologically fruitful, and he has succeeded in
achieving, on that basis, a new way of looking at the divine rule. It
cannot, of course, be understood on the basis of a general system of
value or meaning but can be grasped only in relation to its proper
time and to the need of that time. Then, from man's point of view, the
divine rule can be evaluated as completely negative, in the same way

[20] Presumably Sirach is taking up the 'very good' of Gen. 1.31. Perhaps the
poem is something in the nature of a fanciful interpretation of the Genesis passage.
But by 'works' it does not mean the objects of creation, but God's rule.
[21] Sir. 23.20, see below p. 265.

as fire, hail, plagues, scorpions and snakes. If Yahweh is angry, then they too have their proper time (v. 30), and his power is good and right in this form, too. At their proper time, then, these apparently negative phenomena, too, are 'marvellous' (vv. 21b, 34). Here, Sirach's well-known teaching about the ambivalence of events is expressed at its most rigorous, but expressed also with a surprising theological significance. Even the wholly direct intervention of God in the world of men is regarded by men as marked by that ambivalence. This attempt to tackle the problem of theodicy is new. Certainly it does not neglect to offer man's intellectual need help towards understanding; but it is released from the unpleasant task, with which Job's friends still felt themselves faced, of interpreting God's power in comprehensive terms on the basis of a definite, fixed norm.

Can something now be said by way of a summary about the intentions which Sirach aimed at in his teaching? Certainly he wishes to teach wisdom, knowledge, mastery of life, learning, etc. But the question is precisely on what level he sees all this, and how he interprets, alters or develops the traditional doctrines. This cannot, of course, be summarized in one sentence. In this respect, Sirach is wholly within the tradition of the old teachers: his instruction is human instruction, that is, it does not end up by being a divine command. It does not claim for itself the authority of a direct, divine address. It is not 'proclamation' but discourse between man and man; it is advice, exhortation and warning about all the questions which man found as obstacles on his way. In spite of the authority which Sirach claims for himself, his teaching is always a dialogue, indeed it is, as we have seen, thoroughly dialectical in so far as it happily confines itself to pointing to the two or more sides which any one thing has. The one which is right can be found by the pupil only 'existentially', in the situation of decision. But how does Sirach regard man who is skilled in this kind of dialogue, and how does he, in Sirach's opinion, achieve self-realization and arrive at his destiny?

24   Listen to me, learn insight from me,
           pay attention to my words.
25   I will let my spirit bubble over in full measure,
           and carefully proclaim my knowledge.
26   When God created his works in the beginning
           and, before he created them, gave to each its part,
27   then he established his works for ever
           and their dominion for all generations.

They neither hunger nor grow weary
and never cease from their work.

28 None of them pushes the other,
and for all time they never disobey his word.

29 After this the Lord looked down upon the earth
and filled it with his good things.

30 With all kinds of living creatures he filled its surface,
and to it they return.

17.1 The Lord created man from earth
and lets him return to it again.

2 He gave them a specific number of days and a time,
and he gave them power over everything on it.

3 As was fitting, he clothed them with strength
and created them in his image.

4 He laid the fear of them on all flesh,
so that they might rule over beasts and birds.

5 He formed tongues, eyes and ears,
and he gave them a mind for thinking.

7 He filled them with reason and insight
and showed them the good and the evil.

8 He set his eye in their hearts
to show to them the greatness of his works,

9 so that they might tell of the greatness of his works,

10 and praise his holy name.

11 In addition, he gave them knowledge
and bestowed on them the law of life.

12 He established an everlasting covenant with them
and told them of his laws.   (Sir. 16:24–30; 17.1–12)

It would be tempting to examine, sentence by sentence, word by word, how tradition and interpretation are fused in this didactic poem. Of course Sirach follows the biblical, that is, primarily the Priestly writer's account of creation. But there is a vast difference in the language alone. In contrast to the statuesque immobility of the statements in Gen. 1, there is expressed here at the same time also an emotional quality, a subjectivity occasioned by the pathos of wonder. With the representation of the creation of man, there is now mingled awe at man's intellectual equipment. He is empowered to speak, see, hear and, above all, to think and to differentiate between good and evil (vv.6f.).[22] Sirach is particularly concerned to say some-

[22] The sentence that God has placed his eye in men's hearts to enable them to observe his works correctly is very strange. What can have been the Hebrew form behind the not entirely unambiguous Greek textual transmission? M. Z. Segal, Sēfer Ben-Sira haśśālem (Hebr.), 1958, ad loc., follows the Greek text.

thing about the intellectual relationship between man and God, a relationship which, again, was not mentioned (at least not explicitly) in Gen. 1. There, of course, the concern was to determine the relationship of domination between man and the world. Sirach, however, interprets that old text from the point of view of knowledge of God's works and of the praise which man owes to God for these.

1   God has allotted much toil,
      and a heavy yoke lies on the children of men,
    from the day when they go forth
      from their mother's womb
    until the day when they return
      to the mother of all living:
2   thoughts and inner fears
      and worry about the future till the day they die,
3   from the one who sits high on his throne
      to the one who sits in dust and ashes,
5   jealousy, worry, anxiety, fear of death, quarrelling, strife.
      Even when he lies resting on his bed,
        sleep at night confuses his mind.
6   For a brief moment only does he have rest . . .
    he is confused by the visions of his mind,
      like a man who flees from his enemy.
7   And . . . when he awakes,
      he is surprised that there was nothing to fear.
8   On all flesh, both man and beast,
      and upon the ungodly it comes sevenfold,
9   plague, bloodshed, fever and sword,
      devastation and destruction, famine and death . . .

                                        (Sir. 40.1–11)

The poem begins like one of those laments which deal very generally with the toil and sorrow of human life, something like Job 7.1ff., for example ('Is not hard service man's lot upon earth?'), or Job 14.1ff. But where does Sirach consider man's toil and yoke to lie? Not, as earlier generations complained, in illness, poverty and oppression by enemies; it lies, as v. 2 already says, primarily in his mind, in the intellectual sphere, that is, in his anxieties and emotions. This is why he is so restless. And when he seeks rest at night – what a wonderful passage – then hallucinations and deceptive dreams confuse him. He flees even before phantoms. This picture of man, too – once again a remarkable dialectical contrast with the preceding one – shows nevertheless how strongly the specifically mental aspects have come to the fore.

But these gloomy colours are actually uncharacteristic of Sirach's ideas. The central object of his teaching is not man thrown back upon himself and upon his sorrows; it is much more positive, for it is concerned with man face to face with God, with the possibilities, as well as with the obligations, encompassed by this relationship with God. In his 'Hymn of the Fathers' he demonstrates this, by means of the example of the great men of the past, as it were in an educational picture book (Sir. 44–50). Let us listen to what he says in the instructive prologue which he has prefixed to this historical picture book.

1 I will praise the pious men,
   our fathers in their generations.
2 The Most High has allotted to them great honour,
   and they were great from earliest days,
3 rulers of the earth in their kingdoms,
   men renowned for their power;
   they gave counsel by their insight
   and observed everything by their prophesying,
4 governors of the nations by their cleverness,
   and rulers by their keenness of mind,
   wise thinkers in their learning
   and poets as was expected of them.
5 They composed songs according to the rules,
   made known didactic poems in writing . . .
7 All these were honoured in their generation,
   and in their lives their fame endured.
8 Many of them have left a name behind them,
   so that their fame can be declared.
13 Their memory will remain for ever,
   and their righteousness will never be wiped out.
14 Their bodies were buried in peace,
   but their name remains from generation to generation.
15 Their wisdom is handed down by the congregation,
   and the assembly proclaims their praise.   (Sir. 44.1–15)

Anyone familiar with the older presentations of history in Israel cannot be sufficiently amazed at the difference in the way in which Sirach looks back into history. The concern here is not with the obvious or the hidden examples of God's guidance, nor with his judgments or his decrees of salvation, nor with the relationship of tension between promise and fulfilment, but with great men. They, not God and his plans for history, are the objects of the presentation, even of the praise.[23] One wanders through history here as through the rooms of a hall of fame.[24] On no account, however, should this be taken to suggest that in this retrospective look into history a process of secularization has taken place. It has certainly not become God-less. Only the religious aspects have changed – and that to a considerable extent. It was indeed God – as v.2 says – who brought these men to such great honour. The whole hymn is tuned to the one key: What an amazing variety God has made out of these men! What a lot they are able to achieve, as kings and advisers, as wise men or poets! Occasionally the poet is carried away by sheer emphasis to a second person address of praise. 'How glorious you were, Elijah! Whoever is like you, may well boast' (48.4). Obviously, we are here faced with something new. The man who is empowered by God to political or intellectual achievements becomes an object of admiration, occasionally also of horror. Man in union with God is an aesthetic phenomenon by which Sirach is fascinated. Aaron in his priestly garb is admired as 'the delight of the eyes, perfect beauty' (45.12). But this is true of all the other great men in history.[25]

This, then, is how Sirach regards man, and it is on this basis that we must also understand the whole of his teaching. In the principal

[23] The very old cultic word *hillēl* 'praise' is used.

[24] The hymn in Jud. 16 is entirely in the same key. It celebrates in detail Judith and her action (vv.6–11), but it is nevertheless a Yahweh-hymn. Here, if anywhere, the assumption of the influence of 'Hellenistic' thought is clear. But what does that imply? Obviously that in this intellectual encounter Israel has laid herself open to a new way of looking at man. The co-ordination of this way with Yahwism is completed and rounded off in Sirach. It is unlikely that Sir. 24 is to be understood as a tendentious, i.e. anti-Hellenistic, version of Prov. 8.22ff. (D. Michaelis, *ThLZ* 83, 1958, col. 604), intended to give precedence to Israel's knowledge of the truth. The task undertaken by Sir. 24 was, as we have seen, to provide a link between primeval order and Torah. Nothing more specific can be deduced from the book about Sirach's relationship with Hellenism. There is much to be said for thinking that in his day he was, rather, a 'conservative'. It appears questionable, however, whether one can, in contrast to him, consider the author of the Wisdom of Solomon as a progressive (A. Di Lella, 'Conservative and Progressive Theology: Sirach and Wisdom', *CBQ* 28, 1966, pp. 139ff.). In Hellenistic Alexandria things were different; there the author of the Wisdom of Solomon could perhaps be considered conservative (by contrast with Philo, for example).

[25] After the programmatically ambitious prologue, the presentation of individual personalities falls off. Sirach scarcely achieves more than the quotation of excerpts from older literature, excerpts which must now be read in the light of the prologue. Sirach's idea of prophets is astonishingly inadequate, for he regards the prophets almost solely as wonder-workers (cf. 48.1–16, 22–25). From what (Hellenistic?) literary form can Sirach have borrowed the cry, 'How glorious you were (he was)' (Sir. 48.4; 50.5)?

task which he has imposed upon himself he is still wholly within the tradition of the old teachers: he aims at training the young man (beginning with table manners, 31.12f.) for life. The ways in which he teaches pupils to look at life are, as we have seen, astonishingly flexible. There is nothing here that has been 'legalized' on the basis of Torah. Sirach has not, then, allowed the traditional form of wisdom perception and wisdom teaching to be replaced or restricted by the Torah. And yet much has changed. The example at which training is aimed differs remarkably from the one envisaged by the older teachers. They, too, knew about God; but they regarded him, rather, as a limit imposed on human attempts to master life. The training of young men was – perhaps for that very reason? – much more neutral from a religious point of view. The example which is the goal for Sirach's educational endeavours is that of the pious man. One could almost reduce his teaching to the single sentence, 'Remember the Lord our God all your days' (Tob. 4.5). In any event it is a very interiorized educational ideal; in fact, if one remembers the importance which Sirach attaches to the fear of God and especially to humility, one could really speak of a tendency to pietism. For his attitude to God contains a highly emotional element.[26]

But the scope of Sirach's perceptions is, nevertheless, of an astonishing breadth. He encompasses much more than only the relationship between God and the individual. In him expression is given to ultimate questions and insights: the world as creation, man's relationship to the truth (Sir. 24), the ambivalence of phenomena and occurrences between good and evil. One would dearly love to know the nature of the store of perceptions from which Sirach drew his individual instructions. The possibility of his having in front of him a collection of theological teaching about God, the world and man cannot be ruled out. Compared with the older teachers, this would, then, certainly be

[26] The theme of 'humility' appears in Sirach in the most varied contexts, cf. Sir. 1.27; 3.17f., 20; 4.8; 7.17; 10.14; 13.20; 18.21; 45.4. The question how wisdom changed in this way and concentrated on the religious factor could be answered only after an examination of the intellectual and religious situation in post-exilic Israel. All that appears certain to us is that this change is not to be attributed to the direct effect of Torah. The central religious concepts in Sirach (fear of God, humility) certainly cannot be explained from that direction. Rather, they could point to specific, religious tendencies in later Israel, whose piety had an effect on the wisdom teachers. The most obvious example to be discussed here would be the piety of the so-called 'anāwîm. On this, cf. most recently, Martin Achard, 'Yahwé et les 'anāwîm', *ThZ* 21, 1965, pp. 349ff. D. Michaelis' statement: 'All signs of direct experience of God are absent (from Sirach)' (*ThLZ* 83, 1958, col. 606) completely misunderstands Sirach.

something quite new. At any rate, Hebrew man, in the widely ramified teaching of Sirach, has taken his place before God and in the world in a new and, theologically, very clearly defined way. Surrounded by great mysteries and confronted again and again by insoluble problems, man is nevertheless aware that he is secure in a beneficent divine order. His faith in the protection and life-promoting blessing which God bestows upon those who seek him is so great that not even contradictory experiences can shake him. God tests and tries men, too, *sub specie contraria.*[27]

In this way, then, the instruction of men is undertaken by Sirach on the basis of different presuppositions. The ancients, too, knew that the fear of God, knowledge about God, is the beginning of wisdom. But with them things lay much further apart. The religious components affected the process of perception rather than the content of the teachings. Sirach's educational example, however, is the pious man. This brings the religious components into the centre of the educational system. The man who strives for piety, the one who fears God, that is, the one who gives his heart to God, is man as God wishes him to be.[28] To him alone are the sources of wisdom and knowledge open. It is, then, Sirach's firm conviction that – to put it briefly – faith is also a factor in education. The fear of God is able to make something of a man. It improves a man with regard both to his knowledge of the world and to his behaviour towards others. It forms him, protects him and supports him. Put concisely, 'Whoever seeks God receives instruction' (*mūsār – paideia*, 32.14).

It must, of course, still be said that, from a social point of view, there is something much more strongly exclusive than was the case in old Israel about Sirach's example for man and about his educa-

[27] Sir. 2.1–18; 4.11–18.
[28] J. Haspecker, op. cit., pp. 209ff. This turning towards religious factors also explains the inclusion of detailed prayer models in the instructions (Sir. 23.1–6; 36.1–17; 42.15–43.33; 51.1–12). Particularly interesting also is the section about cultic duties 34.18–35.20. It is certainly amazing that a wisdom teacher should utter sentences about sacrifices, fasts, ritual uncleanness, etc. But Sirach is only interested in the personal and, above all, the moral presuppositions which he considers to be the necessary preliminary to proper cultic activity. Sacrifices ought not to be offered if they consist of dishonestly acquired property such as that of the poor (34.18, 21; 35.12). One should bring one's offering in a spirit not of meanness, but of joy (35.8–10). One can see that Sirach's approach to cultic institutions is a very limited one. For him it is the moral or spiritual element which is the all-important one. 'Whoever repays faithfulness offers a sacrifice and whoever practices mercy offers a thank-offering' (35.1f.). Sirach did not read that in the Torah. He links up, rather, with the world of ideas found in certain psalms.

tional teachings. Sirach very well knows that such a training is not available to all walks and stations in life (38.24–34).[29] He is a scholar, and he forms men to his own pattern. He addresses the intellectuals among the young men, and in his period that means men who can handle books and for whom literature is an important constituent element in life. The impetus of the genuine desire for knowledge, with all its risks, has certainly slackened off compared with old wisdom. Its place is taken more and more by a breadth of training and by literary learning. Is there not sometimes something almost cosmopolitan about this training? To what extent this striving after training is thoroughly religious Sirach shows in the fine portrait which he paints of a teacher of such training. The old teachers, of course, could also handle books. But the literary activity has become more extensive. It also included study of the Torah and a concern with prophetic writings.

> . . . But the man who turns his mind
>   to the study of the law of the Most High
> finds out the wisdom of all the ancients
>   and is concerned with prophecies.
> He pays attention to the statements of famous men,
>   and he penetrates the mysteries of riddles.
> He finds out the secrets of parables,
>   and he is concerned with the secrets of proverbs.
> He serves among great men
>   and appears among nobles.
> He sets his heart to seek his creator,
>   and he prays to the Most High;
> he opens his mouth in prayer
>   and makes supplication for his sins.
> If God most high is willing,
>   he is filled with the spirit of understanding;
> he pours forth words of wisdom,
>   and he praises the Lord in prayer;
> he directs his counsel and his knowledge aright
>   and meditates on the mysteries;
> he reveals the propriety of his teaching,
>   and he glories in the law of the Lord.
> Many praise his understanding,
>   and for all time his name will never be blotted out.
> The nations tell of his wisdom,
>   and the congregation proclaims his fame.

[29] Differently, however, in Sir. 7.15.

If he lives he will be blessed above thousands;
  if he goes to rest, then his name will be enough for him.

                                                  (Sir. 39.1–11)

We saw at the beginning how Sirach wrote his book in order to teach wisdom. It would be wrong, then, to try to understand it simply as a declaration of his faith. Certainly in his day the idea of what wisdom was had changed, and, accordingly, he had clearly and definitely taken up a position in which he was personally committed with regard to questions of faith. But Sirach intends his book to have a specific purpose, and that surely also means that he did not intend to present in it everything which came within the sphere of his knowledge. In this respect, statements in Sirach are significant which, although objects of great theological weight, are touched upon only in passing and are not intended to be subjects of instruction. This is the case, for example, with 'sin' and mortality, which are traced back to Eve (25.24), or with the 'evil urge' which is inherent in all men (37.3).[30] It is especially true of a few references to eschatological events which scarcely seem to be in line with the main teachings of the book, but which leave us in no doubt of the fact that Sirach knew about these concepts and also shared them.[31]

Sirach was aware that he stood in a line of succession. 'As the last' in a long chain of tradition he had worked hard at his part. Was it literary delicacy if he regarded himself merely as the one 'who gleans after the grape-gatherers' (Sir. 33.16)? Or did he sense that the main work really had been completed before him?

[30] On the important doctrine of the 'evil urge', see most recently E. Brandenburger, *Adam und Christus*, 1962, pp. 33f.

[31] Sir. 36.8: 'Hasten the end, be concerned about the time'. In the book of Tobit, practical wisdom is linked much more organically with the eschatological outlook. There are some passages in Sirach which have given rise to the question whether he is not openly advocating belief in a 'retribution in the life to come' and in a 'hope for the life to come' (e.g. 1.13; 2.3; 7.36; 9.11; 11.26–28; 16.12; 17.23; 18.24). The study by V. Hamp, *Zukunft und Jenseits im Buche Sirach* (BBB 1, 1950, pp. 86ff.) has, however, undermined this idea.

XIV

THE DIVINE DETERMINATION
OF TIMES (EXCURSUS)

WE DERIVE THE DEFINITION of the term 'determinism' from those texts to which we must still briefly direct our attention. What is meant by it is the idea of a primeval, divine predetermination of specific events and destinies. It differs from belief in a providence, in a divine guidance of history and fate in being more theoretically orientated. Both beliefs are convinced that all events depend on Yahweh; in the one, this dependence is sought in the presence of the hand of Yahweh, while in the other, the divine will has been active in history long before the appearance of the events. The one concept of history will lay more emphasis on the fluidity of historical events, the other on their unalterable nature. It is scarcely possible to avoid noting a certain loss with regard to the divine presence in history in the deterministic concept. Yet the points of transition are not fixed. Finally, it should be noted that even when the use of the term 'determinism' is justified, it is never a question of a complex of ideas which have been thought through philosophically and logically. Thus, for example, the individual's freedom of decision in religious and ethical matters is, strangely enough, scarcely affected by this determinism.

We recall the old and widespread experience of the appropriate time, as a consequence of which all man's activities and abstentions from activity have 'their proper time'. This idea of appropriate times, in the way in which it was expressed by the earlier teachers and in early Israel generally, cannot possibly be described as deterministic. Like so many of the teachings of old wisdom, it has no theological importance at all; it was, rather, a 'secular' experience of the world, an experience of which the human art of living took advantage. In this context there belongs also the famous passage about the time and the hour which are set for all human projects (Eccles. 3.1–9). In these statements, the Preacher recapitulates what earlier teachers had always known, but he does so only in order immediately to place the old subject of instruction within the realm of the problematical. That is, he understands what was said about times and hours in theological and deterministic terms and asks what it means for man that his life is subject to such constantly changing divine decrees. In this respect – he believes – one cannot reproach God with anything; he makes all things 'good'. But man lacks all the presuppositions necessary for understanding these decrees and for working out an attitude towards them, and therefore the fact that his life is determined is 'trouble' to him and is certainly not regarded as a positive offer to man to make use of a temporary freedom.[1]

Once again we come face to face with that realization which we encounter continually in the analysis of such didactic material, namely that the basic perception – in this case that of appropriate times – is very old and has been handed down through the ages. In this process of tradition, however, it often moves to a new sphere of understanding, it suddenly appears in an altered light and creates new tensions to which the readers then have to expose themselves. This change in the sphere of understanding in Ecclesiastes introduces – as far as we can determine on the basis of the scanty literary deposit from this period – an interesting new phase in the long history of this subject of instruction. It is certainly to be brought into relationship with that general tendency, which we have already encountered, to set the teachings more decisively on a theological foundation, a tendency which, moreover, can also be paralleled in the texts of later Egyptian wisdom.[2]

In the course of this 'theologization', there arose a new interest in 'time' and 'times', an interest which, to mention the cases only of Koheleth and Sirach, is already indicated by a rather sudden increase in the occurrence of the key-word 'ēt .. 'appointed time'.[3] In this respect, Koheleth seems to occupy a specifically transitional position. At the same time, expression is given to unmistakably deterministic ideas, a factor which differentiates it to some extent from the older didactic traditions and connects it with the later ones. Eccles. 6.10 is quite unambiguous, 'Whatever happens has long since been determined (actually 'has long since been called by name'), and it is

---

[1] See above pp. 229f.

[2] Cf. S. Morenz, *Gott und Mensch im alten Ägypten*, 1963, pp. 65, 84.

[3] The table in O. Loretz (op. cit., p. 168) counts forty instances of the word 'ēt in Ecclesiastes, twenty-eight of which, however, occur in the passage Eccles. 3.2–8.

determined what man will be. He cannot dispute with one who is stronger than he.' In fact, however, this awareness of the determination of events lies behind very many of the sentences in this book.

Sirach, who is not very far from the Preacher in time, speaks more clearly of a determination of all destinies which has long since been completed by God. 'From the beginning' he decreed good things for good people (Sir. 39.25), but all kinds of bad things – fire, hunger, plague, wild beasts, snakes, sword – are also created for a specific purpose; they are 'stored up and are summoned forth at the proper time' (Sir. 39.30). God's eyes see everything; 'before it happens everything is known to him, and similarly he sees it before it is finished' (Sir. 23.20).[4] So, too, the angel Raphael could say to the young Tobias that the girl Sarah 'was destined for (him) from eternity' (literally 'made ready', Tob. 6.18). Thus, God sees events twice. In the first instance he sees them in their primeval, predetermined state and then once again when they have appeared in history 'in their time'. The most important factor, however, is that 'all the works of God are good in their time'. (This is almost word for word the same confession as we found in Koheleth, 'He has made everything beautiful in its time', Eccles. 3.11a). One cannot regard one thing as worse than another 'for everything is marvellous in its time' (Sir. 39.33f.). The concern of these sentences is, in the last resort, not a theoretical or a theological one, but an explicitly pastoral one. They are addressed to men who cannot see their way in the chaos of events.[5] The teacher admits to them that it is actually impossible for men to qualify events in any fundamental way as if on an objective scale of values. One can – and this is a profound piece of wisdom – understand them only from the point of view of the respective times which God has set for them. But – and the instruction insists on this – the divine decrees are good and right in their time. How different the questions are here from what they were in earlier periods! In those days, the teachers were concerned with teaching men to observe as far as possible the 'appropriate times' and to let men's lives be carried forward by means of them. Here, however, the teacher faces an attack occasioned by the appropriate times, and he dispenses consolation. Even although it is consolation that the teacher intends to dispense, one must also realize that he sees no reason to examine in detail the problems which he has

---

[4] One could also cite at this point Sir. 42.18: '. . . the Lord has all knowledge, and he sees what is coming in the distant future.' But the translation is uncertain.
[5] See above pp. 250ff.

just banished with his teaching. We are, of course, at once confronted by the question of freedom of will. Was this not a threat to it? Strangely enough, although Israel was so aware of the sovereign actions of God towards men, she was not in the least disturbed by this question. Nor did she, even in extreme cases, ever doubt man's responsibility for his decisions and his actions. However, on one occasion Sirach does envisage the possibility that one could draw erroneous conclusions from this basic, deterministic point of view.

> Do not say, 'My sin comes from God',
>   for he does not do what he hates.
> Do not say, 'He has caused my downfall',
>   for he has no need of people who break the law.
> Yahweh hates evil and abomination
>   and does not let these happen to those who fear him.
> In the beginning God created man
>   and gave him into the power of his own thinking.
> If you wish, you can keep the commandments,
>   and it is his desire to be faithful.
> Fire and water are set before you;
>   stretch out your hands for what you want.
> Before man are life and death,
>   he will be given whichever he wishes.
> He orders man not to sin.
>   and he gives no dreams to those who lie.   (Sir. 15.11–20)[6]

But we must return once again to the idea of the determination of everything that happens, for it opened to the teachers essentially broader horizons than had been expressed hitherto.

> 7   Why is one day better than the others,
>   while all the daylight of the year is from the sun?
> 8   They were separated by the wisdom of the Lord,
>   and he made the times and feasts different.
> 9   Some of them he made exalted and holy,
>   and some he counted as ordinary days.
> 10 Men are all made of clay,
>   and Adam was created from the earth.
> 11 In the fullness of wisdom the Lord separated them
>   and made their destinies different.
> 12 Some he blessed and exalted,
>   and some he made holy and brought near to himself.

---

[6] Even in late texts, man's freedom of decision is maintained, cf. I Enoch 98.4; Jubilees 30.19ff.; II(4) Esd. 8.55f.; Syriac Baruch 85.2.

> Some he cursed and humbled
>   and hurled from their place.
> 13 Like the potter's clay in his hands,
>   to form it as he pleases,
>   so are men in the hands of their creator
>   to give to them as he decides.
> 14 As good is the opposite of wicked,
>   and life is the opposite of death,
>   so the sinner is the opposite of the godly.
> 15 So look upon all the works of the Most High;
>   they are in pairs, the one the opposite of the other.
>   (Sir. 33.7–15)

This text is very skilfully constructed. It begins with trivial daily experiences, behind which the whole problem is already outlined. Every day is ushered in by the same sun, but how different they all are! All men are made from the same earth, but how differently their lives run! Behind this puzzle, there lies the wisdom of God which has made the differences and determined the destinies. Here, then, the thought reaches far in the direction of fundamental questions. In this broad sphere, the election of Israel, that is, a historical phenomenon of great consequence, actually appears as an act of God's determining differentiation (v. 12). But this special existence of Israel before Yahweh is here, interestingly enough, not, as one might have expected, the real point of the discussion; it is, rather, only an example of something quite fundamental, namely of the determination, the destiny and the behaviour of all men.[7] Thus, it is entirely logical that the thought should go right back to the beginning of humanity, to Adam. The question about the primeval order automatically leads to the question about the beginnings. That was the case with the order which, according to Prov. 8.22, was effective in creation; so it is here, too, in the question about the order of the proper times. The conclusion of the discussion is also very significant. One can see that it is devoid of any theoretical or philosophical interest which might have gathered together into a single point the confusion caused by all the possibilities which might occur. The interest is more limited, for it is not concerned with the many possibilities open to divine predetermination but only with two, namely good or evil, life or death.[8]

---

[7] Just as abrupt is I Énoch 41.8: God has divided men's spirits (between light and darkness).

[8] P. Winter, 'Ben Sira and the Teaching of the "Two Ways"', *VT* 5, 1955, pp. 315ff.

One can see that behind this discussion by Sirach there lies the question of salvation, and where that question is raised, only these two possibilities can be discussed.

It should be carefully noted that, in spite of his pastoral and homiletic aims, Sirach applies the doctrine of the divine determination of times to the whole range of events and, on the other hand, that, in the question of divine determination, he is concerned, in the last resort, only with the question of salvation, the question of life or death. For this is precisely the basis on which later didactic writings, especially the apocalyptic ones, also take their stand. In what follows, we gather together a few particularly striking and characteristic passages:

(God) changes times and hours,
    deposes kings and enthrones kings.   (Dan. 2.21)

God created the nations of the world as well as us;
    he foresaw both them and us from the beginning to the end
    of the world,
nothing, not even the smallest detail, was overlooked by him;
    he foresaw everything, predetermined everything.
The Lord foresaw everything that happens in this world,
    and this is how it all happens.   (Assumption of Moses 12.4f.)

(God) knows what the world is before it was created
    and what will happen from generation to generation.
                                        (Enoch 39.11)

The Holy and Great One has determined days for all things.
                                        (Enoch 92.2)

Then (Jacob) saw in a night vision how an angel came down from heaven with seven tablets and gave them to Jacob. Jacob read them and read everything that was written on them, namely what would happen to him and his sons for all eternity.   (Jubilees 32.21)

From the God of knowledge comes everything that is and everything that happens, and before it came into being, he established its whole plan. When they achieve their purpose corresponding to the plan of his majesty, they fulfil their duty, and (there is) nothing to alter.
                                        (1 QS III 15f.)

One can see how the wise men are able, from time to time, to vary the theme very impressively and to approach it from different points of view. The theme itself, however, is everywhere the same. Already before time began, God's decisions about life and death, salvation and judgment have been accomplished, and now the prescribed times materialize precisely in accordance with the order which was given to them. There is something uncanny about this idea, especially when this order is regarded as something which God has decreed from within himself and to which he must now adhere.[9] The times stand, like realities, face to face with God. 'He does not disturb them or arouse them until the prescribed measure has been fulfilled' (II(4) Esd. 4.37). But the idea that events and their times are determined from the very beginning is quite inseparably bound up with the essential nature of the testamentary literature. How else, in such a distant past, could a whole chain of consecutive events have been foretold?[10]

The idea of the determination of times is rather surprising, almost confusing, to anyone even slightly familiar with the ideas about history which were current in early Israel, for even a superficial glance at the older historical works shows completely different ways of presenting Yahweh's sovereignty over history, but never a deterministic one. Whether we read through the Jehovistic patriarchal narratives or the Succession Narrative or the prophetic proclamation of events decreed by Yahweh, the idea of a plan of Yahweh's encompassing a fairly extensive period of time is frequently discernible, and yet, at the same time, it is always thought of as divine intervention which occurs according to the given case and which is completely incalculable. The decision to destroy Ahab is taken initially in the heavenly council (I Kings 22.19ff.). And similarly, in Isaiah's call from then on in the prophets, new decisions of God's in his guidance of history are continually being revealed. But even where theological reflection is concerned with grasping the question of the divine guidance of history more from the point of view of fundamentals, for example in the Deuteronomist's theory of the creative word of Yahweh invading history from time to time, there is nothing that recalls, even remotely, the idea of the primeval determination of times by Yahweh.[11] There is nothing here that could have been known earlier on the basis of any kind of reflection or study. The invasion by the word is, both for the prophet and for his hearers, an unexpected event, and the fulfilment

[9] Thus, e.g., II(4) Esd. 7.74: God was patient with men 'but not on your account, but only on account of the times which he has determined'.

[10] 'In the divine economy, the great principle is: everything has its time and everything has its measure . . . both spatially and temporally; everything has its day, its fixed hour, its duration, so too have eschatological acts and the eschaton. This belongs particularly to the stock of apocalyptic ideas' (P. Volz, *Die Eschatologie der jüdischen Gemeinde im neutestamentlichen Zeitalter*, 1934, p. 138).

[11] More on this 'theology of the word' in G. von Rad, *Old Testament Theology*, Vol. I, ET 1962, pp. 355ff.; Vol. II, ET 1965, pp. 85ff.

of it in the form of a spectacular occurrence is equally unexpected. The divine action is always in flux, and the prophet is continually being faced with new decisions made by Yahweh.

> Sometimes I threaten a nation or a kingdom, to uproot it and demolish it and destroy it; but if the nation which I have threatened turns from its wickedness, then I shall repent of the evil which I decreed for it. Sometimes I promise a nation or a kingdom, to build it and to plant it; but if it does something that displeases me and does not heed my words, then I repent of the good which I had promised to it.   (Jer. 18.7–10)

The gulf between this conception of history and the deterministic-apocalyptic one seems unbridgeable. And yet the historical traditions and, partly, also those of prophecy have joined with the deterministic conception of history. The first wisdom teacher to refer to traditions from his nation's history was Sirach. As we have already seen, he equated the voice of primeval order with that of Torah which was present for Israel first of all in the tabernacle and then on Zion (Sir. 24.10); he mentions Lot, the defeated Canaanites (16.8f.) and the making of the covenant on Sinai (17.12). Above all, in his 'Hymn of the Fathers', he gives something in the nature of a sketch of Israel's history in which he praises the men, from Enoch to Nehemiah, who, as he says in his preface, were honoured by God as rulers, prophets, thinkers, teachers or poets (Sir. 44–50). None of these passages refers to the divine determination of times, a doctrine which Sirach defended so forcefully elsewhere. Obviously the weight of this historical material was still too great for this concept of history which was so foreign to it to have been able to penetrate it. Nevertheless, we encounter in Sir. 33.12 the idea that the election of Israel is also to be attributed to a primeval decision on God's part. Clearer, in this respect, are passages in the Testaments of the Twelve Patriarchs which, in their basic form, are very probably contemporaneous with Sirach. There, for example, Asher reports that the disobedience of his descendants was already indicated in the tablets of heaven.[12] Judith gives still clearer expression to this. In her prayer, she says, with reference, be it noted, to the history of Israel:

> For you have done all that happened previously. You designed what happened earlier and what followed later, what happens now and what

---

[12] Test. of Asher 7; cf. also Test. of Levi 5. On the period to which the 'Testaments' are to be assigned, see E. Bickerman, 'The Date of the Testaments of the Twelve Patriarchs', *JBL* 69, 1959, pp. 245ff.

will happen in the future. What you intended happened, and what you desired appeared and said, 'Here I am'. For all your ways are prepared and your judgment has already taken place. (Judith 9.5f.)

From this point of view, let us also examine the Book of Jubilees. The situation here is particularly interesting because in this book the old tradition is not referred to merely occasionally. The whole book is a massive reinterpretation of the historical narrative from Gen. 1 to Ex. 12 for an age whose religious ideas have radically changed. We hear already in the preface that God has shown to Moses on Mount Sinai 'past and present history' (1.4). He is to write down all of this history (1.26); it is indeed recorded on heavenly tablets from creation 'to the day of the new creation' (1.29). Thus we learn, even with regard to details, that these have happened exactly as has been described in advance on the heavenly tablets, like, for example, the giving of the name Isaac (16.3). Of Isaac's curse on the Philistines (cf. Gen. 26.26), it is said that it 'stands written on the heavenly tablets that this would happen to him (the Philistine)' (24.33).

Concerning Jacob, too, one learns that on seven tablets which an angel from heaven showed to him, he read 'everything that was written on them, namely what would happen to him and his sons for all eternity' (32.21).[13] It is clear that here for the first time, as far as we can see, the concept of divine determination has taken complete control of all historical traditional material. This concept has not simply been attached to the historical material only incidentally and superficially, but it dominates it, not least by its doctrine of specific periods, and has thrust into the background the old idea of history as a sphere of tension between given promises and their fulfilment.

This great change in the way of looking at history can be discerned particularly in the apocalyptic historical summaries.[14] The form of 'historical summaries', that is, fairly short or fairly detailed recapitulations of Yahweh's dealings with Israel, had a long history in Israel. It is not, then, surprising that in earlier ages, too, such historical summaries could be drawn up from very different aspects. Ps. 105 narrates the history of Israel from quite different points of view from those of Ps. 106.

[13] Text above, p. 268. Paul, too, speaks of how the fate of Jacob and Esau had already been decided before their birth by a free, divine choice; cf. Rom. 9.11.
[14] Especially in I Enoch 85–90 (Vision of Beasts); I Enoch 93.3–10; I Enoch 91.12–17 (Apocalypse of Weeks); Assumption of Moses 2–10; II(4) Esd. 3.4–27; Apocalypse of Baruch 53–74 (Vision of Clouds).

But there is a great difference between these older variations and the apocalyptic historical summaries. The very fact that the historical summary is now, in the form of a detailed prophecy, built in to the testamentary address of a man of the past (Enoch, Moses, Ezra, Baruch) of necessity altered the conception of the sequence of events. If these could be predicted, even with regard to details, by divine revelation, if men's actions could be shown one after the other (I Enoch 90.41b), that means that God knew everything in advance. This is asserted over and over again. Moses says that God has foreseen everything in the world and that it happens accordingly (Assumption of Moses 12.4). Before the historical summary in the Apocalypse of Abraham, the reader learns that God's decree is fixed for all the future which is still unknown to man (Apocalypse of Abraham 26.5). By looking at the heavenly books, Enoch gained that knowledge about the future which he expounds in the Apocalypse of Weeks.[15]

These summaries are in agreement with the earlier ones in that they present history as guided by Yahweh and wholly determined by his will. This is, of course, also true of the Apocalypse of Weeks, which mentions divine intervention only with the beginning of the eschaton (I Enoch 91.15), for both the division of time into weeks and the individual events themselves are also no doubt considered to have been decreed by God. God's participation in Israel's history is spoken of in more detail in the vision of beasts (I Enoch 85–90) where God brings the sons of Jacob to Egypt, speaks with Moses, inflicts the plagues, leads the way to Sinai, etc. Finally, he also summons the seventy shepherds who will treat Israel cruelly. Obviously nothing has changed with regard to the old conviction of Yahweh's complete sovereignty over history. But how, in particular, does this sovereignty reveal itself? It reveals itself in the fact that, in accordance with a plan, God leads history to its end, an end where salvation dawns for those who were chosen from the beginning. Basically, this history knows of no manifestations of salvation within history itself. Certainly, it can describe acts of guidance and of deliverance, as well as acts of judgment. But these indications of salvation are actually present to later readers only in the form of a general instruction to the effect that God guides events. Basically, all these acts of deliverance which are described are rather episodic and never reach decisive historical effectiveness. They are incapable of establishing a new relationship between Israel and God. But this was no longer required by this way

[15] I Enoch 93.1f.

of looking at history, for the real salvation-event has moved out to the fringes of history, to the primeval election and determination and to the dawning of salvation at the end.[16] This divine activity, too, needs to be revealed to men. But this act of revelation is a non-recurring one; it lies at the beginning and concerns the whole of history right through to its eschatological conclusion.[17] This eschatological salvation-event is not prepared by God by means of detailed events within history (such as the role of Cyrus in Deutero-Isaiah), nor does God take up earlier, historical salvation-decrees (even if this is untypical). Rather, the end erupts abruptly into a world of history which is growing darker and darker, and the benefits of salvation which have long been pre-existent in the heavenly world – 'until time comes to an end' – (Son of Man, the New Jerusalem) make their appearance. If one compares this conception of history with those produced by Israel in earlier periods, then one will have to speak of a characteristic theological or, to be more precise, soteriological depletion of history. There is surely logical consistency in the fact that Ezra, in his lament with its historical summary, comes to the conclusion that the whole of God's history with his people – and this less as Israel's fault than God's – never reached a goal. It was a plan that had gone wrong.[18] If there is anything at all to hope for, then salvation must make its appearance as something completely new, but the recipient of the salvation – and this, too, is significant – is no longer an Israel renewed, no matter in what form, but only a group selected from Israel, such as the Hasidim, even simply the individual who is being addressed with words of consolation. In the course of an ever-increasing individualism with regard to salvation, even the concept 'Israel' begins to disintegrate.[19]

While this soteriological depletion of history was a consequence of a completely altered doctrine of salvation, in contrast to this, something new appears in the historical summaries, indeed it actually appears in place of the soteriological decrees, namely the division of

[16] D. Rossler, *Gesetz und Geschichte. Untersuchungen zur Theologie der jüdischen Apokalyptik und der pharisäischen Orthodoxie*, 1960, pp. 63ff.

[17] Dan. 7.13; I Enoch 90.29ff.; II(4) Esd. 8.52; 10.54; 13.36; 14.9; Apocalypse of Baruch 59.4–11. The New Jerusalem, prepared from the beginning of time, had already been shown to Adam; Apocalypse of Baruch 4.3.

[18] II(4) Esd. 3.4–27; cf. G. Reese, *Die Geschichte Israels in der Auffassung des frühen Judentums* (Typewritten dissertation submitted to the Theological Faculty of the University of Heidelberg, 1967), p. 131.

[19] G. Reese, op. cit., pp. 86, 149.

history into numbered periods. In every instance, this division into periods has been imposed on the traditional historical material only secondarily. Sometimes it corresponds to the material to some extent (Apocalypse of Weeks), at other times it is forced, because the old material is not capable of such a division (Vision of Clouds).

The decisive question which we had to ask of the older conception of history in Israel, namely to what extent it was still able to make God's dealings with Israel topical, can no longer be asked in this way of the apocalyptic historical sketches. What measure of relevance does the past have here? It certainly requires no lengthy discussion to realize that the historical presentation of the narratives of the patriarchs or of Moses in the Deuteronomistic History, and even in the Chronistic History, had a quite different degree of topicality for its period than one can attribute to the summaries in the apocalyptic books. Even the Chronicler – even if he must stretch himself a little for this purpose – is still able to understand his levitical existence entirely on the basis of the salvation-decree which was revealed in David, and he is, without any hesitation, ready to legitimatize it on that basis. But this interest in history, that is, this endeavour to understand oneself and one's whole existence on the basis of Yahweh's great decrees immanent in history, in a word, this outstanding actuality of what is past, is quite foreign to our summaries, and at the same time – this could scarcely have been avoided – much of the contemporary significance of God's dealings with Israel has been lost. In spite of this, past history is of great importance for the apocalyptists, too. One can recognize God's total sovereignty over history by its precise determination, and its division into periods helps the observer to recognize his own place in history, namely at the end of the world's first age and immediately before the dawn of the new. It has been rightly said that the exact function of these historical apocalypses is to act as a proof. The end is near, and God has things firmly in hand. With this realization they dispense consolation. In the historical sketches in the book of Daniel, this change in the way of looking at history is already in all essentials complete. The recipient of this historical interpretation does not himself appear in the book; we can only deduce the kind of person he is. But there can be no doubt about the fact that from this view of history, consolation and the exhortation to persevere were supposed to emerge.

There is preserved, however, in the so-called Fourth Book of Esdras, an apocalypse which speaks to the period after the great

Jerusalem catastrophe of about AD 70.[20] Here the partner who is attacked takes his full part in the discussion in that, in the great dialogue with the angel, he stubbornly asks the question of theodicy. Both from the point of view of the complex of questions raised and from the point of view of the answers given to them, the book is, like scarcely any other, a document of the most strenuous theological endeavour. The great force with which the theodicy question is posed here anew, but also the dialogue form in which the whole book is clothed, reminds us inevitably of the book of Job. Of course, Ezra's questions are quite different. Unlike Job, he cannot appeal to the integrity of his relationship with God. Quite the contrary. Ezra is aware that since Adam mankind is under sentence of death and is subject to an urge to do evil (both ideas are to be found already in Sir. 25.24). What is one to make of the plans which God seems to have had for Israel, if he has indicated no way of achieving the proffered salvation? He has not taken the evil urge from them (II(4) Esd. 3.20). 'Of what use is it to us that we are promised eternity if we have done works of death?'(II(4) Esd. 7.119). This divine undertaking had to come to grief, and for this reason Ezra is incapable of understanding the terrible judgment which has now come upon the Jews. The Babylonians – by these he means the Romans – are no better, and they are not under judgment (II(4) Esd. 3.28, 31). The intensity of Ezra's despair, but also its intellectual consistency, makes it difficult for the interpreting angel to reply. The answer does not come to the one who doubts in a few, brief sentences. It is not final, because it is always recommencing its instruction, at a different point and also in the way in which it argues, it is fairly free. But all in all, in the replies of the interpreting angel, a reasonably self-contained point of view is contrasted with that of Ezra. With regard to history – and it alone is of interest to us here – he is unable to give Ezra much consolation. He does not contradict him; it is a history of disaster (II(4) Esd. 4.27). For Israel, at any rate, it provides the opportunity of a trial and then of receiving the promised benefits of salvation in the coming age. The

[20] On this most recently, W. Harnisch, *Verhängnis und Verheissung der Geschichte. Untersuchungen zum Zeit- und Geschichtsverständnis im 4. Buch Esra und in der Syr. Baruchapokalypse*, 1969. The second main section of the book is important for our question: 'Die Lehre von der Nezessität des geschichtlichen Ablaufs (Der apokalyptische Determinismus)', pp. 248ff. 'The historical apocalypses in II(4) Esdras and the Apocalypse of Baruch function only as proofs. By means of them, the proof that history is now complete is meant to be provided and the idea of the nearness of the end stimulated' (op. cit., p. 265).

promise of life for Israel – Ezra realized – has not lapsed. God did not create only one age for the world, but two (II(4) Esd. 7.50). That is the angel's great word of consolation. The man who sets his sights on this age can find additional consolation in the fact that in this present age all events, in sequence, are exactly predetermined by God. Nothing will happen that God has not long since envisaged.

> He spoke to me, 'At the beginning of the world,
>   before heaven's gates were set up,
>   I determined it,
> and thus it was created by me and no other;
>   so, too, the end is created by me and no other.'   (II(4) Esd. 6.1–6)
> (God) rules the hours and what happens in the hours.
>   (II(4) Esd. 13.58)

It is unnecessary to point once again to the complete change in point of view by contrast with the older understanding in terms of 'salvation history'. The election of Abraham is certainly mentioned (II(4) Esd. 3.13f.; 5.23ff.). On another occasion, election is mentioned, but in connection with the creation of Adam (II(4) Esd. 6.54). On one occasion a divine promise of protection is mentioned (II(4) Esd. 3.15f.), so too, briefly, the building of the city of Jerusalem by David (II(4) Esd. 3.23). The apocalyptist attributes much greater significance to the revelation of the law to Moses, and this is because of the promise attached to it. But in view of the fact that the benefits of salvation are realized only in the age to come, all these historical facts appear, theologically, in a completely altered light. Thus, for example, the election of Abraham happened for the sole purpose of revealing to him the secrets of the final age (II(4) Esd. 3.23f.). We are, as we have said, unable to point out the inner compulsions which led to this complete change in the way of looking at history. Is it, perhaps, already contained in embryo in the basic ideas of Ecclesiastes, namely in his refusal to recognize in events orders immanent in history? And has not Sirach, too, in his 'Hymn of the Fathers', already basically left behind the old way of regarding history as a 'history of salvation'? The most interesting point is, however, that the really old idea of the determination of times has, in the late period, become strongly theologized and been made a constituent element of a new way of looking at history.

The conviction must be affirmed that God has the power to transpose history from its second-last hour (in which the apocalyptists believe they live) to its final one. In a situation in which one was aware of standing so close to the liquidation of all previous history, how could there still have been any interest in introducing historical material into the present for purposes of self-legitimation? This can be reduced to a simple formula: There has emerged a way of looking at history which does not include any praise for God's historical indications of salvation. Praise emerges only in anticipation of the apocalyptic end.[21] The taste for giving contemporary significance to divine actions in the past is on the wane. History has become material which one knows and which one must use for instruction; above all, however, for the correct evaluation of the moment in which one lives.

This brief investigation which we have carried out into the apocalyptic literature was concerned only with the idea of the determination of times. It was, of course, immediately apparent that we were dealing with an idea which was absolutely constitutive for all apocalyptic thinking. It is another question, however, whether we must describe it as specifically apocalyptic. That all that happens is predetermined, that God knows beforehand about all that is created, that he has determined days for all things, that he has chosen times, that he does not disturb them, that he does not anticipate them – could all this, at least as far as the basic conviction is concerned, not also have been said by Sirach, indeed perhaps even by Joseph with his double seven-years scheme? That the times are unalterably determined and that God's eye sees everything before it happens, we have already read, at all events, in Sirach (Sir. 23.20) and, similarly, in the book of Judith (Judith 9.5). It must be admitted that the idea has developed more strongly in respect of details and that, thereby, its fundamental significance for historical thinking has become essentially clearer. But this was surely more a question of advancing, theological penetration than a real didactic difference. One must also ask whether, within the framework of his teachings, Sirach ever had the occasion to spread himself more extensively on this subject.

This does, not of course, mean that we are trying to understand Sirach as an apocalyptist; but, rather, the apocalyptist as a wise man. When Sirach says that God 'declares what is past and what is still to come and reveals the depths of hidden things' (Sir. 42.19), this is an exact definition of the area within which apocalyptic will then

[21] I Enoch 90.40; Syriac Baruch 75; Dan. 7.14.

develop further. The attempt, convincingly to derive the essential characteristics of apocalyptic from another tradition (such as the prophetic) has not hitherto been successful. If one considers the extension of the range of vision to include universal history to be one of its essential characteristics, that is, that interest in the succession of world powers and its causes, then for this subject, too, we find in Sirach an idea which, especially in the reference to hubris, already anticipates much that is in the great apocalyptic sketches (Dan. 2; 7; II(4) Esd. 11f.).

> Rule over the world lies in the hands of God,
>   and he sets over it the right man for the time.
> Power passes from one nation to another,
>   because of arrogant acts of violence.   (Sir. 10.4, 8)[22]

Of absolutely central significance for apocalyptic is the looking to an end to the present course of events, to a judgment and the dawning of a time of salvation, that is, its thoroughgoing eschatological orientation. One can, of course, scarcely describe as eschatological the idea that events which are predetermined happen in due course, nor the prediction of specific times, nor the division of history into periods. It is, rather, the expectation of a great culmination of history which is already fixed in the divine scheme of determination and in which, as we have seen, the salvation event is realized. But even this idea is not so entirely new that it could be described as the specifically apocalyptic factor.[23] Already Sirach prayed in a lament,

---

[22] The idea of the divine *translatio imperii* has an interesting prehistory in the Old Testament. K. Baltzer has pointed out the profound change which occurred in the messianic idea with the end of the state of Judah ('Das Ende des Staates Juda und die Messias-Frage', in *Studien zur Theologie der alttestamentlichen Überlieferungen*, 1961, pp. 33ff.). Already in Jeremiah, and then in Deutero-Isaiah and in the Chronistic History, this new conception came to the fore: Yahweh gave Nebuchadnezzar world dominion (Jer. 27.5ff.); he awakened the spirit of Cyrus (II Chron. 36.22), he even authorized Cyrus, as his anointed, to be a world ruler (Isa. 45.1ff.). Here, then, the idea suddenly appears for the first time that Yahweh gives universal power to a great monarch for a time. Whether this idea 'arose' at this period is debatable. There was originally no connection between the idea of a succession of world empires and the doctrine of world ages (Hesiod). The combination of the two in Dan. 2 and 7 is a traditio-historical problem on its own.

[23] Against P. Vielhauer, in E. Hennecke, W. Schneemelcher, R. McL. Wilson, *New Testament Apocrypha*, Vol. II, ET 1965, pp. 597f. Vielhauer considers the eschatological element to be the fundamental one in apocalyptic, with the wisdom elements as an outer layer. This impression may indeed be given by individual apocalypses; from a traditio-historical point of view, the situation is very probably the opposite: the wisdom element is the fundamental one.

Rouse your anger, pour out your wrath,
 overthrow the adversary, destroy the enemy,
 hasten the end, establish the time. (Sir. 36.7f.)

The absolute usage of the term 'end' (qēṣ) permits of no other conclusion than that Sirach already knew of and shared in the expectation of a culmination of history. Similarly, Tobit, too, looking into the future, speaks of the temple being rebuilt 'until the times of the future are completed' (Tob. 14.5).[24] One cannot, of course, compare Sirach with the great apocalypses, for the reason that we are dealing there with works of quite varied literary purpose. Quite different branches of knowledge are unfolded in them from those in Sirach. One must certainly also take into consideration an intellectual development in the time between Sirach and the apocalypses, perhaps specifically in the domain of eschatological ideas. Here we encounter the literary form of the testamentary address in which perceptions which were originally secrets are made public. Here is the idea of world ages and of a final judgment which concludes the world ages with an event which is not warlike but solemnly forensic. Here are broadly developed cosmological ideas, both angelological and demonological, in which it is, in part, quite evident that extensive material from Irano-Chaldaean syncretism found expression also in late Jewish writings.[25] It remains only to ask whether all this would not, after all, best be understood as a relatively organic process, that is, as the branching out of wisdom in the direction of widely varied intellectual spheres.[26] It would not have been the first time that Israelite wisdom had laid itself open to foreign intellectual material. Nor do we know the period when this Irano–Chaldaean material was taken over. Sirach, too, already knew a considerable amount about Enoch, whose role has obviously been confused with that of legendary wise men of

[24] The sentence in Tob. 14.5 runs as follows: ἕως πληρωθῶσιν καιροὶ τοῦ αἰῶνος (BA) ἕως τοῦ χρόνου οὗ ἂν πληρωθῇ ὁ κρόνος τῶν καιρῶν (S). On this, cf. B. Reicke, *RGG*³, Vol. III, s.v. 'Iranische Religion, Judentum und Urchristentum', col. 881ff.

[25] On this, cf. the detailed discussion in Bousset-Gressmann, *Die Religion des Judentums im späthellenistischen Zeitalter*, 1926, pp. 469ff.

[26] The role played by the idea of divine determination in the religious thinking of the ancient Egyptians – especially that of their teachers – has been indicated by S. Morenz, *Untersuchungen zur Rolle des Schicksals in der ägyptischen Religion* (Abh. d. Sachsischen Akad. d. Wissensch. zu Leipzig, Phil. Hist. Kl. Bd. 52, Heft 1, 1960). From ancient Ugarit, too, a wisdom text has emerged, the refrain of which is: 'By Ea the (primeval) plans are drawn. According to divine pleasure the fates are shared out.' Nougayrol, op. cit., pp. 294f. See above p. 10, note 8.

the past, as someone who had knowledge of all earthly and heavenly secrets. He calls him 'a marvel of knowledge for all generations' (Sir. 44.16). 'For all generations' means, however, that his knowledge had topical significance far beyond his own lifetime. Is it then no more than probable that this thematically wide-ranging material was taken over only in an age in which it had already appeared in literary form in great encyclopaedic works?

It would, of course, be important to know whether in Israel, too, the foretelling of coming events, particularly through the medium of dreams and through the interpretation of dreams, belonged to the sphere of activity of the wise men. Unfortunately their literary legacy offers no proper clues. But did collections of rules for individual lives afford either room or occasion for such activity? The Joseph story, which was put together in wisdom circles, celebrates Joseph as the authorized interpreter of dreams and of coming events, and Daniel, too, walks in his footsteps. That, to a great extent, we are dealing with *vaticinia post eventum* need not disturb us, for *vaticinia post eventum* are nevertheless only imitations, in fixed literary form, of real predictions. On this subject a whole group of ancient Egyptian texts, namely the so-called Prophecies, could acquire a new significance for us. Till now, they have been compared, one-sidedly, only with the predictions of the Old Testament prophets, with predominantly negative results.[27] Their authors, however, are wise men, that is, in each case a teacher 'who predicts before it has happened, who sees before it has occurred'. This form of prediction – also of a political type – belonged, in Egypt, to the sphere of activity of the wise men. Interestingly enough, in the famous practical wisdom of Merikare a passage of a quite different type has been inserted, in which there is the statement, 'Troops will harass troops as the ancestors have predicted'.[28] Here, as has been rightly said, we are dealing not with a particular charisma which is capable of unveiling a future which is otherwise concealed, but with 'the conviction that the world progresses in accordance with recognizable rules', 'that account is taken of a plan in history, a plan which has long since been determined and which can be discovered'.[29]

[27] S. Hermann, 'Prophetie in Israel und Ägypten: Recht und Grenze eines Vergleichs', SVT IX, 1962, pp. 47ff.

[28] *Merikare* 68–69.

[29] On this range of questions, see H. Brunner, 'Die "Weisen", ihre "Lehren" und "Prophezeiungen" in altägyptischer Sicht', *ZÄS* 93, 1966, pp. 29ff. The suggestions and quotations here are taken from him: 'I examined and foretold what would happen. I understood when I looked to the future, for I had examined yester-

In this connection, one cannot but think of apocalyptic. On the other hand, the difference between the wisdom element in individual rules for life and that involved in looking to the future does not now appear to be so great, for both of them are concerned to read events and both are searching for rules. Perhaps behind the apocalyptic predictions of warlike devastation and the like, for which there are parallels also in the much older Egyptian texts, there lies essentially older, traditional material. If one thinks it probable that prediction of the future, at least occasionally such as in times of distress, also belonged to the sphere of activity of the wise men in Israel, that is, that there were also those 'who knew the times' (Esth. 1.13), then one must accept the fact that the fruits of this activity, for whatever reason, were not collected together. Only the rules of life which were meant for the individual have held the field. Nevertheless, the traditions behind the picture of the four kingdoms in Dan. 2, which are certainly pre-Maccabean and pre-apocalyptic, give us a clue as to the kind of interpretations of the future with which the wise men dealt. Not until apocalyptic did this probably basically old function of the office find literary expression, and this has survived in the form of didactic material.[30] We will be unable to have a clearer picture until a careful comparison between the *ex eventu* predictions of apocalyptic literature and the widely varied form of 'political' predictions which are found

---

day and had thought of tomorrow and knew how to deal with what would happen.' A tutor to princes describes himself as one 'who foretells before it has happened, who sees before it has occurred'.

[30] The dream in the Apocalypse of Clouds in Syriac Baruch 53 is, as far as its imagery is concerned, comparatively simple. Baruch sees a cloud rise out of the sea, full of white water and black water; on its upper edge he sees something like a flash of lightning. This cloud sweeps over the earth and lets the black and the white water rain down upon it. Finally, it hurls the lightning flash on to the earth, and it shines over the whole world. From this dream picture, the description of which occupies 11 verses, an interpretation is woven which includes the whole of history from Adam to the coming of the Messiah (chs. 56–74 = 134 verses). Does this lack of a quantitative relationship between dream and interpretation not show us what we have already learned from the dreams in Daniel, namely that we have to separate dream from interpretation? The dream picture is not, as far as its plot is concerned, derived from political history, but surely arises from older, traditional material, individual elements of which had first to be expanded and particularized before it could be applied to later history. I find such a particularization of the picture in, e.g., the suggestion that the change between white water and black water lasted for twelve periods, for this element provides the scaffolding for the whole interpretation.

in late Egyptian, Greek and Roman literatures has been made.[31]

The idea of the determination of times is, then, pre-apocalyptic.[32] Unfortunately we can say nothing about the particular causes which led to such a far-reaching change in historical thinking. In this case one finds that the great literary hiatus between 400 and 200 BC is particularly distressing (we cannot name with certainty any literary work which emerged in those centuries).

In so-called apocalyptic, the idea of the determination of times becomes strongly theological and develops in various new ways. Here, however, it appears also in close connection with a strongly eschatological type of historical thinking which, as we have seen, was originally not at all constitutive of it. Another new element is its connection with the much discussed doctrine of the two ages of the world. Probably under the influence, in the last resort, of Iranian ideas, two world ages were distinguished, one which is approaching its end and one 'to come' in which the hitherto concealed rule of God would appear with all its salvation benefits. This, however, completed the break with the whole earlier way of looking at history in Israel, for while, for the older way of looking at history, the salvation bestowed on man by God lay in the past and was determinative for the present, now it was expected in the future; to be precise, at the dawning of the new age. In the course of this completely altered idea of divine salvation, the interpretation of history was, so to speak, subjected to a revolution of a hundred and eighty degrees, for now it was interpreted not from the past but from the eschaton.

By way of a footnote, let us add a brief word about a quite different way in which wisdom circles presented history, namely about the course of history as sketched in the Wisdom of Solomon from the first man to the miracle at the Red Sea (Wisd. 10–19). This way of looking at history lacks the eschatological aspect and the division into periods

[31] On these political, *ex eventu* prophecies, see M. Hengel, *Judentum und Hellenismus*, 1969, pp. 330ff.

[32] There is an explicitly deterministic statement in Ps. 139.16. Hab. 2.3 and Ezek. 2.9 also belong, from a terminological point of view, to a deterministic range of ideas, cf. P. v. d. Osten-Sacken, *Die Apokalyptik in ihrem Verhältnis zu Prophetie und Weisheit*, 1969, pp. 48ff. But were they actually understood in this way? In spite of his 'heavenly book', Ezekiel's preaching is extremely indeterministic. Such reminiscences say no more than that deterministic ideas, probably more than we think, were current in Israel too. On the other hand, there is the fact that the proclamation of the prophets had no bearing on this range of ideas. In this respect, a slight change may have taken place in the post-exilic prophets.

and, if seen as a whole, the idea of allotted times.[33] Above all, one cannot in this case speak of the disappearance of a sense of the contemporary significance of history. Quite the contrary. Everything that has happened, even with respect to the details, is available for interpretation, everything had a meaning which can be deduced from the events themselves. This has happened for instruction, that as a warning, a third event as consolation or as judgment. Every individual event readily provides, even for the latest generations, a clearly delineated teaching. The motives of divine action are clear for all to see; history has become, rationally and morally, completely transparent. Thus, the author also succeeds in making it contemporary with a forcefulness which had not hitherto been granted to Israel. Spanning a millenium, history speaks with amazing directness. If one considers how difficult it was for the Yahwist and even still for the Deuteronomist to grasp a divine significance on the basis of the great bulk of traditional material which was available to them, if one considers above all that these two did not do what the author of the Wisdom of Solomon continually does, namely that they did not interpret the individual narratives feature by feature but left them with all those difficulties which they contain and which can never be rationally solved, then one can see how far-reaching in this case, too, the change is which has taken place in the way of looking at history. In the way in which it uses old historical traditions, the Wisdom of Solomon is very close to apocalyptic. In both, history has become teaching material from which one can derive, with comparative ease, knowledge for the present. The question is, however, then justified whether what we have in the Wisdom of Solomon is history made contemporary or simply teachings which can be detached from history. The knowledge of man and of the human psyche which finds expression in this presentation of history is, of course, very subtle, astonishingly so. Especially in the descriptions of how men are ensnared by blindness, anxiety and other dark things, the author ventures into regions which were not accessible in this way before to Israel's psychological knowledge.[34]

[33] On one occasion – thinking about the punishment of the Egyptians – the author admits, 'You have arranged everything by measure, number and weight' (Wisd. 11.20). This shows once again how familiar this idea was to the thinking of the age. One cannot, however, say that the author's whole presentation of history was coloured by it. It is, rather, an incidental argument.

[34] A passage from Wisd. 17 is translated above on pp. 132f.

PART FOUR

CONCLUSION

XV

CONCLUSION

ARE WE NOW able to say something by way of summary without prejudice to the variety of the material dealt with or to the variety of the questions it has raised?

In the first place we must justify the special position accorded to the wisdom texts from which our investigations, apparently uncritically, took their point of departure. They were confined to the group of explicitly didactic writings which are usually described as wisdom writings. It is not our purpose to ask whether the circle of wisdom writings should be enlarged, that is whether the term 'wisdom' itself should be widened in one direction or another. If the question were actually to confront us seriously in a new form, then in our opinion it can certainly be properly answered only once we have understood still better the way of thinking, the specific questions and the perceptions of a wisdom which appears in an explicitly didactic guise. Unfortunately there is much to suggest that the 'wisdom books' which have found their way into the Old Testament are to be regarded as only a perhaps small selection from Israel's didactic productions. Ecclesiastes says of himself that he intended 'to search out all that happens under heaven' (Eccles. 1.13). He has presented us with only a fragment of these studies. And this will be true of many wisdom teachers. One can therefore assume that only a specific selection of didactic books, especially those which appealed to a fairly general circle of readers, that is, particularly the so-called 'practical wisdom', have survived over the centuries. To what sources will the poet of the divine speech in Job 38f. have gone in order to be able to display such a varied 'nature wisdom'? He must have had at his disposal a wealth of literary material. Job and Sirach certainly used *onomastica*. None have survived. But did not specific rules for the interpretation of the future, that is the science of omens, not also belong to the province of the wise men? Apocalyptic, wisdom's immediate successor, certainly did not produce such and similar material out of the blue. In the Wisdom of Solomon, at one point, the fictitious Solomon writes about the significance of wisdom for men. The sentences are interesting because they have precisely the character of a definition which paraphrases the subject.

> Self-control and understanding she teaches,
>   justice and courage,
>   and there is nothing more useful in life for men than these.
> But if anyone asks for wide knowledge,
>   she knows the things of old and infers the things to come;
> she understands the forms of proverbs and the solution of riddles,
> signs and wonders she knows in advance and the outcome of times and
>   seasons.   (Wisd. 8.7b, 8)

In the first half of the text one can easily recognize, behind the Hellenizing diction, the interests of old practical wisdom, the training in composure, understanding, justice, etc. Then, however, there are mentioned areas of knowledge, the science of omens, interpretation of the future, which accrued secondarily to the teachers only in the latest period.[1]

On the one hand, therefore, we are forced to consider the range of sciences pursued in Israel as considerably larger; on the other, however, for lack of extant literary material, we are not in a position to define that range any more closely. That philology, which had been studied in Babylon from ancient times, was cultivated in Israel too, is unlikely; it is, to say the least, uncertain whether the mention of a few constellations allows us to deduce a serious concern with astronomy. An interest in zoology is suggested by some lists of animals and by the precise description of exotic animals. The tables of nations (Gen. 10) are to be attributed to the area of political geography. Here Israel can actually produce an astonishing achievement. The genealogical enumeration of all the nations in the form in which they appear in history is unique, not only in the ancient Near East. The fact that the table of nations exists in an early (Yahwistic) and a late (Priestly) form, permits us to assume a whole tradition of scientific work of which only the results have come down to us. But, of course, we do not know whether this work was in the hands of the wise men. But one could seriously ask whether the 'science of history' which, as is

[1] One would also have to bear in mind the 'catalogue' of fields of knowledge which is found in Wisd. 7.18–20 and which has been briefly discussed above pp. 16, 119.

well known, was pursued in Israel on a very broad basis, is not to be
included in this catalogue. But however ready we are to correct the
faded term 'wisdom', a term which has become no more than a
formal label, at this point there arise considerations to which we must
first turn.

I

Like all nations, Israel was on the search for the 'rational rule'.[2]
'Rule' means something permanently valid, something by which one
can reckon, on which one can rely. 'Rational' means that this rule is
supported by general evidence which can be controlled and confirmed by the mind. That this validity and this evidence are not
absolute, excluding any discussion from the outset, that conflicting
opinions are also possible, that, therefore, if need be the rule must be
modified or, in the last resort, even replaced by a better one – all this
is of the essence of the subject. Here, then, we find ourselves faced
with a first, though still very general definition of the nature of wisdom. Of all the texts with which we have been concerned it can be
said that they were in search of the rational rule or that they were
reflecting on that rule.

This definition, of course, already produces a deep gulf between
the intellectual striving of the wise teachers on the one hand and that
of the narrators, theologians of history, etc, on the other. And this is
justifiable, for the intellectual activity of these two types was quite
different, as were the subjects with which they were each concerned.
In the one case, Hebrew man examined his sphere of life closely for
reliable orders and gathered together whatever could be expressed in
the form of rules. In the other case, he came upon Yahweh's irreversible historical decrees, which certainly could not be expressed in the
form of rules and which, at least at first sight, were actually unique
in character. In the one case it was a question of stating what was
eternally valid, of noting general, human experiences; in the other, of
occurrences which established unique political and cultic facts. There
was yet another difference in that in the one case reason, searching
for rules, found itself beginning to acquire knowledge of the human
environment and to achieve mastery of life, but that in the case of
events in history, as Israel conceived of them, the initiative lay with
Yahweh. With his salvation decrees (covenant with the patriarchs,
exodus, Sinai covenant, Davidic covenant, etc.) he had surprised

[2] H. Fränkel, *Dichtung und Philosophie des frühen Griechentums*, 1962, p. 293.

men, and, as he guided them, they were the object of his visitations. Of course, even in Israel's awareness of history, reason was active in an enquiring and formative capacity. The characteristic element in its contribution is to be seen in the fact that as time went on it became less and less satisfied with the presentation of the episodic and the anecdotal, that is, of isolated facts, but that it sought, with increasing audacity, to encompass longer and longer periods of time. None of the many individual narratives which report an event from that sphere in which man was confronted by God, stands on its own. They must all be understood as part of a larger context. This attempt to see a continuity is so obvious already in the smaller 'compositions' such as the Gideon story (Judg. 6–8), in the description of the events of Israel's settlement (Josh. 2–10) right through to the extensive sweep of the Deuteronomistic and the Chronistic Histories, that one need say no more about it.[3]

If these large complexes were also characterized by quite unparalleled interventions on the part of Yahweh and by a recognition, which was unique in the ancient Near East, of the contingency of all historical events, a contingency which could not be explained away by any ideological theory, Israel, as she tried to find her way in such large historical areas, found herself increasingly faced with a new question, namely the question about the constant factor in history, that is, the question whether the confusion caused by the unique event is not after all only apparent, whether recurring features are not also discernible. It is characteristic of Israel's encounter with history that the awareness of a constant element in history was a second stage for Israel, while the conceptions of history in the rest of the ancient Near East, on the other hand, had the typical and the schematic as their starting point and scarcely succeeded in getting beyond that stage.[4] Not until a comparatively late period did Israel,

[3] That Israel's neighbours were also aware of the intervention of gods in history has never been contested. But did there exist there, too, that obstinate need to recognize extensive historical continuities? No one can maintain that these nations, too, felt themselves forced to legitimatize their existence and their relationship to God in constantly fresh and more ambitious historical sketches. What is surely a very important side of Israelite historical thinking is not discussed at all in B. Albrektson, *History and the Gods*, 1967. We look in vain there for the specific, theological relevance of history. One cannot, then, see why this idea of history which was constantly developing in Israel should not be a 'necessary idea' for the biblical scholar if he wishes to understand how Israel encountered 'revelation' (against J. Barr, *Old and New in Interpretation*, 1966, pp. 65ff.).

[4] H. Gese, 'The Idea of History in the Ancient Near East and the Old Testament', *Journal for Theology and the Church* 1, 1965, pp. 49ff.

too, dare to express the constant elements in history in schematic terms. An example of this is the prologue to the deuteronomistic book of Judges (Judg. 2.6–3.6), in which the author attempts to bring divine judgment into relationship with the constant, recurring disobedience of the people. It was surely Ezekiel who went furthest in such schematism in his outline of Israel's early history (Ezek. 20). Here, too, Israel was in search of a 'rational rule'.

But it is impossible to connect this very specific question, on the one hand about the unique element in history and on the other about the recurring element, a question which the Deuteronomist for example asked himself, with the search for knowledge on the part of the teachers with which we are dealing here. In addition – and this is an important argument – these two groups use a very different language and a very different set of concepts.

Recently the suggestion has been repeatedly made that the term 'wisdom' should be understood in a wider sense and that the older narrative works should also be included in it.[5] Wisdom, it is said, does not indicate a definite literary form of speaking and thinking. That is, of course, correct. But if we take wisdom, with its specific form of thought, seriously, it is precisely then that it becomes difficult to include in it without further question the early 'historical works', for with such an extension of the term, we would certainly not encounter a specific form of common thinking. The teachers' search for knowledge was, as we have already shown, thus specific, but its literary expression was also so specific that we are well advised to regard all of this as a phenomenon on its own. Otherwise where would it be possible to draw a line? It is, of course, true that wisdom perceptions have been widely disseminated and have, occasionally, found expression in the presentation of history. But that is not at all surprising, for these teachings did not arise from any secret doctrine but became part of the common cultural stock. More than elsewhere, this way of thinking seems to have permeated the presentation of the Succession Narrative, which was certainly written by someone at Solomon's court. In spite of this, the religious problem and the objective of these works was different. We must make clear this difference in two respects only.

1. Wisdom teaching was in need of legitimation. In the one case the instructor acquired it in appealing to the tradition with which he

---

[5] Especially by J. L. McKenzie, 'Reflections on Wisdom', *JBL* 86, 1967, pp. 1ff.; J. Barr, op. cit., pp. 72ff.

found himself in accord. It was similar with regard to the voice of primeval order whose call the teachers transmitted because it had invested them with authority. Still more effective, of course, was the appeal to Yahweh himself. Eliphaz and Elihu appealed, at considerable length, to the divine origin of their advice. In doing so, of course, they were dependent on prophetic ideas. What is interesting here is simply the fact that they felt obliged to justify themselves in this way. Also, the statement that the fear of Yahweh is the beginning of wisdom, which is programmatically prefaced to the book of Proverbs, was, in its way, a legitimation of the individual teachings that followed. They could be included only in so far as they contributed to knowledge about Yahweh. What is the situation in this respect, however, with the larger and smaller narrative works? Nowhere do we see any attempt at self-legitimation on the part of an author. That is nevertheless remarkable, for the traditions which are presented were of incalculable significance for Israel. But obviously there was inherent, in a recognizable form, in what was narrated, in the actualized tradition, sufficient evidence to make a legitimation on the part of the narrator superfluous.

2. In the preceding sections much has been said about the sober business of discovering rules and about the didactic evaluation of all the experiences of God's guidance. We also saw, however, how carefully the teachers noted the limits which were imposed on their search for knowledge. The world, knowledge of which they strove to acquire, was included within God's great mystery. It was a world in which it was 'God's glory to conceal things from men' (Prov. 25.2), a world in which God did inscrutable deeds, wonders without number.

> Dominion and fear are with him
>   who creates peace in his heights.
> Are not his hosts without number,
>   and upon whom does his light not arise? (Job 25.2–3)

> Behold, God is great beyond our comprehension,
>   the number of his years is unsearchable.
> When he draws up the drops of water
>   they are scattered in his mist as rain (?),
> which the clouds pour down
>   and drip on many men.
> Who fully understands the course of the clouds,
>   the clap of thunder from his tent . . .? (Job 36.26–29)

God thunders wonderfully with his voice,
  he does great things beyond our comprehension.
Hear this, Job,
  stop and consider God's wonders.
Do you understand how God orders them,
  so that light shines above his clouds?
Do you understand the soaring of the clouds,
  the wonders of one who has perfect knowledge,
you, whose clothes become hot
  when the earth lies quiet under the south wind? . . .
Teach us what we should say to him.
  We cannot produce anything because of darkness.
. . . Him, the Almighty, we cannot grasp;
  he is exalted in power and justice. (Job 37.5, 14–17, 19, 23)

These accompaniments to the advice of Job's friends are important for us, for they are also part of the picture which they had of the world. Reason has little room for manoeuvre. It is surrounded by the insurmountable wall of the inexplicable. These teachers, who have often been credited with trite rationalism, are also hymnists of the divine mysteries. Still more, the divine mystery has itself become a subject of instruction.[6] It was part of these teachers' duty, then, to speak not only of what could be known but also of what could not be known, for what is known has no connection at all with what is hidden from men.

See, these are (only) the ends of his ways,
  and how soft a whisper do we hear of him.
But the thundering of his mighty deeds,
  who can understand it? (Job 26.14)

There is much that is more incomprehensible and mightier than this.
  I see (only) a few of his works. (Sir. 43.32)

The mysteries, so the teachers believe, lead the thoughtful man to adoration. As a rule the mystery is spoken of in the style of the hymn.

---

[6] Even in the later didactic literature there is, from a terminological point of view, no word for 'mystery' that is accorded particular preference. What is meant is, as we could so frequently affirm, described but not defined in conceptual terms. Only in Sirach does the concept of the 'hidden' acquire any weight (nistārōt 4.18; 42.19; 48.25. Cf., however, with Sir. 3.21–24, Deut. 29.28). The wise man thinks about the 'secrets', according to Sir. 39.7. R. E. Brown, *The Semitic Background of the Term Mystery in the New Testament*, 1968, pp. 8ff. For the eschatological mystery, the book of Daniel uses the Persian loanword rāz.

Seldom does it depress man as a hardship, seldom does it ever drive him to the verge of despair.

> I have endeavoured, God, I have endeavoured, God,
>   to be able to grasp it.
> For I was more foolish than a man,
>   and human understanding was not in me.
> I have not learned wisdom
>   so that I might have knowledge of the Holy One.
> Who ever climbed up to heaven,
>   and who ever came down from there again?   (Prov. 30.1–4a)[7]

And once again we ask: At what point does one of the history writers ever let us suspect even only a little of this way of understanding the world? Where does he ever say that round about the events narrated there is a fringe of vast, divine mysteries and that he, the narrator, moves in an area of what is explicable and also of what is inexplicable? And where does a narrator ever let us suspect that he has also taken account of the possibility of his failing in his objective? Events are crystal-clear and sharply delineated in the light of human understanding. The events narrated never appear simply as elements of a divine rule which again and again vanishes into mystery. From this it is again possible to conclude that the wise men thought differently about the perceptibility of their subjects from the 'historians'. These subjects were by no means so clear to them. In the evaluation of the general course of events in the world, the divine incognito was obviously more troublesome, the range of interpretative possibilities greater, and in this way the dimension of mystery achieved such great theological relevance.[8]

All this affords us greater support in distinguishing the wise men's intellectual endeavour from that of those who present Israel's historical experiences.[9] We must resign ourselves to the fact that the

---

[7] The translation given here is the one closest to the Hebrew text. Many scholars, however, doubt its originality and emend; cf. G. Sauer, *Die Sprüche Agurs*, 1963, pp. 97ff.

[8] Here, too, apocalyptic reveals that its roots are in wisdom. It cannot do enough in the expounding of the divine mysteries.

[9] What, however, is the position with the Yahwist who has always been placed in close proximity to 'wisdom' (most recently H.-J. Hermisson, op. cit., pp. 126f., 133)? Undoubtedly there is much in his work that recalls characteristics of wisdom teaching: his enlightened way of looking at man's environment, his interest in psychological factors, his distance from the world of the cult, etc. One must, however, bear in mind that the freethinking atmosphere in the vicinity of Solomon's court can scarcely be regarded simply as the product of wisdom. Many different

intellectual endeavours of the wise men, this discovery and evaluation of rules, was a unique type of activity which was nurtured in the schools. In addition, this dualism is to be found among the ancient Greeks, and there, too, the point of unity can be discovered only indirectly and by way of supposition.[10] If we remain aware of these differences, which were obviously deeply rooted in the subjects themselves, then one must also mention common elements, for these exist particularly in the manner and way in which, by both types, the subjects are approached intellectually. Historical decrees and historical guidance, too, could be presented only in a context of knowledge about Yahweh; thus here, too, 'the fear of Yahweh' was the unalterable presupposition for knowledge. And the guidance and decrees of Yahweh were the ever-changing objects of knowledge. Again and again they present themselves in new forms, so that Israel was sometimes quite unable to adapt them. Is not the late Deuteronomistic History comparable to the later 'theological wisdom' in that it was obliged to present history once again from quite new aspects, that is, that the encounter with history had to be worked through afresh?

---

factors are at work here, that is, we have to reckon with stimuli which, in turn, also affected wisdom. As far as the Yahwist's 'kerygma' is concerned, his references to Yahweh's saving activity which has been operative from the very beginning of Israel's history, there is certainly no bridge from there to wisdom (H. W. Wolff, 'Das Kerygma des Yahwisten', *Gesammelte Studien*, 1964. pp. 345ff.). Rather, one can examine specific material which has been reworked by the Yahwist and ask whether and in what respect wisdom influences can be discerned in it (esp. Gen. 2f., etc.), although there is other material where there can be no question of this. Thus, as things stand today, it is advisable to stress the differences rather than the resemblances.

A strange mixture is presented by the so-called Song of Moses in Deut. 32 with its retrospective examination of the nation's history. It begins with a teacher's opening summons and calls Israel a foolish and senseless people (vv. 6 and 29); this would correspond to wisdom language. And yet not, for the poem is addressed to the nation as a whole, which is quite unlike wisdom, and the teacher's opening summons is not addressed to human listeners but to heaven and earth, and the people are promised (in the form of a divine address) a destructive judgment (vv. 37ff.). This, and above all the presentation of history as proof of Israel's unfaithfulness, clearly stems from prophetic tradition. Precisely because of this unmistakable prophetic influence, the early dating of the song which is sometimes attempted (tenth century) cannot be maintained, so most recently W. Beyerlin in *Tradition und Situation* (*Festschrift* for A. Weiser, 1963), pp. 17ff. Deut. 32 is, therefore, no proof of the fact that the teachers worked with historical materials.

[10] K. v. Fritz, 'Der gemeinsame Ursprung der Geschichtsschreibung und der exakten Wissenschaften bei den Griechen', *Philosophia naturalis* 2, 1952, p. 200. In Israel, the discovery of the common point of origin would be still more difficult.

Thus, history too was not simply the passive object of knowledge; it was itself endeavouring to set Israel to rights, it addressed Israel.

II

That we have such difficulties in defining appropriately the phenomenon of wisdom as a specific form of human intellectual endeavour is largely due to the fact that we cannot shed any light on it by means of a comparison with present-day intellectual life. The question how man should use his reason in his life in community with his fellow men and in all that happens to him in life – especially in a situation of crisis – weighed heavily on ancient man, and he was of the opinion that in this matter he needed to be trained and constantly guided afresh. In Sophocles' *Antigone*, this question is never far away: In what, in specific cases of conflict, does the right activity of reason consist? What would be the right thing to do, in what way would lack of judgment become apparent? These were questions which clearly afflicted men, and to be able to give illuminating replies to these questions was one way in which a man could achieve public esteem – in Greece no less than in Israel.[11]

It is worthwhile considering for a moment how wisdom could lose this position of great worth in intellectual life. Israel and other ancient peoples proceeded from the conviction that in the real, objective world and in its movements truth could be grasped, in fact that this truth was concerned with men. The real problem was not its existence but how one could find one's way to it, for it was, beyond all doubt, a source of knowledge. In the vocabulary of the wise men of ancient Israel there is no single term for human intellect corresponding to *logos* or *ratio* or 'reason'. 'Reason', which has pushed its way forward to become part of wisdom, was for them not simply part of the natural equipment of each single man, but was, rather, basically something like a charismatic gift which was not available to everyone. (Thus the late wisdom teachers were not so wrong when they interpreted wisdom as a charisma; see above 54ff.) A wise and understanding mind, a 'listening' mind – that was the content of Solomon's royal request (I Kings 3.9). What he, the paradigm of the wise man, wished for himself was not the authoritative reason which reigns supreme over dead natural matter, the reason of modern consciousness, but an 'understanding' reason, a feeling for the truth

[11] Sophocles, *Antigone*, ll.683, 721, 727, 1027–30, 1051, 1198.

which emanates from the world and addresses man. He was totally receptive to that truth, but this was not passivity, but an intense activity, the object of which was response, prudent articulation.[12] The discovery of truth on the basis of the modern concept of reason, on the other hand, is, rather, an experience of power. It produces an ability to control in which, basically, everyone can participate. Our reason is technically determined; it is knowledge about what one can do and, as such, is in opposition to the receptivity of wisdom and equally hostile to any attainment of trust. Nevertheless, there has survived, even when today we speak about a 'wise man', something of the understanding of reason which the ancients had. We mean by this a man who has at his disposal knowledge which can be used for other than merely technical ends and who actually also has no method. The judgment of Solomon in the well-known story of the quarrel between the two women about the child can certainly not be attributed to any specific method of discovering the truth; but the king succeeded – we would say intuitively – in removing the veil from an extremely difficult situation and revealing the truth (I Kings 3.16–28). The way by which the wise man arrives at his knowledge remains in obscurity, but in an obscurity that is full of promise. One runs no risk if one trusts it in advance; on the contrary, anyone who refuses to do so, will not even win from it what can, in an objective sense, be known.

The Solomon of I Kings 3 could – regarded objectively – have said that he would yield to Yahweh so that the world might not remain dumb for him but that it might be understood by him. The understanding of reason and of the world of course correspond to one another. Thus the answers which the wise men of old gave only become comprehensible when we understand them, as exactly as possible, from the point of view of the understanding of the world which they presuppose and without which they really are non-committal. All truth is inscrutable; only to the uncritical man does it appear so clear and unequivocal that he thinks he is able, without further ado, to measure the ideas of other peoples and other religions against his own. Israel regarded the reality around her considerably differently from Sophocles. The doctrines with which Israel answered the questions of life arose from an intellectual power which had wholly

[12] The fine saying about the 'listening heart' seems to come originally from Egyptian wisdom. There the heart was 'the organ by which man takes in the meaning and order of the world'. H. Brunner, *Altägyptische Erziehung*, 1957, pp. 111f.

freed itself from belief in mythical powers immanent in the world. This is a search for knowledge with which a keen rationality approached a demythologized world. But with this demythologization of the world, Israel only appeared to approach the modern understanding of the world, for to this radical secularization of the world there corresponded the idea of an equally radical domination of the world by Yahweh, that is the idea of the world as a creation of Yahweh.

If the word 'creation' is deliberately understood in its specifically theological sense, then the statement that Israel's search for knowledge was directed at creation already basically encompasses the problem in all its uniqueness. We recapitulate the three most important points which we have encountered again and again.

1. Creation is, in an ontological sense, something other than 'world' in so far as it is, for the man who observes it, not a neutral object whose 'meaning', whose advantages and disadvantages he could contemplate from the standpoint of an observer. As an object of the highest quality – 'everything was very good' (Gen. 1.31) – it stimulated man in all its manifestations. At the point where the wise men began their endeavours, this was no longer open to discussion. For them it was firmly established that creation was not only worthy of all possible trust, but also that it vindicated every form of trust. The question of trust, we saw, was of absolutely central importance, for there were also forms of false trust – trust in possessions, in one's own wisdom, etc. – which led to destruction. The teachers knew very well that the search for wisdom and for mastery over life could unexpectedly come to grief. How otherwise were the arts of persuasion which they proclaimed to be explained? And it would come to grief – such was the firm conviction of the wise men – if it was not rooted in the proper trust. When Jeremiah says that that man is blessed who trusts in Yahweh (Jer. 17.7), then he is, as far as his thinking is concerned, wholly within the sphere of the sentence which states that the fear of Yahweh is the beginning of knowledge (Prov. 1.7; etc.). The 'fool' was not simply an imbecile, but a man who resisted a truth which presented itself to him in creation, who, for whatever reasons, did not trust in an order which would be beneficial for him, but which now turns against him.[13]

2. That creation was an unlimited sphere of activity for the divine will, that God's attitude towards it could be one of either blessing or refusal, that he could conceal himself in it but also reveal himself –

[13] See above pp. 64f.

this, too, was no longer a subject of debate among the wise men. Equally certain was the fact that the divine will was discernible and here, as we have seen, mystery was accorded its rightful place. It can thus be easily understood that everything that happened in this life that was granted by Yahweh was at the disposal of Israel's search for knowledge. How could the teachers have arrived at the idea of directing their search for knowledge only by those orders which were perceptible as, so to speak, 'inherent laws' in the sphere of things and men and of leaving out of account Yahweh's activity which was, after all, indissolubly linked with everything else? Were Yahweh's blessing and refusal not thought to be experiences? Did not they, too, stimulate the search for knowledge? But how could they talk about the government of the world and its being moved by God in a language appropriate to pure reason? It is only with this question that we approach the specific, theological endeavour of the wise men. The idea that God manifested himself in his world by means of miracles or other occasional incursions had lapsed.[14] What – and this is a fascinating question – what was left, if the possibility of giving divine activity a special place alongside events in the world disappeared? Whatever possibilities may have offered themselves, of speaking of a divine *concursus*, of a divine 'accompaniment', in no case could the idea of the hiddenness of God in the world be avoided.

The business of knowing (and that, as we can now clearly see, always included the duty of speaking about God) was divided in Israel, as we can deduce from the didactic literature, on the whole into two clearly differentiated 'processes'. If one regards, from a certain distance, the work accomplished in both of them, then it is not difficult to realize that the object of knowledge remained basically the same. The results of the one 'process' are to be found above all in the sentences in Prov. 10–29. Here the objects, particularly the experiences of community life, are understood in a predominantly 'secular' way, or, to be more precise, the environment is addressed, in characteristically dialectic terms, as a secular entity governed by Yahweh. One could say that the victory is achieved through good advice (Prov. 24.6), but one could also say that it comes from Yahweh alone (Prov. 21.31). But in the vast majority of the sentences, the order which is discovered in set down as a kind of neutral pattern immanent in the world. Hardly anything was said about 'cooperation' or 'accompaniment' on the part of Yahweh. One knew about

[14] See above pp. 58f, 97f.

him, but in this business of discovering an order, Yahweh only appeared, on the whole, more in the sense of a limitation imposed on men.[15] At any rate his participation in events was not the real object of the intellectual endeavour. The situation, however, was completely different in the other process of intellectual discovery, for here (primarily in Prov. 1–9, in the speeches of the friends in the book of Job and in large sections of Sirach) the question is, 'In God's dealings with men, is it not possible to discover orders which can be recognized as such by reason?' There must have been circles in Israel, or a period, in which it became necessary to rethink the old questions on a more definite, theological basis. On can recognize the shift in the question in the treatment of the act-consequence relationship, but especially in the evaluation of the events to which man is exposed. Formerly, the act-consequence relationship was a more or less objective law, but now it is regarded as involving a personal act of God, directed at the individual. In the one case, knowledge about Yahweh enabled one to understand the world as world, in the other it enabled one to order the experiences which were made available through God's guidance and to examine them with a view to finding rules. On the frontiers of its jurisdiction, reason was at work in the one case as well as in the other. The frequently raised objection, that later wisdom has been 'dogmatically' hardened, would have to be based on the texts with more precise exegesis. It would appear as if the hardness lay more with the exegetes who have drawn up a scheme against which they then examine the teachings of the ancients.[16] This brings

[15] See above pp. 98ff.

[16] We were not concerned with 'saving' the opinions expressed by the teachers, but with looking for proper standards and with warding off inappropriate judgements imported from outside. Thus, I am unable to find corroboration in the texts for the main thesis of H. H. Schmid's book, namely the transformation of an early, genuinely living (i.e. still genuinely related to existence) form of wisdom into a dogmatic system divorced from history (op. cit., p. 196). On what solid basis could the reproach be founded that 'verification by empirical reality was abandoned'? If one tries to interpret the texts against the background of an understanding of reality appropriate to them, then it would be very difficult to show from them such a profound 'shift in structure', for the very reason that each text has an intellectual 'context' and every didactic complex requires a background against which it has to be understood and through which it can find expression. Often it will be impossible to pin it down to one meaning, for it is to be understood not from one standpoint alone. It seems to me to be impossible to point to the break, i.e. the step to secondary, dogmatic wisdom, as Schmid tries to do (op. cit., pp. 155ff.) already within the sentence groups in Prov. 10–29. Could one not see in the 'theologization' of wisdom, i.e. in the endeavour to bring the life of the individual and the movements of his environment back once more to the centre of Yahweh's sphere of

us to the third point in the ontology of the wise men which has particularly caught our attention.

3. The confrontation is almost unbearable for the modern exegete between the idea of reality in which he himself lives and the one which he encounters in the old teachers. Again and again, by means of some kind of criticism, he tries to rid himself of the tension involved. This criticism generally amounts to the reproach that the whole of reality has been rationally violated, particularly by later wisdom.[17] Now, such judgments do not really lead very far as long as the person doing the judging is not also subjecting his own understanding of reality to criticism, for perhaps objections (possibly quite similar ones at that) could be raised against it, too. But it is a serious matter, for, unquestionably, the uncritical absolutism of our modern, popular conception of reality is one of the greatest obstacles in the way of a proper understanding of our texts. One cannot be sufficiently careful in one's use of the term 'reality', for Israel was fascinated by quite specific realities which have become lost to the modern range of vision, and she reckoned, accordingly, with different eventualities in the sphere of reality. The most characteristic feature of her understanding of reality lay, in the first instance, in the fact that she believed man to stand in a quite specific, highly dynamic, existential relationship with his environment. Man – and it was always the individual – regarded himself as bound in a circle of the most varied, outward-looking relationships, in which he was sometimes a subject and sometimes an object. If we occasionally spoke of Israel's search for knowledge being directed at the objects of her environment, that was only one side of the matter. One could equally well say that her search for knowledge was first of all the response to a stimulus, that it only arose from the fact that it felt itself forced to take up a position with regard to circumstances and movements in its environment which were stronger than man. Man was, at the same time, always the object of movements which reached him from men and also from

---

activity, a new attempt to relate the teaching to existence in a new way? The unalterable characteristics of Israel's teachings, which we have encountered along the way and which are rooted in the very origins of her way of thinking, occupy much too small a place in Schmid's book. Schmid does, in fact, say that the understanding which can be derived from Egyptian wisdom cannot be transferred without modification to Israel's wisdom (op. cit., p. 198); but it was there that he worked out the basic idea of the two 'stages' (op. cit., pp. 79f.; etc.).

[17] W. Zimmerli, *ZAW* 51, 1933, p. 204; H. H. Schmid, op. cit., p. 197.

things. But these movements of the environment – and this is the most important factor – did not disappear into an unrelated outer sphere in accordance with some strange law; they were, rather, turned quite personally and in unending mobility towards man; indeed, they corresponded to his behaviour even in areas which we would call 'natural'. In all the endlessly varied forms which they could assume, they were ready to accept man. Everything that happens to you is appropriate to you. The man who has brought his relationship with God into order is himself in league with the stones of the field and is befriended by the beasts of the field (Job 5.20ff.). The environment is not only the object of man's search for knowledge. In so far as it is turned towards him, man is the object of its advance on him. We need only recall the great poems about the fate of the oppressor.[18] All at once, all the elements in his environment rise up against him to destroy him. 'The heavens will reveal his sin, and the earth rises up against him' (Job 20.27). To put it the other way round: If God is pleased with a man, he can even make his enemies be at peace with him (Prov. 16.7). No one has expressed this experience, this benevolent attitude of the environment, more comprehensively and more precisely than Paul, 'We know that to those who love God everything works together for good' (*sunergei*, Rom. 8.28). The ancients also knew that this attitude, this working together of 'everything', could take on for man very complicated forms. Disturbing experiences could also be had of this wisdom of the world which acted benevolently towards man and which we have called primeval order:

> At first she walks in disguise with him,
>   brings fear and trembling upon him
> and tests him by her discipline
>   until she can trust him,
> and tempts him with her statutes (?).
> Then she comes to him again by a straight path
>   and gladdens him
> and reveals to him her secrets.   (Sir. 4.17–18)

At whatever point we approach the teachings of the wise men, we always encounter this experience of the world, this belief that events are controlled, especially, of course, in the idea of the act-consequence relationship. Creation – so the teachers were convinced – has something to say to man. It is certainly not impossible to read her tracks.

---

[18] See above pp. 38ff, 131f.

In the great divine speech (Job 38f.) God leaves it to his creation to bear witness to him. In the teaching of primeval wisdom's clear testimony to herself, this conviction found its keenest expression, in so far as here, reality not only advances towards man but actually addresses him and woos him. To the man who entrusts himself to this order, it is not only that the movements of his environment appear different to him (this we could still understand), but it is actually different things that happen to him. This existential relationship, this turning of the world towards man, first had to be made known by means of special considerations; as a fact, as a reality, it was subjected to all kinds of thought-processes. Thus, this idea was not the sole prerogative of the wise men; their task was simply to give expression to it in didactic terms. Anyone who fails to be aware of the constitutive idea of this reciprocally determined sphere of action between man and his environment and who appraises the sentences by means of the modern understanding of reality, will, of necessity, misunderstand from the outset much of what the wise men say, will indeed feel that their sentences are foolish and capricious postulates. But they were not postulates; they were statements of experiences.[19] This does not, of course, mean that the experience was the same in each of them or that it was always unambiguous. Here there was considerable scope for all sorts of reflections. Indeed, such reflections were indispensable, for Hebrew man laid himself open, with great care, to these movements which advanced towards him, he tried to interpret them for himself, he faced them with great hopes, and he was, correspondingly, of course, open also to specific disappointments and attacks. The scepticism of Ecclesiastes actually arises from the very fact that this living, existential context had become questionable for him.[20]

But the modern observer who is so decisively in sympathy with the (in his day unique) ideas of Ecclesiastes, must also listen to the other

---

[19] On the basis of this ancient understanding of reality, all modern criticism of the act-consequence relationship would need to be revised, for it is dealing with something more than 'wisdom dogmatics' (H. H. Schmid, passim). One could, rather, speak of a 'dogmatic' preoccupation on the part of exegetes. On the destruction of the primacy of the 'real' by the 'possible', on the authority of the 'possible' from the point of view of systematic theology, see most recently E. Jüngel, 'Die Welt als Möglichkeit und Wirklichkeit', *EvTh* 29, 1969, pp. 417ff.

[20] The author of the Wisdom of Solomon felt obliged to provide remarkable explanations for his readers in order to make clear for them, living as they obviously did with the Hellenistic idea of physics, the miracle of the exodus event: 'The world fought for the righteous' (16.17); creation can 'exert' itself in judgment and 'relax' in salvation (16.24); 'the elements changed places with one another' (19.18).

voice which in so many different forms can be heard behind the teachings: The world has something to say; she actually dispenses truth. How could there be, then, an objectively valid standard for what a man hears in the environment which advances towards him? In her 'wisdom', Israel has made the attempt – with the help of a highly flexible set of rules – to make this voice contemporary from the point of view of her religious presuppositions. The exegete must always be on his guard against the naïve error of thinking that 'reality' and the experience of it is something objectively given to all men equally, something against which the teachings can then be measured with comparative ease. If he adopts that position, then, as exegete, he has already obstructed his view of what Israel's concern here really was.

But we must take a decisive step further in our discussion of the wisdom teachers' understanding of reality. When we said that the teachers conceived of reality as having been created by Yahweh, that they looked on it in non-mythical ways, this means that they were completely incapable of even seeing in the world the existence and activity of any evil powers hostile to God. To be more precise, they know nothing of a mythically or speculatively objective evil power. Israel really knew a great deal about evil, and one cannot say that the teachers had wilfully played down a whole dimension of reality. The world which they show to their pupils lacks hardly any of the great misfortunes by which men are constantly being worn down: poverty, illness, folly, strife, etc. All this is experienced and recorded by the teachers in essentials no differently from the way in which it has always been experienced by men. The teachers' experience of the world has, then, no decisive gaps from which one could deduce any deficiencies or perversities in their teachings. They are aware of all the misfortunes, but they understood them in their own way.

This is equally true of what they have to say about death. Israel experienced death quite differently from the way in which modern man experiences it. Much more than by the mere fact that men must eventually die, Israel was assailed by the irruption of death into the sphere of life. Death could thrust deep into life, for even illness, imprisonment, indeed any serious impairment of life were, as the psalms of lament show, already a form of death.[21] Thus, on the whole, the teachers, too, are not greatly concerned with ultimate mortality.

[21] Chr. Barth, *Die Errettung vom Tode in den (individuellen) Klage- und Dankliedern des A.T,* 1947, pp. 53ff.

It is difficult, from our complicated precognitions, to see correctly what the teachers say about death and what they leave unsaid. Are we not already speaking of something else when we speak so objectively about 'death'? In their teachings they often spoke of having to die, but almost always meant by this the premature death which the fool, the lascivious and the lazy bring upon themselves. One can do something to prevent this death, and one can escape the 'snares of death' by living wisely (Prov. 13.14). But death could also approach man in the form of a great fulfilment (Job 5.26). Death was not part of creation; it was not an ordering power. It was not a 'power' in any sense, but an event and, as such, was ambivalent. It could be 'bitter', but it could also be 'good' (Sir. 41.1f.). But let us always remain conscious of the limits of such information. For it is a highly problematic undertaking to start from sentences which are aimed in a specific didactic direction and ask about the general, religious principles which lie somewhere in the background. The fact of ultimate death first finds expression as a real intellectual problem in the teachings at the point where faith in Yahweh's support of life begins to disappear. This new situation, with all its disturbing consequences, is depicted in very impressive terms in the book of Ecclesiastes.[22]

We can retain this: The world contains nothing that could confront man ontologically as an objective evil factor hostile to God. It has been correctly asserted that the division of the world into a benevolent world ruled by God and a malevolent world ruled by evil first becomes discernible in the Hellenistic Wisdom of Solomon. Death is a reality which does not come from God. God has created man for good, but through the envy of the devil, death came into the world (Wisd. 1.13; 2.24). The frail sphere of the flesh is contrasted with the creative wisdom-spirit.[23] One should be clear about the fact that Job, too, for all his despair, still stands on the far side of such metaphysical dualism. There is not even the slightest attempt to convince the friends of the existence of an evil power outside of God. He does not look for the discordant note in the world; it is with God that something is wrong. It is true that the proximity of death troubles him, but only for the reason that it deprives him of the opportunity of coming to terms with God. In no sense is 'death' for him the great evil. If he could only come to terms with God then everything else would be

---

[22] W. Zimmerli, *Das Buch des Predigers Salomo*, 1962, pp. 135f.; N. Lohfink, *Das Siegeslied am Schilfmeer*, 1965, pp. 211ff.

[23] D. Georgi in *Zeit und Geschichte* (*Festschrift* for Bultmann, 1964), pp. 270ff.

restored to order of itself. In this conviction he is in agreement with his friends. The disagreement arises only with the question how and by whom this order has to be restored. But in this respect all who have ever had to react to such questions are in agreement: In any confrontation between man and any of life's great misfortunes, only God is competent to deal with it. The world has no contribution of its own to make. The world is not a battlefield between God and any of the evils found in it. There is no split in the world. From all parts of it – except from the underworld – there arises praise, and all its parts and opportunities are, in their turn, once again the objects of enthusiastic praise. It is a world that is thoroughly worthy of trust, and the understanding of man in these teachings is unquestionably a non-tragic one. Even if life is subject to many different limitations, they are nevertheless not imposed by fate, but can always be accepted.

> He has established the powerful acts of his wisdom.
>   He is one and the same from everlasting.
> There is nothing to be added and nothing to be taken away,
>   and he has no need of anyone to instruct him.
> Everything lives and lasts for ever,
>   and for every purpose they are all ready.
> All things are different, one from the other,
>   but he has made nothing that is incomplete.
> The one confirms what is good in the other,
>   and who can have enough of observing his glory?   (Sir. 42.21–25)

What a view of the world this is! It is no wonder that the teachers who felt obliged to meditate on these things were so often led to expressions of praise. How easily the dry enumeration of the world's resources in the *onomastica* passed into hymnic style! How small a step it was from knowledge to adoration! Of course, the price which Israel had to pay for this refusal to split the world dualistically, to regard it, instead, as a good creation, open, in each of its movements, towards God, might appear to be a high one. Israel was now forced to understand all the disruptive misfortunes as statutes or decrees of Yahweh. On one occasion Sirach broods on the wickedness of the human eye. Nothing more wicked has ever been made. And why was the wicked friend made (Sir. 31.13; 37.3)? Do such sentences betray the first signs of the metaphysical dualism represented by the Wisdom of Solomon? On the contrary, they are the last consequences which had to be wrested from the 'monism' of Yahwism. In what breaking tests Israel's faith could be involved as a result of this monism is sufficiently shown by Job's struggle and despair. But in this matter, Israel had no choice, and in the long run Job also had to admit that his life, too, was in Yahweh's safe-keeping, even if this was one of Yahweh's impenetrable mysteries. We recall the remarkable fact that the wise men had a great deal to say about mysteries, but not about the mysteries of the world. They were all mysteries of God.[24]

III

In view of all this, only a brief answer is still required to the question which we had to raise right at the beginning of all our discussions, namely what Israel's 'wisdom' really was and how it was to be defined. We can begin with the assertion that the wisdom practised in Israel was a response made by a Yahwism confronted with specific experiences of the world. In her wisdom Israel created an intellectual sphere in which it was possible to discuss both the multiplicity of trivial, daily occurrences as well as basic theological principles. This wisdom is, therefore, at all events to be regarded as a form of Yahwism, although – as a result of the unusual nature of the tasks involved – an unusual form and, in the theological structure of its statements, very different from the other ways in which Yahwism reveals itself. But Yahwism was thoroughly imbued with this specific unique quality from the very beginning. In it the responses are laid down in rules which worshippers of Yahweh, challenged by the world around them and confronted by 'life', have made for themselves. The presupposition for being allowed to speak in this matter was knowledge about Yahweh. The presupposition for coping with life was trust in Yahweh and in the orders put into operation by him. Particularly characteristic of the fact that in the teachings of the wise men everything comes from Yahweh and is, in the last resort, directed towards him, was the theme of proper trust, a theme to which the wise men return again and again, and the warning against false trust. All that the wise men say, especially also what they have to say about the beneficent turning of the world towards men, only has meaning if one places one's trust in the orders, and that means, in the last resort, in Yahweh. This is a trust to which Yahweh is entitled and which has long since been justified by experience. The warning not to consider oneself wise pointed in the same direction. The man who

[24] See above, pp. 108f.

lived and thought in partnership with Yahweh could never insist upon his insights but must, rather, always be ready to let his actions, even if they emanated from tested perceptions, be crossed.

To speak of Israel's 'wisdom', as if there were only one kind of wisdom, is always risky. We recall that Israel did not have a comprehensive description which included the whole of her didactic, literary efforts which spanned many centuries. She did not, therefore, regard the productions of the wise men as an entity, nor did she differentiate them theologically from other expressions of Yahwism. Nevertheless, one can discern an important common factor which bound all wisdom efforts together: What was wisdom, if not Israel's attempt to unfold her humanity in the very sphere of a reality which she experienced quite specifically, that is, a humaneness on Israel's part? What goal was served by the many efforts, so characteristic of wisdom, to master the contingent? There was surely only one goal, to wrest from the chaos of events some kind of order in which man was not continually at the mercy of the incalculable. One requires this room for manoeuvre in order to be able to live at all and to make something of one's life. If this room as such, as the wise men believed they had discovered and experienced, was determined by orders in which man could feel secure, then man's humanity was threatened all the more by man himself, by his own lack of order and his own folly. Mysterious, anonymous forces were not, as we have already mentioned, believed by the wise men to be at work. All that lacked order and all that destroyed life emanated from man himself. It was at this point that effort had to begin.

Let us be clear, once again, about what the teachers used and did not use in order to help man to become himself. There is no talk of the divine spark which man alone has within him, as has been taught from the days of the ancient Greeks until today; nor, and this would have been more likely, of his being made in the image of God. One can but marvel at the sobriety with which the teachers set to work. They certainly do not feel themselves called upon to protect things sacred. But they summon the pupil's reason as an ally in order to convince him that he does well not to destroy himself, but to trust himself to the power of good and to fear that which lacks order. They do not appear to have at their disposal any controlling and guiding idea. Have they, then, much more to contribute to the preservation of humanity than here a word advising moderation, there a word about calmness or a few important words about the many limitations, the disregard of which endangers man's humanity, with the limitations with regard to God being treated with particular attention? From a quite different direction – and this was a unique feature – Job was aware that the humanity which had been conferred on him by his creator was being threatened, and that by God himself.

The function of the prophets was different. They, too, were concerned with man, but in a quite different sense, for through them God gave specific messages to man. God had set out to find man. In wisdom, however, man was in search of himself and took things into his own hands without being able to appeal to a specific, divine commission. In the unbroken chain of situations of conflict (and the longer it was, the more he became involved in ultimate questions which threatened existence) he endeavoured to discover what was right in any given situation; but in the last resort he strove not simply to acquire perceptions, but for something that was a totality, for a total attitude, for culture. In a word, he strove to discover his humanity in the sphere which had been allotted to him by God. This endeavour has established itself in the shadow of Yahwism, perhaps because Yahweh started it off or because he taught man the limits of his opportunities or because he trained man to fashion his life through a critical collecting of religious experiences.

In the form of wisdom instruction a certain liberality – perhaps in contrast to the 'apodeictic' divine law – has long been noted. It is directed towards the understanding of the person being instructed; it cannot and will not take away from him the power of decision. Even when man was being urgently addressed, an area was always left which the teacher never entered but which he left free for the pupil to use as he wished; one could in fact say that it was left for a kind of intuition which helped the pupil to transfer correctly the general instruction to his own particular situation, for here it was man who intervened, whether he was endeavouring to hold his forces together, to utilize his opportunities or to cultivate relations with his fellow men.

But this humanity could not be protected by a handful of clever rules. Again and again it had to be established anew from the very heart of Yahwism. More and more we saw the wise men involved in a struggle with fundamental problems which threatened to darken their relationship with God and which called for fairly decisive theological reflection. And finally we even saw them – bordering on hubris – summoned and wooed by the mystery of the world itself and responding to that wooing with an intellectual love. Thus wide, then, was the theological framework stretched within, which the wise men in Israel believed they could begin to understand themselves correctly. To live intellectually in such spheres, to be able to handle such knowledge, really required a *rōḥab lēb*, a 'width', a 'breadth' of heart and mind (I Kings 5.9). In this concept, what was both the task and, at the same time, the presupposition of Israel's humanity found admirable expression. As weapons in the conflict with theological problems, in later wisdom especially, hymnic traditions were mobilized against the attacks.

Any attempt to try to understand this picture of man from a constitutive point of unity and to try to describe it from that point of view, would, however, come to grief. And this not only because the patterns changed with the times. That of the early monarchy was vastly different from that of Sirach. What lasted was only the general demand that man, through knowledge of Yahweh, must learn to become competent with regard to the realities of life. It can certainly be said that the atmosphere of the school unmistakably surrounds the teachings of the wise men. The young man who is open to instruction is the man that the teachers primarily see before them. But this is also true in a wider, more basic sense. The man who listens, who reflects and who then entrusts himself to his perceptions; that is the highest form of human existence in the eyes of the wise men. But that this picture of man had to remain open in many directions was already clear from the presuppositions from which these teachings began, for this desire for education was also aware of God and of the unpredictability of his actions. For this reason, all objects of human knowledge were on the one hand knowable and, on the other, subject to a divine mystery to which God could at any time recall them, thus concealing them from man. Under such circumstances could even a single perception be satisfactorily achieved or a problem acquire ultimate solution? That 'no wisdom, no understanding, no counsel' was valid in Yahweh's eyes is surely one of the most illuminating sentences in the whole book of Proverbs (Prov. 21.30). But it brings out sharply an awareness which lay, more or less, behind all of these teachings. This did not lead to the belittling of what could be and had become known, but certainly to a reticence towards attempting great, sweeping explanations. The theoretical attempt at a total illumination of the world could no longer have been attempted in the face of the specific, intellectual presupposition of the wise men. The perceptions achieved are not built into a comprehensive system. On the contrary, they are basically left in the form in which they were originally expressed, and, without the slightest need for harmonization, perceptions of a different kind could be placed alongside them.

Did not the juxtaposition of different teachings right on until the final composition of the individual collections – we emphasize here yet another characteristic – preserve an element of discussion and debate which belonged to these teachings? The phenomena are never objectified; they are always conceived only from the point of view of their relationship to the man envisaged in each particular case.[25] These relationships, however, were always extremely variable and could certainly never be evaluated unambiguously. Behind the teachings of the wise men there lies, therefore, a profound conviction of the ambivalence of phenomena and events. As a proposition, this scarcely finds expression, but it is practised all the more keenly.[26] Here, too, and not only in her historical thinking, Israel, with great openness, gave precedence to the contingent event over the *logos* achieved by means of abstract calculation. Obviously it created no intellectual difficulties for the teachers to supplement an experience which they had turned into a teaching, by means of another one, sometimes even a contrary one. Certainly wealth is a good thing, but it can also be harmful; certainly poverty is a bad thing, but it can also be good.[27] Every sentence was, in principle, open to any possible amplification. It always had its truth only in a specific sphere in life and in a specific range of comparable circumstances. It was then the pupil's task, one might say, correctly to recognize the time in which the sentence is true or in which it becomes false.[28]

[25] 'The strong interest which wisdom has in man and his world, does not have as its foundation a point of view whereby man is the measure of all things, but the reverse: man is measured against the world in which he is set' (H.-J. Hermisson, op. cit., pp. 150f.).

[26] See above, pp. 72, 247.

[27] A cautious use of words can be a sign of wisdom; but it can also conceal folly (Prov. 17.27f.). Wealth is always something worth striving for, but it is of no use on the day of wrath (Prov. 11.4). Wealth and a large income can open the way to good, but also to sin (Prov. 10.16). The man who is sated despises honey, but to the hungry anything bitter tastes sweet (Prov. 27.7). A blessing which is spoken too loudly can be taken for a curse (Prov. 27.14).

[28] How dangerous this awareness of ambivalence could be is shown by the Old Babylonian dialogue between a master and his slave. The master informs the slave of various plans, but immediately revokes them and says that he will do precisely the opposite on each occasion. Each time, the slave is able to give good reasons for the original plan and for its opposite (cf. Pritchard, *ANET*, pp. 437ff.). The interpretation of this dialogue as a humorous skit on blind obedience is, in my opinion, a serious misunderstanding of this bitterly serious poem.

This was not basically different in later wisdom either, for it, too, began from experiences. While the wise men taught the act-consequence relationship and the 'synergy' of a world turned towards men, Ecclesiastes challenged that fact. While the teachers of old wisdom devoted themselves to the discovery of knowledge and order, later teachers, in the doctrine of the self-testifying of creation, were aware that they were the objects of a desire for order which was directed towards men. The two pictures of the Job who, in spite of the most extreme suffering, is still protected by God, and the Job who falls into the lowest depths of despair, cannot be made to coincide. Thus, it is rooted deep in the nature of this way of thinking that the human dialogue in the book of Job breaks off still unfinished. The question envisaged by the partners in the Job-dialogue is left unresolved. Only Yahweh can, by his decision, put an end to the to and fro of opinions, and it is interesting to note that even this divine decision, for its part, does not take up the themes of the dialogue and lead it to its conclusion.

In all our study we have encountered this element of discussion and dialectic. Man sees himself faced with orders which can be recognized; but he also sees himself faced with God's freedom, in the face of which any attempt of his to think he is wise vanishes. While old wisdom gave instructions as to how property and honour could be acquired and secured, later wisdom understood these worldly goods to be the gifts of primeval order. This means, therefore, that the element of discussion and dialectic which is so clearly a feature of individual works, is also to be found in this literature as a whole. Can one then understand all these works, with their varied teachings, other than as parts of a great dialogue in which truth can be opposed to truth? If one only took seriously the fact that these teachings can be understood only on the basis of their own understanding of God and reality, then (but only then) there is nothing to contradict the assertion that this way of thinking was always subject to doubts into which it was inevitably led by its own presuppositions. We have said that the understanding man is always in conflict with the reality which surrounds him, but the wise men's understanding of reality did not possess the kind of evidence which could satisfy everyone in every situation. The question then was whether what remained unmastered could still be coped with in the face of the orders that were known, whether it could still be calculated – even in terms of mystery – or not. In the case of Job, the friends were of this opinion, while Job, on the other hand, regarded his suffering as an unbearably discordant fact.

'Zeal kills the fool' (Job 5.2). To this perception of theirs the wise men (including those in Job) certainly did not always remain faithful. In the long run one will have to recall the fact that Israel took great pains to learn from experience, that she could not, however, also escape the unavoidable opposite tendency, for perceptions gained can, by contrast, prejudice experience. But, in such teachings, in which the zeal of the wise men threatens to overreach itself, can the exegete still not recognize the truth which they are zealously seeking?

It would also be possible to judge the thinking of these teachers from the general standpoint of the history of philosophy. It cannot be denied that tangible limitations were imposed on it. Compared with Greek thought, the lack of method strikes one at once. But caution is advisable here, too. It may well contain more method than we can observe. At any rate, here, as everywhere, the defects should not be separated from the virtues. Presumably only in this way could Israel tackle the exacting task of looking for rules in a world that was entirely open to God. If anyone thinks that only the Western method of acquiring knowledge, a method which, as everyone knows, goes back to the questions asked in ancient Greece, can be called 'science', if, that is, he equates pre-Greek thinking with pre-scientific, then he will have to invent some other name for what transpired in Israel. But there is no reason why one should withhold that description from the efforts of the wise men, provided one is clear in one's own mind that Israel had a different way of approaching objects in order to gain knowledge from them.

These wholly pragmatically orientated teachings, as we further saw, were not intended to improve man, but, rather, to humanize him. Thus, these rules must be regarded as only a part of ancient Israel's search for culture. In the teachings of the wise men, there speaks a humanity which in no sense tries to liberate itself for a new and better existence, either in a socio-political respect or from the point of view of the individual. Nowhere is man trained to find himself in an ideal picture which transcends his own being. He is, therefore, not a man split within himself, who must first work towards a liberation for an existence which still lies in front of him. From an educational point of view, all of these teachings lack any sense of liberation.

One may ask whether this last statement is still applicable to certain teachings of later wisdom. In the teaching about primeval wisdom the concern, in fact, was not with this or that instruction which might be useful to man in his life, but with an ultimatum to the whole man; it was a question of life or death. The voice which spoke in these terms was not that of some teacher or other; it was the voice of the world-order itself which called man to itself and offered to him every imaginable fulfilment. In fact, the concern here is with the redemption of man, and what the teachers taught in this respect has all the signs of a doctrine of salvation, though perhaps not of a 'doctrine of liberation'. The teachers here are working out only one perception with great keenness: Constitutive for man's humanity is the faculty of hearing. If he is not constantly listening to the order established by God, then he is lost. But, basically, this perception was not new either; for the earlier teachers, too, were convinced that the orders are benevolently turned towards the man who takes refuge in them.

If one speaks here of soteriology, then it would be a soteriology which, in this particular form, could appear to be almost heretical from the point of view of the traditional ideas of the cult and of the historical salvation-decrees. For here, salvation is not brought about by Yahweh descending into history nor by any kind of human agency such as Moses or David or one of the patriarchs, but by specific factors inherent in creation itself. This seems to set up a theological tension with traditional Yahwism: a harsher one could hardly be imagined. It is true that we then also saw the teachers, in Sirach, for example, and in so-called apocalyptic, concerned with history, even with world history. The competence of the wise men at interpreting the future has, at a late period, imposed new tasks on this concern. But however vast the historical sketches drawn by apocalyptic, history could no longer be credited with the specific importance of being the interpreter, unique in its sphere, of decrees which bring about salvation.

But the thinking of the wise men was never, from the very beginning, stimulated by signs of divine activity in history. Rather, they felt themselves stimulated above all by the much older question of humanity. In her practical wisdom, Israel was subject to the ancient stimulation of the world, that is, she asked one of the most elementary questions of human existence. She answered it in a way of which she felt capable, thanks to the particular form of her understanding of God and reality. Without being able to achieve a total picture, the thinking of the wise men circled round the problem of a phenomenology of man, not of man as such, but a phenomenology of man tied to an environment in which he found himself both as subject and object, active and passive. Without this environment to which he is turned and which is turned to him, an understanding of man was just not possible in Israel. Israel only knew a related man, related to other men, to his environment and, not least, to God. Even the doctrine of the self-testifying role of creation is to be understood solely as a contribution to the phenomenology of man and of the world around him. This doctrine is, indeed, perhaps Israel's last word on this subject.

If we look back to the 'subjects of instruction' with which we have dealt here, then one can say that the number of basic perceptions with which Israel was concerned was not at all large. But they were constantly being reflected on and always being expressed afresh, with great fluidity, in the face of the ever-changing possibilities of application. We ought to remain conscious of the fact that in this sphere of man's intellectual life – especially in the ancient Near East – perceptions as such were peculiarly stable. The variable factor, on the other hand, was the stage of reflection at which they were given expression, the background of theological understanding against which they were set and the subjects to which they referred. It is clear that, reflected on in this way by later generations, they were occasionally capable of revealing new and exciting aspects.

As we said right at the beginning of our discussion, the teachers turned towards the perception of what was new, of the well-known, the everyday, what everyone knows and no one tries to prove. We can now say that the teachers did not waver from this task of theirs right to the end, at any rate not until Jesus Sirach. They did, of course, in the process, range fairly far afield, through many different circles of questions. In their efforts to give expression to their knowledge of experience, they became more and more involved in specifically theological problems. There arose teachers who could no longer restrict themselves to keeping the question of God on the fringes, more as a 'limit'. Even the term 'wisdom' – in the older teachers understood comparatively simply and unambiguously as the ability to shape life – now had to prove itself against a more complicated theological background. There was no way back. Thus, opinions in the later period became remarkably richer in contrasts. The evidence for a teaching was now confronted, in dialogue, with other opinions, the evidence for which could not simply be denied. It is impossible to overlook the role of Ecclesiastes as a danger signal. We have, however, declined to see in him the great guardian who led wisdom back to an awareness of her limitations.[29] This dialogue could never be brought to an end. Particularly in later wisdom, it was carried on with great poetic feeling. Its spokesmen, including Job and Ecclesiastes, are carried away by the greatness and majesty of their subject matter. Even the enigmas and terrors of God are invested with majesty. But in old wisdom, with its, in part, less pretentious questions, this was basically no different. There, too, knowledge, the expression of what was known, was always something beautiful, something which one could freely enjoy. The teachers were aware of primeval wisdom's sporting with man (Prov. 8.31) and, in their own way, participated in that sport. The expression of what was true required poetic form; for Israel, too, it was an aesthetic phenomenon.[30] But no one was so filled with praise for the majesty which had been poured out upon creation as was Sirach.[31] The step from teaching to praise became in him a very small one.

In view of all this, Israel's practical wisdom cannot be described as a self-contained entity, or, still less, as a completed intellectual structure. We have reasons for believing that of Israel's didactic endeavour only parts have been preserved. But even if the whole had been more clearly discernible, we might not have appraised it very differently. We believe that we have shown that an intellectual endeavour, working with the presuppositions that obtained in Israel, could never have achieved a comprehensive vision, that this undertaking could not but remain a torso. The intellectual sphere within which this thinking and knowing operated was certainly of an imposing breadth, but the individual subjects of instruction operate within it peculiarly unrelated to each other.

However, within Israel's didactic achievement one can discern a movement which has a certain logical consistency. Dissociating itself sharply from a sacral understanding of the world, this way of thinking

[29] So W. Zimmerli, 'Ort und Grenze der Weisheit', *Gottes Offenbarung*, 1963, pp. 314f.

[30] 'Pleasant words are like a honeycomb, sweet to the soul and healing for the body' (Prov. 16.24). 'Pleasant words' (*'imrē nō'am*) please God and men (Prov. 15.26). We still lack any sound criteria, however, which would enable us to appraise the poetic forms used by the wise men from the point of view of the history of style. Was there not, in their case too, something like a change of style from 'classical' to 'baroque' or 'mannerism'? This would be not at all surprising in productions which were so concerned with cultivating the form of expression and which nourished this art over centuries. Is, perhaps, the polished rhetoric of Elihu (Job 32–37) to be considered at this point?

[31] H. U. v. Balthasar, *Herrlichkeit (Eine theologische Ästhetik)*, Vol. III, Part 2/1, 1967, pp. 319ff.

placed man and his created environment in a measure of secularity with which Israel had never before been thus confronted. With wonderful open-mindedness, the older teachers' way of thinking circles round a man who has been, to a certain extent, newly discovered, man with all his psychological realities and imponderables, his possibilities and his limitations. In later wisdom, on the other hand, there appears what can almost be called a counter-movement. More specialized, theological questions had arisen, and later wisdom saw itself faced with the task, without sacrificing to the secularity of creation the knowledge that had been acquired, the task of bringing the world and man back once again into the centre of God's sphere of activity. This, of course, raised new and difficult questions which demanded answers. It is difficult to decide which of these two movements was threatened with the greater dangers, the placing of creation within the sphere of secularity or the bringing of it back within the sphere of direct, divine action towards man and the world. One could, of course, speak of such a movement, something in the nature of a diastole and a systole, only with great reservation. On closer examination, in both of them, many lines of thought run parallel or even contrary to each other. Sometimes a line of thought never moves away from its original starting-point, for the simple reason that it was never taken up and carried any further.

But almost more important than the differentiation of strong movements within wisdom, is what has continued in it from the very beginning, namely the unwavering certainty that creation herself will reveal her truth to the man who becomes involved with her and trusts her, because this is what she continually does. It is this self-revelation of the orders of creation, and not the convictions of the teachers nor their zeal, that has the last decisive word.

To a greater extent than is the case in any other intellectual or religious sphere, Israel's wisdom has borrowed from neighbouring cultures. Indeed, she perhaps first learned, through her familiarity with foreign wisdom, to see correctly the real importance of many of the basic human questions. But what she borrowed she incorporated into the sphere of a belief in God and an understanding of reality which were different from those of her neighbours. Thus Israel had to accomplish this task faced both with unique opportunities and with unique difficulties. Unique, too, was her confidence that she could recognize God's ways in the world around her as well as the limitations she encountered in this task. Unique was her confidence in the world; unique, too, however, were the attacks to which she was subject. In a word, a whole unique world of experiences was opened up by the wise men of Israel. It would certainly be interesting to reappraise, from this standpoint, the characteristics of other forms of ancient Near Eastern wisdom, especially those of Egypt and Babylon.

Let us, finally, turn back once again to the 'negative' features of Israel's wisdom, which we had occasion to point out above and which, in the long run, are perhaps more characteristic of it than its positive 'achievements'. There is no attempt to achieve a theoretical, self-contained picture of the world, no ideal picture of man to which man was to be led out of himself, no scientific construction of a system, but, rather, a noticeable caution with regard to comprehensive attempts at explanations; in contrast to this, there is an unfinished and even unfinishable dialogue about man and world on the basis of an awareness of the ambivalence of recorded phenomena, preference for the (sometimes contingent) event over any *logos*, etc. But are these entirely negative factors? Did there not lie behind them all a basic knowledge which Israel put into practice with regard to the opportunities presented to her and to the limitations imposed on her? There is the fact that the truth about the world and man can never become the object of our theoretical knowledge; that reliable knowledge can be achieved only through a relationship of trust with things; that it is the highest wisdom to abstain from the attempt to control wisdom in abstract terms, that it is much wiser to let things retain their constantly puzzling nature, and that means to allow them to become themselves active and, by what they have to say, to set man to rights. Equipped with this knowledge, Israel scarcely took any serious part in the philosophical debate, perhaps because she found no partner for dialogue within the popular philosophical movements of the late ancient world, perhaps out of a growing feeling that any complete agreement was no longer possible, linked with an increasingly certain awareness of the unique nature of her own intellectual and religious assets. Without claiming complete knowledge, Israel believed that she had knowledge of a unique kind of truth.

> She has not been heard of in Canaan,
> > nor has she been seen in Teman.
> Even the sons of Hagar
> > who look for knowledge on the (whole) earth,

the merchants of Merran and Teman,
    the authors of proverbs and those who strive for understanding
did not discover the way to wisdom,
    nor had they knowledge of her paths.   (Bar. 3.22f.)[32]

[32] The contrast is still sharper in the prophets, for they see the wisdom of the other nations already under the shadow of divine judgment: Isa. 19.11ff.; 44.25; Ezek. 28.12ff.; Obad. 8.

INDEX OF KEY WORDS

INDEX OF PASSAGES